Transnational Crossroads

BORDERLANDS AND TRANSCULTURAL STUDIES

Series Editors:

Pekka Hämäläinen
Paul Spickard

EDITED BY CAMILLA FOJAS & RUDY P. GUEVARRA JR.

Transnational Crossroads

Remapping the Americas
and the Pacific

University of Nebraska Press | Lincoln & London

Library of Congress Cataloging-
in-Publication Data
Transnational crossroads: remapping the
Americas and the Pacific / edited by Camilla
Fojas and Rudy P. Guevarra Jr.
p. cm. — (Borderlands and transcultural
studies)
Includes bibliographical references and index.
ISBN 978-0-8032-3795-7 (pbk.: alk. paper)
1. United States—Ethnic relations—History.
2. Asia—Relations—United States—History.
3. United States—Relations—Asia—History. 4. Latin America—Relations—United
States—History. 5. United States—Relations—Latin America—History. 6. Islands of
the Pacific—Relations—United States—History. 7. United States—Relations—Islands of
the Pacific. I. Fojas, Camilla, 1971–
II. Guevarra, Rudy.
E184.A1T693 2012
308.800973—dc23
2011046035

Set in Sabon by Bob Reitz.

In loving memory of Louis Baas Fojas,
Consuelo Fernandez, and Raúl Beltrán

Contents

| Illustrations

Transnational Crossroads

Introduction

Camilla Fojas and Rudy P. Guevarra Jr.

Transnational Crossroads explores the contact among Asian, Latina/o, and Pacific Islander cultures and communities in the Americas and the American Pacific that is apparent in key figures, migratory paths, cultural productions, and social and political formations. Perhaps the most infamous example of this transcultural contact is that of Alberto Fujimori, the former president of Peru, who maintains strong ties to Japan and Latin America, evinced by his dual Peruvian and Japanese citizenship. After leaving his self-imposed exile in Japan in 2000, Fujimori was extradited from Chile to Peru, where in April 2009 he was sentenced to twenty-five years in prison after being found guilty of ordering massacres and kidnappings during his tenure as commander in chief. Although the victims' families and human rights groups around the world celebrated his sentencing, it was not without conflict, for Fujimori is still revered by many Peruvians for his legacy in bringing the country out of near economic and political collapse and for his role in subduing the leftist guerrilla group El Sendero Luminoso, the Shining Path; in fact hundreds of Fujimori supporters, or *fujimoristas*, took to the streets to protest his sentence, and his closest ally, his daughter Keiko, once a congresswoman in Peru, was narrowly defeated in the 2011 run-off election for the presidency.[1]

On the popular culture front, the multiethnic band Ozomatli, with Latino and Asian American band members (among others), points to the new kinds of collaboration and political solidarity between Asian American and Latina/o Americans that is created in the music and entertainment media. Their compositions illustrate their multiethnic sound and often feature overtly political lyrics. Similarly the famed Latin pop star Enrique Iglesias, touted for his Spanish songs and crossover appeal in the United States, is of mixed Filipino and Spanish ancestry. These two examples were preceded by the renowned Mexican singer and entertainer Ana Gabriel, who foregrounds her Mexican Chinese heritage in her public image.[2] Twenty years ago Chicano activists and audiences were scandalized when the mestizo Filipino actor Lou Diamond Phillips took major roles in Latino cinematic productions, such as the lead role of Ritchie Valens in Gregory Nava's *La Bamba* and a Chicano gang member in *Stand and Deliver*. Now the protagonist in a recent film about the Chicano student movement, *Walkout* (2006), is openly Filipina Mexican, or as the character's father refers to her, a "Chilipina." And Phillips has been embraced by the Filipino American community; he was recognized by *Filipinas* magazine in 2001 and awarded the Asian Pacific Islander Heritage award in 2005 for his work in the entertainment media.

The collaboration and continuities between these two communities, Filipino and Mexican, in the United States has begun to be recognized in mainstream media. This recognition affects subsequent political, social, and cultural formations and challenges the separation between ethnic and racialized communities, which, as many who study these topics are aware, has always been part of the larger tapestry of Asian-Latina/o relations. Indeed many of the regions of this study—Hawai'i, the Philippines, the Caribbean, and North and South America—have long histories of racial mixing and cross-cultural contact. We seek to bring these lineages to the fore to forge the groundwork for new ways of approaching often disparate fields of study toward the formation of transnational and comparative studies of the Americas and the American

Pacific. *Transnational Crossroads* participates in what Masao Miyoshi calls the "de-disciplining" of geographical spaces and bodies of knowledge as they pertain to Asian and Latina/o America and the American Pacific. Utilizing a comparative and relational framework this collection of essays weaves together narratives of U.S. and Spanish empire; globalization; resistance; social, labor, and political movements; and identity.

Scope of the Book

Transnational Crossroads interrogates "America" as a placeless place that does not neatly index the mainland territory of the United States but instead corresponds to the larger geopolitical boundaries of the Americas and the American Pacific. We use the term "crossroads" to evoke the idea of a place where various lines of inquiry intersect to produce new forms of knowledge and ways of seeing. This study of the Americas adds an east-west dimension to the typically north-south orientation. Thus the focus shifts from the United States as the purported center of American studies to foreground contact and collaboration across the Americas and the American Pacific. American studies has just begun to reflect changes in world dynamics that have impacted the role and function of the United States in the hemisphere and beyond. Though cultural and political contact across and between the American hemispheres and the American Pacific has a long history, there is little academic work that examines the consequences and contemporary conditions of this contact. *Transnational Crossroads* foregrounds the cultural contact and political alliances that have shaped the newly defined force field of America and examines how this region is profoundly affected by a long history of colonialism and imperialism. Recent American studies scholarship has moved away from the exceptionalist model to examine the United States in terms of its naked imperial ambitions while excavating the actual meaning of "America" as inclusive of the entire hemisphere. Scholars such as José David Saldívar, E. San Juan Jr., George Yúdice, Haunani-Kay Trask, Amy Kaplan, Greg Grandin, John Mason Hart, Donald

Pease, Robyn Wiegman, David Stannard, and Rob Wilson have led this charge.[3] *Transnational Crossroads* carries on this critical tradition but adds the South American hemisphere and the American Pacific into the examination of the multiple imperial legacies of the Americas, particularly within a comparative analysis of the U.S. and Spanish empires.

An emergent body of work over the past few years has set the stage for comparative ethnic studies, especially as it relates to Asian and Latina/o America. Books by Mae Ngai, Natalia Molina, Scott Kurashige, Luis Alvarez, Eileen O'Brien, and Laura Pulido provide comparative frameworks for understanding the experiences of both Chicana/os and Latina/os, African Americans, Asian Americans, and Pacific Islanders with regard to issues such as immigration, health, racialization, and social activism in the United States. Similarly studies done by Sandhya Shukla and Heidi Tinsman and by Rob Wilson also expand this comparative approach with regard to national and disciplinary boundaries, expanding notions of what "America" means in a rapidly globalizing world. Shukla and Tinsman's *Imagining Our Americas*, for example, provides a hemispheric approach beyond the confines of an America that is not bound by borders but is a space where transnational realities exist.[4]

Transnational Crossroads brings together many areas of study and disciplines to forge a global perspective around imperial formations in the American hemisphere and the Pacific. Often Latin American, Asian American, and Pacific Islander studies are separate "area studies," just as American studies and Latin American studies had been in the early years of their development. American studies began as a nationalist project about U.S. identity and the formation of the nation-state. Latin American studies in the United States emerged during the cold war to serve the intelligence interests of Washington, though by the 1970s Latin American studies in the United States shifted focus and became inflected with the political work of left-leaning thinkers. U.S. American studies and Latin American studies were mutually exclusive projects that served the same aims: the continued dominance of the United States in the hemisphere and the commanding position of Washington. Recent American studies work links these two projects around a critical and reflexive approach that includes a trans-American perspective and examines the imperial ambitions of the United States.

Asian American and Latina/o studies, like American and Latin American studies, share the same origin; both emerged in a post–civil rights context to examine the histories, cultural productions, political formations, and social movements of Asian Americans and Latina/os. Yet Asian American studies and Latina/o studies have been kept separate, a reflection of the racial stratification of the United States. Moreover ethnic studies has harbored U.S.-centric notions based on exceptionalist ideas about the exemplary case of U.S. civil rights struggles. Often the United States remains at the center of ethnic studies, and U.S. processes of racialization are central to its formation.

Transnational Crossroads engages the colonial and imperial histories of migrations and cultural and political contact across the Americas and the Pacific that displaces the United States from the center of critical analysis. For instance, we include areas of research that have been marginal to recent studies of the Americas. Hawaiian studies is rarely at the center of ethnic and American studies, as it has been to Pacific Islands studies. Yet Hawaiian studies examines issues of sovereignty and native self-determination and U.S. imperialism that set it apart from the larger rubric of Pacific Islands studies. Likewise Filipina/o studies has unique features that distinguish it from Asian or Asian American studies. Filipina/o studies explores the transnational links among Filipinos in the diaspora and the Philippines along with issues of both Spanish colonialism and U.S. imperialism.

This volume seeks to be a foundational text that will bring all of these areas of study together under the same umbrella. We bring together comparative American and comparative ethnic studies while opening up a field of study that compares Asian Pacific American and Latin American studies. Thus academic programs of study might rethink the boundaries and separations among academic units and seek new collaborations and new comparative and relational analyses for pressing concerns related to immigration, borders and national identity, and political coalition building. Our hope is that this volume enables new cross-discipline work and creative collaborations that will help students to think differently and maneuver an increasingly complex and interconnected global world. We bring together work on migration in the Americas, the political solidarity of Latina/os and Asians, political and social movements in the American Pacific, and comparative imperialism to show how these areas of study and the essays that represent these intersecting themes connect in comparative, relational, and global ways.

Part 1. The End of Empire: Spanish and U.S. Imperialism

The southern American hemisphere—from the U.S.-Mexican borderlands to the Southern Cone, and the American Pacific from Hawai'i to the Philippines and Guam—share many issues and concerns relating to national and cultural sovereignty, independent political formations, and socioeconomic and political stability. Each region must deal with the expanding notion of "America" as a term that has been colonized as shorthand for the United States and as an imperial concept—where "America" means, paradoxically, the forced imposition of democratic freedoms and at-will interventions to protect those freedoms. The borderless space of America links the various singularities and seeming incongruities in the hemisphere and across the Pacific. The American Pacific, Latina/o America, and Asian America are at the margins of America, in the places that are part of its territorial identity but not its definitional center. This anthology challenges the invisibility of these regions to the core notion of "America" and connects often disparate areas of study to foreground continuities and trends among places that share an Americanism of culture and name.

Recent work on the analysis of imperialism tends to focus on the role of the United States at the helm of global politics.[5] We argue that U.S. imperialism cannot be extracted from the legacies of Spanish imperialism in the hemisphere and in the Pacific. The comparison of the Spanish and U.S. imperial formations links the Pacific to the Americas while it also reveals how the process and status of empire have changed. The contemporary form and function of empire and its definitional center resides with the United States, but it is the shared history of Spanish subjection that links Latin America, parts of the Caribbean, the Philippines, and Guam.

The Uruguayan thinker Enrique Rodó, in his essay "Ariel" (1900), compared U.S. and Spanish cultural hegemony in a manner that shaped subsequent analyses of this relation.[6] His "Ariel" is a symbol of the intellectual and romantic spirit of Europe, and he implores Latin America to recognize and embrace this lineage. The United States is characterized by cold materialism and the ambitious drive, at all costs, to hegemony. Rodó cautions against the drive to modernization at the expense of cultural and intellectual development and calls for the creation of an elite class of cultural producers. Of course, his rhetorical exhortations were interpreted by later generations as the agenda of the ruling class. After the Cuban Revolution the Cuban thinker Roberto Fernández Retamar would rewrite "Ariel" as "Caliban" and propose the creation of liberatory cultural productions that value working-class contributions to national cultural identity.[7] What each writer from either side of the socioeconomic divide shares is the comparative analysis of postcolonial experience in the shadow of U.S. cultural imperialism. This back-to-back imperialism is more directly experienced by the regions linked by the Spanish-American War. Cuba, Puerto Rico, the Philippines, and Guam were "liberated" from Spain only to be placed directly into the imperial force field of the United States.

In this anthology we argue that it is possible to understand these island histories only within the context of shared and dual imperial relations. The histories of Spanish and U.S. imperialism are deeply imbricated. In many ways the rise to power of the United States is directly connected to the failures of the Spanish Empire. One of the greatest gains in territory occurred after the Mexican-U.S. War in 1848, when the United States annexed a massive amount of land that had formerly belonged to Spain. After 1898 the United States would present itself as a benevolent hero of freedom and independence to the former colonies of Spain. If the two empires were to be compared, as they were in "Ariel," it would be along the axis of modernity. Spanish rule was characterized by brutal conversions to Catholicism, corrupt rule, excessive taxation, hierarchical social relations, and adherence to tradition.[8] At the end of its imperial rule, Spain had remained unchanged for centuries and had acquired the status of being archaic and backward. After the Spanish-American War, the United States promised cultural and economic uplift from the downward pull of Spanish backwardness. The Spanish imperial career in the American hemisphere and the Philippines was finally terminated in 1898, with the Spanish-American War opening the way for the subsequent rise of U.S. dominance in the region and the Pacific. The corrupt and weakening influence of the Spanish Empire left its former colonies prey to U.S. colonial rule and vulnerable to its many promises of cultural and economic uplift. The United States offered modernization of public works and institutions and political restructuring and opened up trade relations. But these benevolent gestures concealed sinister motives to control these new colonies at all costs; the United States would engage in an illegal war against Filipinos from 1899 to 1902 (which led to continued resistance until 1916), slaughtering an estimated one million Filipinos who resisted being "liberated."[9]

The geopolitical boundaries of the United States, far from being natural or predestined by the shape of its territorial space, can be traced back to international wars and conflicts. Those boundaries are an effect of the competition among empires, particularly the Spanish and the French, and the success of the United States in the nineteenth century set the stage for its global imperial image in the twentieth and twenty-first centuries. From the original settlements to the Louisiana Purchase in 1803, the Mexican- and

Spanish-American wars in 1848 and 1898, respectively, the wars in Asia and Central America, and the wars in the Gulf region and the Middle East, the motives for international engagement have shifted from desire for territorial expansion to the promotion and display of influence and "American" values. Washington has reshaped the meaning of empire to something practically unrecognizable and easily disavowed; George W. Bush and his staff often denied the existence of a U.S. Empire, stating plainly on many occasions that "the United States is not an empire." In actuality the United States is the only truly global empire that has created and disseminated a world system based on its principles. The United States is both visible and invisible as the center of world organization; it is the absent center that shapes the whole. The "Americanism" of the world order is most apparent in the shape of "America," which has migrated from the mainland United States to the Caribbean and the Pacific. We use the term "America" to link these disparate locations and spaces, and we do so in a manner that is critical, recognizing the imperial drive that animates it.

The transnational flows that are an effect of empire have recently been marked as sinister routes of terrorism. For instance, the colonial connection between the United States and the Philippines was not a very visible part of popular or public culture in the United States—the opposite is true in Filipino popular culture—until the specter of terrorism forcefully emerged after the tragic events of September 11, 2001.[10] Suddenly the Philippines were targeted as another front on the "war on terror." The Philippines developed internal counterterrorism strategies that reflected those of the United States. This led to new restrictions on travel into and out of the Philippines as part of the 2007 Philippine Human Security Act that authorizes the detainment of anyone suspected of terrorism at will and without due process. Faye Caronan writes of the limitations this places on transnational activists whose work makes them vulnerable to charges of terrorism. She offers the example of the transnational network Gabriela, which advocates for Filipino women's rights in various capacities, particularly as they relate to domestic workers. But members of Gabriela have been deemed terrorists by the Philippine government and put on no-fly lists, severely limiting their ability to act transnationally to protect Filipinas from human rights abuses. Caronan compares the postcolonial roles and work of Filipino and Puerto Rican transnational activist-artists as symptoms of the divergent status of the Philippines and Puerto Rico within the U.S. Empire. The Philippines and Puerto Rico share the double colonial legacies of subjection to the Spanish and U.S. empires, and from these colonial conditions arise similar means of addressing and contesting them. Yet as a colony, the Philippines was deemed unassimilable to the U.S. state, while Puerto Rico was integrated as a commonwealth, making Puerto Ricans U.S. citizens. Caronan describes how Filipino artist-activists suffer more limitations than their Puerto Rican counterparts, yet these artists actively engage in coalition building that serves to break down these limitations.

Camilla Fojas examines the incongruity noted by Caronan between the Philippines and Puerto Rico along with the other islands gained by the United States after 1898, including Hawai'i, Cuba, and the less often mentioned Guam. Fojas describes the imagined space of the U.S. Empire in which disparate island nations were in constant company in U.S. mass media. She argues that travel writings after 1898 promoted empire as a way of life for U.S. citizens by suggesting new opportunities for work and leisure. These travel guides were popular texts that set the terms for subsequent imperial attitudes toward Cuba, Puerto Rico, the Philippines, and Hawai'i. Describing these places together also generates the illusion of imperial control. The guidebooks depict island peoples as uniformly suffering from moral and physical lassitude while exhorting U.S. readers to invest in the colonies and remedy tropical malaise with industrial labor. The Spanish-American War and subsequent rise to empire of the United States intensified the circulation of peoples and goods among these islands and the mainland U.S., a circulation that would include new routes of military travel between Pearl Harbor, Vieques, Manila, and Guantánamo Bay.

Vernadette Vicuña Gonzalez follows one axis of these patterns of travel, taking the route from Pearl Harbor to Manila. She traces recent paths of circulation in Asia and the Pacific through the production of articles of tourism relating to Hawaiian practices and objects. She traces the production of the Hawaiian quilt as it is displaced from the islands to the Philippines and later to China. The quilt is an object that embodies cultural relations and visually depicts Hawaiian stories, but Gonzalez notes that it can be read as an object of different cultural relations telling new stories about the conditions of global capital flows. Gonzalez examines the history of the relationship between Hawai'i and the Philippines in terms of the hierarchies of empire and the gendered relations of the work and politics of quilt making. She finds that the global circulation of the Hawaiian quilt form produces unexpected contact and possible lines of affiliation between colonized peoples across Asia and the Pacific.

Part 2. Comparative Racialization:
Trans-American Pacific Racial Formations

In this anthology we attempt to go beyond ethnic studies as a regional set of debates by placing interethnic and transracial relations in a global context that includes the American hemisphere and the American Pacific. What may seem like a project with an ambitious scope captures the complex and shifting perspective shared by many multiracial and mixed-heritage peoples in a globalized world. The work in this anthology is linked by the common experience of a colonial heritage that can be traced back to the Spanish Empire or to the contemporary force field of the U.S. Empire.

Comparative work on racialization challenges discrete categories of race but is also inherently tied to colonial and imperial histories, giving it a transnational and global focus that displaces any single nation or territory from the center of critical analysis. The contact among races is the result of various kinds of migration, both forced and at will, and it is the outcome of imperial expansion throughout the ages as well as contemporary forces of globalization. Though the work in this anthology is linked by the common referent of "America," we are concerned with how the notion of "racialization" has different meanings in the hemisphere and in the Pacific, particularly in regions that share colonial heritages.

We acknowledge, as many critics have done, that although race is a fiction, it has very real effects, particularly that of differential treatment based on racialization. Like ideology, race is an idea and an image that has changed across time and place and that has been identified as a major shorthand for identity. To get a sense of one of the possible futures of contact among the races, or multiraciality in the Americas, we need only take a page from the history of *mestizaje* in Mexico.

After the Mexican Revolution the mestizo became a symbol of new revolutionary Mexico, a symbol not just of the mixed configuration of cultures but of a future state of social unity and cohesion. The spokesperson for this future was José Vasconcelos; his mestizo is heralded as the "cosmic race" and the future not just of Mexico but also of the world. Yet his theory of the cosmic race retained the taint of racial hierarchies of his day; he talks of *tipos bajos* ("lower types") being absorbed by *el tipo superior* ("the superior type"), the latter describing the Anglo race while all other races were deemed lower. The mixture of the two elevates the lower types, who bring the advantage of the adaptive qualities of the lower races.[11] The postrevolutionary rhetoric about a racial utopia remained just that; the entrenched meanings around race have yet to be eclipsed by some other value system, and whiteness remains a powerful cultural emblem. Later in the twentieth century the borderlands critic Gloria Anzaldúa reclaimed the new mestizo as a sign of how Latina/os, particularly Chicana/os, are between cultures and racial poles in the United States and thereby have already culturally adapted to the future of mestizaje.[12] Nonetheless the overwhelming symbolic force of whiteness emanating from long histories of empire and colonialism maintains Anglo power far beyond efforts at cultural resignification.

In the United States Latina/os and Asian Americans are less likely to be drawn into the same political orbit, and there has been little work on the comparative racialization of both groups. Yet Latina/os and Asian Americans share common experiences related to immigration, internal colonialism, assimilation, and often negative racialization. In the United States these groups have been pitted against each other through the myth that Asian Americans constitute a "model minority" against which all other racialized minorities fall short. For this reason we couch the analysis of race within the American sphere in terms of histories of colonialism and imperialism. We examine circuits of migration in the Americas and the American Pacific; this includes Asian migration to the Americas and Hawai'i and Latina/o migration to the northern hemisphere and the American Pacific. Each instance of cross-cultural and racial contact subtends different racialized and cultural discourses, and these discourses must be read in terms of the history of colonial and imperial interventions. Many of our contributors are interested in the potential for political collaboration across racial and ethnic divides, particularly in the case of Asians and Latina/os. In the relatively special case of Hawai'i, plantation economies and the migration of various groups from Asia, the Caribbean, and the mainland along with the Native Hawaiian population has created a uniquely diverse racialized population. The "local cultures" of mixed peoples of Asian heritage with long histories in Hawai'i often conflict with the indigenous Hawaiian sovereignty movement. Using various cases from diverse regions in the Americas and the American Pacific, we challenge American conceptions of racial polarization by reexamining the color line around the histories and politics of colonialism and imperialism.

One way of reexamining the negative racialization of Asians and Latina/os in the United States is by returning to shared histories of racial denigration and political exclusions. Jinah Kim shows how Japanese internees and Mexican braceros during World War II share similar histories of racialization and cultural exclusion. Yet she warns of the pitfalls of reparations discourse in ethnic studies scholarship since the discourse of state apology or reparation obviates the need to discuss the role of the state in the ongoing production of racial violence. Instead Kim argues that we should move beyond the politics of injury and victimization to the formation of a "just space" in the racial remapping of the Americas. These two cases show how the borders of the United States have realigned to produce what Mike Davis calls a "third border," which effects a pervasive separation and segregation of racialized and immigrant bodies. Kim uses these historical cases to forge new directions in comparative work in Latina/o American and Asian American studies.

Asian Americans and Latina/os have long been separated and pitted against each other in the United States. In their chapter Gilda L. Ochoa, Laura E. Enriquez, Sandra Hamada, and Jenniffer Rojas show how the separation between Asian Americans and Latina/os originates and is perpetuated in the experience of students in middle school and high school in California. Drawing data from 230 open-ended interviews of students, parents, and teachers and other school personnel, Ochoa et al. discovered a profound gap in social and educational experiences based on racialization. Asian American students were perceived as "high achieving" and rule-abiding, whereas Latina/os were considered "low achieving" and more likely to be disobedient. This insidious and persistent gap in perception based on race and ethnicity leads to profound interracial tension and learned social stratification. This study makes apparent the need to reassess the dominant attitudes and ideologies that shape educational policy and practice; moreover all students are negatively affected by such deeply prejudicial and racially determined attitudes, which in turn limit their educational experience. This educational socialization denies the history of collaboration and interethnic work of Latina/os and Asian Americans.

In his essay Rudy P. Guevarra Jr. recovers a vital history in the labor and political collaboration between Filipino and Mexican workers, showing that interethnic labor organizing in Hawai'i was a template for similar efforts in California. Guevarra shows, for example, that Filipino organizers, after being forcibly exiled from

Hawai'i for being "agitators," joined thousands of other workers who left voluntarily and took their work to California, thus beginning interethnic labor organizing efforts. He notes that this occurred a good forty years before the iconic work of the United Farm Workers in the 1960s. The work of Filipinos and Mexicans set the terms and lay the groundwork for subsequent efforts, and although moments of tension existed between them, their common struggle may be seen as a model for interethnic and cross-racial alliances.

Part 3. The American Pacific

The American Pacific is a vast region where cultures and peoples have intersected as U.S. interests spanned the continental United States and reached into the Pacific Ocean and its territories. Within this context, the struggles of Kanaka Maoli (Native Hawaiian) and other Pacific Islanders have been an ongoing process in the realm of U.S. empire. Indeed these movements center on issues of citizenship, sovereignty, land rights, political leadership, labor, identity, and nationhood. Studies such as those by Paul R. Spickard, Joanne L. Rondilla and Debbie Hippolite Wright, Jonathan Kamakawiwo'ole Osorio, Davianna Pomaika'i McGregor, Donald Denoon and Malama Meleisea, Noenoe K. Silva, Haunani-Kay Trask, Candace Fujikane, and Jonathan Y. Okamura speak to the complex, interwoven histories and interrelations that Asians, Filipinos, and Pacific Islanders have to each other and within the context of U.S. empire and postempire relations as colonial and postcolonial subjects.[13]

The Monroe Doctrine of 1823 set the global stage for how the United States imagined its boundaries, beginning in the western hemisphere, which was the impetus to expand overseas as U.S. greed for markets, cheap labor, and military buildup in the region was well under way. The cry of manifest destiny necessitated U.S. expansion, according to its proponents, doubling the size of the United States by 1848, after its war with Mexico, and supporting its imperial ambitions to compete with European powers that were colonizing the world. The Spanish-American War of 1898 catapulted U.S. geographical boundaries across the globe to extend its reach to the Philippines, Guam, and other former Spanish colonies. The United States also set its sights on the Hawaiian Islands, which were already being colonized by missionaries and sugar interests after the Great Mahele (division) in 1848 and a subsequent land law in 1850 ended the traditional Hawaiian system of landownership. This opened the door for foreign interests to control Hawaiian lands for the sake of U.S. capitalism. The illegal overthrow of the Hawaiian Kingdom in 1893 and the annexation of the Hawaiian Islands in 1898 signaled the beginning of U.S. permanency in the Pacific as it established the island of O'ahu as its major Pacific military base. Controlling the Hawaiian Islands was a strategic move of the United States, which could monitor Japan and other colonial powers as they made their way into U.S. territorial waters. Guam and the Philippines were already militarily, economically, and educationally colonized to create other U.S. bases in the Pacific.

In the context of the U.S. military buildup in the Pacific during the late nineteenth and twentieth century, one could argue that the United States was also in an arms and territory race with a rising Asian superpower, Japan, who with the Sino-Japanese War (1894–95) and Russo-Japanese War (1904–5) had established itself as a modern-day military force with its own imperial ambitions. With the entrance of the United States in World War II after Japan's bombing of Pearl Harbor on December 7, 1941, the two imperial powers were fighting for control of the Pacific region, with campaigns in the Philippines, Guam, New Guinea, and the Gilbert, Marshall, Solomon, and Mariana Islands, among other areas. Just as it rose in power amid the ashes of Spain's demise as an empire, with Japan's surrender in 1945 the United States became the most powerful empire in the world, establishing permanent military bases in the Philippines, Hawai'i (which achieved statehood in 1959), Guam, and American Sāmoa (which was under U.S. control by 1904). The Federated States of Micronesia, which includes the Republic of the Marshall Islands, the Republic of Palau, and the

Commonwealth of the Northern Mariana Islands, also came under the umbrella of U.S. control when they signed the Compact of Free Association in 1986. Indeed the presence of the United States in the Pacific and its neocolonial relationships with these countries confirm the continued existence of the U.S. Empire.

However, when U.S. soldiers went from being "liberators" to being "oppressors," the U.S. Empire faced resistance among the populations of these regions. Scholars such as Haunani-Kay and Mililani B. Trask, Kekuni Blaisdell, Keith L. Camacho, and Setsu Shigematsu write critically about the United States and its colonial stranglehold in the Pacific, which has endured nuclear bombings, economic dependence, the destruction of land and water, and U.S. military presence.[14] One cannot discuss the Pacific without critically examining U.S. imperialism and its influence in the continued migration of Pacific Islanders and Filipinos to the United States as a result of the depressed economies and environmental destruction that is occurring in the name of national security and democracy. Indeed these movements of people signal the contraction of geographic space as imperial expansion and globalization have made such journeys a means of survival.

Maile Arvin addresses some of these issues in her chapter, as she explores how Kanaka Maoli (Native Hawaiians) deal with issues of identity and land rights when public discourse markets their cultural and socioeconomic difference and multiculturalism through neoliberal benevolence, thus depoliticizing and minimizing their claims for sovereignty and justice under U.S. rule. Referring to what she calls "spectacles of philanthropy," Arvin evokes the examples of multimillion-dollar homes in an area of Oʻahu being given to eight "deserving" Native Hawaiian families by Genshiro Kawamoto, a Japanese real estate tycoon in 2006, and an episode of ABC's *Extreme Makeover: Home Edition* in 2007 that featured a Native Hawaiian family receiving a mansion. The episode portrayed them as deserving because they embodied a humble "spirit of aloha." These forms of welfare, Arvin notes, worked to silence the voices of Kanaka Maoli struggling for sovereignty and land rights.

Arvin also provides a critical examination of the debates surrounding the Akaka Bill, which also elicits spectacles of philanthropy by rewarding good citizenship with a settlement package
from the U.S. government. The bill has gone through several revisions to address issues such as gaming rights, though it still does
not speak to the issue of land rights in Hawai'i. Although there
are groups in favor of the bill, others, such as Ka Lahui Hawai'i,
advocate for moving the conversation of Native Hawaiian recognition away from a U.S.-centered discourse to one that is international. Arvin explores how this recent debate over the Akaka Bill,
land rights in Hawai'i, and Kanaka Maoli citizenship illustrates
that Native Hawaiians are more than just the "victimized citizenry" that both the media and Congress present them to be.

Continuing the conversation regarding Hawaiian lands and identity, ku'ualoha ho'omanawanui demonstrates the importance of
viewing Hawai'i as a geographical place and a contested space. As
the original inhabitants of the Hawaiian Islands, Kanaka Maoli
must contend with immigrant groups who claim Hawai'i as their
homeland. The use of indigenized identity terms such as *kama'āina*
(child of the land), "local," "hapa," and "Hawaiian at heart,"
ho'omanawanui claims, perpetuates the erasure of Native Hawaiians, who are "First Nations people." She asks whether indigenous
claims to identity, land, and nationhood are still relevant in today's
transglobal world, and whether immigrants and settler groups can
support indigenous claims to land, nationhood, and identity. These
questions probe for a deeper understanding of these identity terms
and the implications they have with regard to the violent dispossession, displacement, and treatment of Kanaka Maoli from the
eighteenth century to the present.

Ho'omanawanui links issues of land and identity to present-day
scenarios, as she examines contemporary erasures in what she calls
both "real and imagined worlds." These include websites that misappropriate the term "hapa" in multiple forms, though what they
all have in common, she suggests, is a lack of historical knowledge
of this Hawaiian word as used by Kanaka Maoli; the Polynesian

Cultural Center and its use of advertisements to play with the notion that settlers are also native; the use of the word *kamaʻāina*
by local business and tourism that normally have no such ties to
Hawaiʻi and, most famously, to describe President Barack Obama,
who is touted as a kamaʻāina because of his ties to Hawaiʻi as a
former settler, which, as hoʻomanawanui notes, ignores the Natives in Hawaiʻi and further erases their indigenous claims to land
and identity.

Bianca Isaki continues the discussion of Asian settlers with a
specific incident. In 1894 Japanese workers trekked thirty-eight
miles from Kahuku plantation to Honolulu to present their grievances regarding a *luna* (foreman) to Goro Narita, the Japanese
chargé d'affaires to the Hawaiian Republic. Rather than listen with
compassion to the workers' issues, authorities arrested them and
fined them five dollars each, then made them walk back to work.
In connecting history with the present, Isaki then recounts how
her grandmother Thelma Shigemitsu shared memories of her ties
to Kahuku while they walked along the Kahuku stretch of Kamehameha highway. In the context of juxtaposing these two stories,
Isaki links past to present, offering a way to re-archive Hawaiʻi
in U.S. history as the history not only of colonial dispossession of
Native Hawaiian rights and land, but also of the position Asian
settlers have in this narrative. She writes, "As Hawaiians decolonize *these* histories, Asian settlers cannot have a history of becoming U.S. citizens in Hawaiʻi anymore." She thus calls for a decolonial archive. Her exploration of this idea is in response to what
she sees as Asian settler state administers who have politically and
economically benefited under U.S. hegemony since World War II.
Citing the former Hawaiʻi governor George Ariyoshi, who stated
that non-Native Hawaiians also deserve a place to rest under the
sun, Isaki exhorts us to critique such notions of political legitimacy and of a moral economy of merit and insensitivity. By contem-
plating and reenvisioning her grandmother's connection to history and landscape, Isaki offers a way to remember and re-archive
such histories of Asian settlers in the context of U.S. hegemony.

JoAnna Poblete examines the relationship between Puerto Rico, the Philippines, and Hawai'i. After the Spanish-American War of 1898, both the Philippines and Puerto Rico become territories of the United States, along with Hawai'i, which was illegally annexed and made into a territory. Because of their status as nationals who could move freely within the United States and its colonial possessions, Puerto Rican and Filipino plantation workers move to the Territory of Hawai'i to live and work on the sugar plantations during the first half of the twentieth century. Poblete calls these workers intracolonials who move in and out of the U.S. Empire. Given that they had no official support to advocate for their grievances, local community leaders, such as labor agents and ethnic ministers, filled that void. Poblete thus explores the complexities of these intracolonial workers, local community leaders, and Anglo sugar planters and how the workers' needs were met in this context.

Part 4. Crossroads of American Migration

The intersectionality between Asians and Latina/os has been the subject of several studies that examine the diaspora and the integration or subjugation of Asians across the Pacific and into the western hemisphere. These interactions are not a twentieth- or twenty-first-century phenomenon, but are part of historical processes in which cultures, bodies, and consumer goods have been in constant motion between Asia, the Pacific region, the Americas, and the Caribbean. The 250-year period of the Acapulco-Manila galleon trade (1565–1815) between Mexico and the Philippines in the context of Spanish colonialism is one example. This period signaled the first global trade network, which brought significant changes to these economies in the form of agricultural produce, forced labor, luxury and other consumer goods, bodies, and ideas. It is in this context that primarily Filipino Indios as well as Chinese (known to the Spanish as *Sangleys*) and Chinese mestizos (*mestizos de Sangley*) from the Philippines were integrated into local Mexican societies. Tens of thousands of Filipino Indios jumped ship once they reached the port of Acapulco, blending into local communities and marrying Mexican Indio and mixed-race women. The descendants of these early deserters still reside in the coastal regions of the Mexican state of Guererro and other parts of Mexico.[15] However, Filipinos were not the only group from the Asian Pacific region to migrate to the Americas and the Caribbean. Throughout the nineteenth and twentieth centuries, thousands of Chinese, Japanese, Asian Indians, and Koreans made their way to Mexico, Cuba, Brazil, Peru, and other parts of Latin America and the Caribbean. There they labored in various industries, established small businesses and communities, and even fought in revolutionary wars in their adopted countries. Studies such as those by Evelyn Hu-De-Hart, Seiichi Higashide, Lane Ryo Hirabayashi, Edward R. Slack Jr., Robert Chao Romero, Walton Look Lai, Floro Mercene, Lok C. D. Siu, and Andrew R. Wilson show the rich, complex history and interactions of Asians and Latina/os in the Americas.[16] Social and political movements, most notably the involvement of Chinese during the Cuban Revolution of the 1950s, illustrate the integration of these communities into their new homelands and their relationship with their Latina/o counterparts. Indeed Asians and Latina/os have been intricately linked by historical events, cultural exchanges, commerce, and personal interrelationships. However these interactions were not always amicable; at times conflict and violence also existed between Asian and Latina/o communities. In Mexico, for example, staunch anti-Chinese sentiment and racism was rampant during the 1920s–30s. Violence and the move to exclude and expel Chinese and other Asians from Mexico were very profound at both local and national levels. Intellectuals, business leaders, and others, such as José Vasconcelos, José Maria Arana, Adolfo de la Huerta, José Angel Espinoza, and even the Mexican revolutionary Francisco "Pancho" Villa, were staunchly anti-Chinese and participated in the expulsion and even extermination of Chinese and other Asians.

In the contemporary era, conflict between Pacific Islanders and Latina/os can be seen in the recent example of the violation of human rights by the Chilean government against the Rapa Nui people, stemming from land and sovereignty issues, which demonstrates the intricacies of colonialism in all its forms.[17] These examples of interaction and conflict show the complexities and intersections that exist in Latin America and the Caribbean among Asians, Latina/os, Africans, and other ethnic groups as they live, work, mobilize, and worship together in their respective societies. Their stories are evidence of the rich historical legacy that continues to unfold in the present time, as Asians and Latina/os continue to build community across boundaries in the Americas.

We begin this section with Erika Lee, who examines a transnational debate over race and immigration policy in the western hemisphere in the nineteenth century, led by the United States, which ultimately influenced how Canada and South America, specifically Brazil and Peru, would treat its Japanese immigrant communities. In what she calls "hemispheric Orientalism," the multiple processes of race made Japanese an unassimilable race and culture. Lee contends that anti-Japanese sentiment and restrictive immigration policies in North and South America "contributed to an unparalleled transnational conversation about race, migration, and national and hemispheric security." A global discussion of the "Yellow Peril" spread from the United States and Canada, eventually influencing how Peru and Brazil would see and respond to its Japanese immigrant communities. Indeed the fear of the Yellow Peril in the United States set the tone for its immigration laws, specifically the 1924 Immigration Act to curtail the Japanese threat. Similar laws followed in Canada, Brazil, and Peru in the 1920s and 1930s. The rhetoric of Peruvian businessmen, intellectuals, policymakers, and ordinary citizens echoed the same prejudices and fears that were running rampant in the United States, portraying the Japanese as an economic threat unwilling to assimilate into Peruvian society. These unfounded fears and animosity culminated in anti-Japanese riots. World War II proved devastating to the Peruvian Japanese community, when Peru sent an estimated 1,800 of its Japanese immigrant citizens to be interned in the United States. These incidents illustrate how racialization and laws of exclusion

occur as transnational processes and policies across borders and
have lasting implications in the western hemisphere. As Lee notes,
these hemispheric Asian migration and exclusion experiences provide us with a way of connecting histories of Asians in the Americas across local, regional, national, and global contexts.

Stella Oh provides a much-needed perspective on the dialogue
concerning the U.S.-Mexican border by illustrating how borders
are dynamic regions that redefine notions of home. In her examination of Karen Tei Yamashita's *Tropic of Orange* (1997), Oh challenges the notions of an exclusive U.S.-Mexican border by tracing
what she calls the "capital flows of poisoned oranges from Brazil to
Mexico to California," and more broadly from South America to
the United States. Utilizing an approach that shows the complexities of transnational flows of capital, culture, and people that extend far beyond the U.S.-Mexican border, Oh's reading of *Tropic
of Orange* illustrates how new approaches to homeland are forged
as people search for their roots in a context of displacement. This
is most evident in the way Asians and Latina/os are exploited in
their home countries, so that they are forced to migrate to the United States, leading to what Oh calls a "commerce of humanity." Using the examples of an Asian-Mexican relationship and a multiracial child, she shows how the lived experiences of people transcend
boundaries and borders, resulting in transnational movements and
cultural connections in an increasingly globalizing world. Borders do not necessarily define us, Oh says, but they contribute to
the complexity of our notions of home, nation-state, and identity.

Claudia Sadowski-Smith engages with the work of both Stella
Oh and Erika Lee, invoking Lee's argument that comparative work
should move beyond the geographical confines of the United States
and the Pacific and incorporate hemispheric perspectives into the
discussion of transpacific connections of families and communities. Sadowski-Smith does this by examining three novels: Cristina
Garcia's *Monkey Hunting* (2003), SKY Lee's *Disappearing Moon
Café* (1991), and Karen Tei Yamashita's *Tropic of Orange* (1997).
These novels portray the movements of Chinese migrants to Cuba,

Canada, and the United States via Mexico and the impact this has had on the formation of Asian American families. As Sadowski-Smith notes, these stories speak to the role that trauma plays in these relationships and how it is passed down through family stories. Historical trauma and memory thus contribute to the formation of these interracial families. The relationship between Chinese men and Afro-Cuban, Native Canadian, and Latina women were based on a shared, collective experience with trauma and multiraciality, thus challenging the long-standing belief that ethnic communities function as separate entities with little interaction with each other. Read together, these novels illustrate how interactions between racialized communities and the multiplicity these families and communities embody have yet to be acknowledged as part of the "narrative of national identity" that was influenced by U.S. imperialism and the migratory movement of Chinese as a result of economic, political, immigration, and racialized policies. In her examination of these novels Sadowski-Smith challenges the reader to embrace the possibility of alternative conceptions of family, community, and nation.

Jane H. Yamashiro and Hugo Córdova Quero provide a comparative account of how Japanese Americans and Japanese Brazilians construct their ethnic identities and cultural ties to Japan based on their cultural, social, and economic capital. In examining the transnational and transpacific migration patterns of these Nikkeijin (Japanese emigrants and their descendants), Yamashiro and Quero argue that although both Japanese Brazilians and Japanese Americans have similar backgrounds, once they are in Japan their social and economic status is based on their national background. Japanese Brazilians lose cultural capital because they come from a Latin American nation; in Japan they are seen as unskilled manual laborers. Japanese Americans occupy a more privileged position; because they come from the United States they can use their cultural and social capital to obtain white-collar work and move into middle- or even upper-class status. The fact that one does not need to know Japanese to get a good job in Japan, and the desire of many Japanese residents to learn English to obtain better employment opportunities and move up in social status, both speak to the power and influence of English-speaking countries in the world today. As Yamashiro and Quero explain, "Simply being an English speaker—and even more so if one is a native speaker—gives one cultural capital in Japan." This translates into economic capital as well, as English-speaking Japanese Americans supplement their income or make their livelihood by teaching English in Japan. These transnational experiences, when taken together, illustrate how Japanese Brazilian and Japanese American ethnic and cultural connections to Japan occur and are situated within a stratified local context and larger global economy.

Ryan Masaaki Yokota speaks to Erika Lee's discussion of the migration of Japanese to Peru; however, his focus is on the experience of Okinawans (Uchinānchu), who composed over a third of those who had migrated to Peru by 1941. Although Japanese and Okinawans maintained separate, independent community institutions, anti-Japanese sentiment by the larger Peruvian population changed their isolation from each other. As Yokota also notes, Okinawans constituted half of the 1,800 Japanese Peruvians to be interned in concentration camps in the United States, to be used as tools for hostage negotiations with Japan. That wartime experience, Yokota points out, started a transnational chain migration, which continues to the present.

As a diasporic community, Peruvian Okinawans developed a distinct transnational identity. Examining the Peruvian Nisei Association, whose members were predominantly Okinawan Peruvians, Yokota shows how these communities in Los Angeles had to deal with the complexities of having four different identities: Uchinānchu, Japanese, Peruvian, and American. They fostered this collective identity, overcoming class, regional origin, and language differences. By focusing on identity and ethnic formation in the context of cultural adjustment to the United States, Yokota shows how Okinawan identity has challenged notions of what it means to be an American, Asian, Asian American, or Latina/o. Their complex, cultural identity has survived despite all of the changes that have occurred since World War II. This identity persists today, and this multiplicity contributes to "a growing appreciation of who the Uchinānchu are."

Transnational Crossroads examines the geographic and imaginary boundaries of "America" across the Americas, the Caribbean, Asia, and the Pacific, weaving topics that address issues relating to the transnational and transpacific movements of goods, bodies, and ideas. By engaging in the interrogation of particular historical moments and contemporary issues, this collection critically examines how these relationships are complex in contested and cooperative interactions, existing as both a product and a mechanism of resistance to colonialism and racial discourses. It is our sincere hope that these essays, taken together, open up new discussions about the role and function of "America" in the world.

Notes

1. Adriana Leon and Chris Kraul, "Former Peru President Fujimori Convicted of Mass Murder, Kidnapping," *Los Angeles Times*, April 8, 2009, http://www.latimes.com/news/nationworld/world/la-fg-fujimori8 -2009apr08,0,1670805.story (accessed May 24, 2009).

2. Margie Brown-Coronel, "Intermarriage, Contemporary," in *Latinas in the United States: A Historical Encyclopedia*, ed. Vicki Ruíz and Virginia Sánchez Korrol (Bloomington: Indiana University Press, 2006), 1:342.

3. José David Saldívar, *Border Matters: Remapping American Cultural Studies* (Berkeley: University of California Press, 1997); E. San Juan Jr., *After Postcolonialism: Remapping Philippines–United States Confrontations* (Lanham MD: Rowman & Littlefield, 2000); E. San Juan Jr., *U.S. Imperialism and Revolution in the Philippines* (New York: Palgrave Macmillan, 2007); Haunani-Kay Trask, *From a Native Daughter: Colonialism and Sovereignty in Hawai'i* (Honolulu: University of Hawai'i Press, 1993); Amy Kaplan and Donald Pease, eds., *Cultures of United States Imperialism* (Durham NC: Duke University Press, 1993); Greg Grandin, *Empire's Workshop* (New York: Metropolitan Books, 2006); John Mason Hart, *Empire and Revolution: The Americans in Mexico*

since the Civil War (Berkeley: University of California Press, 2002); Donald Pease and Robyn Wiegman, eds., *The Futures of American Studies* (Durham NC: Duke University Press, 2002); David Stannard, *American Holocaust: The Conquest of the New World* (New York: Oxford University Press, 1992); George Yúdice, *The Expediency of Culture: Uses of Culture in a Global Era* (Durham NC: Duke University Press, 2003); Rob Wilson, *Reimagining the American Pacific: From South Pacific to Bamboo Ridge and Beyond* (Durham NC: Duke University Press, 2000).

4. See Mae M. Ngai, *Impossible Subjects: Illegal Aliens and the Making of Modern America* (Princeton NJ: Princeton University Press, 2004); Natalia Molina, *Fit to Be Citizens? Public Health and Race in Los Angeles, 1879–1939* (Berkeley: University of California Press, 2006); Scott Kurashige, *The Shifting Grounds of Race: Black and Japanese Americans in the Making of Multiethnic Los Angeles* (Princeton NJ: Princeton University Press, 2008); Luis Alvarez, *The Power of the Zoot: Youth Culture and Resistance during World War II* (Berkeley: University of California Press, 2008); Eileen O'Brien, *The Racial Middle: Latinos and Asians Living beyond the Racial Divide* (New York: New York University Press, 2008); Laura Pulido, *Black, Brown, Yellow and Left: Radical Activism in Los Angeles* (Berkeley: University of California Press, 2006); Sandhya Shukla and Heidi Tinsman, eds., *Imagining Our Americas: Towards a Transnational Frame* (Durham NC: Duke University Press, 2007); Wilson, *Reimagining the American Pacific.*

5. See Andrew J. Bacevich, ed., *The Imperial Tense: Prospects and Problems of American Empire* (Chicago: Ivan R. Dee, 2003); Andrew J. Bacevich, *American Empire: The Realities and Consequences of U.S. Diplomacy* (Cambridge MA: Harvard University Press, 2002); Niall Ferguson, *Colossus: The Price of America's Empire* (New York: Penguin, 2004); John Carlos Rowe, *Literary Culture and U.S. Imperialism: From the Revolution to World War II* (New York: Oxford University Press, 2000); Noam Chomsky, *Hegemony or Survival: America's Quest for Global Dominance* (New York: Metropolitan Books, 2003).

6. José Enrique Rodó, *Ariel*, ed. Belén Castro (Madrid: Cátedra, 2000).

7. Roberto Fernández Retamar, *Caliban and Other Essays*, trans. Edward Baker (Minneapolis: University of Minnesota Press, 1989).

8. The corruption of the Catholic Church was epic, particularly in the Philippines, where priests had the reputation of having forced relations with the young women of the pueblo, characterized at length in

José Rizal's critical novel *Noli me Tangere* (Manila: National Histori-cal Commission, 1975).

9. See Dylan Rodríguez, "A Million Deaths? Genocide and the 'Fili-pino American' Condition of Possibility," in *Positively No Filipinos Al-lowed: Building Communities and Discourse,* ed. Antonio T. Tiongson Jr., Edgardo V. Gutierrez, and Ricardo V. Gutierrez (Philadelphia: Tem-ple University Press, 2006), 158–61; Paul A. Kramer, *The Blood of Gov-ernment: Race, Empire, the United States and the Philippines* (Chapel Hill: University of North Carolina Press, 2006), 157–58; Luzviminda Francisco, "The First Vietnam: The U.S.-Philippine War of 1899," *Bul-letin of Concerned Asian Scholars* 5, no. 4 (1973): 10–14; Abe Ignacio, Enrique de la Cruz, Jorge Emmanuel, and Helen Toribio, *The Forbidden Book: The Philippine-American War in Political Cartoon* (San Francisco: T'Boli, 2004), 13; Angel Velasco Shaw and Luis H. Francia, eds., *Vestig-es of War: The Philippine-American War and the Aftermath of an Impe-rial Dream 1899–1999* (New York: New York University Press, 2002).

10. See San Juan, *U.S. Imperialism and Revolution in the Philippines,* xi.

11. José Vasconcelos, *The Cosmic Race,* trans. Didier T. Jaén (Balti-more: Johns Hopkins University Press, 1997); José Vasconcelos, *La Raza Cósmica* (México D.F.: Espasa-Calpe Mexicana, 1948).

12. Gloria Anzaldúa, *Borderlands/La Frontera: The New Mestiza* (San Francisco: Aunt Lute Books, 1987).

13. See Paul R. Spickard, Joanne L. Rondilla, and Debbie Hippolite Wright, eds., *Pacific Diaspora: Island Peoples in the United States and across the Pacific* (Honolulu: University of Hawai'i Press, 2002); Jona-than Kamakawiwo'ole Osorio, *Dismembering Lahui: A History of the Hawaiian Nation to 1887* (Honolulu: University of Hawai'i Press, 2002); Davianna Pomaika'i McGregor, *Na Kua 'Aina: Living Hawaiian Culture* (Honolulu: University of Hawai'i Press, 2007); Noenoe K. Silva, *Aloha Be-trayed: Native Hawaiian Resistance to American Colonialism* (Durham NC: Duke University Press, 2004); Donald Denoon and Malama Meleisea, *The Cambridge History of the Pacific Islanders* (New York: Cambridge University Press, 1997); Trask, *From a Native Daughter*; Candace Fuji-kane and Jonathan Y. Okamura, eds., *Asian Settler Colonialism: From Local Governance to the Habits of Everyday Life in Hawai'i* (Honolu-lu: University of Hawai'i Press, 2008); Jonathan Y. Okamura, *Ethnicity and Inequality in Hawai'i* (Philadelphia: Temple University Press, 2008).

14. See Mililani B. Trask, "Historical and Contemporary Hawaiian Self-Determination: A Native Hawaiian Perspective," *Arizona Journal of International and Comparative Law* 8, no. 2 (1991): 77–95; Trask, *From a Native Daughter*; Fujikane and Okamura, *Asian Settler Colonialism*; Setsu Shigematsu and Keith L. Camacho, eds., *Militarized Currents: Toward a Decolonized Future in Asia and the Pacific* (Minneapolis: University of Minnesota Press, 2010); Kekuni Blaisdell, "The Indigenous Rights Movement in the Pacific," *In Motion Magazine*, May 25, 1998, http://inmotionmagazine.com/pacific.html (accessed March 5, 2009); Kekuni Blaisdell, "Kanaka Maoli Self-Determination and Reinscription of Ka Pae-Aina (Hawai'i) on the U.N. List of Non-Self-Governing Territories," *In Motion Magazine*, November 22, 1998, http://inmotionmagazine.com/ngo2.html (accessed March 5, 2009).

15. See Rudy P. Guevarra Jr., "Mexipino: A History of Multiethnic Identity and the Formation of the Mexican and Filipino Communities of San Diego, 1900–1965" (PhD diss., University of California, Santa Barbara, 2007), 19–61; Floro L. Mercene, *Manila Men in the New World: Filipino Migration to Mexico and the Americas from the Sixteenth Century* (Honolulu: University of Hawai'i Press, 2007); Edward R. Slack Jr., "Sinifying New Spain: Cathay's Influence on Colonial Mexico via the *Nao de China*," *Journal of Chinese Overseas* 5 (2009): 5–27; Edward R. Slack Jr., "The *Chinos* in New Spain: A Corrective Lens for a Distorted Image," *Journal of World History* 20, no. 1 (2009): 35–67; John M. Headley, "Spain's Asian Presence, 1565–1590: Structures and Aspirations," *Hispanic American Historical Review* 75, no. 4 (1995): 623–46.

16. See Evelyn Hu-Dehart, ed., *Across the Pacific: Asian Americans and Globalization* (Philadelphia: Temple University Press, 1999); Evelyn Hu-Dehart and Lane Hirabayashi, eds., "Asians in the Americas: Transculturations and Power," special issue, *Amerasia Journal* 28, no. 2 (2002); Mercene, *Manila Men in the New World*; Slack, "Sinifying New Spain"; Slack, "The *Chinos* in New Spain"; Walton Look Lai, *Indentured Labor, Caribbean Sugar: Chinese and Indian Migrants to the British West Indies, 1838–1918* (Baltimore: Johns Hopkins University Press, 2004); Walton Look Lai, *The Chinese in the West Indies, 1806–1995: A Documentary History* (Kingston, Jamaica: University Press of the West Indies, 1998); Seiichi Higashide, *Adios to Tears: The Memoirs of a Japanese-Peruvian Internee in U.S. Concentration Camps* (Seattle: University of Washington Press, 2000); Lane Ryo, Akemi Kikumura-Yano, and James A.

Hirabayashi, eds., *New Worlds, New Lives: Globalization and People of Japanese Descent in the Americas and from Latin America in Japan* (Stanford: Stanford University Press, 2002); Lok C. D. Siu, *Memories of a Future Home: Diasporic Citizenship of Chinese in Panama* (Stanford: Stanford University Press, 2005); Andrew R. Wilson, ed., *The Chinese in the Caribbean* (Princeton NJ: Markus Wiener, 2004); Robert Chao Romero, *The Chinese in Mexico, 1882–1940* (Tucson: University of Arizona Press, 2010).

17. Ron Crocombe, "Latin America and the Pacific Islands," *Contemporary Pacific* 3, no. 1 (1991): 115–44; Max E. Stanton, "I'm Not a Chileno! Rapa Nui Identity," in *We Are a People: Narrative and Multiplicity in Constructing Ethnic Identity*, ed. Paul Spickard and W. Jeffrey Burroughs (Philadelphia: Temple University Press, 2000), 142–52; Mark Briggs, "U.N. Urges Chile to Halt Evictions of Indigenous Protestors on Easter Island," *Santiago Times*, January 14, 2011, http://en.mercopress .com/2011/01/18/u.n.-urges-chile-to-halt-evictions-of-indigenous-pro testers (accessed January 15, 2011).

Part 1
The End of Empire

| Spanish and U.S. Imperialism

Chapter 1

Postcolonial Im/migration and Transnational Activist Practices
Filipino American and U.S. Puerto Rican Performance Poet Activism

Faye Christine Caronan

On August 5, 2007, Annalisa Enrile, the national chairperson of Gabriela Network, a Philippines-U.S. women's organization focused on issues concerning Filipinas globally, was prevented from returning to the United States at the Manila international airport because her name was on a Philippine government hold list for undisclosed reasons. The hold list was a product of the 2007 Philippine Human Security Act (HSA) that authorized the government to indefinitely detain terrorist suspects without due process.[1] The HSA ambiguously defines terrorism as any act that "sow[s] and creat[es] a condition of widespread and extraordinary fear and panic among the populace, in order to coerce the government to give in to an unlawful demand."[2] Prior to the HSA, someone leaving the Philippines could be detained only if charges against him or her had been filed in court.

The Gabriela Network is one among many transnational Filipino organizations that have criticized the Philippine government's human rights violations of activists who oppose its policies. The inclusion of Enrile and two other founding members of Gabriela Network on the hold list can be understood as a political tactic designed to harass critics of the Philippine government and discourage others from voicing their criticism. However, this hold list can also potentially influence the possibilities for Filipino American activism in the Philippines. This and other considerations, such as the lengthy and expensive flights, hinder physical collaborations between Filipinos in the Philippines and Filipino Americans.

Like Filipino American activists, U.S. Puerto Rican activists organize against the continuing inequalities of U.S. imperialism in Puerto Rico. However, it is generally easier for U.S. Puerto Rican activists to organize and participate in activist events in Puerto Rico because of its commonwealth status. Travel between Puerto Rico and the United States is considered domestic travel. Though U.S. Puerto Rican activists may also have their travel inconvenienced by the U.S. "no fly" list, for the most part, the affordability, availability, and convenience of air travel between the United States and Puerto Rico facilitate the formation of mutual, physical activist coalitions between Puerto Ricans in the United States and on the islands.

This essay examines the activist practices of Filipino American performance poets in Los Angeles and U.S. Puerto Rican performance poets in New York City. I argue that their common commitments to challenging racial and global inequality combined with their common histories of colonialism result in their use of similar organizing strategies at the local level, but their transnational organizing differs because of the different trajectories of the Philippines and Puerto Rico as U.S. colonies. The Philippines' and Puerto Rico's colonial legacies partly determine how Filipinos and Puerto Ricans in the United States can engage with homeland politics.

My findings are based on personal interviews with thirty performance poets, attendance at open mics and special events in Los Angeles and New York City, and textual analyses of these artists' poems. First I will discuss the similar organizing strategies Los Angeles Filipino American and New York Puerto Rican performance poets deploy in their local activism. These strategies are based on building interracial coalitions through shared histories. Then I will illustrate the different forms their transnational organizing takes given the migratory possibilities enabled by their colonial legacies.

Taken together, these groups illustrate how the differential processes of U.S. imperialism affected and continue to affect Filipino American and U.S. Puerto Rican lives in their interrelated creative work and organizing.

Forging Local Interracial and Interethnic Coalitions

In *Methodologies of the Oppressed,* the cultural theorist Chela
Sandoval charts the different forms that minority movements in
the United States assumed in the past and argues that the most effective social movements are ones that deploy a differential form
of consciousness, that is, "a consciousness that perceives itself at
the center of myriad possibilities all cross-working," one that produces strategically shifting subjectivities.[3] In her analysis of Asian
American writers Lisa Lowe similarly argues that a coalitional politics based on the specificities of ethnicity is more productive than a
cultural politics based on a homogeneous construction of panneth-
nic identity.[4] The ability to shift subjectivities allows social movements to build temporary coalitions with other movements as necessary to adapt to the shifting processes of hegemony.[5] New York
Puerto Rican and Los Angeles Filipino American performance poet
activists enact differential forms of consciousness to build coalitions with other people of color based on their shared experiences
of oppression by global power inequalities. Studies on the formation and popularization of hip-hop illustrate how Puerto Ricans
in New York participate in a black Atlantic culture, one that follows the historical routes of the slave trade and the current routes
of migration from former colonies to former imperial metropoles.[6]
Likewise Filipinos in Los Angeles can be located within an Asian
Pacific culture, one that follows U.S. imperial and economic expansion across the Pacific and that traces the migrations that followed
such expansion.[7] These transnational cultures can be understood
as a result of and a response to global power inequalities. In their
local communities they perform poetry that emphasizes the histories and experiences they share with other people of color to build
interracial coalitions and work toward social change together. At

all times these poets use their experiences and understanding of
Puerto Rico or the Philippines as a way to understand and connect to other anti-imperialist struggles and to the struggles of other people of color in the United States. Despite this similar organizing tactic, the coalitions that these poets work to forge differ
according to their location and their racialization.[8]

In their local organizing New York Puerto Rican performance
poet activists use the history of U.S. imperialism in Puerto Rico as
a basis for building coalitions with other people of color in New
York, particularly African Americans, Afro-Caribbeans, and other U.S. Latinos. The dynamic nature of performance poetry makes
it an especially useful tool for bridging communities because regardless of how a poem is written on the page, the poem can be
modified during a performance to more effectively reach the audience. In a published collection of his poems, Shaggy Flores ends
his poem "Oye Lo Boricua" with a centered, italicized list of activists who have worked to improve the lives of Puerto Ricans on
the island and in the diaspora:

> *Yuri Kochiyama*
> *Antonio Maceo*
> *The people of Vieques*
> *Dr. Ramón Emeterio Betances*
> *José De Matta Tereforte*
> *Don Pedro Albizú Campos*
> *Mariana Bracetti*
> *Lola Rodriquez de Tío*
> *Eugenio María de Hostos*
> *Lolita Lebrón*
> *Rafael Cancel Miranda*
> *The Young Lords*
> *Los Macheteros*
> *F.A.L.N.*[9]

This iteration of the poem consists mostly of Puerto Ricans,
with the notable exception of the Asian American activist Yuri

Kochiyama. However, in other versions of this poem, Flores adds more names to the list, including African American figures like the Black Panthers and Malcolm X, Latino revolutionaries like Che Guevara, Chicano figures like César Chávez, and even the Filipino American labor activist Phillip de la Cruz. In the printed version the line following this list reads "And all the Puerto Rican political prisoners that kept it real." When he adds names to this list, he also changes the line to "And all the Puerto Rican, Black, Latino, Diaspora political prisoners that kept it real." On the stage Flores strategically tailors the poem to the audience or the event. By including other people of color and other third world revolutionaries in a poem that focuses on the history of Puerto Ricans, he connects Puerto Rican experiences to the experiences of other Latinos and African Americans and encourages interracial coalition building. The explicit inclusion of Latinos and African Americans reflects the population of color in the Northeast and Mid-Atlantic regions of the United States, where Flores does most of his performance, activist, and academic work. However, the emphasis on the shared experiences of Puerto Ricans with other Latinos and African Americans also underscores that Puerto Ricans are at times racialized as Latino or black in the United States. There darker skinned Puerto Ricans are often racialized as black, whereas lighter skinned Puerto Ricans are racialized as Latino or pass as white. The rigid nature of U.S. racial categories does not fully recognize the racial diversity of Puerto Ricans, who represent all colors of the racial spectrum.

The strategy of using Puerto Rican history as a lens for understanding the experiences of other people of color is particularly effective because the United States often tests policies on the Puerto Rican population before implementing the policies in communities of color in the United States, as they did with the sterilization of Puerto Rican women and women of color in New York City. U.S. pharmaceutical companies first tested birth control pills on Puerto Rican women. Between 1930 and 1970 Puerto Rican women were encouraged or coerced to be sterilized as part of a population

control program. By 1970, 20 percent of the island's women had
been sterilized as part of the program. The "success" of this sterilization program led to its importation to the United States, to help
the nation deal with problems of overpopulation. In the United
States such programs targeted working-class African American and
Latino households. Similarly racial ideologies, such as the "culture
of poverty" thesis and the myth of the underclass, were developed
in Puerto Rico prior to their use to describe people of color in the
United States. These myths about the deficiencies of Puerto Rican
culture explained the Puerto Ricans' inability to be economically
successful and justified the lack of social welfare programs to help
them. These discourses were then applied to working-class communities of color in the United States.[10] Acknowledging the links
between inequality in Puerto Rico and the mainland United States,
the poet Ray Ramirez equates life in New York City barrios with a
military occupation. His poem "Drop the Bomb" encompasses police brutality against people of color in the United States and their
disproportionate imprisonment. He begins the poem by describing
the poor health conditions resulting from U.S. military bomb testing on the Puerto Rican island of Vieques: "I'm going to drop the
bomb about Vieques how the navy harms Viequenses. Simple living is cancerous. The U.S. government is a scientist dumping toxic
pollutants on this island."[11] The phrase "drop the bomb" is a double entendre that signifies the slang definition of imparting important, often unexpected knowledge, but also likens his performance
of the poem to a weapon in the fight for an end to U.S. military
bomb testing. To explain how conditions in Puerto Rico and New
York are connected, Ramirez likens the U.S. government's low regard for Puerto Rican living conditions to its low regard for the
living conditions of people of color in New York City: "Vieques is
like Hunts Point. Our children are wheezing, most are Puerto Rican, Dominicans, Africanos, poor people in the ghetto. Wherev-
er we're from, you know we're having problems from the police,
the army, the navy, the marines."[12] Harlem and the South Bronx,
home to a large population of underprivileged Latinos and African

Americans, houses multiple bus depot stations and waste transfer stations. The rates of asthma among residents of Harlem and the South Bronx are the highest in the United States and are often attributed to these stations and air pollution caused by automobile traffic crossing the bridge between the two areas. Within this area the highest concentration of asthma cases is in Hunt's Point, a South Bronx neighborhood that is predominantly Puerto Rican.[13] By juxtaposing the cancer rates in Vieques to the asthma rates in Hunt's Point, Ramirez illustrates how Puerto Ricans, whether in Puerto Rico or in New York City, fall victim to environmental racism. Furthermore, in grouping the police with branches of the U.S. military, Ramirez argues that poor Puerto Ricans and other people of color reside under conditions similar to a military occupation regardless of where they live. The shared conditions of occupation are underscored at the end of the poem, when Ramirez exclaims, "The Navy, they've got to go from Vieques and the barrio."[14]

Ray Ramirez is part of an activist Latino hip-hop group, the Welfare Poets. Their mission is to "bring information and inspiration to those facing oppression and to those fighting for liberation" by offering workshops, grassroots activism, and musical performances that combine hip-hop with Latin rhythms.[15] Not only do they offer creative writing workshops for elementary and high school students, but they also offer workshops on the poetry of resistance and community organizing. In keeping with their mission statement, the Welfare Poets always schedule performances in African American and Latino communities. When the group is invited to perform at the University of Illinois, Chicago, they make the time to perform also for the Puerto Rican community in that city. When they perform in Los Angeles they perform also in Compton and East Los Angeles. By doing so Ramirez hopes that their art can make "positive change and [be] accessible to the community, to the people that [the Welfare Poets] work with."[16]

Recently the Welfare Poets and other Puerto Rican performance poets have been actively organizing against police brutality and capital punishment. They relate the interactions between police

and people of color in the United States to the experiences of Puerto Rican political prisoners. The poet Meagan "La Mala" Ortiz
helped organize a large rally on Fifth Avenue after the acquittal of
four NYPD officers who shot to death an unarmed Guinean immigrant, Amadou Diallou.[17] Diallou was sitting on the stoop of his
building on February 4, 1999, when the four officers approached
him. As Diallou retreated inside, the officers fired forty-one shots
at him, hitting him nineteen times. They claimed that they thought
he was armed. In the past two years the Welfare Poets have focused on prisoners' issues and on ending the death penalty, inspir-
ing them to perform at a rally on behalf of four African American men on death row in Texas. One of these men has since been
executed. They also began filming a documentary on the remaining four prisoners and the Texas prison system, particularly death
row.[18] Their latest CD, released in February 2007, *Cruel and Unusual Punishment*, reflects these efforts, with songs dedicated to
the executed Texas prisoner.

In their organizing, Los Angeles Filipino American performance
poets likewise relate the history of and current situation in the Philippines to their own experiences in the United States as well as to
the history and current situations of other third world countries
to build interracial coalitions. Balagtasan Collective's Faith Santilla performed at a January 2005 event for the nonprofit organization Strategic Actions for a Just Economy. Dedicated to economic
justice and popular education, the event raised money and awareness for the low-income tenants of the Morrison Hotel in downtown Los Angeles. At the time, the Morrison Hotel was in danger
of being torn down to create a new development. The event drew
a young crowd of local artists invited to perform, academics from
local universities, local activists, Morrison Hotel tenants, and some
hip-hop enthusiasts there to see KRS-One (Knowledge Reigns Supreme over Nearly Everyone), an influential, progressive MC. The
program began with guest speakers who spoke about the Morrison
Hotel dilemma and the plight of people of color in cities and ended
with a series of featured performers, including Santilla.

During the evening a Native American woman spoke of her experiences as one of Morrison Hotel's residents. She spoke of the little respect she received as a low-income person and appealed to the crowd to help prevent the closure of her home. Santilla performed a piece called "Mirror Images," which she dedicated to this woman. This poem illustrates the continuity between 1898 and current U.S. foreign policy to emphasize women's shared experiences of struggle and the need for solidarity:

So now,
Where are the warriors that we once were?
Where is Gabriela who fought alongside Diego?
Where is Malinxe?
All of whom drove out the Spanish
While Uncle Sam was on his way
To hand you NAFTA
And to me, APEC
Cause Presidents Estrada and Zedillo got
American dog collars around their necks
Trained to sit, heel and stay.[19]

Santilla references resistance to Spanish colonialism in the Philippines and Mexico. Gabriela Silang was the wife of Diego Silang, who led a revolt against the Spanish in 1792. After Diego's assassination, Gabriela took control of the revolt and was later captured and executed. Malinche was the Spanish conquistador Hernán Cortés's interpreter, cultural intermediary, and lover. As such she is generally constructed as a colonial collaborator who aided Cortes in the conquest of Mexico. However, she has recently been reclaimed by feminists as a revolutionary figure. Instead of framing her as a collaborator, feminists focus on her shared power with Cortes. They argue that she acted more like a diplomat who helped to craft a new world, in this case the mestizo nation of Mexico.[20] Santilla portrays Gabriela fighting to free her people from Spanish control and Malinche exerting her influence to prevent the extermination of her people; thus Santilla encourages women of color to resist U.S. control and actively imagine a different world. By linking the North American Free Trade Agreement (NAFTA) and the Asian-Pacific Economic Cooperation forum (APEC), she demonstrates how both Mexico and the Philippines are influenced by U.S. neocolonialism. Both NAFTA and APEC promote open trade that ultimately exploits third world labor to the benefit of U.S. corporations. Santilla emphasizes that economic trade agreements reproduce global power inequalities by representing former Mexican president Ernesto Zedillo Ponce de León and former Philippine president Joseph Estrada, whose governments agreed to these trade agreements, as the trained domestic pets of the United States. She provides concrete examples of how the United States maintains its economic control of both Mexico and the Philippines and links colonial struggles to contemporary neocolonial struggles. By dedicating her performance to the Native American woman she strategically links indigenous claims for sovereignty and justice to Filipino and Mexican resistance to neocolonialism to highlight shared struggles of people of color in Los Angeles. She invokes the history of resistance to colonial violence to empower people of color today.

As an organizing tool used in Los Angeles, "Mirror Images" strategically compares the past and present experiences of the Philippines and Mexico to target the large Filipino and Mexican populations there. In 2002 Santilla performed "Mirror Images" alongside the other women of the Balagtasan Collective at the annual Mujeres de Maiz live art show commemorating International Women's Day. Mujeres de Maiz is an organization of Chicana and Latina artists based in Los Angeles. The set performed by the women of the Balagtasan Collective began with a projected screen reading "Makibaka! Luche!" These are the command forms for "struggle" in Tagalog and Spanish, respectively; thus the women set the stage for translating their shared struggles. The first screen is replaced by a projection of a woman and a map of the Philippines. Alison de la Cruz performs a poem allegorizing the Philippines as seven thousand daughters of the sea and sky, making clear to the audience the specific social positions from which they speak.

Santilla's performance of "Mirror Images" follows de La Cruz's performance, making explicit the histories they, as Filipinas, share with the members of Mujeres de Maiz and with the largely Chicano and Latino audience. The other women of the Balagtasan Collective read poems representing World War II in the Philippines, Filipinas as a global labor force, and the Filipina American experience. The performance ends with all of the women singing "Bayan Ko," a patriotic Filipino song, in front of a screen projecting the words "International Women's Day." After establishing their common histories and experiences, the women of the Balagtasan Collective share their specific histories and struggles to teach and find other people of color who will join and support their activist pursuits.

Filipino American performance poets also participate in Asian American activist events. In November 2005 METHODOLOGY, "a monthly jam of community, consciousness, and culture" in Los Angeles's Chinatown, featured Kiwi, a Balagtasan Collective founder and Native Gun member. This particular METHODOLOGY served as a fundraiser for a Los Angeles delegation to protest at the December 2005 World Trade Organization (WTO) Conference in Hong Kong.[21] METHODOLOGY takes place at Chow Fun, a Chinatown restaurant that is transformed into a late-night dance and lounge space one Saturday every month. On this particular night Kiwi's performance attracted a large crowd consisting mostly of young Asian Americans. Once he took the stage, everyone packed the dance floor and faced him, transforming the dance space into a mini concert space. His high-energy set kept the audience dancing and waving their arms in the air when he did. One poem he performed that night, "Work It," dealt specifically with the labor conditions that globalization creates for workers in the third world, one issue that the Los Angeles delegation wished to highlight by protesting at the WTO conference. The poem links exploited labor conditions in Africa, Latin America, and Asia: "I keep my wrists ice cold with the shiny stone fresh picked by some workers in Sierra Leone, or some Filipino kids that have their futures postponed, twelve years old looking like they could be one of my own, that

made my phat kicks on my cellular phone, or the way the cap fit-
ted on top of my dome, blood stain right beneath where the stitches were sewn, hidden from the crowd when I'm reading my poem.
. . . What Guatemalan family picked them coffee beans, broke their
back for my broccoli and artichoke."[22]

He references the diamond miners in Sierra Leone, Filipino factory workers, and Guatemalan farmers, who are all exploited to
produce commodities for a typical U.S. American lifestyle. In doing so he argues that the average U.S. American is complicit in creating the poor working conditions these workers suffer from. At
the end of this performance, he encouraged people to take action
by buying T-shirts in support of the Los Angeles delegation and to
learn more about the WTO and other ways they could contribute
to the protests. Santilla's and Kiwi's choice of events and poems illustrates their efforts to build Asian panethnic and interracial coalitions that reflect Los Angeles's population of color.

At the local level New York Puerto Ricans and Los Angeles Filipino Americans both deploy their homelands' own histories of imperialism and their ethnic groups' own histories in the United States
to foster interracial and interethnic activist coalitions. However, the
Philippines' and Puerto Rico's specific relationships to the United
States influence their transnational activist possibilities. The current manifestation of U.S. imperialism facilitates physical collaborations between New York Puerto Rican performance poets and
Puerto Rican activists on the island but does not facilitate physical
collaborations between Filipino American performance poets and
Filipinos in the Philippines. This difference is rooted in economically and racially based U.S. colonial policies that put the Philippines and Puerto Rico on different colonial trajectories.

Colonial Legacies and the Quality of Transnational Activism

After centuries of Spanish colonial rule, in 1898 the Philippines and
Puerto Rico were among the first possessions to become part of an
overseas U.S. empire, following the Treaty of Paris ending the Spanish-American War. In the Philippines and Puerto Rico, as in all of

its new island possessions, the United States established political and government institutions modeled after its own. Although the United States had similar colonial intentions for Puerto Rico and the Philippines shortly after acquiring them, it began to differentiate its colonial projects in the two territories. In "The Chains of Empire: State Building and 'Political Education' in Puerto Rico and the Philippines," Julian Go argues that U.S. domestic groups pressured Congress to implement different economic policies in Puerto Rico and the Philippines.[23] U.S. capitalists were much more adamant about securing free trade with Puerto Rico rather than the Philippines because of its proximity to the United States, which resulted in more restrictive colonial policies for Puerto Rico than for the Philippines.[24] In the early twentieth century the U.S. Congress also differentiated between Puerto Ricans and Filipinos on the issue of citizenship based on their race. The 1916 Jones Act made Filipinos wards of the United States and promised the Philippines independence in the future. The 1917 Jones-Shafroth Act granted U.S. citizenship to Puerto Ricans with no specific plans for political independence, insinuating Puerto Rico's incorporation into the United States. Congressional debates over whether or not to grant Puerto Ricans U.S. citizenship emphasized their Spanish roots, characterizing them as civilized and nearly white, and thus capable of assimilating into the United States. But congressional debates racialized Filipinos as either Asians or black, characterizing them as a heterogeneous people consisting of many uncivilized tribes who could not be assimilated.[25] Thus economic concerns and racial anxieties put the Philippines on a path toward political independence in 1946 and Puerto Rico on a path toward U.S. commonwealth status.

These different colonial paths resulted in different patterns of migration and immigration to the United States for Puerto Ricans and Filipinos. Puerto Ricans' U.S. citizenship allows them to migrate freely to the United States. However, beginning in 1934 with the passage of the Tydings McDuffie Act, Filipinos became subject to immigration restrictions.[26] This effectively halted Filipino immigration from 1934 until the 1965 Immigration Act passed, with the exception of Filipino men who became U.S. citizens through the 1947 Philippine U.S. Military Bases Agreement.[27] Today tight immigration quotas and widespread Filipino desire for visas make it difficult for Filipinos to get U.S. visas.

The ease of circular migration facilitates physical collaborations between Puerto Ricans in the diaspora and on the island, whereas immigration restrictions limit the possibilities for on-site physical collaboration between Filipino Americans and their Philippine counterparts. On May 3–5, 2002, more than a hundred Puerto Rican, U.S. Puerto Rican, and other artists against the U.S. military bomb testing gathered in Vieques to participate in Viequethon 2002: Poetry and Concert for Peace. The international group of artists joined the local community in protesting and demanding an end to U.S. military bomb testing on the Puerto Rican island of Vieques. Despite President Clinton's agreement to put an end to U.S. military testing in Vieques by 2003, President George W. Bush deemed more testing necessary after the September 11, 2001, attacks on New York City and Washington DC. The Viequethon was organized by two New York Puerto Ricans, the poet Pedro Pietri and the photographer Adal Maldonado, to demand the withdrawal from Vieques of the U.S. Navy, as promised. In addition to poetry readings and performances, there were seminars and children's storytelling and poetry readings at a local public school.[28] The ability of New York Puerto Ricans to organize and participate in an event in Vieques points to the collaborations between Puerto Rican activists in New York and those in Puerto Rico enabled by Puerto Ricans' U.S. citizenship.

In another example of transnational collaboration City University of New York (CUNY) students organized a strike against tuition increases and the end of open admissions in 1999. Lenina Nadal describes how students from Puerto Rico with experience organizing workers in Puerto Rico came to New York to help the CUNY students' organizing efforts. During the 1998 general strike these students helped organize hundreds of thousands of Puerto Rican workers to go on strike against the privatization of the Puerto

Rican Telephone Company.[29] They used their organizing experience to help CUNY student enlist the support of the local health care workers union (SEIU 1199) and the transit workers union. The relationships established during the CUNY strike led to more activist collaborations between CUNY students and University of Puerto Rico (UPR) students. After the CUNY strike, Nadal returned the favor by participating in student activist struggles at the UPR while visiting the island, helping students organize for smaller class sizes and more parking spaces.[30] Such collaborations and sustained relationships of students of the same generation in Puerto Rico and the United States confirm Georges E. Fouron and Nina Glick Schiller's assertion that transnational social fields simultaneously shape the identities of immigrants and their children in the United States as well as their counterparts in the homeland.[31] These particular transnational practices that Nadal describes are remarkable because they provide examples of a circular "long-distance nationalism," which Fouron and Glick Schiller define as "ideas about belonging that link people living in various geographic locations and motivate or justify their taking action in relationship to an ancestral territory and its government."[32] The transnational activist coalitions between CUNY and UPR show not only U.S. Puerto Ricans taking action in their home islands, but Puerto Ricans taking action to aid Puerto Ricans in the diaspora.

In contrast to the circular cultural and activist exchanges between Puerto Ricans in New York and in Puerto Rico, such exchanges between Filipinos and Filipino Americans in Los Angeles are less feasible. As Philippine citizens, Filipinos cannot come to the United States without a visa. Obtaining a tourist visa is especially difficult for young Filipinos, whom the U.S. government believes are likely to become undocumented immigrants. These conditions make the circulation of activists and artists less possible. Filipino Americans can travel to and from the Philippines as they please, but the expense of a round-trip ticket and the length of the transpacific flight to the Philippines limit the number of trips that Filipino Americans in Los Angeles can make.

The cultural exchanges that can occur between Filipinos in Los Angeles and Filipinos in the Philippines depend largely on Filipino American travel to the Philippines. Filipino American performance poets must perform in the Philippines to introduce their work to Filipinos. To introduce Philippine performance poetry to Filipino Americans, poets returning from the Philippines must either recount their experiences or bring back examples of Philippine performance poetry to share. This is precisely what Johneric Concordia did. He is a Filipino American performance poet and the chair of Kabataang Maka-Bayan USA, also known as Pro-People Youth. In 2004 he spent four months in the Philippines to experience firsthand the conditions that people living in Mindanao face as a result of joint U.S.-Philippine military operations there. While there he performed a poem titled "Do You Want to Know?" The poem debunks the American Dream, often packaged for Filipinos who long to immigrate to the United States. Johneric begins his poem by asking the audience, "Do you want to know what's happening in my town?" In his answer he paints an image of misunderstanding, distrust, and violence in an inner city: "This kid was shot with a glock by another kid who would not appreciate the statement the other kid wouldn't talk. The bullet lodged in his heart and bloodless died on the spot. No second chance to advance for a future. All that it got: sixteen buried and wasted, lifer incarcerated. The concrete conditions we live in rarely debated. Up in Congress, I guess our life is worthless, feel no justice, peace, solace."[33]

Whereas Filipinos in the Philippines often hear stories about higher wages and economic success from their Filipino American counterparts, Concordia represents the life that low-skilled immigrants and their families face in the United States. The desire to secure a better future for their children often motivates Filipinos to immigrate to the United States. By representing two youngsters whose futures are cut short by violence, Concordia argues that the United States does not always offer a better future for immigrant children. Likewise he insinuates that the conditions that foster such violence are unlikely to change because U.S. lawmakers do not value

the lives of young Filipinos. The image he paints for Philippine audiences contrasts starkly with immigrant success stories that reproduce the United States as a land of opportunity for anyone.

To complete the Philippine–Filipino American cultural exchange,
Concordia wrote a second verse to this poem representing the struggles of the indigenous minority in the southern Philippines. Upon
returning to the United States, he embarked on a twelve-city tour
to perform the new version of "Do You Want to Know?" and report back on what he observed during his time in the Philippines.
He intended to perform his poem for Filipino American audiences, so he chose to perform at major U.S. and Canadian cities with
large Filipino populations. The second verse of his poem begins
with the question, "Do you want to know what's happening back
home?" To respond to this question, Concordia describes how one
man's family was murdered by the Armed Forces of the Philippines
(AFP): "Here's the story of one father. His child ripped from the
womb. The mother died pretty soon, an example to anyone who
would dare to assume, challenge AFP goons will bring about your
own doom. They'll destroy all you love and keep whatever they
can, too. Mother, daughter were buried. The rotten smells carried, found by the husband. They were just recently married. It's
a nightmare he swears he can never wake from, so he hikes up the
hills with a pack and a gun."[34] By representing the circumstances that compel Filipinos to join guerrilla resistance movements in
the mountains, Concordia illustrates that guerrilla fighters have
legitimate reasons for opposing the Philippine government. This
representation challenges the construction of guerrilla resistance
in Mindanao as terrorists by the Philippine and U.S. governments
and the international media.

Kabataang Maka-Bayan (KmB) USA is one among several U.S.-
based activist groups with ties to Philippine radical activist groups.
Bearing the same name as the decades old youth organization of
the National Democratic Front of the Philippines (NDFP), KmB
USA was established in Los Angeles in 1999. KmB USA, its Philippine counterpart, and NDFP all advocate for the disempowered

peasants and working class in the United States, the Philippines, and globally. The Balagtasan Collective's founding members were all part of the League of Filipino Students, a transnational organization working toward goals similar to those of KmB USA. BAYAN-USA, the international chapter of Bagong Alyansang Makabayan (BAYAN-Philippines), is an alliance of progressive Filipino groups across the nation devoted to disseminating information about the national democratic movement in the Philippines and serves as a campaign center for Filipino American anti-imperialism efforts. In the greater Los Angeles area there are also two Gabriela Network chapters, a Philippine-U.S. women's solidarity organization that focuses on issues that Filipinas face worldwide. In particular they are dedicated to securing rights and protections for Filipina domestic workers and participate in anti-U.S. imperialism campaigns like the other transnational organizations. Just as New York Puerto Rican performance poets participated in an ideoscape that challenged U.S. definitions of democracy and freedom, these organizations likewise reimagine what democracy should look like in the Philippines. U.S. institutionalized history often describes the Philippines as the oldest democracy in Asia.[35] KmB, BAYAN-USA, Gabriela, and other radical Philippine and Filipino American organizations challenge this assertion by focusing on the plight of low-wage Filipino workers in the Philippines and in the diaspora to underscore that the Philippine government does not represent or adequately provide for all of its people. In this way they question the Philippines' characterization as a democracy.

U.S.-born Filipino American poet activists' understanding of the plight of Philippine workers is often framed by these activist organizations, community events, and university classrooms and is not based on their own experiences. Concordia's trip to the Philippines is a rare example of second-generation Filipino American activist travel to the Philippines, although increasingly organizations like KmB and BAYAN-USA sponsor exposure trips to allow Filipino Americans to travel to the Philippines to witness the living conditions of underprivileged Filipinos. Although all of the

Filipino American performance poets I interviewed had traveled to the Philippines, a majority of them went on vacation or to visit their family members, not to perform or participate in activist events. Among my interviewees, only one poet, Dorian Merina, had performed in the Philippines. He and one other poet, Wendell Pascual, met with Philippine performance poets and brought back with them C D compilations of their poetry.[36] Pascual broadcasts tracks from Philippine performance poetry C D s on his public radio show, *Aziatic Arts*, which features Asian Pacific Island music, community events, and news. The show is broadcast from 3 to 6 on Saturday morning, targeting youth out late on Friday night, and can also be accessed online.[37] For the most part these compilations of Philippine performance poetry do not circulate. Thus in contrast to the New York Puerto Rican experience, Philippine–Filipino American cultural exchange occurs unevenly; only occasionally do Filipino Americans perform in the Philippines, and Philippine performance poetry is being exchanged only as a commodity, not for the sake of building activist coalitions.

Other activist performance poets' organizing work consisted of participating in U.S.-based rallies and campaigns put together by KmB, BAYAN-USA, the League of Filipino Students, or the Gabriela Network. In her study of second-generation Filipino Americans Diane Wolf found that they experience an emotional transnationalism based not on their own experiences in the Philippines but on an imagined sense of the Philippines provided for them by their parents and their parents' transnational practices.[38] I would add to Wolf's argument that U.S.-born Filipino Americans' imagining of the Philippines culls from community and university resources as well. The concerns that this emotional transnationalism creates for Los Angeles Filipino American performance poets compel them to work toward social change in the Philippines by joining transnational activist organizations. Unlike New York Puerto Ricans, Los Angeles Filipino American performance poets participate in an imagined transnationalism because their activist organizing occurs mostly, if not completely, in the United States. For the most part they can only imagine the benefits that their U.S.-based actions can make in the Philippines. Transnational activist organizations provide an additional emotional link to the Philippines, but these links do not necessarily involve the physical collaborations of all Filipino American activists with Filipinos.

Filipino American activists have actively organized against the overt manifestations of U.S. imperialism following the attacks on the World Trade Center and the Pentagon on September 11, 2001. In addition to military operations and occupations in the Middle East, the U.S. military declared the southern island of Mindanao another site in its war on terror and launched Operation Enduring Freedom–Philippines. In January 2002 the United States sent troops, mostly Special Forces, to advise and conduct joint training exercises with the Philippine military, over a year before the U.S. invasion and military occupation of Iraq in March 2003. President Bush used institutionalized narratives of U.S. colonial success in the Philippines as a metaphor for the future of Iraq under U.S. occupation. Filipino American activist groups, such as BAYAN-USA, deploy the same metaphor, but use the metaphor to envision how the U.S. occupation of Iraq will lead to the continual U.S. neocolonial subjugation of Iraq. Thus both President Bush and Filipino American activists use different versions of Philippine history to foretell Iraqi future. In doing so they both underscore the constructed nature of historical narratives. Lisa Yoneyama argues that by narrating history as prophecy "the remembered event is dislodged from the past and transfigures into a future happening in a fictive timespace."[39] While Bush projected a constructed history of U.S. colonial benevolence into the future, Filipino American activists wish to ensure that their history is not repeated in the form of "benevolent assimilation" policies for Iraq and Afghanistan. Thus Filipino activist groups in Los Angeles and nationwide have mobilized against U.S. imperialism in the Middle East, but also military activity in Mindanao and the suppression of dissension in the Philippines in an attempt to imagine the end of U.S. imperialism.

The activist coalitions and events that Los Angeles Filipino

American performance poets participate in take place mostly locally. The limited visas available to Filipino citizens to travel to the United States and the expense and length of a round-trip flight between Los Angeles and Manila restrict the formation of physical transnational activist coalitions and poetry exchanges between Filipino Americans and Filipinos in the Philippines. Instead Los Angeles Filipino American performance poets participate in transnational activist organizations that host events in the United States for the benefit of the Philippines. They also build coalitions with other people of color in Los Angeles by performing poems that reveal their shared histories and current shared struggles.

Conclusion

Toward the end of both verses of "Do You Want to Know?" Johneric Concordia states, "So I ask of you, you can ask me, too. In what direction we're headed for a world that's brand new?"[40] In this question he encourages the audience to become actively involved in finding solutions to problems facing people of color in the United States and peasants in the Philippines. Ray Ramirez also asks his audience to take action by stating, "It's war. Which side you joining?" in his poem "Drop the Bomb."[41] Directly addressing or questioning the audience in their performances is a tactic New York Puerto Rican and Los Angeles Filipino American performance poets often use to organize their communities. They impart knowledge about ongoing struggles and specify what actions can be taken to aid in these struggles to convince people to join in their local and transnational struggles. Though both New York Puerto Ricans and Los Angeles Filipino Americans build interracial coalitions based on their colonial histories and histories of discrimination in the United States, their migratory possibilities determine the shape of their transnational activism in their homelands. U.S. citizenship allows for easy circular migration between Puerto Rico and New York City and for physical transnational coalitions with reciprocal participation. Expensive flights and "no fly" lists discourage the formation of such physical transnational coalitions for Filipinos, and immigration restrictions prevent their participation in activist events held in the United States. As a result Filipino American transnational activism remains largely imagined.

Notes

1. Jeanette Andrade, "U.S.-based Gabriela Exec Stopped from Leaving; HSA Cited," *Philippine Daily Inquirer*, August 12, 2007.

2. Philippine Congress, *An Act to Secure the State and Protect Our People from Terrorism*, RA 9372 (Manila: National Printing Office, 2007).

3. Chela Sandoval, *Methodologies of the Oppressed* (Minneapolis: University of Minnesota Press, 2000), 31.

4. Lisa Lowe, *Immigrant Acts* (Durham NC: Duke University Press, 1996).

5. Lisa Yoneyama, *Hiroshima Traces: Time, Space, and the Dialectics of Memory* (Berkeley: University of California Press, 1999). Yoneyama describes how third-generation Koreans in Japan formed coalitions with people of different backgrounds to advocate for antidiscrimination and the construction of Japanese citizenship and civil rights independent of nationality.

6. George Lipsitz, *Dangerous Crossroads* (London: Verso, 1994); Joseph Roach, *Cities of the Dead: Circum-Atlantic Performance* (New York: Columbia University Press, 1996); Paul Gilroy, *Black Atlantic: Modernity and Double Consciousness* (Cambridge MA: Harvard University Press, 1993).

7. John R. Eperjesi, *The Imperialist Imaginary: Visions of Asia and the Pacific in American Culture* (Hanover NH: University Press of New England, 2005). Rob Wilson, *Reimagining the American Pacific: From South Pacific to Bamboo Ridge and Beyond* (Durham NC: Duke University Press, 2000) calls this space the American Pacific.

8. There is little interaction and no sustained coalitions between the Filipino American and U.S. Puerto Rican performance poets I interviewed. A couple of the Filipino American poets from Los Angeles had been to the Nuyorican Poets Café. In my New York fieldwork I found a Filipino poet community, but there was not widespread interaction between Filipino and Puerto Rican poets there as of 2006.

9. Shaggy Flores, "Oye Lo Boricua," in *Sancocho* (Springfield MA: Dark Souls Press, 2001), 5.

10. Laura Briggs, *Reproducing Empire: Race, Sex, Science and U.S. Imperialism in Puerto Rico* (Berkeley: University of California Press, 2002).

11. Welfare Poets, "Drop the Bomb," *Rhymes for Treason*, CD, 2005, my transcription.

12. Welfare Poets, "Drop the Bomb."

13. Ray Ramirez, personal interview, January 19, 2006.

14. Welfare Poets, "Drop the Bomb."

15. Welfare Poets, http://www.welfarepoets.com/ (accessed March 27, 2007).

16. Ray Ramirez, personal interview.

17. Meagan Ortiz, personal interview, February 28, 2006; William K. Rashburn, "Marchers Protest Diallou Verdict, Taunting Police along the Way," *New York Times*, February 27, 2000.

18. Ray Ramirez, personal interview.

19. Faith Santilla, "Mirror Images," in *Legacy to Liberation*, ed. Fred Ho (San Francisco: AK Press, 2000), 361.

20. Cordelia Candelaria, "La Malinche, Feminist Prototype," *Frontiers* 5, no. 2 (1980): 1–6.

21. Benji Chang, e-mail to author, November 16, 2005.

22. Native Guns, "Work It," *Barrel Men*, CD, 2006, my transcription.

23. Julian Go, "The Chains of Empire: State Building and 'Political Education' in Puerto Rico and the Philippines," in *The American Colonial State in the Philippines: Global Perspectives*, ed. Julian Go and Anne L. Foster (Durham NC: Duke University Press, 2003), 182–216.

24. Go, "The Chains of Empire."

25. José A Cabranes, *Citizenship and the American Empire* (New Haven CT: Yale University Press, 1979).

26. Roger Daniels, *Guarding the Golden Door: American Immigration Policy and Immigrants since 1882* (New York: Hill and Wang, 2004).

27. Yen Le Espiritu, *HomeBound: Filipino American Lives across Cultures, Communities, and Countries* (Berkeley: University of California Press, 2003).

28. Associated Press, "Poets Invade Vieques," *Puerto Rico Herald*, May 4, 2002.

29. Juan Gonzales, "'Puerto Rico Had Never Seen Anything Like It'. The Meaning of the General Strike," *Progressive* 62, no. 9 (1998): 24–28.

30. Lenina Nadal, personal interview, February 9, 2006.

31. Georges E. Fouron and Nina Glick Schiller, "The Generation of Identity: Redefining the Second Generation within a Transnational Social Field," in *Migration, Transnationalization, and Race in a Changing New York*, ed. Hector R. Cordero et al. (Philadelphia: Temple University Press, 2001), 58–86.

32. Fouron and Glick Schiller, "The Generation of Identity," 61.

33. Johneric Concordia, "Do You Want to Know?" *The Next Best Thing*, CD, 2005, my transcription.

34. Johneric Concordia, personal interview, September 28, 2005.

35. Maura Reynolds, "Bush Briefly Visits Asian Ally," *Los Angeles Times*, October 19, 2003; David E. Sanger, "Bush Cites Philippines as Model in Rebuilding Iraq," *New York Times*, October 19, 2003.

36. The Philippine performance poetry Merina and Pascual shared with me diverged from Filipino American performance poetry in its lack of any political content and its focus on sampling of other recordings. I am not sure if these CDs are representative of performance poetry in the Philippines or even in Manila.

37. Wendell Pasqual, personal interview, December 24, 2004.

38. Diane L. Wolf, "There's No Place Like 'Home': Emotional Transnationalism and the Struggles of Second-Generation Filipinos," in *The Changing Face of Home: The Transnational Lives of the Second Generation*, ed. Peggy Levitt and Mary C. Walters (New York: Russell Sage Foundation, 2002), 255–94.

39. Yoneyama, *Hiroshima Traces*, 212.

40. Concordia, "Do You Want to Know?"

41. Welfare Poets, "Drop the Bomb."

Chapter 2

Imperial Works
Writing the United States after 1898

Camilla Fojas

At the turn of the nineteenth century, four island nations from different parts of the globe were in constant company in the U.S. press. Though the United States had been gaining territory for years in the Southwest, the acquisitions in the Pacific and the Caribbean were new and fascinating outposts in the North American imagination. By the end of 1898 the United States had annexed Hawai'i and, as a result of the Spanish-American war, ceded Puerto Rico, Guam, and the Philippines and held Cuba under semicolonial rule; this turn of events marked the emergence of the United States onto the global stage as a full-fledged empire. While public fascination with Hawai'i had begun much earlier, after the victory over Spain the "American public" was anxious for information about the new island "acquisitions," and a number of travel writers and historians were willing to oblige. The writings about the new U.S. possessions took part in the legacy of travel writing as a function of empire: they disseminated the idea of U.S. empire while cultivating adventurist desires for experiential knowledge of the new colonies.

The writings from the new acquisitions revisited earlier colonial portraits of indigenous immorality and lassitude, portraits that were central to European travel writings and to the cultural conquest necessary to the foundation of empire. The portrait

of the former Spanish colonies emanated from the bad press given
to Spain leading up to the Spanish-American War, while the portrait of Hawai'i was shaped by accounts of indigenous immorality and the "cruelty" and arbitrariness of Queen Lili'uokalani. According to the popular press, Spanish cruelty and backwardness
contributed to the degenerate and primitive conditions of the Philippines, Puerto Rico, Cuba, and Guam; it was the responsibility
of the United States to unhinge these colonies from the backward
pull of its former master. In all of the colonies gained in 1898, it
was also the U.S. racial and messianic duty—the white man's burden, to borrow from Kipling's 1899 poem about the U.S. role in
the Philippines—to civilize and morally uplift Natives from their
savagery. This would be achieved through North American capital investment and its attendant way of life.

North American travel writings and guidebooks were distinctly "American," using the long-standing tropes that characterize
the United States: industriousness, heroic individualism, can-do
optimism, and benevolent capitalism; they invested the discourse
of Americanism with the moral obligations of cultural, political,
and economic uplift. Moreover they outlined various kinds of opportunities for an ambitious (male) public, giving all the necessary
information for successful capital investment and employment of
inexpensive Native labor.

Travel writings from the United States in the late nineteenth century have a distinct tone and tenor, and they dramatize an image
of U.S. prominence in the region that anticipates an uncontested
hegemony that will not have purchase until after World War II.
These writings were essential to the popular understanding of the
new role of the United States in the world since few North Americans knew anything about the Philippines, Cuba, and Puerto Rico
and had only a limited view of the Hawaiian islands. The public
would discover much about these new acquisitions, especially regarding the benefits to commerce and industry; some guidebooks
offer histories of these regions, but little in the way of the ongoing struggles for independence or of the real importance of these

islands to the U.S. military, a major motivation for the enlargement of U.S. territories. In fact in all of the new colonies, U.S. military bases would become major anchors of cultural infiltration and the consequent rise to global power.

There are numerous travelogues and handbooks about the new U.S. territories—*Our Island Empire, Our Islands and Their People, Everything about Our New Possessions*, and single national tracts like *Pearl of the Antilles* and *Industrial Cuba*—that were published within a few years after the Spanish American War. To get a sense of the main tropes and preoccupations of these writings, I turn to two examples, both published in 1899, that offer the most lengthy and in-depth descriptions of all four island nations: *Our Island Empire* by Charles Morris and *Our Islands and Their People: As Seen with Camera and Pencil* by José de Olivares. These texts differ in many ways, particularly in target audience, style, and address, yet both offer a sense of these island nations for the purpose of engendering capital relations between the colonial center and the island periphery. José de Olivares was a writer and war correspondent noted for his fictional works, and Charles Morris was a prolific historian and travel writer. Of the many handbooks of the era, I found the literary work of Olivares and the proto-ethnographic work of Morris to have the clearest accounts of U.S. imperial ambitions and overall plans for these islands. Morris's work is meant to be a quick reference handbook about the islands but seems to offer more by way of historical narrative and social analysis, with a clear ideological mooring, and thus seems closer to the imperial discourse of travel writing. Olivares's work is more literary and "artistic" and aimed at an intelligent public or the lettered class; it seeks to shape an elite cultural agenda regarding these islands. Regardless of style or tenor, these guidebooks are primarily concerned with civilizing Native populations through the discourse of work and transforming local cultures with the development of "American" institutions. They will inspire U.S. citizens to perform the work of settling and setting up households and businesses in these new island frontiers in fulfillment of the messianic duties of "manifest destiny," the exhortation to populate and civilize ever more territories to expand the mission and destiny of the United States across the globe.

Travel Guides to Our Island Empire and Their People

In order to examine the form and function of travel and guide literature of the late nineteenth century, I turn to one of its prolific authors and, fortuitously, one of the authors of the works of this study. Charles Morris was an exemplary and prolific late nineteenth-century North American travel writer and historian who wrote, among many other works, *The Aryan Race* (1888), *Civilization: An Historical Review of Its Elements* (1890), *Our Island Empire* (1899), *Heroes of Progress in America* (1906), *The Marvelous Career of Theodore Roosevelt* (1910), and *The Story of Mexico* (1914), and who, with Oliver H. G. Leigh, edited the seven-volume tome *The World's Great Travelers* (1901). Morris and Leigh write that travel writing is "the highest form of intellectual recreation" and that "next to actual travel, the reading of first class travel stories by men and women of genius is the finest aid to broadening of views and enlargement of useful knowledge of men and the world's ways." Though Morris's texts lack the legacy of Henry Adams, Mark Twain, or Henry James, he published at an incredible pace and with expansive breadth. His impetus for writing about travelers and writing his own travel narratives was ideological: to jump-start relations between the U.S. mainland and island domains. He decries this lack of contact, which the edited travel volume would change: "The fact that ocean voyages are now called mere 'trips' has not made us over-familiar with even our own kinsfolk in our new dependencies." He adds, "Foreign people and lands are still strange to us," which seems to suggest a cosmopolitan rapport with the world as an antidote to national isolation while it hints at more insidious designs. His friend and coeditor Oliver H. G. Leigh, writing in the essay that inaugurates their edited collection, encourages this enlargement of "geographical knowledge" by focusing on the "new dependencies of the

United States" in order to make "Americans more intimately acquainted with the communities now linked with the most powerful of nations."[1] In the case of the "new possessions," guidebooks
and travelogues served several purposes. They would not only provide key information for industrialists for investment, trade, and
business purposes; they would override the critical rhetoric of the
anti-imperialists who were caught up in raging debates on imperialism in the U.S. press. Imperialism would be framed as a noble
venture of capital investment and entrepreneurialism and thus an
"American" activity par excellence.

Morris considers travel writing to be a patriotic activity of the
most necessary kind, the duty to survey U.S. territories and its ad-
jacent allies for the North American imagination, to make empire
a popular event of public interest. In his work on the career of Theodore Roosevelt he makes his ideological position baldly apparent
as he expounds on the role of the United States to solve world issues, referring once again to the propitious outcome of the Spanish-American War:

> It was not until 1898, after a brief war for the liberation of Cuba from
> the cruelties of Spanish rule, that the world fairly woke up to a full
> realization of the fact that a nation to be reckoned with had risen in
> the West, a power which was ready to take a full part in the affairs of
> the world. Previously the United States had given its attention strictly
> to the affairs of the western hemisphere, while Europe took upon it-
> self the task of managing the rest of the world. But the rapidity with
> which the American colossus disposed of Spain and its evident stand-
> ing as a great naval and financial power, with the interest in Eastern
> affairs which it gained from its possession of the Philippines, gave a
> new aspect to the situation. Evidently the United States would take
> part in the future in moving pieces on the chess-board of the world.[2]

This sudden change in the order of the world was cause for rapid cultural readjustment at home. "Americans" needed to know
about their new status and act accordingly. This new world order is viewed as something thrust upon the United States, almost

unexpectedly, not the culmination of almost a century of imperial expansion. U.S. businessmen had been working for years to cede control of the sovereign nation of Hawai'i to further their capital interests. Likewise the United States entered the war with Spain ostensibly with the altruistic aim of "liberating" Cuba from the "cruelties of Spanish rule" but had other, less disinterested motives. In fact the United States had clear self-interest with designs on Cuba for many years prior to the war, having made a few unsuccessful attempts to purchase the islands from Spain. Morris's description of American disinterest was part of the contemporaneous discourse about U.S. intervention as an altruistic dedication to the principles of democracy. Locating the cruelties of Spain as the origin of the war, rather than some larger imperial design, is what Andrew Bacevich describes as the "myth of the reluctant superpower." Bacevich traces this myth to the observation of the historian Ernest May regarding the events of 1898: "Some nations achieve greatness, the United States had greatness thrust upon it."[3] Regardless of the official stance of the state, the public, perhaps thanks to the boosterish discourses of the tourist manuals and guidebooks, would become enthusiastic imperialists, eager to seek out new opportunities for economic gain and new locales in which to spend their leisure time.

For Frank Ninkovich, the U.S. drive to empire was energized by "public opinion" influenced by the "newly aggressive communications media," apparent not just in the technologies of the telegraph and the telephone but in the creation of global news-gathering organizations like the Associated Press and the United Press.[4] In the 1890s the U.S. public became accustomed to a daily dose of international news and began to develop and assert opinions about foreign policy and the place of the nation in the rest of the world; foreign affairs had become a national obsession. The guidebooks would transform this interest into something actionable; they would give all the information not found in newspapers necessary to set up industries and households and plan touristic ventures to these locations.

The post-1898 travel writings and guidebooks convey the tone, tenor, and idiom of discovery and often deploy the narrative gaze of the explorer who happens upon vast unpopulated lands, primitive peoples, and untapped resources. Morris's *Our Island Empire* exploits the national romance with exotic foreign locales, but immediately acknowledges a shift in alliance: what was once foreign is now familiar, and the fascination with elsewhere is replaced by paternal concern and responsibility. Morris writes after the many national debates about the moral meaning of U.S. imperialism in the annexation of foreign territories. By 1899 the conclusions were clear: there was no turning back from the fate of empire, and it was Morris's aim to help it along. He begins the preface by announcing this new historical turn in the "career" of the United States: "The United States of America, after more than a century of continental growth and development, has, upon the threshold of the Twentieth Century, taken a new and radical step forward in its national career, having added to its dominions a large number of tropical islands, situated on opposite sides of the earth, and inhabited by peoples strikingly distinct from those of the great republic of the West." He continues, "The question, What shall we do with them? is one which necessarily arises." The answer, he concludes, will become clear with time and experience, the latter being the aim of the guidebook: to send readers out to discover "our" island empire. His work serves the public interest: "It is for this purpose, in part, that the present work has been prepared, —to give the people of the United States a general knowledge of the problem they have taken in hand, through succinct description of these new island dominions, their natural conditions, physical resources, and the character and modes of life and thought of their populations, as a guide to an enlightened decision as to what had best be done with them."[5]

Unlike the more literary genre of travel writing, *Our Island Empire* has more facts and statistics than personal story and serves as a manual for rapid acculturation with little of the trappings of impressionistic musings. But all of this information is meant to act as a "guide to an enlightened decision as to what had best be done" with these islands. With this sensibility in mind, Morris writes with an expediency and anxious drive to disseminate as much information as quickly as possible. And unlike the piecemeal information offered in daily newspaper accounts of foreign lands, *Our Island Empire* is both guidebook and handbook that collates many fragments of disparate sources of information to draw a comprehensive account of Hawai'i, the Philippines, Puerto Rico, and Cuba for various constituencies and interests, "to give in a single volume of moderate size the information which elsewhere would need to be sought in many distinct works."[6]

Our Island Empire is aimed at the social classes with less means, those for whom the cost of the guidebook is a factor in its consumption. The elite and lettered classes would seek out the work of José de Olivares. *Our Islands and Their People* has loftier ambitions and even claims to be of high aesthetic value and addresses the higher classes. Moreover it is a hefty opus of two large volumes for the prohibitive price, in 1899, of fifteen dollars. The title page asserts that the "perfect photographic and descriptive representations of the people and the islands lately acquired from Spain" is "so complete as to practically transfer the islands and their people to the pictured page."[7] Unlike the other tomes, which give facts and figures about each place as a prelude to visiting the islands, this volume offers historical narratives and contemporary observations and images that substitute for the trip itself. The publisher of *Our Islands and Their People*, N. D. Thompson, wrote the following preface to the text:

> Our Islands and Their People are the subjects of interest and of the most thoughtful inquiry on the part of every patriotic and public spirited America. Cuba[,] Porto Rico, and the Isle of Pines; the Hawaiian group, the Philippine Islands—embracing territory large enough for an Empire—what of their topography, geography, their agricultural, mineral and other resources? What of their improvements and what of their people? What of their cities, towns, villages and country

homes? In dress and appearance, in their every-day life and occupation, what is known of them?

We have sought herein to satisfy all these inquiries, and in a manner at once practical, artistic, comprehensive and exhaustive. . . . The work combines high art with descriptive and statistical fact of the greatest practical value, to an extent, it is believed, never before undertaken. It is done with the belief that it will meet with the hearty appreciation of every intelligent American who would acquaint himself with our Islands and their people—and with the wonderful producing possibilities of those possessions.[8]

Our Islands and Their People is a hybrid of the travel and guidebook; it is a literary account of travels that stands in for travel itself, while it also offers extensive history and practical details about the "producing possibilities" of the islands. This work is no doubt for the creative capitalists of the elite classes, for whom this rich and deep knowledge would enable the development of a commandeering position in each new colony. In the introduction Maj. Gen. Joseph Wheeler (who would later be involved in the atrocities of the Philippine-American War) describes the successes in the military campaign against Spain and gives the fullest account of the war, with accompanying photographs, of both travel guidebooks. He notes that the author engages the literary genre of the travel guide in an account of the imaginative voyage of reading along with images meant to elicit the voyeuristic gaze of the tourist:

The reader will be taken on a series of systematic tours through every part of the new possessions; he will become the daily companion and intimate associate of the genial artist and the talented writer; with them he will view the hazy outlines of the azure mountains and gaze with delight upon the fertile valleys, covered with the verdure of the tropics and beautified by the stately grandeur of the palmetto and cocoanut trees; he will become a guest of the generous-hearted and hospitable natives, entering into their humble home or resting himself beneath the colonnaded verandas of their stately mansions; he will observe their varied industries, endowed by the blessings of peace with renewed life and hope, rising out of the wreck and ruin of war, and will listen enraptured to stories of heroic patriotism that form so splendid a setting to their romantic history.[9]

This language of the hospitable and welcoming Native is evident in these guidebooks and is part of the discourse that justifies colonialism. Wheeler accuses the Spanish of "jealous domination"; though these islands remained unknown to the rest of the world, this travel book and pictorial would remedy this. He ends his introduction with lofty rhetoric about the United States: "Be it ours to lift them from the low estate of unwilling subjects to the high plane of independent citizenship, to extend to them the knowledge of our beneficent institutions, and to help them onward and upward to the realization of the loftiest ideals of perfection in human government and the universal happiness of mankind."[10] The guidebook is fully immersed in the ideology of the white man's burden to civilize and colonize. *Our Islands and Their People* sets a political agenda, offered by the military's Major General Wheeler through cultural means. The presentation of the islands is meant to inspire a sense of responsibility in the form of benevolent paternalism while providing the illusion of full knowledge of the peoples, cultures, climate, and geography of each location.

The Repeating Island

In *Our Island Empire* and *Our Islands and Their People*, each island nation is described with the same tropes; these tropes link these locations in ideological portraits that seek to manage diversity for the purpose of control. In fact in his description of these places, Morris does not distinguish one island from the other: "There is a natural feeling of interest concerning these islands, based partly on the usual desire to know, partly on more personal motives, which it is important to gratify. There are some who have it in view to visit one or more of these islands, for business or observation, or for permanent residence; others who desire to enter into business relations with their merchants or producers; and many others who are moved by the natural thirst for information, which recent events have directed strongly towards these oceanic lands."[11]

There is a distinct tone of excitement about the new position of the United States in the world order; the potential for world power status seemed within reach, and new opportunities for average North Americans promised an immediate elevation of social status. Regardless of the distinct histories and plain differences among these island nations, the popular press used the same language to describe them all. What strikes the modern reader is the unreconstructed evolutionary rhetoric in vogue at the time, apparent in the continual emphasis on the constitutional weaknesses of the colonized peoples, where those native to Hawai'i, the Philippines, Cuba, and Puerto Rico share the same inborn desires for a sensual life unencumbered by the worries of work or business. They are preoccupied with gambling, music, dancing, sexual pleasure, and in the case of Hawai'i and the Philippines with surfing and diving. These islands are ripe for exploitation; they are rich in resources but ruined by the oppressive taxation and commercial restrictions of Spanish colonization. Moreover their peoples are ruined by the unchecked proclivities for vice. Both the world of letters and the world of politics shared the fear of social and cultural degeneration and decadence and concern for how the United States might combat moral decline once it entered into more intimate relations with these island outposts.

There is a wealth of literature and critical work on the travel writings that bolstered European empires; however, critical work on U.S.-origin travel literatures from the turn of the century is less abundant. Terry Caesar's *Forgiving the Boundaries: Home as Abroad in American Travel* (1995), one of the first major works about travel writing from the United States, claims that early U.S. travel writings tend to share a similar feature: they are writing "against something," typically against England and often against the lesser genre of the guidebook. The empire handbooks perhaps do not meet the high, often literary standards of the travel genre, and Morris's guidebooks are certainly not bound by any aesthetic sensibility, but neither are they free of rhetorical style. They do not resist earlier portraits of empire, but tacitly call forth the empire exemplar of England. The modern U.S. Empire in these guidebooks is a derivative of its European forebears; it echoes the European ideology concerning the noble cause and responsibility of empire to civilize. But there is a distinctly "American" tone and tenor to the flurry of texts generated at the turn of the century; these popular writings, ripe with exceptionalist rhetoric and nationalist fervor, were fundamental to the reimagining of the United States as a center of global power. In these works the United States is characterized by its materialism and unrelenting commitment to work.

In *Heroes of Progress in America*, published in 1906 and again in 1919, Morris describes the process of nation building as ongoing, involving the continual work not just of "warriors" and "pioneers," but of "heroes of daily life" who have "nobly helped to make the United States great among the nations of the earth."[12] These figures are the symbolic coordinates of American history who established the criteria for assessing American character, including but not limited to Roger Williams, William Penn, Benjamin Franklin, Samuel Adams, John Marshall, Cyrus H. McCormick, Charles Goodyear, Charles Sumner, Susan B. Anthony, Booker T. Washington, and Theodore Roosevelt. Morris's work surveys this history, sums it up, and sends it out to readers, thus setting the terms and values of "American" history and national identity, including innovation, pioneering spirit, industriousness, and leadership. These values inform the ideal type of American traveler, the tourist and tour guide who will represent the mainland United States while exploring the outer limits of its empire. Morris reminds the post-1898 reader of the now defining connection to its colonies and the regions just beyond its borders.

Later, in *The Marvelous Career of Theodore Roosevelt* (1910), Morris writes of the exemplary type of travel writer, one whose travels provide the raw materials and ideals for political leadership, Theodore Roosevelt—the same figure that Hardt and Negri describe as exercising a European-style imperialism, whereby the responsibility to civilize justified colonial expansion. In *Heroes of Progress in America*, Morris describes Roosevelt as the hero of the Spanish-American War, whose career as colonel of the Rough Riders in Cuba, his success at the battle of San Juan Hill in the Philippines, and his travels to the "African wilds" provide an exemplary itinerary of a life dedicated to the forces of civilization. The empire handbooks promote Roosevelt's brand of tourism, where travel carries the force of U.S. diplomacy and a refreshing escape from the centers of civilization. For Morris, though Europeans admire Roosevelt, perhaps for his colonial ideological affinity, "only in America can he be fully understood, for he is one of ourselves, an American in grain, in the fullest aspect an example of the most modern Americanism." The "American way" is industriousness and incessant work; indeed Roosevelt has "none of the European sense of repose," but rather "to do things is his forte." Morris adds that he is able to "make the world spin around him" and "to win his way by main strength, and without regard to precedent or convention." U.S. imperialism may look like its European forebears, but it is defined more thoroughly by the ideology of work and labor. Morris defines Roosevelt along these lines: "The word 'strenuous,' which he has bound up with his own name, aptly illustrates his character. His was a true example of the 'strenuous life.' There was always 'something doing' in his neighborhood." The language of the "strenuous life" is drawn from Roosevelt's speech at the Hamilton Club of Chicago in 1899: "I wish to preach, not the doctrine of ignoble ease, but the doctrine of the strenuous life, the life of toil and effort, of labor and strife; to preach that highest form of success which comes, not to the man who desires mere easy peace, but to the man who does not shrink from danger, from hardships, or from bitter toil, and who out of these wins the splendid ultimate triumph."[13] Even before he took the helm, Roosevelt was admired and feted as an exemplary public figure. His emphasis on work as the founding principle of U.S. national culture, as its cardinal virtue, would become the linchpin of the critical anti-Americanism, or rather anti-pro-Americanism, central to the

Uruguayan José Enrique Rodó's critique of North American materialism in *Ariel* (1900), and later, and much more stridently, in the Cuban José Fernández Retamar's "Caliban" (1971).[14]

Work is not simply the defining feature of U.S. culture; it is the mode and value with which U.S. culture extends its reach. The United States has always been and continues to be the promised land of labor, where hard work yields success, where success is defined simply as the accumulation of capital. For the cosmopolitan capitalists prophesied by Marx there is no limit to the potential to spread the beneficent ideology of work and wealth around the world. American industry would travel the globe to induct listless Natives on the edges of civilization into the world of wage labor. Work would be just one of the benevolent services of empire.

American industrialists had conquered the Southwest and Hawai'i piecemeal through industry, yet after 1898 the "American way" could be transported wholesale on a larger and more complex scale. Cuba, Puerto Rico, the Philippines, and Hawai'i were the testing grounds for the expansion of the American way of life to other parts of the world. The United States ceased being simply a location and became a way of producing and consuming the world; this was accomplished through industrial technologies that put the Natives to work in conjunction with the industries associated with leisure that kept the colonial mainland in a state of ease. The responsibility of the mainland U.S. audience of Morris's text was to consume and thereby support this new dynamic. This readership was the first to set sail to the new tropical outposts, to understand how capital and its machinery would liberate the Natives from their decadent sloth and inevitable degeneration, to use the parlance of the late nineteenth century. *Our Island Empire* and *Our Islands and Their People* would enable the public to participate in the process of capitalist deliverance of the slothful Native; this same public would be rewarded with the transformation of their social and economic status and with new opportunities for leisure and rejuvenation in the tropical clime.

Imperial Work and Native Indolence

Our Island Empire and *Our Islands and Their People* are handbooks that offer general information about industry, climate, geography, religion, and culture in the new imperial outposts that
would prove useful to North American capitalists. Primarily mer-
cantile handbooks written in an imperious tone, they promote investment and leisure ventures alike. Each suggests that the Natives
are docile and ready to serve the new colonial masters. In *Our Island Empire*, each section ends with future directions for foreign
enterprise and commerce along with a description of the salubri-
ous benefits of the tropical climate. But for Morris it is capitalism
with a conscience, since the "natural feeling of interest concerning these islands" invokes a U.S. duty and a sense of the tremen-
dous work of empire: "We have primitive populations to civilize,
indolent populations to stimulate, hostile populations to pacify, ignorant populations to educate, oppressed populations to lift into
manhood and teach the principles of liberty and the art of self-government." Unlike the European travelogues aimed at an elite metropolitan population, Morris urges all levels of the North American public to get involved in the new empire. He argues that the
people are at the helm of the civilizing project, since public opinion will determine the course of history and only those equipped
with knowledge, those enlightened readers of his text, will provide
the answer to the cardinal question regarding these islands: "What
shall we do with them?" The question is rhetorical since the solution is evident to Morris: "In gaining these tropical islands, the
United States has entered into a new and important business and
political relation with the nations of the world. Widely separated
as they are, they possess a remarkable similarity in production. . . .
Sugar is the leading product of most of them and an important
product of them all. . . . Its commerce with these countries bids fair
to gain a great development, and their productiveness to be enor-
mously enhanced under the stimulus of American capital and enterprise. Politically, the outlook may prove a similarly broad one."[15]

Sugar is not the only common feature of these tropical locations; each place could be exchanged for the other in this guided
tour of the degraded moral life of the colonies. The moral lassitude
of the Natives, their lack of a work ethic, and the combination of
underdevelopment and a wealth of natural resources makes each
place fertile ground for imperial expansion. In every island nation,
Morris finds the same exact conditions, and using the same language to describe them all he creates continuities across territories that hitherto had been completely isolated from one another.
This "factbook" of island society presents its case as an objective
history, yet all four locations are united by a common trope and
rhetoric of laziness and its various tributaries: indolence, dissipa-
tion, leisure, amusement, enervation.

Both guidebooks begin not coincidentally with the colonial subject of Cuba. For years the United States had been trying to gain
control of Cuba and its sugar industry, and the events of 1898 satisfied this ambition. As early as 1823 John Quincy Adams had declared that Cuba and Puerto Rico were "natural appendages to the
North American continent" but that Cuba in particular, being "almost in sight of our shores, from a multitude of considerations has
become an object of transcendent importance to the political and
commercial interests" of the United States.[16] Indeed Cuba would
become a coveted object of the expansionist cause. For this reason
both texts lead with Cuba as the symbolic origin of empire and a
point of reference for the other island colonies. *Our Islands and
Their People* begins by affirming the legend of Don Diego Velas-
quez, who, five centuries earlier, had claimed that Havana was the
"llave del Nuevo Mundo," the key to the new world. José de Olivares revises this legend to proclaim Havana "key to the new possessions," citing its proximity as justification. Later he remarks, "Under a stable form of government, the enactment of wise and just
laws, and with the progressive spirit which will speedily infuse itself in a land within five hours' steaming distance of our coasts, the
future is full of promise and great possibilities." U.S. government
administrators are cast as heroes engaged in the reconstruction of

the city and its institutions, cleaning up the pestilent waters near Havana that made it unsuitable for "surf bathing," ridding neighborhoods of the illnesses resulting from unsanitary conditions, reforming the corrupt police force, and transforming the educational system and the attitude among Cubans that "study in any form" was "an unnecessary tax upon [their] energies." The section ends with the prophetic musing that Havana, though burdened by "sanitary and moral" shortcomings, will be transformed to become "one of the most attractive and popular winter resorts of the world." Olivares promotes Cuba as a place of winter health resorts "for the fashion and wealth of North America." In language that will be continually reiterated, he writes that "its future could hardly be more promising," noting its Native "hospitality" and plentiful opportunities for industrial investment.[17]

Olivares's account is the most thorough and aims, in places, to disabuse the North American of common prejudices about Cubans:

The reproach has been made against the Cuban that he is unenterprising, uninventive, and lazy. Nothing could be farther from the truth. Is it to be wondered at that he was not enterprising in developing the resources of the country when such instances as the foregoing are considered? To say that the Cuban is lazy, is to utter one of the cruelest calumnies. The laboring man in Cuba rises at four in the morning, and works until sunset. On the sugar estates there is nothing but unremitting work for everybody, from the owner down, from day to day, and from week to week, and from month to month, until the crop is harvested. Only a breakdown of the machinery of the mill will stop the wheels of this tireless, ceaseless energy. Business men in Cuba have been known to toil day after day for years, without any holiday. They had no Holy Thursday, Good Friday—no Sunday, even. The Anglo-Saxon people, unfortunately, get their ideas of the Cuban's laziness, and his fondness for the daily siesta, and the general notion that Southern people think only of the *dolce far niente* of life, from fiction. Such picturesque impressions are gained by travelers who have seen but little more than the rosy side of the picture.[18]

For Olivares, the Cubans are tireless workers, and any ideas to the contrary are the stuff of fiction. Of all the colonies, Cuba is the crown jewel; it is the only one that Olivares finds fit to disabuse the reader of the prejudice of tropical malaise. He makes a strong case for the integration of Cubans into the United States as embodiments of its defining value. Cubans lack only the social structure and institutions that would efficiently harness their labors. The "Americans" brought a new order of technological innovations that demanded the engagement of Native labors. Olivares notes, "Ever since the Americans entered the city the population of Santiago has been in a state of astonishment. The chief thing which the Americans have introduced into Cuba has been work, and the people are kept guessing what innovation they may expect next."[19]

Morris, on the other hand, finds indolence in Cuba, though it is limited to the higher classes. His diagnosis of cultural sloth serves ideological purposes equal to those of Olivares. Morris finds pure idleness among the women of the higher classes, while elite men busy themselves with socializing in clubs and cafés. According to our esteemed author, this social situation, along with the lack of intellectual pursuits, leads to a generalized cultural condition of degraded morality. This description is nothing short of an exhortation to bring the institutions of modern education, home economics, and industry to the island, an exhortation that leads to the same conclusion—Cuban annexation: "The average Cuban rarely takes his meals at home, his spare hours being given to his club, while cafés and restaurants flourish under his constant patronage. As a result of this neglect of home life, the domestic virtues are at a low ebb in Cuba. The almost utter absence of books and reading matter, the lack of occupation for women of the higher class, the neglect of their homes by the men, all tend to such a result, and a lowered condition of morals is naturally to be expected under such circumstances."[20]

The lack of attention to home is overshadowed only by neglect of business, to which Cubans only attend in the mornings, spending the rest of the day, Morris writes, "in festive relaxation, in the cafés or worse places, yielding to the enervating influence of the climate and passing their time in lassitude and luxurious ease." Since, as Morris claims, "love of music is universal, as with the natives of warm climates generally" much time is spent enervating in its noisy din.[21] The portrait of Cuban society is that of a people who will not object to an afternoon foreign intervention into the island's business affairs, since they would be loath to abandon the cafés or worse places. In fact the wholesale takeover of the sugar industry by U.S. companies will be the fate of the island. Writings such as this one would not only justify this exploitation; they would invite it.

Native Cubans who are not of pure Spanish descent, but either mixed-race or indigenous, are at the lowest rung of the social scale, not for structural reasons reaching back to colonialism, but for a "hereditary love of ease": "The enervating climate of the island seems to have taken the disposition of hard work out of those of native ancestry and given them a hereditary love of ease." Unlike Olivares's account, Morris finds Cubans take a "naturally" leisurely approach to their daily lives. This is not merely the state of affairs in the city but the way of being for the rural population, who are "none too fond of labor." "Lazy comfort is the rule of the day" on the plantation mansions. Although hard work is not hereditary, Morris finds that the opposite of productive labors, gambling, is an innate propensity in Cubans: "Cubans are born gamblers. In the clubs, the cafés, all places of relaxation, games of chance are in constant activity, and betting is the universal custom." Gambling in itself is merely described as an unfortunate inclination; the truly pernicious activity belongs to the colonial government, which "instead of seeking to check this propensity, has taken advantage of it and done its utmost to encourage it."[22] The United States, unlike Spain, is concerned with elevating the "moral" climate of the island by encouraging work and industry. In keeping with this ethos, this island pastime is curtailed as a public event in 1898 by U.S. general Leonard Wood, though Morris speculates that prohibition has likely turned gambling into a secret practice.

The final word on Cuban industry in the section reporting on the island's "future outlook" forecasts a complete sale of all industries and an American industrial redevelopment of Cuba through the revival of the sugar estates and intensification of coffee production. This is not just a forecast but an exhortation to North American businessmen: "With skill, energy, and enterprise, such as may be applied to this rich land in the near future under American powers, its productive powers can be greatly increased, and it may be made one of the garden spots of the earth." Likewise Olivares promulgates Cuba as a new market for the United States: "Cuba, under an American protectorate, pending reconstruction, would throw open her markets for the importation of American pork, products, flour, corn, potatoes, beans, fish, canned goods and all food products, of which she stands in urgent need."[23]

For Morris, the promulgation of Cuban commercial enterprises is buttressed by the selling of Cuba as a "garden spot" and a "winter resort for health or pleasure." The island, he suggests, will prosper under the benevolent rule of the United States and the energetic command of U.S. business interests. Yet it is the mainland United States that will prosper with the expansion of commercial interests. He declares that all profitable existing industries have fallen to ruin through mismanagement and lack of capital, all but openly exhorting U.S. enterprise to exploit Cuban resources. This is the fate of the island, whose sugar industry was entirely controlled by U.S. companies until the mid-twentieth century. Morris ends by reasserting the chief advantage of the new colony as a commercial and undoubtedly colonial region: "While taking more from Cuba than ever before, our exports thither must be largely enhanced, and the sum of exports and imports approximate far more closely than in the years of the past."[24] This cultural assessment is not in itself extraordinary in a handbook of this sort, but the tropes of Native indolence and U.S. enterprise exploit a thematic unity usually reserved for literary efforts.

Each of these island locations in many of these guidebooks is virtually interchangeable. Island peoples are characterized as suffering the same vices and naïve virtues. According to Morris, like Cubans, Puerto Rican men of all classes share a proclivity for gambling combined with a disinterest in business affairs: "The lottery, cock-fighting, and other gambling devices serve as ready means with numbers of them to dispose of their last dollars. The people indeed, are fond of amusements of all kinds; steady devotion to business being the only thing to which they are not addicted."[25] Likewise for Olivares, the cardinal motto of the Puerto Rican is "Excelso Indolencia." Olivares describes this in the following anecdote:

> In the interpretation of this quaint solecism, as employed by the Porto Rico cavalier who accompanied me on my first stroll about San Juan, I recognized a thoroughly appropriate description of the serene old capital's prevalent characteristic. Literally, the idiom signified "lofty indolence," which translation, without detracting in the slightest from its current adaptability, I forthwith resolved into "sublime laziness." Everywhere throughout the length and breadth of the city is this languorous, sedentary element emphasized, personified. . . . You are sure to encounter the same invariable types of an inherent, imperturbable lassitude—the same apathetic conditions and customs that have become crystallized by century after century of inviolate observance.[26]

It should be noted that Olivares focuses on San Juan as the engineering center of the new colony and thus the primary site of evaluation. Though each island is interchangeable with the next, they differ only in the intensity of the description of tropical ills. Puerto Ricans seem, at least to Olivares, to be unrepentantly lazy and slothful and will do anything to avoid all manner of irksome labor—so much so that they prize indolence as a lofty virtue. For instance, he describes a favored pastime as sailing on the harbor, which he relates to a general desire to evade work: "The intense popularity of the pastime, while doubtless in a measure due to the actual enjoyment derived therefrom, is probably more directly ascribable to its exemption from a demand upon the physical energies." The same is true for those on terra firma, for whom the concept of work is banished from the conscious mind: "The average

denizen of San Juan is a silent, but most eloquent, exponent of ha-
bitual somnambulism. He appears to be perpetually wrapped in
slumber. I have sometimes thought his ambulatory hours, if anything, the more restful, because therein he need never so much as
dream of having to work." Yet Puerto Ricans are marked by a pas-
sivity that translates into loyalty, making them desirable potential
members of the union of states. They readily assumed their role
as colonial subjects of the United States, and Olivares hopes to reward them with the dubious virtues of U.S. citizenship: "In our
war with Spain, the Puerto Ricans were our true and loyal friends;
they welcomed the advent of the 'flag of the stars' with demonstra-
tions of the most extravagant joy. We should not, therefore, treat
them in such a way as to cause them to regret their union with the
great Republic. The good work begun by the military authorities
should be continued by our legislators at Washington, in order that
the Porto Ricans, at the earliest practicable date, may become not
only good citizens, but also firm friends of our nation."[27]

Later Olivares prophesies the swift entry of Puerto Rico as a
"State of the Union" and its future as "an unusually bright commercial horizon." Like Cubans, the Puerto Ricans are grateful to
the United States for their liberation: "The people seem to be abun-
dantly satisfied with their transfer to the care of the United States,
and upon every opportunity give free expression to their loyalty
and devotion to the Government which relieved them from Spanish oppression."[28] The role of Puerto Rico in 1899 had already been
determined; thus the only problem noted by both Morris and Olivares is a lack of investment in the value of work and a tendency
to idle occupations and amusement, which, rather than a source
of trouble, are viewed as signs that Puerto Rican annexation and
subjugation would occur with little resistance or difficulty of any
kind. This attitude toward Puerto Rico shaped by these guidebooks would ensure investment in the continuation of its colonial
dependency.

In these handbooks Puerto Ricans and Cubans are not alone;
Filipinos also love amusements of all sorts and are not interested

in business. According to Morris, the Filipino "has the faults of the half-civilized—improvidence and shiftlessness, and the indolence that seems characteristic of all tropical peoples, and is an almost necessary result of the enervating climate." Moreover the Filipino is described as lacking ambitions: "He works when he must, but takes every opportunity to rest." "He lacks ambition, unless to make a fine display in a procession or other social event; and is sober, patient, and always clean, being as fond of bathing as the Hawaiians." And like the Puerto Ricans, the favored Filipino pastime is gambling: "Gambling of one sort or another is widely indulged in, and the lottery and the cock-fight have long flourished in the land."[29] If they are not at the cockfights, they are whiling away their time enjoying dance and music.

Olivares goes beyond Morris's bland rhetoric of tropical malaise and work-averse pleasure seeking. He expresses contempt for the Filipino and tacitly suggests the exclusion of the Philippines from the union of states. This devaluation of the Philippines and Filipinos is evident not only in the placement of the Philippines at the end of his tome, but in the very tone of his narrative:

They are a dark people—some are distinctively black—and our soldiers have fallen into the habit of calling them "niggers" (negroes), but there is probably less African blood on these islands than in almost any other part of the world. Many of the people resemble the negro in appearance, but that is as far as the similarity goes. For all the practical purposes of civilization, the mirthful, easy-going African is superior to these treacherous and blood-thirsty hybrid Malays. They have been pirates from the earliest eras, and their vengeful disposition is written indelibly on their sullen faces. No civilized nation has anything to gain by associating with them or endeavoring to govern them. Spain tried the experiment for four centuries, and smiled broadly when she sold the hot tamale to us for twenty millions of dollars. The lamented General Lawton knew them well; a green mound in Arlington Cemetery attests his intimate acquaintance with these people, and he declared that the only good Filipinos were the dead ones. But are we ready to

go into the business of national extermination? That is a question for
the people of America to answer for themselves. It is not our place to
advise. We have undertaken the more agreeable task of showing them
the kind of people they have to deal with, in order that they may see
their way clearly before proceeding with the slaughter.[30]

Olivares's narrative reflects public ambivalence about retaining
the Philippines as a colony and ire over Filipino resistance to U.S.
rule. Filipinos are described as "treacherous and blood-thirsty hybrid Malays" to justify the illegal takeover of their country and the
subsequent violent subjugation of the Native population, citing, as
justification, the murderous language of Gen. Henry Lawton, who
fought in the Spanish-American War and would fight against Filipino "insurgents" in the subsequent Philippine-American War. Olivares avoids depicting resistance to U.S. occupation, but the spirited Filipino insurrection is no doubt reason for the dismissal of
the Philippines. Unlike in other accounts, there is no description of
the happy and grateful Natives throwing themselves at the feet of
their liberators. Rather, many of the negative connotations associated with domestic racialized populations are found in this portrait of the Filipino, described variously as "negros" and "blood-
thirsty," while using the language of the "hot tamale" to describe
the Philippines. Like the Puerto Rican, the Filipino is lazy, but laziness is not a sign of docility or a special kind of charm, as with
the Puerto Ricans and the Hawaiians. For Olivares, Filipino laziness is a sign of willful resistance. The Filipino is a "large child"
who is both unruly and uncontrollable:

Gatherings at festivals and at cock-fights are frequent, but the Tagalog is not ordinarily gregarious. He is nomadic, and delights in ab-
solute autonomy, subject to no laws except such as he is disposed to
make for himself. He has often been called a "large child," and, in fact,
no words could describe him more accurately. Much has been said of
his traditional laziness, but this has been greatly exaggerated. In the
field, it is true, his labor is worth but little, for he does not take kindly to agricultural pursuits, but in the cities and villages, employed at

the various trades and industries, domestic tasks and even rough labor, he is not more indolent than the average inhabitant of tropical
climes. He lives in an enervating atmosphere. . . . His indolence is the
result of generations of tropical ancestors. . . . Moreover, the native
was deprived by the Spaniards of all participation in the affairs of his
own government, and he fell into the habit of listlessly yielding to the
conditions of his environment, preferring the pleasures of indolence
to laboring for the benefit of his oppressors.[31]

In many ways the Philippines, like the other colonies, suffers many
of the problems associated with "tropical climes." Yet Filipinos
had a different status in Olivares's guidebook. They were deemed
unfit for entry into the United States for reasons attributed to race
and character, but which seem to relate more to the spirited manner of their resistance to colonialism.

The Philippines is no contender for colonial status, and entry
into the union of states is not an option. It is, however, a key strategic site for U.S. military campaigns and a source of rich material
resources. Olivares and Morris inventory the abundant resources
of the Philippines with a covetous gaze, but the people remain undesirable and real colonial intimacy is resisted. For Olivares, the
women lack appeal: "After seeing Puerto Rican and Cuban maid-
ens, a man entering Manila will expect to be thrilled again by great,
lustrous dark eyes; but the glance of the Filipino woman will never
thrill you."[32] While the Philippines will remain an important port
and military outpost, the role of the Philippines and Filipinos in
the U.S. imaginary will never extend beyond this limited view. In
the case of the guidebooks, the Philippines has little to offer in the
way of a workforce or vacation spots and the Native population is
deemed too volatile and unfriendly. North Americans are tacitly
guided away from the Philippines and directed toward the more
hospitable new territories of the United States, ones that are more
exploitable, with populations waiting to serve their new masters.

The Native peoples of all of these locations are continually described as lacking entrepreneurialism and initiative to harness the

resources that surround them. Like the Filipinos, the Puerto Ricans, and the Cubans, Morris finds that Hawaiians shirk responsibility, opting for the pursuit of pleasure over business: "They are a good-tempered and light-hearted race, given to mirth and laughter, fond of pleasure, and of the most genial disposition. Friendly and forgiving, the Hawaiian meets every one with a smile, and is genuinely hospitable. He is free from malice, harbors no treachery, and is natively simple-minded, kindly and benignant. Though seemingly unfit to conduct business, he makes a faithful and trusty employee."[33] This "hospitality" and friendliness were exploited by American industrialists to create the conditions for annexation. Morris goes further by describing the (Native) Hawaiian as a "faithful and trusty employee," suggesting to the reader that a workforce awaits the adventuring capitalist. Olivares describes Hawaiians in much the same manner as hospitable pleasure seekers who are "not naturally an industrious race" and "passionately fond of music and dancing."[34]

Olivares tacitly inculpates the Hawaiians for their loss of sovereignty and self-rule. The illegal overthrow of the nation of Hawai'i by U.S. capitalists is justified in the portrait of the reigning monarch, Queen Lili'uokalani, as culpable for "her monstrous actions as a sovereign." Citing her conflict with the cabinet and their subsequent removal and her attempt to promulgate a new constitution, Olivares intones, "Through her stubborn opposition to the rights of the people, her selfishness, bigotry and immorality, she brought about such a feeling of revulsion, unsafety, and disgust, that her government was overthrown." All of these actions are attributed to her low morality and childlike arbitrariness. The queen is ousted and a provisional government of the major businessmen of Honolulu is installed. The illegal overthrow is described as a welcome liberation from her tyranny. The Hawaiians, he suggests, annexed themselves: "The first American troops, on their way to Manila, landed at Honolulu some days before the passage of the resolution of annexation, but they were welcomed as cordially as if the islands had already become part of the American territory. The Hawaiian Republic was then in existence, and we were at war with Spain, but there was no consideration of the question of neutrality. The Hawaiians annexed themselves and literally went mad in their extravagant welcome to our soldiers." Elsewhere Olivares writes at length about Hawaiians' lack of appreciation of the leasehold system of landownership set up to restore land to Native peoples. He then gives a detailed description of how investors might acquire land since "no previous acquisition of territory by the United States [was] more desirable or of greater value."[35]

Hawai'i is depicted as naturally belonging to the United States. Even the volcano Mauna Loa conspires to anoint this union, the eruptions of which were taken as a natural sign of the predestined union of Hawai'i and United States: "Eruptions from Mauna Loa have taken place at various intervals of years, the latest and most terrific having occurred on the 4th of July, 1899, as if in commemoration of the union with the great American Republic."[36] The swift takeover of the Hawaiian nation was anything but an act of nature, one that, as Noenoe K. Silva has argued, was strongly resisted by Native Hawaiians.[37] The colonial portrait of Hawai'i is similar to that of Puerto Rico and Cuba; all are places that offer industrial opportunities along with possibilities for leisure travel with little regard for Native populations.

In the late nineteenth-century propaganda of empire—guidebooks, travel books, newspaper articles, and literary texts—the diverse locations of Hawai'i, the Philippines, Puerto Rico, and Cuba are linked by the imperative to transform these locations, to change the deleterious activities of leisure and pleasure to productive work, to counter tropical malaise with the machinery of capitalism and an attendant work ethic. It should be noted that Guam is conspicuously missing from these writings, perhaps for its size and location and the U.S. government's strictly military designs on the island; only one text mentions Guam briefly as a source of copra (coconut meat). Unlike the other locations, Guam had little to offer the U.S. capitalist.

The colonies make for a convenient international division of labor; ever the faithful employee, the Filipino, Cuban, Puerto Rican, and Hawaiian will perform labors unfit for their Anglo-American counterpart. Unlike later tourists tracts, these writings issued a descriptive expediency, an abridged knowledge of the colony that would serve industrial pursuits. The relentless collapse of distinctions in the description of these diverse locations is part of the cultural agenda of U.S. empire, as all colonial subjects are elided under the imperial gaze. The originary epoch of U.S. empire is marked by the pervasiveness of this representational gloss; empire is generated as an idea, disseminated through the discursive totalization of those represented as beyond its operational centers. Treating these places in the same manner would give the illusion of efficiency and control, an illusion that would convince the most nativist and noninterventionist North American of the virtues of empire. The modern reader is an American pioneer who shares in the imperative to civilize through industrialization and its attendant regime of work. In modernity, empire is an idea, an abstraction, while it is also a location, a place to be traversed and experienced, places that were in dire need of the commandeering sensibilities of the typical industrious North American. Each colony is populated by workers awaiting orders, raw resources awaiting extraction, and tropical landscapes that beckon the exhausted U.S. industrialist to luxuriate in their warmth.

Notes

1. Charles Morris and Oliver H. G. Leigh, eds., *With the World's Great Travelers*, vol. 1 (New York: E. R. Du Mont, 1901), 5, 9.

2. Charles Morris, *The Marvelous Career of Theodore Roosevelt* (Philadelphia: John C. Winston, 1910), 124.

3. Quoted in Andrew J. Bacevich, *American Empire: The Realities and Consequences of U.S. Diplomacy* (Cambridge MA: Harvard University Press, 2002), 7.

4. Frank Ninkovich, *The United States and Imperialism* (Malden MA: Blackwell, 2001), 14.

5. Charles Morris, *Our Island Empire* (Philadelphia: J. B. Lippincott, 1899), ix, x.

6. Morris, *Our Island Empire*, xi.

7. José de Olivares, *Our Islands and Their People as Seen with Camera and Pencil* (New York: N. D. Thompson, 1899–1900), n.p.

8. Olivares, *Our Islands and Their People*, n.p.

9. Olivares, *Our Islands and Their People*, 6.

10. Olivares, *Our Islands and Their People*, 7.

11. Morris, *Our Island Empire*, x.

12. Charles Morris, *Heroes of Progress in America* (Philadelphia: J. B. Lippincott, 1919), iv–v.

13. Morris, *Heroes of Progress in America*, 22, 23, 68, 73.

14. See José Enrique Rodó, *Ariel*, ed. Belén Castro (Madrid: Cátedra, 2000); Roberto Fernández Retamar, *Caliban: Apuntes sobre la cultura en nuestra América* (México D.F.: Diogenes, 1971).

15. Morris, *Our Island Empire*, xii, xi–xii.

16. John Quincy Adams, "Cuba: 'An Apple Severed by the Tempest from Its Native Trees,'" in *Latin America and the United States: A Documentary History*, ed. Robert H. Holden and Eric Zolov (Oxford: Oxford University Press, 2011), 10.

17. Olivares, *Our Islands and Their People*, 44, 23.

18. Olivares, *Our Islands and Their People*, 125.

19. Olivares, *Our Islands and Their People*, 231.

20. Morris, *Our Island Empire*, 100.

21. Morris, *Our Island Empire*, 100.

22. Morris, *Our Island Empire*, 59, 116, 122, 112.

23. Morris, *Our Island Empire*, 124, 44.

24. Morris, *Our Island Empire*, 164.

25. Morris, *Our Island Empire*, 206.

26. Olivares, *Our Islands and Their People*, 257.

27. Olivares, *Our Islands and Their People*, 263, 257, 274.

28. Olivares, *Our Islands and Their People*, 311, 326, 347.

29. Morris, *Our Island Empire*, 417, 417–18, 421, 428.

30. Morris, *Our Island Empire*, 559.

31. Morris, *Our Island Empire*, 565.

32. Olivares, *Our Islands and Their People*, 590.

33. Morris, *Our Island Empire*, 288.

34. Olivares, *Our Islands and Their People*, 471.

35. Olivares, *Our Islands and Their People*, 463, 521, 519.

36. Olivares, *Our Islands and Their People*, 487.

37. Noenoe K. Silva, *Aloha Betrayed: Native Hawaiian Resistance to American Colonialism* (Durham NC: Duke University Press, 2004).

| Chapter 3

Hawaiian Quilts, Global Domesticities, and Patterns of Counterhegemony

Vernadette Vicuña Gonzalez

In 1959 the Stearns and Foster Company released a print advertisement for Mountain Mist, its commercial quilt batting.[1] While this in itself was not an unusual practice—Mountain Mist had been synonymous with quilting for a century and had helped standardize quilting patterns in the United States through the quilt patterns printed on its packaging paper—the occasion was unique.[2] The ad, in essence, commemorated and commercialized a historical moment: the admission of Hawai'i as a state into the United States of America. Illustrated by a photograph of a bedroom interior and a bed on which a Hawaiian quilt was neatly laid, the ad urged the reader, "Bring this far away enchantment of Hawaii to your own home," paralleling Hawai'i's new status as part of the national polity with its invitation into the intimate space of the American home. On the lower left corner of the ad, a (presumably) Native Hawaiian woman stands behind another displayed Hawaiian quilt. She is dressed in a mu'u mu'u, with an elaborate lei draped around her shoulders. She gazes out at the reader, smiling. She embodies the subject described by the text of the ad: "the native" who was "intrigued by the usefulness and beauty" of the quilts first brought to the continent by "our ancestors" on the *Mayflower* then by "the Missionaries" to Hawai'i and who has since created the hybrid "Polynesian quilts, with the brilliant color and the magic charm of the islands"—the future consumer-citizen of the Mountain Mist republic. In 1959 the images and rhetoric that form this ad were completely intelligible: Hawai'i had long been a crossroads for U.S. imperialist and capitalist projects in Asia and the Pacific. By the time statehood was official, the United States had formally occupied Hawai'i for six decades, Pearl Harbor and World War II were still a fresh and powerful memory, and mass tourism was turning Hawai'i into a hypervisible tropical destination for more and more American tourists.[3]

The Mountain Mist ad participated in contributing to an overdetermined representation of Hawai'i as a welcoming place: a tropical land defined by its hospitality to U.S. projects of empire and capital. Just as the putative *Mayflower*-descended subject of Stearns and Foster's ad welcomed Hawai'i to statehood, Hawai'i is positioned as receptive to the gift of statehood and legitimate belonging.[4] The details of the historical conditions that made statehood possible (and seem inevitable), including massive population collapse, the protracted dispossession of inalienable lands through capitalism's hijacking of the legal machinery and due process, the illegal overthrow of the sovereign Kingdom of Hawai'i, its transformation into what was essentially a colonial branch economy, and the long-established military occupation of the islands, are details that do not disturb the placid image of paradise projected by the ad.[5] The domestication of Hawai'i as occupied territory, ultimately made possible by U.S. military might and its induction into the circuits of capital, secures the scene of the Mountain Mist ad: the tranquil bedroom with a view that looks out into a lush tropical garden, and the friendly wahine with her welcoming smile who guarantees the agreeable transaction of statehood. In this scene the quilt that decorates the bedroom's interior not only signals a native authenticity that can be circulated in commodifiable ways in Hawai'i's growing tourist industry; it is evidence of a civilization project gone right—proof of the power of the domestic arts.

The ad's story of the quilt's origins, which is decidedly not a story

about missionary impositions, periodizes the Hawaiian quilt's be-
ginnings as necessarily coinciding with the arrival of New England
missionaries ("our ancestors"), performing the double duty of soft-
ening the colonial story by substituting a narrative of tutelage and
erasing an independent history of Native Hawaiian domestic production in its own right. It is merely a repetition of a familiar Puritan narrative, albeit on different shores, and with a different set
of Natives. Bracketing the other end of this periodization is 1959:
Hawai'i's inclusion in the cultural and political nation. Having finally achieved acceptable domesticity, Hawai'i can now count itself among the locales in which Mountain Mist products are available. In tandem with Stearns and Foster's eager celebration of the
Hawaiian quilt as the symbol of a successful project of expansive domesticity, the company simultaneously attended to the details of a corporation whose primary interest was to create more
consumers. At the very bottom of the ad, the company states that
Mountain Mist is available "in Hawaii as well as every State of the
Union," followed by Stearns and Foster's guarantee that the corporation will penetrate the most remote corners of the United States
to deliver its commodity. Naturalizing the progression from the
colonial missionary project to inclusion in a global economy, the
ad produces a teleology of capitalism and empire. The quilt's centrality in this ad ultimately demonstrates an imperial domesticity
that has successfully abstracted the Native into commodity form.

　　This chapter engages with dialogues about power, identity, and
gender in Asian and Pacific circuits through the specific materiality
and metaphor of the Hawaiian quilt. It examines the contemporary
lives of the Hawaiian quilt and the old and new relations of power
in which it comes to exist. The most popular and homogenized image of the Hawaiian quilt—an abstract silhouette of leaves, fruit,
or flowers appliquéd onto a white background—is a product of
the state's tourism industry, symbolizing not only the islands' natural iconography, but also the innate hospitality attributed to the
assumed makers of the quilt: Native Hawaiian women. Yet today
the bulk of quilt production no longer takes place in Hawai'i; like

most textile and garment manufacturing around the world, quilt making has moved to Asia, in particular the Philippines and more recently China. In other words, the colonial-tourist romance of Native Hawaiian women sewing—as properly trained, happy colonial subjects—is what sells the product of Filipina and Chinese women's labor and domesticates the exploitation of their labor as part of the regime of transnational capitalism. Understood to be handmade by the bearers and makers of Native Hawaiian culture, the quilt serves as a portable symbol of aloha that naturalizes and makes desirable the intertwined projects of U.S. empire and tourism in Hawai'i, even as it is tangled up in the multiple and overlapping webs laid out by global capital.

Locating the quilt and tracing its roots and routes, however, does not mean painting an overwhelming picture of commodification and neoliberal forms of governance. In tandem with the imperial domesticity that obscures the conditions that give rise to the quilt, the ad also promotes, albeit not for the purposes of radical critique, gendered narratives of creativity and expression. The "patterns and techniques" conceived by Native Hawaiians, while artifacts of empire, were also idioms rooted in the productive life of the islands. That is, even as the quilt commodity (and the ad) is a story in shorthand about the domestication of Hawai'i, the quilt form recalls a history of alternative and inventive juxtapositions and disruptive patterns and partnerships. Stearns and Foster's insistence on standardized patterns, on the "full directions for making it in the Hawaiian Manner," signals an anxiety about acts of creativity that do not fit established and recognized patterns of domesticated indigeneity. These possibilities and creative acts that exceed the constraints of the pattern—that are not about "fun," "magic charm," or the "far away enchantment of Hawaii"—haunt the domestic tranquility that Stearns and Foster stages. Contrary to the culture of Native Hawaiian island hospitality evoked by the quilt as souvenir-commodity, its historical roots and present-day routes tell a range of stories about adaptations, exploitation, survival, and resistance under conditions of global capital in Hawai'i, Asia, and the Pacific. Departing from the narrative of modern gendered technologies intersecting with the natural and authentic charm of the islands framed by the Stearns and Foster ad, the argument I present traces a more complex set of gendered relations negotiated around the quilt form. While the commodification of the Hawaiian quilt manufactures a domesticated indigeneity friendly to tourism and neoliberal entrepreneurship that obscures the uneven racial and class geographies constituting the material realities of life in U.S.-dominated Hawai'i, the realities of how different women work through the quilt demonstrate a wide range of creative critiques and perversions of the pattern.

I begin with the fabrication of the Hawaiian quilt in order to restitch the story that Stearns and Foster relates. With the Hawaiian quilt as material, method, and metaphor, I highlight the gendered modes of production that operate in Hawai'i and in Asia and the Pacific. In foregrounding a transnational feminist analysis of gendered labor, I seek alternative ways to think about possible affiliations and politics in these neocolonial spaces and to examine situations where these affiliations and politics are curtailed and deflected through updated missionary values of developmentalism. Thus gendered labor and creativity are the fulcrum of this project: the Native Hawaiian women who are imagined as the makers of the quilt, the Filipina women (and men) who actually stitch the quilt together, the Asian immigrants who participate in its sale in the marketplace, and even the New England missionaries who helped pioneer Hawai'i's colonization. What are the multifaceted and sometimes contradictory social relations that enable and are enabled by the production and circulation of this quilt as a standardized commodity in late capitalism, and how do these relations complicate how we theorize the politics of life in Hawai'i today? By first looking to the usefulness of the quilt as a metaphor for transnational feminist critique, then examining the social relations and material realities linked to the Hawaiian quilt's production and circulation, I piece together a contingent, feminist framework for understanding how different subjects negotiate the complexity of living in the shadow of U.S. occupation and neocolonialism. Last, by offering up examples, historical and contemporary, I seek to also provide a story of the patterns of counterhegemony enabled by the quilt in the hopes that these expressions of dissent and alternative futures always accompany our theorizations of power.

Quilting Circles and Patterns: Domestic Technologies and Colonial Projects

In this section I provide an analytical framework based on the materiality of the quilt itself, its history as a domesticating colonial apparatus, and the relations that it continues to manifest in its contemporary circulations. I link the familiar contours of its present-day commodification with its history as a marker of the "soft" imperial project. At the same time, I explore the possibilities of closely reading the materiality of the quilt itself as a method and a framework in which the quilt and the quilt's history can be situated. While the Hawaiian quilt is primarily an appliqué quilt, the three arts of quilting (patchwork, appliqué, and stitching) make for productive and interlinked metaphors for feminist analysis.

In deconstructing the act of quilt making, I begin with the last and perhaps most foundational act and art: stitching. Stitching is both decorative and functional. The most valuable quilts, Hawaiian or otherwise, are those that are hand-sewn with stitches that are small and even. Most important, stitching is the act that makes the quilt a quilt: one needs good, strong thread to pierce through and securely connect the top layer, the batting, and the backing. In this case, empire is the historical thread that draws together Hawai'i and the Philippines in the same analytical lens. Dispossessed by population-decimating diseases, the steady imposition of capitalist models of landownership, and political disenfranchisement, Kanaka Maoli suffered the theft of their national sovereignty in 1893 with the illegal overthrow of Queen Lili'uokalani by a cadre of American businessmen backed by an American warship docked in Honolulu waters.[6] Its fate—as sovereign nation or American territory—was debated for several years, but with the

outbreak of the Spanish-American War in 1898 Hawai'i was quickly annexed to guarantee a coaling station for American ships on
their way to the war front in the Philippines. When the Philippine-
American War broke out in 1899 as a result of U.S. imperial occupation, U.S. warships continued to dock at Pearl Harbor, carrying soldiers to a new tropical frontier. Soon after, Filipinos arrived
in Hawai'i, the latest Asian group recruited as manual laborers by
the sugar plantation industry: liminal subjects brought in to liminal territories. A feminist approach to examining this thread that
historically sutures together Hawai'i and the Philippines pays attention to the ways colonialism and decolonization are gendered
processes that establish overlapping patriarchies.[7] As a product
crafted by racially feminized, transnational labor, the Hawaiian
quilt brings together the lives of women in relation to each other,
both synchronically and diachronically. Following the threads of
their lives sheds light on the layered stories, choices, and relationships that are stitched together by the hierarchical threads of empire and global capital.

The patchwork involves creating motifs from geometrically shaped
fabrics of contrasting colors, textures, and designs. This idea of ar-
ranging and rearranging demonstrates a model of analysis that values paying attention to patterns, juxtapositions, and connections
to make sense of a whole. First, this patchwork feminist method
de-centers any one privileged position and pays attention to multilocational theorizing and an eclecticism of method that adapts
to particularities of time and space. The quilt's deployment as the
sign of inclusion in the Stearns and Foster ad is symptomatic of
how imperial stories are told about Hawai'i: that U.S. occupation
was a benevolent project, was understood as such by Native Hawaiians, and continues to benefit the people of Hawai'i. Under a
patchwork lens, an alternate reading of this narrative suggests that
the Hawaiian quilt was a disciplinary tool (to domesticate bodies,
notions of productive time, and formations of historical knowledge)
that softened and covered over the brutally sharp edges of the colonial project. Stearns and Foster's origin story of the Hawaiian

quilt fits a Eurocentric narrative; in this familiar tale, without the New England missionary women to introduce the art of quilting, the Hawaiian quilt would not exist. However, paying attention to these stories reveals that these familiar patterns are themselves the product of colonial imaginings that center the colonial narrative while obscuring Native women's creativity.

The origins and the origin story of the Hawaiian quilt embody the notion of hybrid (if highly asymmetrical) cultures of empire. Yet according to the missionary story, missionaries introduced the skills necessary to create the Hawaiian quilt: they are central to the genesis of this art form. Lucy Thurston, a missionary wife, writes a typical narrative of this sort in 1820, with the first arrival of missionaries in Hawai'i: "Monday morning, April 3rd, the first sewing circle was formed that the sun over looked down upon in this Hawaiian realm. Kalakua, queen-dowager was directrice. She requested all the seven white ladies to take seats with them on mats, on the deck of the Thaddeus. Mrs. Holman and Mrs. Ruggles were executive officers to ply the scissors and prepare the work. . . . The four native women of distinction were furnished with calico patchwork to sew—a new employment to them."[8]

In Thurston's journal entry, missionary women were instrumental teachers who introduced the "employment" of the sewing circle, a pivotal detail because the importance of their domestic contribution to the project of civilizing was key to their inclusion. What this familiar narrative ensures is the erasure of productive time before the arrival of New England missionaries. The romance of the missionary women's domestic tutelage obscures the long-existing practices of *kapa* making in Hawai'i.[9] Native Hawaiian women had long been working in collective fashion, collaborating on the labor-intensive production of kapa. Making cloth from the inner bark of native trees, Native Hawaiian women produced smooth and soft cloth that was then stitched together in layers to make *kapa moe*, a bedcovering, on which the top layer was stamped with a design in vibrant colors. The complexity of patterning, textures, and colors, just like the practice of collective labor, was already part of the craft and not a modern contribution of white missionary women. The only new thing that the arrival of the *Thaddeus* brought was cotton fabric and thread. Thus although some quilt historians periodize the emergence of the Hawaiian quilt in the 1870s, after the arrival of the missionaries, and credit the quilt's invention to a hybrid culture produced by colonialism, it is clear that the creative and practical arts of *tapa* making were foundational to the Hawaiian quilt.[10] Thurston's self-conscious perspective of her historical intervention is typical of the Eurocentrism of missionary women, as well as of histories of the Hawaiian quilt.

At the same time it is crucial to historicize the regional practices of women's creativity within a framework of global processes: the missionary movement in Europe and the United States was a primary site in which white middle-class women could participate in the project of empire by optimizing the civilizational potentials of the domestic arts. Thurston understood herself as part of this larger mission; the historian Patricia Hill notes that the women's foreign mission movement "offered [women] a role in a worldwide enterprise that claimed ultimate significance yet was entirely consistent with their ideology of home and motherhood and their theology of sacrificial service."[11] The labor of these women in the service of both God and country also recast a violent process of disenfranchisement and dispossession into one of tutelage and benevolence. In the late nineteenth century, during what Ann Laura Stoler and Frederick Cooper have called the "embourgeoisement of imperialism," the focus of the imperial project shifted from political and social reformation to the moral improvement of colonized peoples.[12] Mary Taylor Huber and Nancy C. Lutkehause suggest that the Christian ideals of missionaries "inevitably encoded a whole range of cultural experience" that was powerful and hegemonic in its own right, imposing foreign values of proper behavior for women, for instance, which would have ramifications in Native Hawaiian society.[13]

In Hawai'i conversion to "civilization" entailed the missionary impositions of monogamous sexual relations and models of nuclear marriage as well as domestic pedagogies, the arts of which were imparted by wives of missionaries.[14] These missionary interventions, carried out in the intimate contact zones of body and home, involved clothing the heathens of Hawai'i and the other Pacific colonies of the United States, as well as teaching them the properly domestic institutions of New England culture.[15] The Hawaiian quilt, as a text and a practice, encoded and introduced alien concepts of domesticity and propriety to colonized subjects. As a cultural technology, the quilt was an ideal vehicle for imparting moral domestic values that missionaries cherished, and its ability to penetrate the more intimate spaces of the home and insinuate itself into the everyday practices of colonial subjects' lives made it a powerful medium for disseminating colonial (and Christian) values to Hawaiian and Philippine households. Quilt making articulated Native Hawaiian women's existing practices to notions of New England domesticity and homemaking practices that happened to revolve around the textile industry and cloth and clothes making.

These gendered interventions also brought the Puritan work ethic into the overall spaces of the colony, transforming them into economic outposts of empire and introducing capitalist modes of production, values, and habits to the "lazy" natives. Anna Johnston points out that these themes abounded in missionary writing: "Tropes of industry and idleness dominated evangelical representations of native women, and Polynesian women's labour in the manufacture of bonnets became a crucial indicator of success . . . requir[ing] a disciplined, quiet body, which could be contained indoors, and produced an object that was specifically feminine, useful, and indicative of a preferred Christian subjectivity."[16] In Lucy Thurston's origins story, the use of the term "employment" is no accident: the arrival of New England missionaries would accelerate the assimilation of the Kingdom of Hawai'i into global capitalist circuits. Thus the history of the Hawaiian quilt is tangled up in the missionary interventions that were foundational to the cultural front of the U.S. imperial project in Asia and the Pacific and the crucial role that these women played in establishing the

U.S. Empire there and especially in Hawai'i and the Philippines. Not incidentally these exported domestic technologies of properly outfitting the body and home had the side effect of benefiting the emerging New England textile industry. Creating a new market for cotton cloth produced in British and New England mills, and later on for the metropole's manufactured clothing, these missionaries fostered dual new practices of consumption and production, further pulling the colony and more of its subjects into closer orbit with the imperial centers.[17] Not only did they inculcate new domestic habits of civilization, but they also perpetuated and exploited existing patterns of economic imperialism in Asia and the Pacific. At the same time, the cheap labor available in the colonies established a pattern of outsourcing that has familiar contours today; even as the garment industry began to flourish in the United States in the early twentieth century, hand sewing and particularly fine embroidery were exported to colonial labor. In the Philippines attention to sewing as a productive and disciplining activity produced a cottage industry of hand-embroidered clothing for the metropole, a crucial detail in the life of the Hawaiian quilt today, as I explain below.[18]

This detour on the domestic colonial politics of the Hawaiian quilt is necessary because of the ways this history is redeployed today: reifying indigeneity while also simultaneously repeating the centrality of missionary labor. Stories that reiterate this narrative are the selling points of the quilts; for those who market, sell, and buy the quilts, the imagined gendered labor of Native Hawaiian women placidly sewing these heirlooms are key to the quilt's status as a popular souvenir-commodity. The violent histories of empire, as well as its sly subversions, are shrouded in the rhetoric of uplift (both colonial and historic and touristic and contemporary), such as the following typical advertisement for Hawaiian quilts from the website of the Hawaiian Quilt Store (which has several stores statewide): "The first recorded introduction of quilting to Hawaii was in 1820 when the first missionaries arrived in Hawaii. A group of royal Hawaiian ladies sat on the deck of the sailing ship

Thaddeus, dressed only in wrapped tapa, where missionary ladies gently showed the art of quilting. The very creative and innovative Hawaiians soon developed a unique quilting style which closely reflected their own culture and traditions, giving birth to the beautiful, more intricate Hawaiian quilt."[19] In the economy of tourism, the Hawaiian quilt's history exists only through the tourist-friendly narrative of early colonizers as benevolent proto-tourists and Native Hawaiians as welcoming hosts. Seamlessly merging with Lucy Thurston's portrayal of her gentle missionary tutelage, this framing of the quilt's origins reinforces themes of Native hospitality, adaptability, and tourist-worthiness.

These familiar, digestible narratives of Hawai'i and its Natives permeate the tourist industry. Yet the stories embedded in the quilt—beyond its symbolic importance for Hawai'i's tourist industry—demonstrate multiple tensions. The Hawaiian Quilt Store's missionaries stand in for today's settlers and tourists, who likewise imagine their stay in Hawai'i as a noninvasion of Hawaiian lands. The gentle tutelage received by the royal Hawaiian ladies onboard the *Thaddeus* is portrayed as an instance of Native Hawaiian sophisticated resourcefulness that is nonetheless dependent on the arrival of the missionaries. The story of women welcoming each other and sharing a domesticated and domesticating moment is crucial to this historical narrative of hospitality: colonialism was not a violent invasion; rather it occurred by mutual invitation   hosts welcoming guests.

Another quilt company, Aloha Quilts, stationed in a small kiosk in a Honolulu mall and owned by an immigrant Asian American woman, savvily taps into discourses of Hawaiian authenticity in its "brand-tag": "Our unique quilt designs are quilted in the traditional Hawaiian quilting appliqué method. Legend says the first Hawaiian quilt was created when a breadfruit tree cast a shadow on a piece of cloth."[20] Pulling back the layers of Hawaiian history of colonial violence and dispossession, the quilt becomes a story merely of natural accident and development. The domestication of the Hawaiian quilt under the regime of tourism and its standardization as a souvenir-commodity are best captured by the recourse to the natural invoked by the brand-tag and the tone of the advertisements that tend to accompany the sale of Hawaiian quilts. While the Hawaiian quilt's design has a long, complex, and nuanced history, the homogenized form with which it is most commonly associated is a product of the tourism machine. The outline of abstracted nature conveys a Hawai'i that is naturalized for tourism: landscape, flora, and people are softened for the hospitality industry.

Picking apart this quilt as souvenir-commodity—deconstructing its materiality—entails paying attention to the stories beyond its homogenized aesthetic, to the conditions of labor that produced, circulated, and consumed the quilt and its associations with touristic aloha. The third art of quilting that contributes to explaining this concept is appliqué. Appliqué is a technique that entails sewing smaller pieces of fabric, embroidery, or other materials onto a larger piece of fabric. Like patchwork, this is a way of creating unique designs on a quilt's surface. Hawaiian quilts have a snowflake-like symmetrical design in a bold color appliquéd onto a paler background with "echo quilting . . . done in white thread, in rows around the appliqué design, like ripples or waves in the water."[21] Appliqué work is best seen from a distance; as a feminist method, this means assessing the larger patterns of what Arjun Appadurai calls "the social life of things" and taking into account overlapping territories, imaginaries, and histories not only in Hawai'i but in the larger Asia Pacific world.[22] The Hawaiian quilt's itineraries around Asia and the Pacific demonstrate the big picture of gendered and racialized American empire that feminist inquiry must consider.

At the same time, seen up close, appliqué illustrates the technique of joining smaller pieces to a larger whole by folding the edges over and stitching. This attention to detail at different levels illustrates the work feminists must do in understanding the lives of individual subjects against the larger backdrop of local, regional, and global forces. Thus while keeping in mind the military and neocolonial developments in Hawai'i and the Philippines that enable the quilt to be produced and circulated, it is just as important to examine the stories of individual women whose lives are shaped by their association with the Hawaiian quilt. While examining how the exportation of Hawaiian quilting techniques to the special economic zones of the Philippines takes advantage of a neocolonial economy's cheap, feminized labor force, it behooves us to ask what the women themselves think about these circuits. How do they understand their lives and their choices as isolated from or connected to each other? What are the frameworks of intelligibility they invoke in order to aspire to citizenship in the neoliberal regimes of global capital? Centralizing women's labor, from the missionary impositions of domestic education in the Philippines and Hawai'i as outlined in the previous section to the continuing "manifest domesticity" of global capital in Philippine special economic zones and in the highly fraught contact zones of migrant, local, and indigenous communities in Hawai'i allows us to examine the social life of this commodity.[23]

Joyce Hammond's scholarship on the flag quilt follows the changing social and political contexts in which it circulated. After World War II, which heralded the rise of mass tourism in Hawai'i, quilts began to perform the work of representing authentic Hawaiian culture and history in more commoditized circuits.[24] Their display and promotion by the Hawaiian Visitors Bureau in publicity photographs from the 1970s indicate their value in signifying Native authenticity within a rapidly expanding tourism industry on the islands. In the tourist-dominated economy and culture of Hawai'i, the quilt functions as a souvenir (though not for *really* remembering, as the etymology of the term suggests) and less obviously as what Oscar Campomanes might call an artifact of empire, those things that are the product or detritus of imperial processes.[25] As a safe marker for indigeneity (as a symbol of the domestic education of and substitute for actual Native Hawaiian bodies, which were less reliably friendly), the Hawaiian quilt in these nascent tourist circuits promised an uncomplicated consumption of aloha. Its conversion into a souvenir-commodity illustrates what Barbara

Kirshenblatt-Gimblett calls the "alienability of inalienable posses-sions" under conditions of capitalism.[26] As a souvenir—an arti-fact of tourism—the quilt becomes a text(ile) of selective memory. Its circulations in Hawai'i point to the ways Native Hawaiian cul-tural forms have been deployed in the service of attracting tourist capital. Nativeness is abstracted from its context and becomes a free-floating signifier on which new meanings can be sewn.[27] Thus the quilt when produced for tourist consumption is not about Ha-waiian ingenuity and technology but about domestication, empire, and the soft sell of the domesticated tropics.

Today the Hawaiian quilt and its derivative forms are sold in ex-clusive boutiques in Waikīkī patronized by tourists from the Unit-ed States, Europe, and Japan, as well as booths and stores in the malls that cater to both locals and middle-class American and Jap-anese tourists and the massive thrice-weekly Aloha Swap Meet at the football stadium, where more enterprising locals and in-the-know tourists gather. Most of the quilts targeted for tourist con-sumption in Hawai'i are made by Filipina women, who labor in export-processing zones in the Philippines. More recently some pro-duction is moving to China. Overwhelmingly the Hawaiian-pat-tern quilts circulated today in Hawai'i as souvenirs are not made by Kanaka Maoli. How can we understand the new social relations brought into relief by the quilt's new circuits? At the same time, how do we also note the barriers of class, race, and nation erected by global capital, even as the quilt itself circulates with more flu-idity across borders? How is Asian womanhood as *the* marker of cheap textile labor today, rendered within these shifting circuits of labor and domesticity, and in particular against the vexed poli-tics of ethnic and indigenous identity in Hawai'i? Tracing the quilt and examining the stories and histories it enables is a story of how gendered labor was central to the colonial project and continues to shape neocolonial economies and imaginaries.

The translation of racialized labor and ideas of domesticity from colonial missionary projects of "civilizing" to postcolonial discours-es and structures of developmentalism forges dense links between

different modes and subjects of labor over time and space. Indeed
the moral rhetoric of colonial domestic ideologies continues to be
reflected in the ways that the quilt circulates and frames the dominant ways it is understood to work under the neoliberal regimes of
global capital. In Hawai'i the quilt's marketing is a means to entrepreneurial immigrant domestication, while in the Philippines the
quilt's production embodies the long success of labor outsourcing.
In both cases the seller and producer's relationship to the quilt is an
updated form of the missionary project, inviting participation in the
economic and perhaps even political structure while withholding
actual social equality and citizenship. Complicating the contemporary circulation of the Hawaiian quilt is the commodification of
indigeneity by Asian migrants, settlers, and nationals and even by
Native Hawaiians themselves, even as Asian women are increasingly the primary producers of the quilt as commodity-souvenir.

At the thrice-weekly Aloha Stadium Swap Meet in Honolulu,
hordes of people circle the parking lots around the stadium, where
booths boast tourist kitsch, jewelry, local snacks, T-shirts, aloha
wear, temporary tattoos, imported "native" products made in various places in Asia, and of course Hawaiian quilt products. The
booths that sell quilts are owned and staffed by Asian immigrants,
mostly Koreans and Filipinos. The entrepreneurs stated that they
contracted the quilts from the Philippines, tapping into an established industry, an experienced labor force, and English-speaking Filipino intermediaries. These quilts, and others made in similar factories in the Philippines, were sold everywhere in Hawai'i.
As one of the Swap Meet sellers explained, essentially the same
quilts were being sold in the tourist boutiques and on the Internet as were in the swap meet. One alleged that in these venues, the
"Made in the Philippines" tags are cut from quilts (which is illegal) to contribute to the narrative of the quilts as Hawaiian-made
products. Indeed at one of the stores in a Honolulu shopping mall,
these tags were missing, yet the saleswoman readily answered that
the quilts were made in the Philippines. Likewise online retailers
such as DBI, Inc. do not advertise the fact that the quilts are made

in the Philippines.[28] Instead the company website waxes at length about the authenticity of the design by a Native Hawaiian quilter and her grandmother. Like the Hawaiian Quilt Store, small-scale entrepreneurs at the swap meet exploit certain symbols of Native Hawaiianness (such as the terms 'ohana and "aloha") to slide the authority of authenticity into the Filipina-made "hand-crafted" Hawaiian quilt.[29]

Their ability to lay claim to the moral value of small business capitalism as immigrants within the context of Hawai'i's tourism economy, as well as their opportunities to piece together transnational family relations, rests on the alienation of the quilt from Native Hawaiian culture and the continual denial of sovereignty to Kanaka Maoli. In the framework of neoliberal globalization, the quilt operates to soften the narrative of tourism and hospitality; it is circulated within a tourist industry that invokes while disavowing Native Hawaiian bodies, while simultaneously allowing immigrant Asians entry into the economic landscape of the United States. As "good" subjects petitioning for inclusion, Asian immigrants and settlers actually embody the successful missionary project of the entrepreneur as American Dreamer. One of the swap meet entrepreneurs, a recent Filipina immigrant, described a transnational network of middle-man entrepreneurship that was family-based: her mother stayed in the Philippines, scouting for good products to export, while she and her uncles and father participated in different venues selling the goods. The owner of the Aloha Quilts kiosk chose the quilts as her commodity because they were "different" and "Hawaiian" and would sell to her target market, of whom 90 percent are Japanese tourists. In her brand-tag, which she created herself, an interesting tension exists in the recourse to a naturalized Hawaiian fruit (to appeal to the tourists); the declaration anchoring the brand-tag, which states, "Hawai'i, U.S.A." (an identification with both "local" and "national" citizenship by an immigrant); and the production tag on the quilt product itself, which states, "Made in the Philippines."

Enabled by the absent presence of Native Hawaiian women

and Filipina labor, the quilt's marketers capitalize on gendered labor to survive in a similarly gendered tourist economy. Indeed this project began with a conversation that took place in 2003 while I was interviewing the curator of a small center for Native Hawaiian history and culture in Hana, often advertised as the "last Hawaiian place" on Maui. While talking mostly about how a scenic highway regulated tourist traffic to her town, she mentioned that the tourists who visited her small town were interested in Native-made crafts, exemplified by the Hawaiian quilt (on display in the museum). She then mentioned the possibility of starting a locally managed business that would export Hawaiian quilting patterns and techniques to the Philippines, where they could be made more cheaply, and then selling the end product in Hawai'i tourist centers (essentially the model this project examines). She indicated that she already knew of similar successful business models of Native Hawaiians and locals actually making the trip to the Philippines and negotiating contracts within the existing export-processing textile industry. The mobility granted these women under global capital, however, comes with conditions. Just as Filipina and Korean immigrant entrepreneurs in Hawai'i participate in a global market that exploits Native Hawaiian cultural forms and Filipina labor, Native Hawaiians themselves are required to undergo multiple erasures in order to participate in an economic and social regime that produces tourist nostalgia as its main commodity. These women, in the places that they occupy vis-à-vis the quilt, are complex subjects, mobile and cosmopolitan and also participants in global capitalism. That they are able to be migrant entrepreneurs is a result of the erasure of Kanaka Maoli dispossession and Filipina labor.

Through the homogenizing tourist narratives of the Hawaiian quilt and its rearticulation under the regimes of neoliberal capital, not only is the actual labor and the disciplining of the labor that stitches these products erased, but the success story of missionary domestication is continued. In the Philippines, as in Hawai'i, the missionary injunction to become productive laborers is echoed in the act of sewing and in the rhetoric that accompanies it. Just as

New England missionaries "brought" the art of sewing to Hawai'i, the Philippines was similarly a beneficiary of this colonial discipline. With the increasing outsourcing of garment and other textile manufacturing to Asia, the Philippines was ideally situated to be the recipient of new investments. At Hibiscus Quilts, located just outside the Clark Freeport Zone in the Philippines, workers are busy at their stations, at different stages in quilt production.[30] The location of Hibiscus Quilts, one of the main producers of Hawaiian quilts in the Philippines, in the Clark Special Economic Zone is significant: just under two decades ago Clark was one of the largest U.S. air bases in Asia. Upon Clark Air Force Base's conversion to Philippine control in 1992, the territories, buildings, and other infrastructures and resources (including the base labor) of this former military reservation were subsumed under a partnership between state agencies and private development companies. In its reincarnation as an export-processing zone, and later as a free port, the former military reservation retooled the old disciplinary routines and technologies of control and management to "new" industries. Hibiscus Quilts is located on a main perimeter road just outside the fenced-in free port zone. Its neighboring buildings are hotels, restaurants, and bars that were established during the U.S. military's "R and R" heyday and that today cater to mostly male tourists from Australia, the United States, and Asia looking for familiar kinds of entertainment on their holidays.

The Hawaiian quilt produced in this space is imbricated in the neocolonial asymmetries that break down along, yet sometimes resist, familiar racial and gendered fault lines. Amelia Aguilar, the owner and manager of Hibiscus Quilts, describes her specialization in Hawaiian quilts as an accident, as something she "fell into," although the itineraries of the U.S. military reveal a different story. Originally a producer of soft toys (such as baby books and quilted toys), the company began to make quilts when visiting American military contractors and American military personnel began to request reproductions of quilts, which they could get at lower-than-retail prices in the Philippines. Hibiscus Quilts first began making

Hawaiian-pattern quilts in the mid-1980s for Hawaiian Airlines employees who were on layovers in Clark. (The airline was chartered by the U.S. military.) The owner employed labor that had previously been drawn to the area during its military days, and did so even before the military had left. Thus even as she "fell into" producing Hawaiian quilts, such a decision was initially made possible by the U.S. military occupations of Hawai'i and the Philippines.

Aguilar understands herself in altruistic terms, as a U.S. citizen who provides safe employment options for the workers in the area that is otherwise dominated by a tourist trade that has picked up where the red-light military R and R trade has left off. Her factory employs forty full-time, in-house workers, most of them women, and provides them with a regular salary ("I don't use quotas"), Social Security, and health insurance, even when most private-sector employers do not recognize their workers as "regular labor." She states that when the base closed down, she was also going to shut down, as there was little local market for her products, but she stayed on for the sake of the workers, saying, "Kawawa naman" (I pitied them). She asked her friends in Hawaiian Airlines to do some direct selling for her in Hawai'i in order to sound out the existing market, and that was the beginning of her large-scale retail business. As a Filipina American providing much-needed jobs in an area that suddenly found itself without its largest employer, she framed herself as participating in familiar discourses of development and benevolence, yet she undeniably also provided real opportunities for women and men to supplement their income in flexible ways. She insists that her workers are like her family, and that her regular buyers give money and donate items to her workers: "Tinutulungan lang namin ang mga tao dito" (We are just helping the people here). According to Aguilar's brother, "Matagal na sila dito. Hindi na sila magkakaiba" (The workers have been here so long. They don't know how to do anything else). In addition, Aguilar assists with personal problems, to the point of affecting her own profit margin: "Nag-gipit siya sa mga expenses" (She's being squeezed by the expenses), says her brother.

My conversations with Aguilar over the course of four years have complicated any kind of straightforward critique I have had of factories operating in or around export-processing zones and my expectations of their exploitation of a feminized workforce. In some ways she occupies a position similar to that of the early missionaries to Hawaiʻi. The company website describes the process of quilt making as a "labor of love," extending the notion of aloha embedded in Hawaiian quilt making's pseudo-history to these Filipina workers. This labor of love on Aguilar's part as the benevolent employer softens the harsh realities of the low-paying, repetitive factory work undertaken by the exploited labor of the global South. Yet Aguilar does not fall easily into the category of exploiter. A sincere belief in the message of the Hawaiian quilt—as an expression of aloha—infuses her worldview. She insists that her reluctance to do commercial work is based on her belief in the individuality of the Hawaiian quilt's spirit. Aguilar is a quilter herself and has done extensive research to "authenticate" her quilts, taking quilting classes and traveling to Hawaiʻi to meet with master quilters. She suggests that they have vetted her commodification of the Hawaiian quilt by agreeing to help her with patterns and sharing other knowledge about quilting. Her personal research into the Hawaiian quilt extends to her retailing philosophy: she stated that she turns down commercial orders instead taking single or double orders, with the occasional bulk order for stores in Hawaiʻi that she has approved in person. She claims that she charges just enough to keep the business going and to produce a quality product: "I don't cheat the quality of the quilts." Deeply believing that this is part of what has made her business a success, Aguilar tells of other examples of ventures that failed in the Philippines because they were "after money," misunderstanding the message of the quilt. Occupying this thin space of business owner and cultural translator, she attempts to frame her business along nonexploitive lines.

The factory itself was clean, well-lit, safe—a space mostly used for cutting and preparation of the fabric for quilting and for packaging the end product. It was also a place where the workers had

meaningful connections with each other through mentorship and
gossip networks. Aguilar pointed out that the lack of competition
between the workers was because she did not employ a quota system. Indeed the workers themselves testified to helping each other during rush orders. Aguilar noted, "We are trying to build up
a family." It may be completely different at the homes of the contract workers, where much of the actual stitching takes place, and
certainly one does not need an actual sweatshop to require workers to work sweatshop hours or produce sweatshop-level output.
Sending labor home has been known to further exploit women's
and children's labor, as has subcontracting, particularly in the textile and garment industries. Aguilar's brother oversees the homework and monitors the children working at home. According to
him, "Karamihan tumulong sila pag bakasyon. Hindi sila pinipilit"
(Many of them help during school vacation. They are not forced).
He suggests that they save their earnings for school expenses, a
service then attributable to the work the factory provides. As for
quality control of the 150 workers who do homework (rather than
work at the factory), he notes that the company develops a close
relationship with those workers, understanding their mutual dependence; the factory has no power to compel these contractors
to do work, and it does not employ the services of a subcontrac-
tor, working directly with the workers themselves.

   As I toured the workplace, it *was* difficult to dismiss the existence of Hibiscus Quilts with facile recourse to the image of the
neocolonial bourgeoisie pimping Native subjects, though that image could describe other factories in the area. At the same time,
Aguilar's self-understanding of her mission lines up in rhetorical-
ly familiar ways that are easily accommodated by the ideological elasticity of neoliberal entrepreneurship. What is increasingly
clear is the way that the quilt, as what James Clifford might call a
tainted text of traveling subjects and ideologies, represents a complex analytical site of gendered exploitation, complicity, domination, and survival that continues to follow recurring patterns and
rationales. Almost two centuries away from its putative origins

in the collision of culture, the Hawaiian quilt remains embedded in the kind of complex negotiations opened up by its initial "missionary impositions."

Other Quilt Stories: Counterhegemonic Patterns

Over the course of this research, it was often clear from my interviews that neoliberal entrepreneurship was a rearticulation of missionary ideologies of uplift, updated for the new circuits and subjects of global capital. Every now and then, however, I was reminded that at the very heart of the act of quilting is a creative impulse. While conducting interviews at the Hibiscus Quilts factory, workers freely related stories about how, despite the owner's devout Catholicism and aversion to queer sexual identities, young gay men were accepted as paid laborers and forged a supportive community within the disciplined confines of the factory. While these stories demonstrate the resilience and flexibility of capitalism when it comes to finding (and not discriminating against) cheap labor, they simultaneously illustrate that contingent communities of creativity and survival exist alongside gendered exploitation and complicity, accounting for the workers in the factory describing their working environment as "magkakapatid" and "parang pamilya" (like siblings, like family). For these young gay men, working in a factory space protected them from the sexual harassment and exploitation of the space abandoned by the U.S. military and tourists and gave them livelihoods that improved their social status and economic chances. Such stories were important reminders that even though the Hawaiian quilt is a product of the colonial process, quilting itself is a *creative* process based deeply in community ties and collective struggle. One of the few accepted creative outlets for women, particularly in early America, quilting was both a necessity and a mode of expression.[31] As such it offers ways to think about power, governance, social relations, and social justice that are not based on colonial, hierarchical models. Feminist scholarship on quilting has noted the creative space carved out by quilters, as well as the radical politics expressed in quilts themselves.[32] The quilt is thus not only a metaphor of but also an expression of the creativity of feminist analyses, in particular the challenges and tensions of simultaneously formulating theories of oppression and theorizing modes of resistance.

In the contemporary context of Hawai'i's mass tourist industry, the quilt's complex and contradictory history, particularly during the Native Hawaiian struggle to maintain sovereignty, is often lost. Its routes, both historical and present-day, illuminate the colonial and neocolonial complexities of the Asia Pacific as a space of violence, survival, and creativity. In considering the interventions wrought by missionary wives in Hawaiian culture, Patricia Grimshaw has argued that these colonial domestic technologies aided Native Hawaiian women in navigating the changes wrought by colonial violence: "Utterly ethnocentric as the American women clearly were, they nevertheless offered Hawaiian women something valuable. Faced with a new order which remorselessly invaded their world, Hawaiian women were offered by the mission wives an introduction to a range of skills and a model of feminine behavior which could provide them with a competency to survive and negotiate their changing environment . . . the cultural forms of New England society."[33]

In feminist analyses of gendered colonial labor, and in the emphasis on recognizing the subtle agency of American missionary women, however, the agency of Native Hawaiian women sometimes gets swept aside. Other historians in contrast point out that Native Hawaiians were not passive recipients of the domestic technologies that missionary women happened to offer. In the early 1820s Native Hawaiian women were already cosmopolitan subjects, adept at bringing together indigenous and outsider technologies and practices. Lisa Kahaleole Hall notes that during the time of European contact, Hawaiian women had more power than their European peers, including missionary women, and were not in need of a "model of feminine behavior" that would otherwise encroach on their established rights and roles.[34] Joyce Linnekin likewise argues that when taken up by some Native Hawaiian women, these

domestic arts were rearticulated in ways that added to their status and authority in Native culture; the clothing fashions and the
practice of domestic arts were not foreign practices to Native Hawaiian women.[35] However, the overwhelming success of the missionary project eventually eroded the position of Native Hawaiian women by the end of the century. Thus the civilizing face of
the colonizing project worked by enforcing new standards of gendered behavior that encroached on traditional women's rights and
roles, while giving them access to others.[36]

Native Hawaiian appropriation of these domestic missionary
cultures did not, however, mean wholesale acceptance of the imperial project. Indeed quilting provided an outlet, albeit a limited
one, for anticolonial sentiment, and not just navigation of the new
world order that faced Native Hawaiians. During the territorial
era (1898–1959), Hawaiian quilts were seen as a symbol of Hawaiian political pride in the face of assimilation policies. For instance,
one of the most revered patterns was My Beloved Flag, which became a way for Hawaiian peoples to express their continuing political support for the Hawaiian monarchy after its overthrow in
1893. After the Hawaiian flag was lowered over 'Iolani Palace in
Honolulu, its presence, often in quilts and canopies, remained in
intimate domestic spaces and outside of the public political realm.
As Joyce D. Hammond suggests, flag quilts were often an expression of aloha as well as "concern with the political future of the
Hawaiian nation."[37] Seen as a domesticating and disciplinary technology, transgressive quilting often escaped the colonial gaze because women's work was seen as nonthreatening.

Because the domestic arts were seen as promoting docility and
discipline, even the most dangerous subjects in the republic were
allowed access to quilting. In the tumultuous years following her
overthrow, Queen Lili'uokalani created perhaps the most famous
Hawaiian quilt of all. While imprisoned in 'Iolani Palace for alleged knowledge of a counterrevolutionary coup by her supporters against the Republic of Hawai'i (formed by the core members
of the overthrow) and for her dangerous symbolism of Hawai'i's

previous status as a monarchy, she was allowed to sew. Starting in
1895, the queen and her companions created an expression of political protest and historical record in quilt form that helped her
communicate with her supporters outside the palace walls.[38] This
quilt, which is not the standardized form of the souvenir-commodity promoted by Stearns and Foster, is a 97-by-95-inch "cra-
zy quilt" that narrates the story of her imprisonment in 'Iolani Palace in 1895 following armed attempts at recovering the Kingdom
of Hawai'i from its colonizers. Paralleling the political creativity
of the madwoman in the attic — and reflecting the insanity of the
illegal overthrow's logics — Queen Lili'uokalani's quilt employs a
profusion and kaleidoscope of colors, media, materials, and images, held together by a narrow border. The center panel of nine narrates significant (and nondomestic) political events: stitched messages such as "Imprisoned at Iolani Palace . . . we began the quilt
here" insist on the historical specificity of the coup. The quilt is,
in essence, an alternative historical document that narrates the existence of massive and sustained anticolonial resistance. The center block features the Kalākaua coat of arms framed by Hawaiian
flags. Stitched into the panel is a timeline of historical theft and rebellion, including the date that Queen Lili'uokalani was forced to
step down by the provisional government and the date of the ill-
fated and aborted Wilcox Rebellion that led to her arrest. Coun-
tering the narrative of inevitability, the queen's quilt also lists the
names of her supporters and friends and displays patriotic badg-
es and the date when a garden was planted in Pauoa Valley by her
supporters.[39] These "perversions" of quilting exhibit the power
of storytelling and demonstrate that for many women, the act of
quilting is about suturing stories into the fabric. Making the quilt
form work for her and turning its mission of domestication on its
head, Queen Lili'uokalani recorded the fierce and sustained struggle against illegal occupation. A deeply political project, the queen's
quilt became a statement about the thefts carried out by the collu-
sions of the United States, missionary and plantation economies,
and military occupation.

While the circulation of the Hawaiian quilt as souvenir-commodity in Hawai'i's tourism industry limits the kinds of political expression possible in the queen's quilt and the flag quilts of an earlier era, contemporary artists have pushed the form of the quilt itself to challenge its standardization under the regime of tourism. Quilt artists produce individual, one-of-a-kind cloth quilts inspired by stories about family, images of life in the islands, and nature. Others use the quilt form but forgo the traditional materials to weave alternative narratives and histories that deliberately unsettle and reject any domestic aspirations that quilting technologies aspired to.

The artist Trisha Lagaso-Goldberg exemplifies the kind of aesthetic innovation that links history and politics in Hawai'i, Asia, and the Pacific in a transnational framework. A Hawai'i-born and -raised Filipina American artist, Lagaso-Goldberg sews together the grammar of the Hawaiian quilt with the vocabulary of U.S. imperial and Filipino immigration plantation history in creating her art. In 2006 an exhibit titled *Alimatuan: The Emerging Artist as American Filipino* opened at the Contemporary Museum of Hawai'i, commemorating the centennial year of the arrival of Filipinos in Hawai'i. Curated by Koan-Jeff Baysa, *Alimatuan* ("the soul of the spirit" in one of the Filipino tribal dialects) is meant to evoke a connection to traditional culture and Filipino indigeneity and the cultural innovations that link the Filipino diaspora. As one of twenty-seven artists chosen for the exhibit, Lagaso-Goldberg wrestled with the question of what it means to be a Filipino subject in a postcolonial and postmodern world, and specifically what it means to be Filipino in a Hawai'i that was similarly occupied and colonized by the United States.[40]

In her *Sakada* series, Lagaso-Goldberg pays homage to her grandfathers, who first came to Hawai'i as *sakadas* (contract agricultural laborers) to work the sugar plantations. A trio of Plexiglas panels 3 feet square, meant to recall Hawaiian quilts, cleverly replaces Hawaiian patterns such as breadfruit with plantation tools such as machetes and hoes. The *Sakada* series positions this memory of migrant labor squarely within a form associated with Native Hawaiian colonial creativity. Lagaso-Goldberg's reinvention of the Hawaiian quilt subversively points out the commonalities between Filipino migrant workers and the Native Hawaiian peoples they were brought in to replace. Squarely positing a story of gendered labor in a colonial economy, she points out that the piecework of her quilt is made possible by the connections between itinerant and indigenous labor wrought not only through imperial violence, but through choice and creativity. In her political appropriation of the Hawaiian quilt form, she reflects on the less tourist-friendly narratives of the Hawaiian quilt but includes the history of imported Filipino labor alongside that of Hawai'i's colonial history, not merely in juxtaposition but as intertwined histories. Thus her quilts ask us to rethink how we remember this history.

In the neocolonial tourist-military occupations of the Philippines and Hawai'i, the disciplinary regimes that limit the social, economic, and political horizons for laboring subjects discourage the kind of multilocational theorizing that Lagaso-Goldberg is performing in her quilt pieces. Here she perverts the quilt form in her deliberate choice of juxtaposing the potentially dangerous plantation implements with the domestic expectations of the quilt. Honoring both Filipino immigrant history and the economic and political expropriation of their labor and the dispossession of Hawaiian lands and sovereignty, Lagaso-Goldberg's quilts link the discrete histories and material realities of the Philippines, Hawai'i, and the United States in unsettling ways. In this jarring contrast she follows the tradition of the flag and aloha quilts, which contain a latent menace in the ordered discipline of the quilt form. Most important, she suggests alternative formations of community outside identity politics and affiliations forged by mutual interests and overlapping perspectives.

The strategic appropriation of the Hawaiian quilt form—thrusting it outside the commodified circuits of Hawai'i's tourism—demonstrates the quilt's potential for inhospitality. It refuses both the historical and the updated missionary history for which the Hawaiian quilt has stood, and instead perverts the pattern, creating the possibilities for counterhegemonic creativity and affiliations that do not serve the interests of neoliberal governance. In this iteration, the quilt itself is an object that simultaneously locates its production within the relations of U.S. empire in Asia and the Pacific and the ever-expanding reach of global capital and finds in those histories the inspiration and opportunity for unexpected ties of affiliation forged between colonized peoples in these neocolonial spaces.

Notes

Writing, like quilting, is deeply collaborative work. To my writing *hui*, Pensri Ho, Roderick Labrador, and especially Hokulani Aikau, whose incisive and constructive comments disciplined this project into a semblance of order, my gratitude. Many thanks also to Camilla Fojas and Rudy Guevarra, who have been the most supportive of editors.

1. My thanks to Gaye Chan for originally providing me with the Stearns and Foster advertising image.

2. Elise Schebler Roberts, *The Quilt: A History and Celebration of an American Art Form* (Minneapolis: M BI Publishing and Voyageur Press, 2007), 306. Mountain Mist batting was first sold commercially in 1846. The patterns did not accompany the batting wrappers until the 1920s.

3. For a detailed and nuanced analysis of the cultural politics of the statehood transitional period and tourism's role, see Christine Skwiot, *The Purposes of Paradise: U.S. Tourism and Empire in Cuba and Hawai'i* (Philadelphia: University of Pennsylvania Press, 2010).

4. Skwiot makes a convincing argument that Hawai'i's acceptability as a potential state hinged on the successful marketing of its acceptable whiteness—a whiteness that worked in tension with indigenous claims and Asian immigrants. Paulette Feeney likewise points out that haole elites managed this potentially thorny racial situation in periodicals such as the *Paradise of the Pacific*, which portrayed Hawai'i through a settler or tourist lens. See Paulette Feeney, "Aloha and Allegiance: Imagining America's Paradise" (PhD diss., University of Hawai'i at Mānoa, 2009).

5. David E. Stannard, *Before the Horror: The Population of Hawai'i on the Eve of Western Contact* (Honolulu: Social Science Research Institute, University of Hawai'i, 1989). For an early history of Hawai'i to the 1887 Reciprocity Treaty, see Jonathan Kay Kamakawiwo'ole Osorio,

Dismembering Lāhui: A History of the Hawaiian Nation to 1887 (Honolulu: University of Hawai'i Press, 2002). For the legal history of colonialism, see Sally Engle Merry, *Colonizing Hawai'i: The Cultural Power of Law* (Princeton NJ: Princeton University Press, 2000).

6. J. Kēhaulani Kauanui, "Native Hawaiian Decolonization and the Politics of Gender," *American Quarterly* 6, no. 2 (2008): 281–87. My use of Native Hawaiian and Kanaka Maoli (real or true people) follows the usage laid out by J. Kēhaulani Kauanui in *Native Blood: Colonialism and the Politics of Sovereignty and Indigeneity* (Durham NC: Duke University Press, 2008), xi.

7. Andrea Smith and J. Kēhaulaini Kauanui, "Native Feminisms Engage American Studies," *American Quarterly* 6, no. 2 (2008): 241–49.

8. Lucy Thurston, *Life and Times of Mrs. Lucy G. Thurston, Selected and Arranged by Herself* (Ann Arbor MI: S. C. Andrews, 1882).

9. *Kapa* specifically refers to the art of creating bark cloth in Hawai'i. *Tapa* is a broader term that refers to a Polynesian tradition. For an exhaustive history and discussion of contemporary kapa artists, see *Kapa Hawai'i: The Art of Native Hawaiian Kapa*, http://www.kapahawaii .com/ (accessed November 27, 2010).

10. See Reiko Mochinaga Brandon and Loretta G. H. Woodard, *Hawaiian Quilts: Tradition and Transition* (Honolulu: University of Hawai'i Press, 2005).

11. Patricia Ruth Hill, *The World Their Household* (Ann Arbor: University of Michigan Press, 1985), 60.

12. Ann Laura Stoler and Frederick Cooper, eds., *Tensions of Empire: Colonial Cultures in a Bourgeois World* (Berkeley: University of California Press, 1997), 31.

13. Mary Taylor Huber and Nancy C. Lutkehaus, eds., *Gendered Missions: Women and Men in Missionary Discourse and Practice* (Ann Arbor: University of Michigan Press, 1999), 10.

14. For the legal history of colonialism and how the twin mechanisms of law and Christianity remade Native Hawaiian family and sexual relations, see Merry, *Colonizing Hawai'i*.

15. By 1915 more than three million American women from over forty different denominations were members of missionary societies, and by that time missionaries had been in Hawai'i for close to a century. See Hill, *The World Their Household*, 3.

16. Anna Johnston, *Missionary Writing and Empire, 1800–1860* (New York: Cambridge University Press, 2003), 151.

17. Rossie Moodie Frost, "King Cotton, the Spinning Wheel and the Loom in the Sandwich Islands: The Story of a Missionary Spinster, an Ambitious, Wealthy Hawaiian Chief, and an Island Industry That Never Quite Made It," *Hawaiian Journal of History* 5 (1971): 110–24, available at http://evols.library.manoa.hawaii.edu/bitstream/10524/374/1/JL05122 .pdf (accessed November 27, 2010).

18. Kristin Hoganson, *Consumer's Imperium: The Global Production of American Domesticity, 1865–1920* (Chapel Hill: University of North Carolina Press, 2007).

19. Hawaiian Quilt Collection (ca. 1999–2000), http://www.hawaiian-quilts.com/ (accessed April 8, 2005).

20. The name of this business has been changed to protect the identity of the owner.

21. Linda Arthur, *Contemporary Hawaiian Quilting: At the Cutting Edge* (Waipahu HI: Island Heritage Publishing, 2003), 28.

22. Arjun Appadurai, ed., *The Social Life of Things: Commodities in Cultural Perspective* (New York: Cambridge University Press, 1988).

23. Here I play with Amy Kaplan's term "manifest domesticity," relocating it in time, if not space, to the neocolonial economy of the Philippines, which is heavily subsidized by the exported domestic labor of its working-class women, and the updating of colonial structures of gendered and racialized labor in the tourist and manufacturing industries, in particular.

24. Joyce D. Hammond, "Hawaiian Flag Quilts: Multivalent Symbols of a Hawaiian Quilt Tradition," *Hawaiian Journal of History* 27 (1993): 14–16.

25. Oscar Campomanes, "Casualty Figures of the American Soldier and the Other: Post 1898 Allegories of Imperial Nation-Building as 'Love and War,'" in *Vestiges of War: The Philippine-American War and the Aftermath of an Imperial Dream, 1899–1999*, ed. Angel Velasco Shaw and Luis H. Francia (New York: New York University Press, 2002), 134–62.

26. Barbara Kirshenblatt-Gimblett, *Destination Culture: Tourism, Museums and Heritage* (Berkeley: University of California Press, 1998), 149.

27. This idea of the abstract Native comes from Rona Tamiko Halualani, *In the Name of Hawaiians: Native Identities and Cultural Politics*

(Minneapolis: University of Minnesota Press, 2002). Thanks to Hoku-lani Aikau for the citation.

28. Personal communication with their customer service confirmed that the quilts are made in the Philippines.

29. *'Ohana* refers to "family" or family-like relations.

30. The names of the factory and the identities of its owners and work-ers have been altered for their protection.

31. Patricia Mainardi, "Quilts: The Great American Art," *Radical America* 7, no. 1 (1973): 36–68.

32. See, for example, Gladys-Marie Fry, *Stitched from the Soul: Slave Quilts from the Antebellum South* (Chapel Hill: University of North Car-olina Press, 2001); Mary Rose Williams, "A Reconceptualization of Pro-test Rhetoric: Women's Quilts as Rhetorical Forms," *Women's Studies in Communication* 17, no. 2 (1994): 20–44.

33. Patricia Grimshaw, *Paths of Duty: American Missionary Wives in Nineteenth-Century Hawaii* (Honolulu: University of Hawai'i Press, 1989), 155.

34. Lisa Kahaleole Hall, "Strategies of Erasure: U.S. Colonialism and Native Hawaiian Feminism," *American Quarterly* 6, no. 2 (2008): 273–80.

35. Joyce Linnekin, *Sacred Queens and Women of Consequence* (Ann Arbor: University of Michigan Press, 1990).

36. See Kauanui, "Native Hawaiian Decolonization."

37. Hammond, "Hawaiian Flag Quilts," 6.

38. Tim Ryan, "The Queen's Quilt," *Honolulu Star-Bulletin*, March 10, 2003. Ryan writes that the "Queen's quilt," as it was known, includes in its center square the words "Imprisoned at Iolani Palace. We began the quilt here." At http://archives.starbulletin.com/2003/03/10/features/story1.html (accessed May 1, 2009).

39. Rhoda E. A. Hackler and Loretta G. H. Woodard, *The Queen's Quilt* (Honolulu: 'Iolani Palace, 2004).

40. The exhibit was curated by Koan-Jeff Baysa and reviewed by Marcia Morse in "Point of Departure: The Contemporary Museum Honors the Centennial Year of the Arrival of Filipinos in Hawai'i," *Honolulu Weekly*, July 19, 2006, http://honoluluweekly.com/entertainment/2006/07/point-of-departure/#.TkLwWovACfU.email (accessed April 6, 2009).

Part 2
Comparative Racialization

| Trans-American Pacific Racial Formations

Chapter 4

Dismantling Privileged Settings
Japanese American Internees and Mexican Braceros at the Crossroads of World War II

Jinah Kim

The creation (or production) or a planet-wide space as the social foundation of a transformed everyday life open to myriad possibilities — such
is the dawn now beginning to break on the far horizon. . . . I speak
of an orientation advisedly. We are concerned with nothing more and
nothing less than that. We are concerned with what might be called
a "sense": an organ that perceives, a direction that may be conceived,
and a directly lived movement progressing towards the horizon. And
we are concerned with nothing that even remotely resembles a system.
—HENRI LEFEBVRE, *The Production of Space*

Tanforan Assembly Center, a black-and-white photograph by Dorothea Lange, commemorates the first bracero workers as they came
into Los Angeles on September 27, 1942, just in time for the sugar beet harvest. Braceros (arms) are Mexican immigrants and nationals recruited to work in U.S. agricultural and railroad jobs by
an official guest worker program started in 1942, soon after the
United States formally entered World War II. Braceros arrived by
train to Mexico's northern border; their arrival altered the social
environment and economy of many border towns such as Ciudad
Juárez, Tijuana, and their border twins El Paso and San Diego. This
photo features these men as they disembark and walk away from

1. Dorothea Lange, *Tanforan Assembly Center*, San Bruno, California, April 29, 1942. (War Relocation Authority, courtesy of the National Archives)

the train. They are well dressed, hats in hand or on their head, and they are carrying suitcases. Some are smiling, perhaps symbolizing the hope they felt at the opportunity to work and earn a wage.

A passenger train looms in the background and fills the entire horizon, an uncanny and unwelcome comparison to dispossessed Japanese Americans who just months earlier rode perhaps these same trains into desolate desert camps. After the bombing of Pearl Harbor, President Franklin Roosevelt issued Executive Order 9066 on May 3, 1942, which authorized the forced displacement of all people of Japanese ancestry, whether citizens or noncitizens, to "relocation centers" located throughout the Southwest and the mountain states. Seen in this light the workers filing out of Lange's picture seem to be framed as much by danger as by possibility. The train is an important symbol that lends the event the sense of modernity.[1] However, the juxtaposition reminds us that linearity and development over time is a privileged fiction.

This chapter aims to provoke a re-visioning of these two events, which are "privileged settings" in Asian American and Latina/o studies, to vastly broaden a notion of justice toward something collective and transformative.[2] The internment of more than 120,000 Japanese immigrants and Japanese American citizens and the exploitive contract labor bracero program highlight how the state deploys spatial mechanisms of displacement, resettlement, deportation, and incarceration to manage its racial subjects, redraw territorial boundaries, and broaden its sovereign domain. More broadly a commitment to theorizing space in relation to race and power contributes to our understanding of the complex, multidimensional racial order that existed in the United States during and after World War II. For example, a consideration of the spatial mechanisms that managed braceros and internees has the potential to differentiate the treatment allotted to racialized immigrants from the treatment of Jim Crow policies for African Americans and of reservation policies for Native Americans.

Highlighting the shared state and capitalist logics by which these two programs were managed also unearths shared practices of resistance, histories, and experiences as bracero workers and internees occupied similar and sometimes the same spaces in the U.S. West and Southwest. A comparative analysis that spatially plots racial domination will help to shake up and decenter the parallel narratives that tend to get set up in separate ethnic studies fields. As Ann Laura Stoler has written, however, "Attention to the historical categories of comparative practices refuses the comfort of discrete cases, highlighting instead those uneven circuits in which knowledge was produced and in which people were compelled to move. Not least, it brings into 'sharper resolution' the kinds of knowledge generated—and on which people might draw—across imperial terrains and within them."[3] Thinking about how the white imagination constructed Mexicans and Japanese relative to each other and relative to whites, blacks, and Native Americans provides a "sharper resolution" in thinking about why braceros were invisible and why the Japanese were hypervisible, especially after

the start of the war. A comparative analysis, then, has the potential to create the conditions for a critical practice based on rap-
prochement that can move critical race studies beyond the hegemonic contest between sameness and difference that defines liberal
multiculturalism.

This turn toward studying the oppressive spatial mechanisms
by the state, and the radical critical spatial practices and imagina-
tions enacted and engendered in response, departs from traditional scholarly considerations of Japanese American internment and
the bracero program. Scholars have looked to these events to call
for the reassessment of the treatment of immigrants and ethnic minorities during wartime and to contest the dominant framing of
the United States as a land of immigrant opportunity.[4]

In addition these events have given rise to movements for redress that dovetail with civil rights and racial reconciliation frameworks. For decades some braceros' wages were withheld by the U.S.
and Mexican governments, and braceros demanded redress and
apologies from both governments for these back wages, human
and workers' rights violations, and unlawful deportation. Their
cause did not reach sympathetic federal ears until the late 1990s.
In 2008, after decades of filing and fighting cases in Mexican and
U.S. courts, braceros living in the United States who worked from
1942 through 1964 were able to file claims for back wages from the
Mexican government.[5] The U.S. government has yet to acknowledge the money it owes.

In a span of four years, from 1988 to 1992, two U.S. presidents,
George H. W. Bush and Ronald Reagan, apologized to what remained of the Japanese American internee community for the injustices of illegal incarceration. The logic of these concentration
camps was upheld by the U.S. Supreme Court at the time. Fifty
years later Bush characterized the events as deplorable and "un-
American" and authorized the awarding of over $1.6 billion dol-
lars to 82,210 Japanese Americans or their heirs.

The language of these reparation claims, citing unjust denial
of rights due to national subjects, highlights the need to bridge

concerns about the necessity and pitfalls of reparations and rights discourse, which tends to limit scholarship to the bracero program and Japanese American internment, with a critical spatial imagination that presses past individual, single ethnic, and national claims and thus broadens the boundaries of justice. Leti Volpp, Iris Marion Young, Kimberle Crenshaw, Wendy Brown, Kevin Johnson, Linda Bosniak, and others remind us that the nation-state encourages the formation of political identities invested in maintaining an injured status that disaggregates linked claims and a priori relieves the nation of its burden as perpetrator of racial violence.[6] Differently problematic, state-level reparations foreclose international adjudication and claims pressed against other nonnational bodies based on broader categories of human rights and workers' rights violations. Politics that are based on injury can be contained by the very geography it seeks to oppose. Thus a critical spatial imagination forces a revitalization of traditional civil rights paradigms that have framed Japanese American internment and the bracero program and animates connections that can enable racial coalitions and expand concepts of rights from the liberal nation-state model.

Japanese American Internment, the Mexican Bracero Program, and the "Third Border"

Seen comparatively, Japanese American internment and the Mexican bracero program animate the "the third border," the policing of citizenship and belonging within national borders by architectural and legal mechanisms, as one of the defining methods of modern U.S. racial domination. I borrow the idea of the third border from Mike Davis and Alessandra Moctezuma, who describe how the international border has "penetrated daily life far north and south of *la linea* itself." According to Davis and Moctezuma, the third border's main function is not to reinforce the international (first) border but to police the movements of immigrants and racial citizens, to maintain residential segregation and discourage immigrants' purchase of private residential property in middle-class and wealthy white communities.[7] The legal and surveillance technologies that Davis and Moctezuma describe that maintain third borders between white and heavily immigrant communities in southern California, such as establishing racial covenants, barricading streets, setting up guardhouses, and restricting the use of public spaces, are eerily similar to the legal and architectural mechanisms that segregated and incarcerated Japanese American internees and Mexican laborers.[8] And of course the denial and dispossession of private property, the hallmark of a subject's belonging and the basis for accessing the full benefits of citizenship in liberal nation-states, is a shared mechanism by which Japanese Americans and Mexican braceros were kept in an abject position by the state.[9] Thus while Davis and Moctezuma use the third border to describe "crabgrass apartheid" in southern California, I extend its conceptual reach beyond the region to map instances in which third borders reified, through spatial domination, whites as American and racial others as enemy aliens.[10]

A novelistic elaboration on the ways that these camps were organized around and elaborate the operations of the third border can be found in *The Plum Plum Pickers*, Raymond Barrio's seventh and most famous book, considered by most critics to be the first novel about bracero workers to be published in the United States.[11] The opening lines— "Bang bang. Crash"—that smash in the door and wake the "blubbery" steward of the migrant camp, the Western Grande (and by extension the reader), set the stage for Barrio's attention to the relationship between the architecture of the camp compound and the operations of the third border as a mechanism of domination. The Western Grande is located at the outer limits of the fictional town Drawbridge, and its name draws on the largesse promised workers in the U.S. West, invoking images of a timeless utopic land of opportunities. Drawbridge is explicitly anachronistic and feudalistic, conjuring images of a gate that separates the modern time and place inside the fortress from the field laborers outside. A mapping of the third border reveals not only how proximate international borders are to the center of the nation—both the physical center of the Midwest and the metaphorical center of the family—but also how unsuccessful the border is in maintaining the strict line between white and nonwhite, citizen and immigrant. The third border in fact highlights that these borders were never meant to keep out workers but function to "reinforce the extra-economic coercion of immigrant labor in the non-union sectors of the U.S. economy."[12]

Japanese Americans were removed from the Pacific coast states of California, Oregon, and Washington after President Roosevelt sign Executive Order 9066. Mexican braceros and Filipinos filled the labor demands created by the internment and the draft. During the middle of World War II the War Relocation Authority slowly began allowing "loyal" Japanese Americans to leave the camps to do farmwork and housework on the East Coast and in the Midwest. After the war some Japanese did return to California and the West Coast, but for many the fear, trauma, and loss of property made return too painful. These Japanese Americans dispersed throughout the United States, many settling in the Midwest and East, as recounted in the works of Shelley Ota, Monica Sone, David Mura, John Okada, Naomi Hirahara, Seijii Higashide, Hisaye Yamamoto, and others.[13] By imagining that the border constituted by the Pacific Coast and the line between the United States and Mexico can meet in Arizona and Chicago also fundamentally challenges the West Coast bias in Asian American and Chicana/o studies.[14] Critics contend that scholarly paradigms based on the experiences, cultures, and histories of Asians and Mexicans in California shape the prerogatives in these fields. This serves to silence or elide alternative ways of knowing that can emerge from studies of archives and histories elsewhere, such as the Pacific Islands, the Midwest, and the South.[15]

Thus when Elaine Kim, one of the founding figures of ethnic studies and Asian American studies, exhorts scholars to go "beyond railroads and internment," she "may be more importantly urging them to reconsider the nationalist basis of these topics."[16] I extend Kim's important interventions into the "privileged settings" of Asian American studies by arguing for the need to jointly address iconic spaces and the meanings these sites are allotted by U.S. and ethnic American studies.[17] Attention to how Japanese American internment and the bracero program make up "a small list of privileged settings" does not mean that these events have no oppositional possibilities. For example, while Pearl Harbor might be a privileged setting that consolidates the U.S. nation—including the authorization of interning and deporting subjects deemed dangerous to national coherence—the bracero program and internment camps as different wartime icons fiercely delegitimize the maintenance of spatial dominance and allow other narrates to emerge. As such, reading these privileged settings necessitates attention to interpolating impulses that "narrate or block other narratives from forming and emerging" in order to redirect our energy toward a recognition of border poetics, "bringing forth a setting on the path toward revelation, truth, being or essence."[18] Thus I have two goals for this comparative study of the cultures of the bracero program and Japanese American internment using the analytic of space and borders. First, I hope to intervene in how these privileged settings are used or abused by examining their shared border politics and poetics. Second, I hope such a study challenges the current limitations on the critique of social inequality, which needs to overcome the "impossible insistence on a uniform ethnic subject" and to move past the politics of authenticity and ownership.[19]

In addition to similarities in styles and narratives between the bracero and internment narratives, both sets of texts reveal important ways of revisiting how we see space. The cultural theorist and Latina studies scholar Maria Herrera-Sobek and Asian American literary scholars such as Kandice Chuh and Traise Yamamoto have noted that the historical events and symbolism tied to these two events occupy significant narrative trends in Mexican and Chicano/a literature and Japanese American literature.[20] From literature about the internment and bracero experiences to legal documents produced to manage the nation's "others" during a period of flux in racial meanings, the cultures of internment and the bracero program offer a critical redrawing of the nation through a remapping of borders. To borrow from Mary Pat Brady, this allows us to consider how Asian American and Latina/o texts operate from the desire to "lose" or become "lost" to America.[21] By foregrounding shared and contingent understanding of space, borders, and extranational practices, texts such as "Fire in Fontana," *No-No Boy*, and *Barrio Boy* show how seeming racially and ethnically isolated spaces and spatial practices are interconnected and anxiously monitored by the nation-state. To shift the terms of critical practice significantly it is crucial that we recognize that in these texts migrant and internment camps, borders in the Southwest, desert landscapes, and "whites only" segregated space are not only places on a map, but also places in history.

Dismantling Privileged Settings

The start of the bracero program was relatively quiet; not until braceros became more visible by agitating for higher wages and better working conditions did anger over Mexican "foreign labor" heat up. The use of vulnerable, flexible, and mobile migrant workers helped shift U.S. agriculture from family to factory farms, which in turn made contract labor a permanent part of the southwestern landscape. According to an *El Paso (Texas) Herald Post* article on April 28, 1956, "More than 80,000 braceros pass through the El Paso Center annually. They're part of an army of 350,000 or more that marches across the border each year to help plant, cultivate and harvest cotton and other crops throughout the United States." Braceros were Mexico's migratory agricultural proletariat, a racialized, transnational workforce that, according to Mae Ngai, "comprised various legal categories across the U.S.-Mexico boundary—Mexican Americans, legal immigrants, undocumented migrants and imported contract workers—but which, as a whole, remained external to conventional definitions of the American working class and national body."[22] The bracero program (1942–64) was America's largest experiment with a "guest worker program," a rhetoric that still surfaces today as we discuss federally sponsored importation of contract labor, usually with explicit limitations on the rights of laborers.[23]

An important cross-current of U.S. immigrant legal history is visible here. Instituting the bracero program meant that the U.S. Congress had to overturn existing laws outlawing contract labor, that is, laws created to stop contract Chinese labor, or "coolies." Moon Ho Jung in *Coolies and Cane* argues that public discourse on contract labor was not a disinterested argument about cheap labor. Anti–contract labor factions argued that contract labor is antithetical to free labor.[24] It encourages large-scale farming and monopolies that create a "wage-slave" labor class. Chinese contract labor also threatened what Americans saw as the future and the just rewards America has to offer—an empty land for free white males. Chinese coolies defamiliarized a white male working-class sense of self, replacing fulfilling visions of entrepreneurial glory with dystopic images of competition for menial jobs with third world hordes.

This passage by Pauline Kibbe captures how the subjugation of contract labor depends on a hegemonic spatial imaginary: "Judging by the treatment that has been accorded [the Latin American migratory worker] . . . one might assume that he is not a human being at all, but a species of farm implement that comes mysteriously and spontaneously into being coincident with the maturing of the cotton, that requires no upkeep or special consideration during the period of its usefulness, needs no protection from the elements, and when the crop has been harvested, vanishes into the limbo of forgotten things—until the next harvest season rolls around. He has no past, no future, only a brief and anonymous present."[25]

"Bracero" is a metonym for the migratory working self that in turn is reified as a "species of farm implement that comes mysteriously, and spontaneously into being coincident with the maturing of the cotton," then "vanishes into the limbo of forgotten things." Importantly both space (the land) and the worker become intertwined as part of a techne that allows the real drama to unfold, a fruitful "harvest." To deny the bracero subjecthood and humanity, in other words, requires a simultaneous dehumanization, for lack of a better word, of the land on which he or she labors. As opposed to a colonial ward that is supposed to be "saved" by the colonists, the contract laborer is imagined as truly out of history. Braceros, like coolies, were treated and represented as an "alien" race without any capacity for control or ownership over their own bodies because the site of their labor was imagined as being outside of civilization, despite, it almost goes without saying, the fact of intense citizenship regulation, border manipulation, and dispossessions that underwrite this image of the Southwest.[26] Thus theorists of the Southwest and agricultural labor argue that the separation of worker from rights is the single greatest reason the Southwest remains a backwater postcolonial space.[27]

If the bracero is taken out of history paradoxically by being redrawn as an essential part of the southwestern landscape, an excerpt from *No-No Boy* demonstrates the pull of the internment camp as a spatial referent for post–World War II Japanese America. In the passage below we see varied temporal and spatial barriers that need to be severed to contest the demand that Japanese Americans see home and camp as commensurate spaces:

> He walked toward the railroad depot where the tower with the clocks on all four sides was. It was a dirty looking tower of ancient brick. It was a dirty city. Dirtier, certainly, than it had a right to be after only four years. . . .
>
> For Ichiro, Jackson Street signified that section of the city immediately beyond the railroad tracks between Fifth and Twelfth avenues. That was the section which used to be pretty much Japanese town. It was adjacent to Chinatown and most of the gambling and prostitution and drinking seemed to favor the area. Like the dirty clock tower of the depot, the filth of Jackson Street had increased.[28]

When the novel's protagonist, Ichiro, returns to Seattle after serving time for refusing the draft, he is confronted with the clock tower, a constant spatial referent throughout the novel that functions as an unwelcome reminder of the guard towers that ringed the internment camps. Other spatial referents, such as the "big wonder bread bakery way up on Nineteenth" and Ichiro's family taking over the

Ozakis' store "further down the block," add to the sense of danger in the postinternment landscape for Japanese Americans. For example, how did the Ozakis become dispossessed, and what does this mean about the security of Ichiro's family's livelihood? How is the logic that enables the disappearance of hundreds of thousands of Japanese Americans from the West Coast ingrained into the geography of these cities themselves? We might read Ichiro's description that the tower and Jackson Street have both become "dirtier, certainly, than [they] had a right to be after only four years" as a search for reconciliation between mental space and real space. We might see how this dialectical practice of bridging ideological considerations of the meaning of space with its experience in everyday life contests the interpolating pull of the internment camp as a privileged setting just like home.

Like the bracero program and its attendant institutions, Japanese American internment was also a social project, a rare opportunity to experiment with Foucauldian discipline, afforded to social scientists by the appearance of approximately ten thousand people crammed into one square mile and isolated from other inputs.[29] In addition to internment the U.S. State Department and the War Relocation Authority begin to craft new ways to segregate the "patriot" from the "traitor." When it was shown that loyalty questionnaires failed in separating loyal from disloyal Japanese Americans, the State Department pushed for renunciation and denationalization of Japanese Americans as the next course of action.[30] World War II was also a time when African Americans began agitating for the second end of a double victory: the end of fascism abroad and the end of racist authority at home. There was a general reactionary push to limit the franchise from the other direction as well, mainly by intensifying Jim Crow: "Last time must have been before Pearl Harbor. God, it's been quite a while, hasn't it? Three, no, closer to four years, I guess. Lotsa Japs coming back to the coast. Lotsa Japs in Seattle. You'll see 'em around. Stupid, I say. The smart ones went to Chicago and New York and lotsa places back east, but there's still plenty coming back this way."[31]

The preceding passage quotes Edo, a member of the 442nd all-Japanese infantry regiment, and marks Ichiro's first conversation in the novel. As opposed to Ichiro, whose frame of reference for World War II is the camps and prison, Edo's spatial marker is Pearl Harbor, a "privileged setting" in U.S. jingoistic history. However, what both passages share is a sense of unsettledness, a lack of spatial and temporal commitment to a place or narrative—three or four years? Pearl Harbor or internment camp? West Coast or "lotsa places back east"?—that underwrite Japanese American remembrances of the World War II era.

We might think here about the sense of being unsettled as an important characteristic of the World War II era, as Japanese Americans and Mexicans, as well as others dispossessed and made orphans by the war, negotiated the procedural aspects of becoming and unbecoming citizens and immigrants. Bonnie Honig reminds us that domestic questions about the meaning of citizen, immigrant, and alien happen in a time when questions of statehood are paramount. World War I created the problem of people without national citizenship, as people became displaced throughout Europe or were deemed enemy aliens and denationalized, like people of Japanese descent in the United States and Peru.[32] The potential for statelessness that World War I and World War II made evident is an important entry point for a critique of the nation-state. As Hannah Arendt envisioned in the 1930s, the nation-state form inaugurates a new terrain in which inequity can be enacted, as citizenship is the only way to have rights.[33] For example, during the 1920s a new category of belonging, "national origins," emerges and creates different de facto levels of citizenship. National origin is a quota system and a social engineering mechanism that Congress imagined would keep the United States white. Studying the bracero program and Japanese American internment in a comparative context can tell us a great deal about how the World War II era inaugurated a new procedural framework of disciplining, classifying, naming, filing, and organizing created by the crisis of unwelcome and uninvited subjects in the midst of war.

I have been suggesting that the bracero program and Japanese American internment seen in a comparative context highlight key similarities and disjunctures that have the potential to redraw and "transnationalize" the United States. As a theoretical lens transnationalism has a fraught relationship within Asian American, Chicana/o, and Latina/o cultural theories. The history of being denied citizenship rights, being racialized as a foreigner within, and being seen only as a labor implement has justly made Asian American and Latino cultural critics concerned about insisting on "foreign" or extranational ties. African America, on the other hand, has a long internationalist streak. For example, in 1852 Martin Delaney published *The Condition, Elevation, Emigration, and Destiny of the Colored People of the United States, Politically Considered*, agitating for a separate African American nation, possibly in Africa, but more probably in Canada or Latin America.[34] It's only since the 1990s that Asian American studies and Latina/o studies scholarship really made visible the limitations of a purely ethnic nationalist focus.[35] I suggest that a turn to comparative practices may help build bridges between transnationalism and empire, to help construct a transnational spatial analytics that does not seek to incorporate more and more disparate lands into "America," but rather locates the global as already embedded in the fiction of the nation. The intersections of the bracero program and Japanese American internment generate knowledge that foreground new terrains and new analytical practices to make legible the overlaps between U.S. empire, the American Century, and citizenship technologies, a shared racial landscape in which "borders are incomparably messier and more complex than our comforting image of precise black lines on maps."[36] Pushing beyond U.S. exceptionalism and centralized imperialism in studies of U.S. history, politics, economy, and culture destabilizes the nation as the agent of history and highlights the constitutive role that immigrants and migration play. Unmoored from demands for full adherence to a bounded body, whether corporeal or territorial, in Asian American and Latina/o studies, U.S. and transnational literary and cultural studies, ethnic nationalist and postcolonial theories unite.

Notes

I would like to thank Rudy Guevarra, Camilla Fojas, Francis Aparicio, Claire Jean Kim, and Dwight MacBride for their immensely thoughtful comments on earlier drafts of this chapter. Versions of this chapter were presented at the Borderlands and Latino/a Studies Newberry Library Seminar Series moderated by John Alba Cutler and Gerry Cadava in October 2009, as well as a meeting of the Race and Ethnicity Study Group organized and hosted with aplomb by Dwight MacBride in October 2008.

1. As a symbol, the transcontinental railroad highlights how the linear is a privileged geometry for Euro-American visions for modernizing the Americas. The train schedule introduces a shared routine and temporality across its route, while its route offers a new organizing principle for the construction of communities. This shared time, by enabling the sharing of values that starts in the East and extends west and southward, particularly capitalist work relations and the European culture of the East Coast, is also imagined to modernize and tame the unruly hinterlands and its denizens, preparing them to join the modern nation as proper citizen-subjects.

2. According to Philip Fisher, "Every history has, in addition to its actual sites, a small list of privileged settings." These privileged settings, such as the World Trade Center, carry intense symbolic weight beyond their "actual" use and are keystones in the myths and narratives that the nation tells about itself. Philip Fisher, *Hard Facts: Setting and Form in the American Novel* (New York: Oxford University Press, 1985), 9.

3. Ann Laura Stoler, *Haunted by Empire: Geographies of Intimacy in North American History* (Durham NC: Duke University Press, 2006), 18.

4. The myths surrounding World War II play a powerful role in impeding the reassessment of the treatment of internees and braceros. It is "the good war" and its soldiers the "greatest generation." During World War II America defeated fascism, Nazism, and authoritarianism and thus won the right to lead an international battle against communism. Domestically World War II introduced a period of unprecedented wealth and growth in the United States, putting memories of the Great Depression to rest. U.S. modernization projects in Latin America and Asia garnered additional surplus capital for U.S. coffers. Finally, as the attacks on September 11, 2001, remind us, the idea and memory of the United States being attacked on its own soil — Pearl Harbor and the World Trade Center — can be used to justify almost any injustice.

5. A federal court on October 10, 2008, approved a settlement for a class action lawsuit that will allow thousands of Mexican farm and railroad laborers to file for collection of monies withheld from their paychecks for work they performed in the United States during World War II.

6. For example, redress for Japanese American internees has raised very passionate and critical dialogues. Some of the generative discussion has been over the ways that Japanese American internees have used their loyalty to the U.S. government during incarceration to win sympathy for their position, as well as the relative success of Japanese Americans compared to the denial of reconciliation claims by African Americans and Native Americans. For more on this, see Leti Volpp, "Righting Wrongs," UCLA *Law Review* 47 (2000): 1815–38; Chris K. Ijima, "Reparations and the 'Model Minority' Ideology of Acquiescence: The Necessity to Refuse the Return to Original Humiliation," *Boston College Law Review* 40 (1998): 385–429.

7. In "Policing the Third Border," *Colorlines*, November 22, 1999, http://www.colorlines.com/archives/1999/11/policing_the_third_border.html (accessed January 23, 2008), Mike Davis and Alessandra Moctezuma write, "Over the course of 150 years, the U.S.-Mexican border has grown sadistic teeth of razor wire and concrete, reinforced by state-of-the-art surveillance technology and a stealth army of border police. At the same time, the border has penetrated daily life far north and south of *la linea* itself. Its ramifications have become complex and despotic. Increasingly, we need to distinguish three separate but interrelated systems of cultural control, each expressed in a distinctive landscape." The first border, according to Davis and Moctezuma, is the U.S.-Mexican international border. The second border, which the Border Patrol calls a "second line of defense," is composed of automobile dragnets inland from the international border. The third border, the *tercera frontera*, is architectural and legal barriers that have been constructed at "precisely those points where blue-collar Chicano or new immigrant communities connect with upper-income Anglo communities."

8. And of course the denial and dispossession of private property, the hallmark of a subject's belonging and the base for accessing the full benefits of citizenship in a liberal nation-state, are a shared mechanism through which Japanese Americans and Mexican braceros were disenfranchised by the state.

9. In a different way, descriptions of hand-built wooden huts that housed both internees and braceros feature centrally in both fictional and journalistic accounts of their lives. The denial of permanent and private dwellings highlights in a different way the operations of a "third border" that separated whites from braceros and internees.

10. A brilliant novelistic example of this can be found in *The Plum Plum Pickers*, Raymond Barrio's 1968 novel about bracero workers who pick prunes in northern California. The fictional town in which the migrant camp, the Western Grande, is situated is named Drawbridge. Drawbridge is a point of no return, a gatekeeping structure that is part of a fortress to regulate movement. This metaphorically suggests that the town is a passageway into the camp, which is an anachronism, a feudalistic state. While the Western Grande conjures images of a utopic land of opportunities, the Drawbridge temporally, as well as physically, separates the migrant camp, and the workers, from modernity.

11. Raymond Barrio, *The Plum Plum Pickers* (Binghamton NY: Bilingual Press, 1984).

12. Davis and Moctezuma, "Policing the Third Border."

13. Stephen H. Sumida's excellent analysis of the "hidden" role of the Midwest even in novels that are iconic for their depiction of the West Coast is instructive. He points out that John Okada wrote *No-No Boy* while in Detroit, and his experience during World War II in Nebraska is described in the novel's first pages, demanding that we more deeply investigate the impact that the sojourn in the U.S. interior has played in iconic Asian American novels. Stephen H. Sumida, "East of California: Points of Origin in Asian American Studies," *Journal of Asian American Studies* 1, no. 1 (1998): 83–100.

My own research contributes to the need to decenter the West Coast in a different manner. While the bracero program and Japanese American internment certainly are centrally related to the southern California region, my research has shown that the Midwest, including Iowa, Illinois, Ohio, and metropolitan centers like Chicago, has a dialectical relationship with the border. From Frederick Jackson Turner's vision of the Midwest as a stopgap of racial immigration to the quiet relocation and settlement of Japanese Americans and Mexicans, the third border as an analytical apparatus makes the connections between these different regions more apparent.

14. For an excellent discussion on the paradigmatic status of California to Asian American studies and Asian American identity, see Sumida, "East of California"; Stephen H. Sumida, "Centers without Margins: Responses to Centrism in Asian American Literature," *American Literature* 66 (December 1994): 803–15; Lisa Lowe, "The International within the National: American Studies and Asian American Critique," *Cultural Critique*, no. 40 (Autumn 1998): 29–47.

15. In this way California is both paradigmatic—experiences there are universal to all Asian and Mexican immigrants to the United States—but also exceptional, as a unique place in the United States, which fosters conditions that enable Asian and Mexican immigration.

16. Elaine Kim, "Beyond Railroads and Internment: Comments on the Past, Present, and Future of Asian American Studies," in *Privileging Positions: The Sites of Asian American Studies*, ed. Gary Y. Okihiro, Marilyn Alquizola, Dorothy Fujita Rony, and K. Scott Wong (Pullman: Washington State University Press, 1995), 1–9; Rachel Lee, "Asian American Cultural Production in Asian-Pacific Perspective," *boundary 2* 26, no. 2 (1999): 231–54.

17. For more on how the state has commercial and national interest in producing certain places as objects of desire and how the monumental status of public structures reflects a social commitment to the entrenched logic of the gendered, racialized, sexualized, and classed public/private binary, see Marita Sturken's discussion of the AIDS epidemic in *Tangled Memories: The Vietnam Wall, the AIDS Epidemic, and the Politics of Remembering* (Berkeley: University of California Press, 1997).

18. Martin Heidegger, "The Question Concerning Technology," in *Basic Writings*, ed. David Krell (New York: Harper Collins, 1993), 321.

19. Kandice Chuh, *Imagine Otherwise: On Asian Americanist Critique* (Durham NC: Duke University Press, 2003), ix. The desire for an "authentic" Asian American hero and past can be seen in many different arenas, such as in mixed-race studies. In one of my classes students wondered whether Asian America has a Malcolm X, which I took as a crisis in origins and anxiety, a desire for a stable rooted subject to which Asian America can look.

20. Some of the works that are paradigmatic of such trends are the short story "Kelly" by Monique Truong; *No-No Boy* by John Okada; the stories of Hisaye Yamamoto; the documentary *History and Memory*

by Rea Tajiri; Barrio's *The Plum Plum Pickers*; Rose Castillo Guilbault's *Farmworker's Daughter: Growing Up Mexican in America* (Berkeley: Heyday Books, 2005); and Alex Rivera's mockumentary *Why Cybraceros?* (1997).

21. Mary Pat Brady, *Extinct Lands, Temporal Geographies: Chicana Literature and the Urgency of Space* (Durham NC: Duke University Press, 2002).

22. Mae M. Ngai, *Impossible Subjects: Illegal Aliens and the Making of Modern America* (Princeton NJ: Princeton University Press, 2004), 128–29.

23. While the program (i.e., recruiting and shipping labor) ran from 1942 to 1964, the braceros themselves continued to work for many decades after that.

24. Moon Ho Jung, *Coolies and Cane: Race, Labor, and Sugar in the Age of Emancipation* (Baltimore: Johns Hopkins University Press, 2006).

25. Pauline R. Kibbe, *Latin Americans in Texas* (Albuquerque: University of New Mexico Press, 1946), 11.

26. To date, the Mexican bracero population is the largest of the contract worker groups in U.S. history.

27. As opposed to going to war, Mexico would send its immigrants to work as braceros in the United States. By 1954 "Operation Wetback" had deported more than one million people of Mexican descent. This project was meant to make farmers understand the seriousness of INS intent to raid noncompliant farms and send their workers back to Mexico.

28. John Okada, *No-No Boy* (Seattle: University of Washington Press, 1976), 1, 4.

29. For more on this, see Lawson Fusao Inada, ed., *Only What We Can Carry: The Japanese Internment Experience* (Berkeley: Heyday Books, 2000).

30. Many historians of World War II–era Japanese Americans, such as Eiichiro Azumi, highlight how nationalism and loyalty to both countries were weak among those who renounced their claim to American citizenship; they were being practical and pragmatic as well as being led by intense feelings of anger, demonstrating how loyalty and nationalism are political, not cultural. Thus internment did not function to culturally assimilate Japanese Americans, but rather was a practice of political incorporation but only through a denial of rights.

31. Okada, *No-No Boy*, 2.

32. For more on this, see Bonnie Honig, *Emergency Politics: Paradox, Law, Democracy* (Princeton NJ: Princeton University Press, 2009). According to the historian Mae Ngai, the Johnson-Reed Immigration Act of 1924 was the first comprehensive restriction law, establishing numerical limits on immigration situated on a racial and national hierarchy designed to increase the number of some immigrants over others. This policy remained in effect until the 1960s and "articulated a new sense of territoriality, which was marked by unprecedented awareness and state surveillance of the nation's contiguous land borders." Ngai, *Impossible Subjects*, 3.

In the meanwhile restrictions on European immigration between 1890 and World War I created conditions under which European immigrants to the United States assimilated (became white) and became further divorced from their homeland, forming the base of a European-rooted American national identity and culture.

33. Arendt argues that political equality is not rooted in nature or a pregiven state, but is man-made. She saw its constructed nature as central to the egalitarian potentials of political belonging, or citizenship. However, this egalitarian state is possible only if citizenship is not based on ethnic identity but in furthering civility and political ties, which is contrary to the historical realities of World War II and the postwar period. For more on Hannah Arendt and citizenship, see *The Human Condition* (Chicago: University of Chicago Press, 1958). Within U.S. immigration law the term or designation "alien" is more specific than terms that connote belonging, such as "sovereignty," "citizen," and "nation." It is easier to name people noncitizens than to decide that they are nonpeople. Within the U.S. legal lexicon the immigrant is very different from a visa holder. An immigrant implies someone who plans to stay; the law allows for stay without citizenship, and there are many places in the world where a person does not transition from immigrant to citizen and yet is a resident there (e.g., Koreans in Japan). The category or term "immigrant" itself is not supposed to be an abject position within the law. One of the main promises of immigration is the promise of naturalization. The bracero program and Japanese American internment show that within the U.S. practical context, even if not in the legal lexicon, the differences between naturalized citizen, immigrant, and alien are very slippery.

34. Martin Delaney, *The Condition, Elevation, Emigration, and Destiny of the Colored People of the United States, Politically Considered* (1852; repr., New York: Arno Press, 1968).

35. Kandice Chuh reminds us that transnationalism is a "cognitive analytic that traces the incapacity of the nation-state to contain and represent fully the subjectivities and ways of life that circulate within the nation-space. In this second sense transnational refers to border crossings without literal movement, to a conceptual displacement of a national imaginary in order to allow for discursive and critical acknowledgement of those political and cultural practices illegible in the official discourse of the U.S. nation-state." Chuh, *Imagine Otherwise*, 62.

36. Davis and Moctezuma, "Policing the Third Border."

Chapter 5

(De)Constructing Multiple Gaps
Divisions and Disparities between Asian Americans and Latina/os in a Los Angeles County High School

Gilda L. Ochoa, Laura E. Enriquez, Sandra Hamada, and Jenniffer Rojas

Administrator Berk remembered, "When I was applying for [this position], I said that there were two campuses at this same school—a high-performing campus, which is predominantly Asian, and a low-performing one which is predominantly Hispanic. . . . This is not a [southern California high school] phenomenon. Hispanics, in general, emphasize putting food on the table over education. —Field notes, February 1, 2007

While at Southern California High School (SCHS), we frequently heard about "high-performing students," "low-performing students," and "the gap," in reference to an achievement gap determined largely by standardized tests.[1] Students more commonly used the descriptors "smart" and "stupid" to describe themselves and their schoolmates. These constant distinctions were made between the two largest panethnic groups at the school—Asian Americans and Latina/os—oftentimes referred to by school officials and students as Asians and Hispanics.[2] By glossing over student differences by class, ethnicity, and generation and ignoring the multiple factors fostering disparities in schools, these broad panethnic categorizations and general designations of high-performing and low-performing students reproduced dominant racialized assumptions.

Asian Americans and Latina/os were cast in opposition to each other, and analyses of their academic performances were often rooted in supposed differences in cultural and parental values, as when Mr. Berk describes an emphasis among Latina/os on working to survive over achieving an education. Likewise the school's narrow conceptualization of an achievement gap focused attention away from the everyday dynamics at the school that were perpetuating more than an achievement gap. Although they were rarely discussed, racialized and classed opportunity and social gaps were woven into the fabric of the school in ways that divided students and reproduced disparities.

Using qualitative research, we apply a case study approach to uncover how academic, opportunity, and social gaps are constructed and reinforced. In particular, school practices and racialized constructions prepare students for unequal life chances and influence their interactions.[3] Among the results of such dynamics is a binary and hierarchical relationship that places Asian Americans as a group above Latina/os academically. While many SCHS school officials and students perceive Asian Americans as academically hardworking, smart, and determined, Latina/os are seen as less academically able and less invested in education. These pervasive conceptions intersect with school practices to reinforce academic, opportunity, and social gaps at SCHS. Collectively these racialized conceptions and practices reinforce one another, but the sources of disparities and students' divisions are largely overlooked because of the general acceptance of dominant ideologies surrounding Asian Americans, Latina/os, and meritocracy.

Underlying our analysis are the ways that dominant ideologies and systemic hierarchies reinforce and are kept intact by school practices and personnel and then manifested in students' achievements, opportunities, and relationships. We also consider how narrow approaches to an achievement gap exclude consideration of the social components of schooling and the significance of racism and class disparities on educational opportunities. By combining an analysis of school-level practices with students' experiences and not losing sight of the larger factors influencing today's schools, we adopt a macro-meso-micro approach to understanding educational experiences and group relations. As one of the few comparative studies to focus on the fastest growing panethnic groups in the United States, we disentangle the structuring of an educational gap and consider how students' opportunities for academic growth and their development of cross-racial/ethnic social and cultural capital are stunted at schools such as SCHS.

Literature Review

The experiences and relationships of Asian Americans and Latina/os must be understood in the context of the dominant conceptions of race/ethnicity and inequality.[4] Power-evasive frameworks that emphasize being color-blind and overlooking structural inequalities have shaped popular discourse.[5] These perspectives assume that the United States is a meritocracy and that racism and other forms of discrimination are something of the past. So the significance of class inequality and individual, institutional, and structural racism on educational experiences and life chances are largely dismissed. Instead individualism and free choice are emphasized, along with the ideology that some groups lack the supposed cultural attributes for progress and success.[6] In general, Asian Americans have been praised for their believed cultural emphasis on education and academic hard work, especially in comparison to African Americans and Latina/os, who are assumed to lack such traits. Within this framework, panethnic heterogeneity and various forms of exclusion faced by these diverse groups are ignored or minimized.

Working in tandem with a power-evasive framework and influencing the dynamics at SCHS is a binary construction that positions Asian Americans as a "model minority" in contrast to Latina/os. This binary is rooted in historical ideologies whereby Asian Americans — often without regard to differences in migration histories, class positions, or ethnicities — have been deemed quiet, hardworking, and long-suffering.[7] In comparison, as part of the enduring and unequal relationship between the United States and

Latin America, Latina/os in general, but Mexican Americans in particular, have been cast as peons, inferior, lazy, and criminal.[8] As a result of the prevalence of these constructions, diverse Asian Americans and Latina/os have been homogenized into these two broad panethnic categories and false images.[9] By casting Asian Americans as models, this construction perpetuates the myth of a meritocracy, pits groups against each other, and undermines the significance of racism and class disparities. Therefore these images of Asian Americans and Latina/os are not simply isolated stereotypes. They are part of larger systems that maintain and reproduce social, economic, and political inequality. It is because of the magnitude of such constructions that Patricia Hill Collins refers to them as "controlling images."[10] They permeate all aspects of our society, including schools, and they reinforce a racial hierarchy whereby the U.S. public views Asian Americans, as a group, more favorably than they do Latina/os.[11]

Schools are ideal places to explore the role of institutional practices and everyday exchanges on educational outcomes and group relations. With students spending about one-third of their waking hours in school, they serve as important places of socialization, and due to the historical pattern of neighborhood segregation, schools are one of the first places where youth have extended and intimate cross-racial/ethnic contact.[12] Likewise, as schools are microcosms of society, their policies and practices mirror and reproduce dominant values, ideologies, and inequalities.[13]

Despite extensive scholarship on the factors influencing students' educational outcomes, research on how schools shape cross-racial/ethnic relations has been relatively limited.[14] It was not until the late 1960s and early 1970s that a body of research on race relations in schools began to develop.[15] However, much of this early research quantitatively explored the impact of desegregation on black and white peer groups, largely avoiding analyses of the school factors structuring students' relationships as well as the experiences of Asian Americans and Latina/os. Responding to gaps in this early work, scholars in the 1970s and 1980s expanded their qualitative research on desegregation and race relations.[16] Some of this research was significant for detailing how school practices such as curriculum tracking, classroom pedagogy, and extracurricular activities foster student racial/ethnic divisions or collaboration.[17] However, in general this work continued to focus on the experiences of blacks and whites.

Since the 1990s there has been a slow movement away from the exclusive focus on black-white relationships and a greater focus on the effects of school factors on multiple racial/ethnic relationships.[18] For example, in *Subtractive Schooling*, Angela Valenzuela details how a Eurocentric curriculum and curriculum tracking limit relationships between Mexican Americans and Mexican immigrants. Not only are students separated by tracking, but they engage in a politics of difference by forming friendships around those who are in their classes and who they perceive to be like themselves. As a result of such separation, students are less able to tap into the social and cultural resources that each group possesses.[19] In her work on Asian Americans, Stacey Lee also demonstrates how schools influence student relationships.[20] She documents how admissions policies, curriculum tracking, student ranking, participation in high-status extracurricular activities, and the belief that Asian Americans are "model minorities" foster racial tensions among students. Consequently Asian Americans are blamed for taking coveted slots in prestigious classes and programs from whites, and they are used to prove to African Americans that they too can achieve if they just work hard. The results of such practices are anti–Asian American jealousy, the invisibility of white privilege, and the blaming of African Americans.[21]

Even with this newer research, comparative studies focusing on the relational aspects of both Asian Americans and Latina/os remain scant. When Asian Americans and Latina/os are included, scholars often focus on whether their experiences are more like those of whites or African Americans, not considering Asian Americans and Latina/os on their own terms or in relationship to one another.[22] In general such approaches are limiting and incomplete, especially in places like California, where Asian Americans and Latina/os often share schools and may be defined in relation to each other. Given the importance of understanding how schools structure group relations and moving beyond a black-white binary, this study heeds the call for research that "explores[s] the diverse experiences of urban, ethnic minority students in multicultural schools, particularly where White students are not the dominant population."[23]

Methodology

This chapter is based primarily on seventy-eight in-depth, semistructured, and open-ended interviews with Asian Americans and Latina/os at a public school in the eastern section of Los Angeles County that we refer to as Southern California High School.[24] The interviews averaged fifty minutes in length and were conducted from May 2007 through June 2008. After interviewers gave brief introductions, they asked students about their personal interests, family background, schooling experiences, perceptions of peers, the culture at SCHS, and career and educational aspirations. The interviews were audiotaped, transcribed, and coded for recurring themes and patterns. Throughout this chapter, all quotes are verbatim from the transcripts, and the names of participants and their schools have been changed.

In addition to these tape-recorded interviews, we spoke informally with students and school personnel and completed ethnographic observations in classrooms and during school activities. These dialogues and observations increased our understanding of some of the dynamics at SCHS.

The Setting

The school we call SCHS is a public high school in the eastern part of Los Angeles County. The school is known for its high standardized test scores and rates of college attendance. Among the nearly two thousand students attending SCHS, relatively equal numbers of Asian Americans and Latina/os predominate. Most students identify as Chinese or Mexican American, and the remaining student body is about 10 percent white, 2 percent African American, and 1 percent Native American. Thirty-three percent of the students are eligible for free and reduced lunch, and about 10 percent are English-language learners. The school personnel do not reflect the racial/ethnic demographics of the community and student body; about 50 percent of the teachers and administrators are white, 33 percent are Asian American, and 20 percent are Latina/o.[25]

In addition to honors and advanced placement (AP) courses, SCHS boasts an international baccalaureate (IB) program with about thirty to forty students. Along with access to their own counselor, IB students enroll in courses such as Theory of Knowledge, Art History, and Twentieth-Century History. Students completing the required advanced courses, international examinations, an extended essay, and community service and extracurricular activities graduate SCHS with an IB diploma. The majority of IB seniors are the children of college-educated Asian immigrants primarily from Taiwan and Hong Kong; during the time of our research, fewer than 5 percent of the IB seniors were Latina/o.

Student Participants

On average the students included in this study were in the middle of their sophomore year and were slightly more likely to be female than male (56 percent compared to 44 percent). Thirty-five were Latina/o, identifying primarily as Mexican, Mexican American, Hispanic, or Latina/o. Most of these students were children or grandchildren of Mexican immigrants, but the families of several had been in the United States for four or five generations. About 33 percent came from homes where one parent had received a college degree, but on average their parents had high school degrees and jobs in construction, trucking, and sales. In contrast, of the forty-three Asian Americans included in this study, most had moved to the United States as children or were the children of Chinese or Korean immigrants, the majority coming from Taiwan or Hong Kong. Over 70 percent came from a home where at least one parent had received a college degree. On average their parents had over

fifteen years of education and were likely to have middle-class professions in accounting or management. Several had construction,
computer, or restaurant businesses. Thus while the Latina/o students were more likely to come from working- and lower-middle-
class households than their Asian American peers, racial/ethnic
background and class position did not always correlate. Thirty-
three percent of Latina/os had at least one parent who had graduated with a BA, and 33 percent of the Asian Americans had one
parent who had not completed college.

Constructing Gaps and a Racial/Ethnic-Class Hierarchy

> There is a major problem between the disparity between Asians and
> Latinos. . . . All honors classes are like all Asian, and all the regular
> classes are like Latino. It's sort of like two subcultures that are mutual-
> ly exclusive from one another. I don't think it's like a healthy environ-
> ment for kids to be around 'cause it's not reality. (Art Chen, Chinese)

> You grow up in a world where some people are just stupid and some
> people are smart. You assume that Asians are smart and that Mexi-
> cans are always stupid. (Monique Martínez, Costa Rican, Mexican,
> and American)

Together SCHS students Art Chen and Monique Martinez capture
the overarching sentiments shared by a majority of the students
we interviewed. They name the school structures and controlling
images shaping their experiences. Art highlights how school practices such as curriculum tracking are dividing students. Monique
describes a sentiment expressed by most of the participants, who
either believe that Asian Americans are "smart" and Latina/os are
"stupid" or feel that some of their teachers or schoolmates support
such racialized perceptions of intelligence. Their analyses, when
combined with their schoolmates' narratives, reveal a racial/eth-
nic hierarchy where "smartness" is associated with being Asian
and "stupidity" with being Mexican. Although class differences at the school are mostly overlooked, class intersects with race/
ethnicity to perpetuate disparities and divisions among students.[26]

Overall students' experiences reveal the interlocking effects of school structures and everyday messages that come together to (re)produce academic, opportunity, and social gaps. These practices, inequalities, beliefs, and interactions are rooted in unequal systems of power and privilege and have been shaped by history and justified by dominant ideologies. They often persist because of their normalization; they become perceived as "the tradition" and are rarely challenged.[27] At SCHS controlling images foster student separation and reproduce binary, racialized, and hierarchical constructions of Asian Americans and Latina/os. These racialized arguments are internalized and become pervasive in explaining what comes to be seen as "the achievement gap," and unequal school practices and class disparities are largely unnamed and are allowed to fester. As a result the controlling images and divisions and disparities continue to exist.

School Structures: Geographic and Academic Segregation

School segregation and curriculum tracking keep students apart from one another, inhibiting them from developing mutual understanding as equals and hampering friendships.[28] At SCHS middle schools, academic paths, and student divisions are racialized, classed, and disparately perceived such that Asian Americans and middle-class students are generally concentrated in one middle school and in the high school honors and advanced placement courses while Latina/os and working-class students are predominantly in a separate middle school and in non-honors courses. With students in one middle school and in SCHS's top classes experiencing greater educational opportunities and academic achievement, a binary, racialized, and hierarchical construction of students is fostered.

Middle School Disparities

By the time students arrive at SCHS, most have attended one of two feeder middle schools in Los Angeles County: La Montaña or Maple Grove. Located less than two miles from each other in distinct neighborhood, these schools differ by race/ethnicity, class,

and academic performance, narrowly defined as students' scores
on standardized state tests. La Montaña is attended primarily by
middle- and upper-middle-class students; nearly 60 percent of the
students are Asian American, about 30 percent are Latina/o, and
12 percent are white. It also boasts the highest Academic Performance Index (API) score of the middle schools in the district, a 10.
Maple Grove is attended primarily by working- and lower-middle-
class students who are nearly 70 percent Latina/o and 25 percent
Asian American. About 7 percent are white. On a scale of 1–10,
the school's API score is a 5.

With statements such as the following, students conveyed their
awareness of these differing demographics and the skewed reputations that accompany their middle schools:

> La Montaña is known as a pretty good school like in the district be-
> cause some schools [referring to Maple Grove] are kinda like ghetto,
> or they say stupid people go there. Our school [La Montaña] was ac-
> ademically higher. (Mary Hwang, Chinese)
>
> They probably think [Maple Grove] is a boring school that's not rich;
> [it's] like a poor school. (Dianna Muñoz, Hispanic)

The extensive attention at the federal, state, and district levels giv-
en to API scores as the key factor determining school quality reproduces students' perceptions of the two middle schools, but as
Mary Hwang and Dianna Muñoz's comments attest, the significance of class and the role of racialized images are also paramount
in shaping public opinion.

The stark association of Asianness, smartness, and a high API
score with La Montaña and the equation of Mexicanness and stu-
pidness and a poor school with Maple Grove was pervasive. In a
group interview, self-identified Hispanic and mixed Hispanic and
European females who attended La Montaña offered the following analyses of such conceptions and their implications:

> VICKI PARDO: Our school was like ninety-seven percent Asian. Yeah,
> so everyone thinks that our school is smart just because of the Asians.

JENN VANDERHOL: Yeah, it's like we [Hispanics] could be smarter than *them*, and they wouldn't even notice.

VICKI PARDO: It sucks for other schools 'cause like when our school sees other schools, they are always like, "Oh my god. They are so dumb." It kind of sucks because everybody is getting judged just because of their race, and then they eventually fall into it.

As the minority in a predominantly Asian American student environment, these students are cognizant of the way that race and academic ability are correlated in the minds of their peers. While the controlling images of Asian Americans as smart made these two students feel invisible, such images and a competitive school climate also reproduce the racialized academic and social rifts between middle schools.

Students who began SCHS unaware of others' perceptions of their middle school were likely to learn fairly early in high school what others thought. A few students shared what teachers had conveyed to them about their middle school and in turn about them as students. One Maple Grove alumnus, Christopher Bonilla, who was a senior when we interviewed him, will "never really forget" when his ninth-grade teacher pulled him aside to discuss the low B that he was receiving in her class and said, "Oh, you know, you're not doing too well. It's probably because you're from Maple Grove." Christopher respected this teacher who was trying to reach out to him, but he believes that she was implying that "'cause that school's majority is Mexican over there, they kind of have a bad rep." Students from Maple Grove may deduce from such comments that their school is stigmatized because Mexicans attend it, and as products of these schools and as Mexicans they too are labeled with a "bad reputation." By racializing middle schools, students and school officials maintain power-evasive discourses. Rather than contest the middle school reputations, deconstruct the limited criteria used for ranking schools, or name the disparities in class resources and the dominant ideologies that accompany skewed images of the middle schools and the students who attend them, many school officials and students casually accept and reinforce the racialized middle school reputations and controlling images. Additionally the apparent academic gap between the middle schools paves the way for the academic gap at SCHS by differentially preparing students and fostering perceptions of unequal student abilities based on race and class and middle school attendance.

For many students, peer relations are also formed before beginning high school. With SCHS doing little to address student divisions, some students speculate that they may have a difficult time crossing middle school and racial lines in high school. Tommy Huie, a Chinese-identified SCHS junior, explains, "Going to La Montaña, we kind of grew up with each other. . . . Pretty much, we knew all the Asians. So coming here we didn't really know anyone, and we stuck together in our own cliques." Such experiences suggest that the racial/ethnic and class segregation of the middle schools helps produce the segregation of peer groups at SCHS and thus fuels social gaps.

Curriculum Tracking

As students begin SCHS, standardized test scores, middle school courses, and school officials' recommendations are used to place them into college preparatory and honors or advanced placement (H/AP) courses, or a combination of both college preparatory and H/AP courses; students may also sign-up as pre-IB students. However, these criteria, used by schools across the nation, are not neutral.[29] Instead track placement has been found to be racially skewed such that Asian American and white students are more likely to be placed into rigorous courses than Latina/o and black students with similar standardized test scores.[30] A couple of school personnel believe that because of "the school's reputation," La Montaña students are often given the "benefit of the doubt" when determining which ninth graders to place into honors courses. Given the differing demographics of the schools that feed into SCHS, Asian American and middle-class students are dramatically overrepresented in H/AP courses and in the IB program. Differential access to these disparate courses and academic paths fundamentally shape multiple opportunity, achievement, and social gaps. As such they foster a racialized and hierarchical academic binary.

With curriculum tracking sorting and dividing students into different courses, these student divisions infiltrate friendship groups.[31] Not only do students tend to form friendships with students who are in their courses, but as captured in the following comments by Art Chen, a senior, students in the highly touted IB program seem largely unaware of other students, even those enrolled in another one of the school's academic programs, Advancement Via Individual Determination (AVID), designed primarily for first-generation college students: "IB is sort of like the elite group but some of the elites don't chose IB because it is so much work, and then I don't know about AVID, but I know they exist. . . . Regular students, umm, yeah, I'm not too sure about what they are up to or what they are into."

The peer groups for such students are so clearly delineated that they often do not know about one another. These social gaps are created in part by academic and opportunity structures, but are also reinforced when students such as Art adopt normalizing and hierarchical language to describe different students as "elite" or "regular." Given the racial/ethnic and class patterns in course placement, for many, labels such as "elite" and "regular" become synonymous with Asian American and Latina/o, respectively. Albert Ortiz, a sophomore in college-preparatory courses, is aware of these divisions and believes, "They probably won't be talking to me, if they're in honors." These stark divisions maintain racist and classist assumptions about students; they reduce students' social capital by keeping students apart from one another; and they reinforce an opportunity and achievement gap wherein students receive different types of college and career preparation.[32]

Students noted that teachers and other school officials not only have distinct expectations for students in different classes, but they also unequally restrict students' movement by academic programs. In particular several students in IB shared how being given a "free pass" by campus security guards is one of the privileges that comes with participating in the program. Mark Song explains, "When I used to get in trouble, I'll be like, 'Oh, I'm an IB student.' Security guards are like, 'Oh, okay.' Like one time I was out of class 'cause I had to go talk to my counselor, and it was like, 'Oh, you're not supposed to be here. . . . You can't meet with your counselor unless you have an appointment.' 'Oh, I'm an IB student.' Then, they say, 'Oh, you can come in.'"

These unequal experiences are commonplace and send messages to students about who is trusted and valued, thereby placing such students in a privileged position relative to their classmates. In comparison, students who lack a "free pass" find that they are suspect and their whereabouts questioned by school officials in ways that reinforce constructions of who belongs on campus and who does not. Since course placement and program involvement at SCHS vary by race/ethnicity and class position, these disparities are even more troubling because they intersect with controlling images to reproduce racial/ethnic and class divisions and hierarchies.

Overall the racial/ethnic and class separations in courses perpetuate the perception that Asian Americans are smart because students see which students are in the top classes. Ashley Cordero, a junior previously enrolled in the IB program, describes how this process becomes self-fulfilling: "IB students could get kind of big-headed at times because it's only Asian . . . and then I'm Hispanic. It's kind of recognized as like the Asian thing because the Asians are supposed to be the smarter ones." Clearly such curriculum tracking reproduces the cycle of dominant perceptions, unequal course and program participation, the establishment of peer networks, and multiple gaps — opportunity, social, and achievement.

Dominant Ideologies and Everyday Messages

Dominant tropes about educational success, Asian Americans, and Latina/os permeated student interviews. Students either drew upon or recounted others' multiple messages that standardized tests are a crucial indicator of academic success and that Asian

Americans—compared to Latina/os—are a model minority. These messages were conveyed to students by the emphasis placed on testing, teacher-student dynamics in the classroom, and students' own interactions. Together these messages (re)produce a racial/ethnic and class hierarchy and the dominant ideologies of meritocracy and individualism that assume equal opportunities and neutral practices.

Standardized Tests and the Framing of an Achievement Gap

Due to the high stakes associated with standardized test scores, schools such as SCHS spend significant time discussing quantitative data on student and school performance. As reflected in the excerpt beginning this chapter, much of the focus is on what is characterized as an "achievement gap." While grades and rates of high school graduation and college attendance are sometimes considered part of this gap, scores on standardized tests are increasingly the primary measure of achievement. This emphasis on standardized tests in K–12 emerged during the Reagan-Bush era and intensified with the policies of No Child Left Behind (NCLB), approved in 2001. At the core of NCLB is accountability, whereby test performance is used to evaluate and make important determinations on students, schools, and teachers. In general, tests are often presented as fair and accurate measurements of students' abilities.[33] The results are a narrowing focus in education on test performance and school ranking based on test scores. Differences in opportunities, the role of school practices, and students' general well-being are often absent from this focus. As such, class disparities are overlooked, and dominant beliefs that Asian Americans are a model minority and that the United States is a meritocracy are sustained.

Illustrating the pervasive focus on test scores at SCHS is the way that some students, typically those enrolled in honors and AP courses, specifically commented on the school's Academic Performance Index, a summary measurement used to evaluate school performance and progress on statewide assessments.[34] Without prompting, students explained that teachers' comments, administrators' announcements, posters around campus, and public rankings of schools have made them aware of the value the school places on doing well on standardized tests. Carmen Chu, a junior, said, "We know about our API scores because we have video bulletins every Monday, and sometimes they'll talk about how the API scores are going down. 'We want to bring them up. This is our goal to have this certain amount when it comes to STAR [Standardized Testing and Reporting] testing.'" Students have felt the pressure to do well for the school and have heard racial/ethnic and immigrant correlations for test performance.

Given the pervasiveness of testing and the constant discussion of the academic achievement gap, the two issues are correlated with racialized and cultural arguments about which groups are impacting the school's ranking. Patty Song, a senior, says that some of her teachers even joke in class that "the Asian kids help us have a high API." She believes that "teachers and the administration kind of have it in their heads that the Asians are the smart ones, like they are the ones that make our API go high." In contrast, a couple of students, such as Tommy Huie, a junior, are "hearing from people outside our school that our API is kind of low because the Mexican people are dragging it down." Drawing upon racialized assumptions of academic ability, teachers, administrators, and even some community members blame the school's declining prestige on falling test scores caused by Mexican American students.

Comments equating race/ethnicity to academic performance and school ranking send powerful messages to students about their supposed abilities and differences. For Patty Song, who wants to be judged "as an individual," teachers' comments "kinda hurt": "We can't be different. We have to stick to a certain crowd." It is assumed that Asian American students are not only smart and good students but that they will befriend other supposedly smart and dedicated Asian American students. Likewise when Latina/os are blamed for lowering the school's test scores, a form of racialized lumping occurs that reinforces white supremacist beliefs that Latina/os are biologically and culturally deficient. An analysis of class disparities and racism is largely excluded, and the assumption is that these tests are fair, objective, scientific, and precise assessments of student learning; therefore something must be wrong with those groups who are supposedly responsible for lower scores.

The high stakes and almost exclusive focus placed on test scores and the correlation of these scores with racial/ethnic background can foster scapegoating and increase student divisions. As the researchers Rosenbloom and Way found, teachers' preferences for Asian American students may fuel anti–Asian American sentiment by Latina/o students.[35] Likewise the equation of diverse panethnic categories with test results lumps together large groups of students with varied histories, class positions, and ethnicities. Thus with scant attention paid to these differences or to unequal access to rigorous classes, the focus on test scores and how various groups perform reproduces stereotypes that Asian Americans as a group are smarter and more valuable to the school than are Latina/os, who are cast as liabilities.

School Officials' Racialized Messages

Students such as April Lee, a sophomore, are keenly aware of teachers' expectations and the ways that they draw racialized boundaries around students and demarcate the academic expectations they have for them: "I think when a teacher looks at you and your face, 'Oh, you're Asian.' 'She must be really smart, or she must be really good at math or something like that.' . . . They have that expectation that Asians have to be in honors. If they're not in honors, something's wrong." Similarly Jenn Vanderhol and Fran Padilla reflect on the power of such expectations by recalling a teacher's comments:

> JENN VANDERHOL: He would just talk about how Asians are smarter. How we are not smart 'cause we're not Asian.
>
> FRAN PADILLA: He was always joking around, but it's like even if you're always joking around there is always some form of truth to it. It has to come from somewhere.

These racialized messages from authority figures influence students' thoughts about one another, and they may limit the roles students can play within the school. As Fran suggests, these messages may then be internalized and reproduced. Albert Ortiz's comments are illustrative: "I feel stressed out, and sometimes I don't feel like I can do the stuff. . . . I just don't try 'cause I feel like I'm not good at anything except football, 'cause I can hit people." Like many of the Latina/o students we interviewed, Albert questions his academic abilities. He even scales back his educational aspirations. While some students note the limitations of these racialized stereotypes and struggle to defy others' expectations, most incorporate them into their discussions.

Several students reported that perceptions and high expectations of Asian Americans—in comparison to Latina/os—manifest into what we refer to as racialized second chances. In particular students noted unequal treatment in the areas of discipline and academics that stem from larger controlling images. The following exchange during a group interview with Asian American sophomores captures the differential experiences of discipline and punishment that both Asian American and Latina/o students perceive:

KATHY HSIN: Some teachers only like Asians because they're Asian.

NAT SASITHORN: Yeah, like if you come late to class, and you tell them like your PE [physical education] teacher let you out late, they'll be like, "Oh, it's okay." Then a Mexican guy comes and says that, and they're like, "Oh, go to the office!"

Albert Ortiz also recounts differential disciplinary policies but correlates them with course placement or academic ability: "[Students in higher classes get] more liberty, I bet, and more choices to get more stuff around here. They probably have more, [a] better chance of staying out of trouble if they do something wrong, or if they do [something wrong, it's] like 'Oh, let them just go.' Like, they'll just have a free pass through all high school."

Kathy's, Nat's, and Albert's comments demonstrate the connections between race/ethnicity, course placement, and discipline. It appears as if Latina/o students are more likely to be unfairly disciplined. Such unequal treatment may stem from pervasive controlling images of Latina/o students as being disengaged from education and troublemakers within school.[36] As a result Latina/o students are relegated to the lower end of the academic hierarchy, with its accompanying lowered expectations, opportunities, and freedom of movement.

While some students believe that Asian Americans receive more second chances when it comes to discipline, they suggest that the myth that all Asian Americans are studious may have the opposite impact academically. During the same group interview, the following two students share how Asian Americans may have fewer chances when it comes to submitting late schoolwork:

NAT SASITHORN: We mess up one time, and [teachers] go like anal-retarded on us.

MARK KU: You're an A-plus student, why aren't you good at . . .

NAT SASITHORN: If it was like a Mexican guy, if he gets a good grade, they're like, "Wow, this guy's so good."

These racialized expectations do not leave space for students to be understood as individuals with their own interests and capabilities. Experiencing such preferential or exclusionary treatment has multiple impacts on students. Individually, while some Latina/os admit to "giving up" because their teachers seem to have "given up on them," several Asian American students explain how these messages reinforce other negative messages they receive about Latina/os. Collectively, as detailed below, the impacts of such racialized messages from school personnel often negatively influence students' relationships by creating animosity.

Peer Expectations and Relationships

In their everyday exchanges, many of the students we interviewed seem to reinforce the vast social divisions and hierarchical constructions at their school. When asked about their interactions with other students, most revealed that their friendship groups were both racially distinct and dependent upon who was in their classes. The following comments are exemplary:

> Asians hang out with Asians. Mexicans hang out with Mexicans.
> (James Tuan, Chinese)

> Well, like obviously, I'm friends with everybody in AVID, but I don't
> think I have any friends in AP or IB. (Felipe Perez, Latino)

While James notes the specific race/ethnicity-based divisions among
peer groups, Felipe suggests that friendships are tied to tracking
practices within the school, which are also racialized and classed.
The academic and opportunity gaps that exist at SCHS help determine the social gaps that students identify within their friendship groups. Additionally the racialized messages that students
receive form the basis for their expectations and relationships, or
lack thereof, with peers.

Students have little cross-racial/ethnic or class interaction due to
segregated middle schools and racialized and classed tracking and
are provided with scant knowledge in their courses about racial/
ethnic histories and experiences. As a result they are often forced
to rely on stereotyped messages as their main source of information
about one another. The following two comments are illustrative:

> It might just be because like an Asian, like an Asian tradition since
> like for thousands of years, like education has been the thing, like for
> millions of years. Chinese dinosaurs probably took school seriously.
> (Sandra Wu, Chinese)

> We [Asians] have the concept that we have to work—get good grades
> to have a good life after you graduate, and well, non-Asian races, I'm
> not saying they're not working hard enough, but they're not as moti-
> vated. (Margaret Wang, Chinese)

Given the school's academic structure, many of the Asian American students who are in the top classes where Latina/os are a minority have little opportunity to counter their presumptions. Mary
Hwang, a sophomore enrolled in honors courses, explains, "Most
of the time, I don't really get a chance to interact with Hispanics because like in my classes, I don't really have that many of them. . . .
But when I do, they're all really like—I know there are stereotypes

that say they don't really work hard in school, but a lot of them work really hard and are smarter than like a lot of people." Yet controlling images remain because tracking practices limit cross-racial and cross-class interactions and opportunities to discredit stereotypical claims, and most students are not provided with alternative discourses to deconstruct such assumptions.

Similar to Mary Hwang, when students like Rose Gonzalez, one of the few Latina/os in the AP and IB classes, are provided with structured opportunities to engage in cross-racial/ethnic interactions, they may develop a greater sense of comfort and understanding: "At first I guess it was like really intimidating because of all the Asians, and a lot of them didn't talk to me at first. I was like kind of a loner. And I was like, 'Ehhhh.' Especially in IB, it was kind of me and then everybody else. But like a lot of them warm up to you, and everyone warms up, like it's just really nice." Later in her interview Rose reveals marginalizing experiences, demonstrating that such racial skewing in the IB courses was not ideal, but her cross-racial/ethnic interactions through this academic program eventually enabled the building of mutual relationships.

Despite the generally positive learning experience Rose encountered, interracial peer relations alone do not necessarily lead to a sense of mutual understanding.[37] Controlling images of academic success are so pervasive that they cannot always be undone with interracial collaboration and peer relationships. In the absence of community-building strategies and courses offering counterhegemonic discourses, one of the most enduring stereotypes is that Asian American students are more strongly oriented to science and math due to supposed cultural and sometimes even biological proclivities for numbers. As the following excerpts reveal, this stereotype often persists despite proof of mathematically talented Latina/o students and struggling Asian American students:

> In my [math] class, this one kid's all, "Oh, wow, this is rare, a Mexican [student] is teaching an Asian person how to do math." (Jennifer Cortez, Latina)

I hear these jokes a lot. If you are Asian, you have to be smart. It is like the most common thing at this school. . . . I am not the smartest kid out there, but if I discuss what I got on a test and I got a D, my Hispanic friend goes, "What, but you are Asian?!" (Jessica Su, Korean American)

Jennifer's mathematical abilities are marveled at because she defies the racialized assumptions that suggest that her Asian American peers should be teaching her, and Jessica's Latina/o peers are confounded by her lack of mathematical prowess. Jennifer's and Jessica's comments reveal that their peers' perceptions of mathematical abilities are grounded in racialized assumptions. In both cases, cross-racial/ethnic peer interactions alone have done nothing to deconstruct the pervasive assumptions that are used to racialize academic ability; instead they perpetuate the academic gap at SCHS.

Besides preventing mutual understanding, an academic gap, and its associated stereotypes, perpetuates the social gap by generating animosity between Latina/o and Asian American students. Jennifer Cortez expresses frustration with racialized academic constructions: "I've noticed that with a lot of Asian kids at school, they try to make it seem as though all Hispanic kids are dumb. That really aggravates me. I'm like, 'Dude, you guys can't even drive a car, and that's common sense.' If you don't have common sense, that doesn't make you smart." To counter the negative stereotypes used against her, Jennifer invokes an equally harmful stereotype about the driving abilities of Asian Americans. Angered by their inability to productively and effectively counter such assumptions, students are often forced to invoke similar negative stereotypes in order to defend themselves. Most likely this is due to the lack of a systemic understanding provided at SCHS of the institutional processes that perpetuate academic inequality.

In some cases, singular incidents come together to build up animosity and discourage future cross-racial interactions. Mark Song, a Korean IB student, explains, "I don't like Mexicans for some reason. I know I'm making a hasty generalization about this one

incident, but then these incidents multiply. . . . There's lots of cases where like some Mexican girls always used to touch my butt or
something. It's so random. I know they're messing around, but I
don't know." Because he has had few experiences with Latina/os,
Mark is forced to understand them only in the context of this perceived threat to his masculinity. If he and the Latina students he
describes had other, more consistent, structured, and collaborative
interactions, it is possible that they would be better able to understand such incidents and form more productive peer relationships.
Restricting interactions through stratified courses negatively impacts peer relationships and does not provide spaces for future interactions that might be able to break down dominant beliefs and
negative messages that are being structured by school practices
and relayed by others.

Conclusion

While most school personnel and students at SCHS focus on what
they describe as "the gap" between Latina/o and Asian American
students in reference to academics, we find that this narrow focus
camouflages other gaps. It also normalizes dominant ideologies
and the criteria used to ascertain academic performance.

There are significant opportunity, academic, and social gaps
between students that are structured in schools such as SCHS and
maintained by controlling images. Students first arrive at SCHS
from two distinct middle schools with different reputations that
are connected to race/ethnicity, class, and test performance. They
then experience raced and classed skewing in tracked courses in
high school that foster race- and class-based peer groups, maintaining the academic, opportunity, and social gaps that were apparent in middle school. Simultaneously students face dominant
messages about their academic abilities. The binary construction
of Asian Americans as smart and Latina/os as stupid leaves little
space to deconstruct cultural norms and pits students against one
another, and they perpetuate social gaps between students, especially considering that students' cross-racial/ethnic contact is

limited. With inhibited student contact, social and cultural capital is differently developed by race/ethnicity and class and course placement and rarely shared.

All of these gaps limit the experiences of both Asian American and Latina/o students and prepare them to maintain dominant ideologies and a system of inequality. The hindering of student interactions across race/ethnicity, class, and perceived ability prevents students from knowing what opportunities and experiences are open to other individuals. This then limits their ability to deconstruct the hegemonic and homogenizing stereotypes that are being used to perpetuate the gaps. As a result students often internalize controlling images and begin to perpetuate the gaps among themselves. At the same time, the meritocratic discourses of capitalism and individualism are used to suggest that their successes and failures are deserved, so they mask the substantial structural, institutional, and interpersonal effects that school practices, controlling images, and class disparities have on students' experiences. Larger ideologies go unnamed and unexamined so that few challenge the systems of segregated middle schools and academic tracking. Additionally meritocracy and the emphasis on standardized tests focus attention on an achievement gap as the most significant factor driving education, rather than opportunity and social gaps.

We need to begin addressing multiple gaps and the dominant discourses and images that are used to maintain them. The model minority stereotype should not be the image that is used to describe and limit the educational experiences of Asian Americans. Latina/os should not be confined to being good at sports and lazy or uncaring in the classroom. We need to fill in these gaps by continuing to examine the heterogeneity within panethnic groups and social classes. School officials and students need counterhegemonic discourses that deconstruct power-evasive frameworks and facile representations of racial/ethnic groups. By eliminating segregated and unequal schools and expanding access to rigorous courses and a multicultural power-aware curriculum for all students, we can construct more complete, well-rounded, and gap-less educational experiences for Latina/os and Asian Americans alike.

Notes

1. All names related to the research site, including the names of schools, are pseudonyms assigned to reflect the gender and racial/ethnic backgrounds of the participants.

2. We use these panethnic terms to be inclusive. However, we acknowledge the vast heterogeneity that exists within each of these categories. Most of the students who participated in this study identified as Chinese, Asian, Korean, Mexican, Mexican American, Hispanic, or Latina/o.

3. Differences in school-sanctioned cultural and social capital are also paramount, but given space restrictions, they will be explored in future work.

4. We use "race/ethnicity" and "racial/ethnic" not to conflate them or to assume that they are biological, cultural, or static categories but instead to acknowledge that they are two interrelated systems and social, political, economic, and cultural constructs that influence life chances and perspectives.

5. Ruth Frankenberg, *White Women, Race Matters: The Social Construction of Whiteness* (Minneapolis: University of Minnesota Press, 1993); Michael Omi and Howard Winant, *Racial Formation in the United States* (New York: Routledge, 1994).

6. Eduardo Bonilla-Silva, *Racism without Racists: Color-Blind Racism and the Persistence of Racial Inequality in the United States* (Lanham MD: Rowman & Littlefield, 2006).

7. Stacey J. Lee, *Unraveling the "Model Minority" Stereotype: Listening to Asian American Youth* (New York: Teachers College Press, 1996).

8. Charles Ramírez Berg, "Stereotyping in Films in General and of the Hispanic in Particular," in *Latin Looks: Images of Latinas and Latinos in the U.S. Media*, ed. Clara E. Rodríguez (Boulder CO: Westview Press, 1997), 104–20.

9. Bernadete Beserra, "Negotiating Latinidade in Los Angeles: The Case of Brazilian Immigrants," in *Latino Los Angeles: Transformations, Communities, and Activism*, ed. Enrique C. Ochoa and Gilda L. Ochoa (Tucson: University of Arizona Press, 2005), 178–96.

10. Patricia Hill Collins, *Black Feminist Thought: Knowledge,*

Consciousness, and the Politics of Empowerment (New York: Routledge, 2000).

11. Thomas J. Espenshade and Maryann Belanger, "Immigration and
Public Opinion," in *Crossings*, ed. Marcelo M. Suarez-Orozco (Cambridge MA: Harvard University Press, 1998), 365–403.

12. Janet Ward Schofield, "School Desegregation and Intergroup Relations: A Review of the Literature," *Review of Research in Education* 17
(1991): 335–409; Judith Goode, Jo Anne Schneider, and Suzanne Blanc,
"Transcending Boundaries and Closing Ranks: How Schools Shape Interrelations," in *Structuring Diversity: Ethnographic Perspectives in the
New Immigration*, ed. Louise Lamphere (Chicago: University of Chicago Press, 1992), 173–213.

13. Samuel Bowles and Herbert Gintis, *Schooling in Capitalist Amer-
ica: Educational Reform and the Contradictions of Economic Life* (New
York: Basic Books, 1976); Henry Giroux, "Theories of Reproduction and
Resistance in the New Sociology of Education," *Harvard Educational
Review* 53 (1983): 257–93.

14. See Robert Rosenthal and Lenore Jacobson, *Pygmalion in the
Classroom* (New York: Holt, 1968); Jeannie Oakes, *Keeping Track: How
Schools Structure Inequality* (New Haven CT: Yale University Press, 1985);
Gilbert Gonzalez, *Chicano Education in the Era of Segregation* (Philadel-
phia: Balch Institute Press, 1990); Jonathan Kozol, *Savage Inequalities:
Children in America's Schools* (New York: Crown, 1991); Gloria Ladson-
Billings, *The Dreamkeepers: Successful Teachers of African American
Children* (San Francisco: Jossey-Bass, 1994); Gary Orfield, "The Growth
of Segregation," in *Dismantling Desegregation: The Quiet Reversal of
Brown v. Board of Education*, ed. Gary Orfield, Susan E. Easton, and the
Harvard Project on School Desegregation (New York: New Press, 1996),
53–71; Angela Valenzuela, *Subtractive Schooling: U.S. Mexican Youth
and the Politics of Caring* (Albany: State University of New York Press,
1999); Nilda Flores-González, *School Kids/Street Kids: Identity Development in Latino Students* (New York: Teachers College Press, 2002);
Nancy Lopez, *Hopeful Girls, Troubled Boys: Race and Gender Disparity in Urban Education* (New York: Routledge, 2003); Gilda L. Ochoa,
Learning from Latino Teachers (San Francisco: Jossey-Bass, 2007).

15. Schofield, "School Desegregation and Intergroup Relations."

16. Schofield, "School Desegregation and Intergroup Relations."

17. See Thomas W. Collins, "From Courtrooms to Classrooms: Managing School Desegregation in a Deep South School," in *Desegregated Schools: Appraisals of an American Experiment*, ed. Ray C. Rist (New York: Academic Press, 1979), 89–113; Maureen T. Hallinan and Ruy A. Teixeira, "Students' Interracial Friendships: Individual Characteristics, Structural Effects, and Racial Differences," *American Journal of Education* 95 (1987): 563–83; Janet Ward Schofield and H. Andrew Sagar, "The Social Context of Learning in an Interracial School," in *Desegregated Schools: Appraisals of an American Experiment*, ed. Ruy C. Rist (New York: Academic Press, 1979), 155–99.

18. See Peter N. Kiang and Jenny Kaplan, "Where Do We Stand: Views of Racial Conflict by Vietnamese American High School Students in a Black-and-White Context," *Urban Review* 26 (1994): 95–119; Susan Rakosi Rosenbloom and Niobe Way, "Experiences of Discrimination among African American, Asian American, and Latino Adolescents in an Urban High School," *Youth and Society* 35 (2004): 420–51; Maria Eugenia Matute-Bianchi, "Ethnic Identities and Patterns of School Success and Failure among Mexican-Descent and Japanese-American Students in a California High School: An Ethnographic Analysis," *American Journal of Education* 95 (1986): 233–55; Valenzuela, *Subtractive Schooling*; Gilda L. Ochoa, *Becoming Neighbors in a Mexican American Community: Power, Conflict, and Solidarity* (Austin: University of Texas Press, 2004); Cynthia L. Bejarano, *Qué Onda? Urban Youth Culture and Border Identity* (Tucson: University of Arizona Press, 2005); Stacey J. Lee, *Up against Whiteness: Race, School, and Migrant Youth* (New York: Teachers College Press, 2005).

19. Valenzuela, *Subtractive Schooling*.

20. Lee, *Unraveling the "Model Minority" Stereotype*; Lee, *Up against Whiteness*.

21. Lee, *Up against Whiteness*.

22. For exceptions, see Tomás Almaguer, *Racial Fault Lines: The Historical Origins of White Supremacy* (Berkeley: University of California Press, 1994); Leland T. Saito, *Race and Politics: Asian Americans, Latinos, and Whites in a Los Angeles Suburb* (Urbana: University of Illinois Press, 1998); Eileen O'Brien, *The Racial Middle: Latinos and Asian Americans Living beyond the Racial Divide* (New York: New York University Press, 2008).

23. Rosenbloom and Way, "Experiences of Discrimination," 447.

24. This chapter is part of a larger study in which 230 open-ended interviews were conducted with high school students, school personnel, and parents.

25. Data accessed from www.ed-data.k12.ca.us.

26. At SCHS there are also divisions, disparities, and hierarchies within the panethnic groups that will be considered in future work.

27. Oakes, *Keeping Track*.

28. Valenzuela, *Subtractive Schooling*.

29. Oakes, *Keeping Track*.

30. Jeannie Oakes and Gretchen Guiton, "Matchmaking: The Dynamics of High School Tracking Decisions," *American Educational Research Journal* 32 (1995): 3–33.

31. Valenzuela, *Subtractive Schooling*; Ochoa, *Becoming Neighbors in a Mexican American Community*.

32. See Oakes, *Keeping Track*; Valenzuela, *Subtractive Schooling*.

33. Jozi de León and Linda J. Holman, "Standardized Testing of Latino Students," in *Educating Latino Students*, ed. María Luisa González, Ana Huerta-Macías, and Josefina Villamil Tinajero (Lancaster PA: Scarecrow Press, 2002), 177–94.

34. In comparison to the H/AP students and Asian Americans, college preparatory and Latina/o students were more likely to discuss the California High School Exit Exam, which is required for high school graduation, rather than the school's API score.

35. Rosenbloom and Way, "Experiences of Discrimination."

36. Lopez, *Hopeful Girls, Troubled Boys*.

37. Lisa Sullivan, Ditra Edwards, Nicole A. Johnson, and Kim McGillicuddy, "An Emerging Model for Working with Youth: Community Organizing + Youth Development = Youth Organizing," http://www.fcyo.org/media/docs/8141_Papers_no1_v4.qxd.pdf (accessed December 10, 2008); Natasha D. Watkins, Reed W. Larson, and Patrick J. Sullivan, "Bridging Intergroup Difference in a Community Youth Program," *American Behavioral Scientist* 51 (2004): 380–402.

Chapter 6

Mabuhay Compañero
Filipinos, Mexicans, and Interethnic Labor Organizing
in Hawai'i and California, 1920s–1940s

Rudy P. Guevarra Jr.

My offense was not against any law of morality or against any political statute, but against a system of industrial exploitation. I was railroaded to prison because I tried to secure justice and a square deal for my oppressed countrymen who are lured to the plantations to work for a dollar a day. I was kept in prison far beyond my minimum sentence because I refused to curry favor or seek concessions from those who held the power. I would not sacrifice my self-respect even for the sake of liberty. — PABLO MANLAPIT's "Farewell Statement" in the *Honolulu Advertiser*, August 14, 1927, before leaving for the U.S. mainland

Pablo Manlapit, a Filipino labor organizer in Hawai'i during the 1920s, believed his countrymen deserved a "square deal" while working in Hawai'i's sugar plantation system. He and other Filipinos rallied the rank-and-file workers to unite with Japanese labor leaders and workers in a series of labor strikes throughout the Hawaiian Islands during the 1920s and 1930s. They demanded higher wages, shorter working hours, and fewer workdays per month, as well as improved living and sanitation conditions in plantation housing, from the Hawaiian Sugar Planters' Association (HSPA).[1] As a result, Manlapit and other Filipinos were labeled "agitators" and blacklisted from working on the islands. Many of these agitators, including Manlapit, were deported to the U.S. mainland.[2]

In addition to deportations and forced migrations, thousands of Filipinos also left Hawai'i voluntarily, primarily for California and the Pacific Northwest, to find jobs in agriculture and fish cannery work.[3] California provided the most opportunities, and Filipinos flocked there to work with other coethnics and relatives who had secured employment during previous migrations to the U.S. mainland. They brought with them their organizational skills in labor unionizing. However, instead of organizing with the Japanese, who by this time were making their move to truck farming and becoming growers themselves, Filipinos allied themselves primarily with Mexicans, who were also resisting poor working conditions in California's agricultural fields.[4]

Manlapit's movement of Filipino laborers and organizing took place long before the rise of the United Farm Workers movement of the 1960s, which is often credited as *the* movement that organized Filipino and Mexican farmworkers for social and economic justice in the fields. Moreover, although both groups have a history of labor organizing, I contend it was Filipinos who first initiated and led the charge for interethnic labor organizing with Mexican agricultural workers. Coming from a sugar plantation culture, Filipinos had more experience in interethnic labor organizing as a result of their experiences with the Japanese in Hawai'i. When thousands of Filipinos left Hawai'i's sugar plantations to work in California's agricultural fields, they brought this philosophy with them. They utilized these experiences to organize with Mexicans, California's dominant ethnic labor group at the time. Through interethnic labor organizing and striking, both groups were able to have some of their demands met, such as higher wages; more important, they were able to see the value of coalition building across ethnic lines.

This chapter explores the interethnic labor organizing of Filipinos in Hawai'i and California and its vital importance to their alliance with Mexican workers. Hawai'i was the focal point for interethnic labor organizing among Filipinos, who brought the philosophy of interethnic unionism with them to California. Common experiences and struggles against racial oppression became the impetus for interethnic organizing, as Filipino and Mexican workers rallied together to combat the unfair labor practices of their employers.

Filipinos and Mexicans have been the dominant labor force in California agriculture since the early twentieth century. As farmworkers, they have been the targets of racial oppression and injustice by their employers; they endured long hours of intense labor only to be rewarded with meager pay and poor living and working conditions. Growers considered Filipino and Mexican workers to be dispensable brown bodies who were suited for hard labor and thus would be content with their conditions. Although they experienced exploitation on many levels, neither group stood by passively. In fact both groups have a long history of labor organizing and striking throughout California's agricultural fields. Though they initially organized as separate ethnic labor unions, eventually they found common ground on which to organize together. In order to understand the role that Filipinos and Mexicans played in organizing under interethnic unions, we must first examine the historical forces that influenced this relationship, beginning in Hawai'i, and its eventual fruition in the state of California. This historical perspective will help us appreciate the labor activities and daily lives of Filipinos in these two locations, as well as how they were interconnected despite being thousands of miles and an ocean apart from each other.

Filipino Immigration to Hawai'i

Hawai'i's economy saw an increase in production from its growing sugar industry, with booming profits from the 1860s through the 1890s.[5] The rise of sugar plantations and their corporate consolidation into the "Big Five" (Castle & Cooke, American Factors, Alexander & Baldwin, C. Brewer & Co., and Theo H. Davies & Co.) ensured that all industries were dependent on this product. Their power was unchallenged during this period, as native production systems and populations were supplanted by foreign settlers and technology.[6] Labor was commodified as immigrants poured into the Hawaiian Islands to meet the demand required for the production of sugar.

Sugar exports to the U.S. mainland continued to increase throughout the early twentieth century. Hawai'i's sugar plantations were
playing a vital role in what became the territory's most important
and profitable export product.[7] Various ethnic groups were recruited to supply the growers' insatiable demand for cheap labor,
among them the Chinese, Portuguese, Puerto Ricans, Koreans, Japanese, and Filipinos. The number of Filipinos grew so large that
they eventually outnumbered most ethnic groups on the plantations, including Japanese workers, who made up a large segment of
the workforce by the early 1920s. Depending on the island and the
plantation, ethnic/racial populations of workers varied. As workers
in Hawai'i's sugar plantations, Filipinos were considered the "ideal
labor force" because in the planters' eyes, they were "accustomed
to subordination and modest expectations of livelihood." In other
words, Filipinos were the perfect workers because they were cheap,
docile, plentiful, and poor.[8] Moreover, as U.S. nationals, Filipinos
did not have immigration restrictions, as did other Asian groups.
They could travel freely to the U.S. mainland and its territories to
meet the labor demands of various industries. With immigration
exclusions and restrictions being implemented against the Chinese
in 1882 and the Japanese between 1907 and 1924, Filipinos were
thus their logical replacement in the fields.[9]

Although Filipino laborers only trickled in at first, by the 1910s
and early 1920s they began pouring in by the thousands to replace
the Japanese in the sugar plantations. Filipinos who came to work
on Hawai'i's sugar plantations were known as *sakadas*. Between
1909 and 1934 approximately 118,556 sakadas were recruited to
work in Hawai'i.[10] By the 1920s and well into the 1930s Filipinos
had become the largest ethnic group working on the plantations, often outnumbering the Japanese and other workers by at least three
to one.[11] In the early 1920s Filipinos protested that their living and
working conditions were worse than what the HSPA had promised
in their labor contracts; they organized with the Japanese, who
had struck against the sugar planters between 1905 and 1909.[12]

During those earlier strikes Filipinos had been used as

strikebreakers. Now they and the Japanese, as well as other community and labor leaders, worked to promote interethnic cooperation so that the combined efforts of both groups could succeed in gaining higher wages, better working and living conditions, and union recognition.[13] It is in this context that labor leaders like Pablo Manlapit emerged and, along with other Filipinos, became a major threat to the HSPA.[14] Although it was a risky coaltion, Filipino labor leaders saw the advantages and importance of working with the Japanese in terms of an interethnic class struggle against the HSPA.[15] The Filipinos had their own union at the time, the Filipino Labor Union of Hawai'i, while the Japanese had the Federation of Japanese Labor. Of the 43,618 workers in all the sugar plantations in Hawai'i, 19,474 were Japanese and 13,061 were Filipino.[16]

The Japanese reluctantly joined Filipinos in a strike against the O'ahu sugar planters in 1920, which lasted six months. Although the strike ended in defeat for the workers, some of their demands were met, including wage increases and equal pay for equal work, bonuses, and social welfare and recreational programs for the workers. Despite initial tensions, Filipinos learned the value of interethnic struggle and unity with the Japanese. In 1920 the two separate ethnic unions united with other ethnic groups to become the first interethnic union, called the Hawai'i Laborer's Association, which later became the United Workers of Hawai'i.[17]

Their victory, however, was short-lived. With the global economy dictating the price of sugar, a recession began in 1921 that resulted in wage cuts for plantation workers and a failing bonus system.[18] In response Filipinos went on strike at several plantations on various islands. Thus began the Filipino Piecemeal Strike of 1924–25. In all, more than two thousand workers participated in work stoppages and strikes on twenty-three of the forty-five plantations.[19] The HSPA responded with extreme violence. On the Hanapēpē plantation in Kaua'i, for example, sixteen Filipino strikers and four policemen died as a result of gunfire and knife attacks in the Hanapēpē Massacre.[20] Although no one knows who fired the first shot, it was likely one of the inexperienced police officers who were hastily deputized by local law enforcement to suppress the strikers. According to a reporter who covered the incident immediately after it occurred, goat hunters were sworn in as police to break up the strikers and release some "prisoners" that the strikers had taken, who also happened to be Filipino. After killing several of the strikers, the deputies continued to take "pot shots" at the strikers. An eyewitness recalled, "They had rifles and the Filipinos had nothing but pistols. It wasn't a real battle, it was a slaughter, really." Another eyewitness also suggested that the police started the incident: "The police were looking for a fight from the very first, when they arrived at the camp."[21]

The plantation-friendly press demonized the Filipino workers and their leadership. Clearly the HSPA had the instruments of government and the press at their disposal, which influenced public opinion against individuals like Manlapit, who was blamed for the incident even though he was not even there when it occurred.[22] The Filipinos who were killed were buried together in a mass grave, and another 161 were arrested. No police were tried for the killing of the Filipino strikers, including the deputized goat hunters.[23] The strike ended in defeat. A report issued by A. W. T. Bottomley, the president of the HSPA, alleged that the "so-called strike of 1924" was unjustifiable. He contended that Filipinos were paid well and were well accommodated with amenities such as free medical care, housing, fuel for food, sanitary living conditions, and water. They also had a plantation store that offered products "almost" at cost.[24] Bottomley tried to prove his point by comparing workers' wages in Hawai'i and the U.S. mainland, asserting, "Notwithstanding the higher standards of living on the mainland, the average laborer of a sugar plantation in Hawai'i earns more than the average farm laborer throughout the United States." He went on to suggest that worker compensation in Hawai'i was the highest in the world. He blamed global competition and the world market for current wages and saw no reason to raise them, claiming, "Wages cannot be increased without endangering the industry which is vital to the welfare of the islands." Yet at the same time he acknowledged that labor was the most vital element of sugar production in Hawai'i. Without it, every other aspect of the industry was affected. He never rescinded his argument that the workers made more than a living wage. Bottomley and the HSPA continued to argue this point throughout the 1930s. He also alleged that the strike was caused by outside "agitators" and not the workers themselves.[25]

In Bottomley's eyes, the workers were content and had no real grievances.[26] But if this was the case, why did thousands of workers strike on the plantations? Why did the Hanapēpē strike and the violence that followed occur if not for the discontent of the workers? Outside agitators only pointed out what was wrong; they could not force the workers in such mass numbers to strike unless they also felt this way. As one plantation worker stated, "Pablo Manlapit, a labor organizer, came here to Kaua'i, and he gave talks, too. Basically, his talk was that we Filipinos have to pull together, be united, and then we can raise our salary. Manlapit was going around the plantations and encouraging people to strike so that they could ask for two dollars per day. His purpose was to help workers get higher salaries to better support our families. Inside my heart, I felt the same as Manlapit. I wished our salaries could be raised — if the plantations would give it."[27] Why would Filipinos strike and even face violent confrontations with the HSPA and law officials if they were paid and treated fairly? As the labor historian Edward D. Beechert eloquently wrote, "The behavior of the Filipino worker in this and other labor actions suggested that a high premium was placed on dignity and respect. To assume that Filipino militancy was caused by 'agitators' is to underestimate the movement's strength. The persistence of the Filipino effort suggests, rather, that there was a deep-rooted discontent with the fundamental organization of the industry."[28]

Filipinos worked extremely hard in the sugar cane fields, only to be paid an insulting wage, which added to their discontent and resentment toward the HSPA.[29] In addition plantation owners identified the workers by their *bango* numbers rather than their names, thus wiping away their identity as human beings.[30] The Japanese had already experienced this dehumanizing treatment and had struck against the HSPA. When striking did not improve their conditions, they began moving to the U.S. mainland for better opportunities. Between 1900 and 1907 more than thirty-five thousand Japanese relocated to the West Coast, attesting to the discontent of the plantation workers. It is only logical to assume that Filipinos saw this act of defiance and followed suit as time and circumstance allowed.[31]

Despite Bottomley's assertion that Hawai'i's sugar plantations paid better than the U.S. mainland, the reality was that mainland agricultural workers earned twice as much as those in Hawai'i. As a result, between 1920 and 1929, 56 percent of the Filipinos who migrated to the U.S. mainland arrived from Hawai'i.[32] Thousands came of their own accord, to seek a better life, while countless others were forced to leave to find work and better opportunities. Once they arrived in California they continued the struggle for the rank-and-file worker. Only this time, instead of allying themselves primarily with the Japanese, Filipinos had new allies: Mexican agricultural workers.

Filipino and Mexican Labor Organizing in California

Many Filipinos were encouraged by labor recruiters to work in California's agricultural fields with the promise of better pay and working conditions. These workers began coming to California during the 1920s and continued through the 1950s.[33] These labor recruitment practices, however, were not extended to Japanese workers.[34] The result was an exodus of Filipino workers to the U.S. mainland to work primarily in California's agricultural fields. Between 1920 and 1929 approximately 31,029 Filipinos were admitted to California, with an average of 4,177 arriving per year beginning in 1923. By 1940 there were approximately 32,338 Filipinos in California alone.[35]

Filipinos were utterly disappointed, however, when their dreams of wealth and better economic opportunity on the mainland were shattered by the harsh realities of the country's racist views toward

them and other racial minorities.[36] Although they had suffered under these conditions in Hawai'i, the problems that they faced in
California were even greater. There Filipinos had to contend with
a white working class who did not want economic competition
from nonwhites and would utilize violence to ensure their control
over the labor market.

As in Hawai'i, Filipinos were relegated to working the most back-
breaking jobs because racist beliefs held that Filipinos were better
suited for "stoop labor" due to their size and other inherent characteristics.[37] In California's agricultural fields they picked grapes,
asparagus, melons, strawberries, lettuce, and other crops. They
also worked in the fish canneries in the Pacific Northwest and in
Alaska, where they were known as Alaskeros, in service jobs, and
in the U.S. Navy as stewards. But it was agriculture that provided
over 59 percent of the jobs for Filipinos.[38] Those who worked in
California agriculture faced very poor working conditions. They
lived in overcrowded shacks with inadequate outdoor facilities and
no running water. Often they had to share the same bathwater after working in the fields all day. These conditions were not much
different from those in the Hawaiian sugar plantations.[39]

Despite working and living conditions that were similar to those
in Hawai'i, Filipino laborers felt they could earn higher wages and
thus improve the economic conditions for themselves and their families back home in the Philippines. Once Filipino labor leaders and
workers settled in the U.S. mainland, they sent letters to friends
and relatives in Hawai'i, urging them to come labor in the fields of
California.[40] As they did in Hawai'i, labor leaders also began organizing rank-and-file workers for better wages, improved living
conditions, and union recognition. They organized as the Filipino Labor Union. Work stoppages and small labor disturbances by
Filipinos throughout the 1920s were part of their ongoing effort
to secure a living wage and decent living conditions.[41]

California growers wanted a labor force that was passive, powerless, and unorganized to replace Japanese and Mexican workers, who struck as early as 1903 in the sugar beet fields of Oxnard,

California. The interethnic alliance between Mexican and Japanese laborers in Oxnard was distinct in its own right. As the historian Ronald Takaki noted, "For the first time in the history of California, two minority groups had come together to form a union."[42] Their working-class solidarity is worthy of note. Although the American Federation of Labor (AFL) was vehemently anti-Asian and did not want to bring Japanese workers into their union, their Mexican counterparts stood by in solidarity and refused their charter unless both groups were included.[43] In other instances, Mexicans struggled on their own, combating the growers over wages and living conditions. In areas such as the Imperial Valley, Mexican laborers organized under the Confederación de Uniones Obreras Mexicanas.[44] Similar to what the HSPA did in Hawai'i, California growers in the late 1920s and early 1930s initially used Filipinos as scabs against other ethnic groups, particularly Mexicans. Their intention was to pit Filipinos against Mexicans, thus keeping wages low and hindering any form of solidarity between the two groups. Moreover growers initially considered Filipinos to be ideal workers, "more docile, low paid, and hard working, unlike the Americanized Mexicans." One grower stated, "The Filipino workers are preferred by this company because they are considered more careful workers and because they are not averse to having as many men employed per acre. . . . The Filipinos are also considered very desirable workers because they are willing to work under all sorts of weather conditions."[45]

As in Hawai'i, however, Filipinos proved to be other than docile. In a report titled *Labor Unionism in American Agriculture*, Stuart Jamieson of the U.S. Department of Labor documents the activities of Filipino militancy in the agricultural fields of California. According to Jamieson, the exploitation and racial oppression of Filipinos fueled their militancy, which resulted in the formation of agricultural labor unions and strikes. Filipinos fought the wage standard they received as stoop laborers, which was often the lowest rate of all ethnic groups. Their militancy included wildcat strikes that caused disruption in the fields. As a result of these tactics, growers soon considered Filipinos to be "the most unsatisfactory [workers], for they were the essence of independence and quarrelsome over contract prices." These strikes, although not always successful in earning them union recognition, did provide them with higher wages. According to the historian Howard DeWitt, "Filipino unionization was a serious part of California agriculture."[46]

Although Mexicans had numerical strength in the fields, by the late 1920s and early 1930s Filipinos were fast becoming the majority in skilled labor in California, constituting up to 80 percent of the total workforce in asparagus and other crops.[47] Filipinos were preferred over whites and other ethnic groups because of the skill and knowledge they developed in other specialty crops, such as melons, lettuce, rice, celery, figs, and grapes.[48] In addition to gaining skilled labor positions, Filipinos had another weapon in their organizing arsenal: they knew when to strike in order to have their demands met, which was another tool they borrowed from their Japanese counterparts in Hawai'i. If the growers did not meet their demands, the workers walked out. As a result, whole crops could be lost. In many instances the growers conceded.[49]

Although Filipinos were becoming a threat, growers still tried to use them as scabs against their Mexican counterparts. The growers' strategy failed, however, as Filipinos continued to strike and often initiated the organization of interethnic unions. Seeing the common struggle that they had with Mexicans, Filipinos forged an alliance, striking together under the Cannery and Agricultural Workers Industrial Union, which was affiliated with the Communist Party as a farm labor organization.[50] Because Filipinos and Mexicans also formed mutual aid societies and other social organizations that worked together, they were able to unite all the workers under a single interethnic union. This provided the self-protection and camaraderie required to collectively fight for improved working conditions for all farmworkers, thus perpetuating the interethnic unionism that they knew in Hawai'i.[51] These interethnic unions continued their struggle with growers well into the 1930s, with approximately 140 strikes occurring in California alone during this time.[52]

Jamieson's labor report provides an interesting account of Filipino and Mexican interethnic unionism in California, which was
often under the leadership of the experienced Filipinos. In 1932,
for example, Filipinos in Vacaville struck with Mexican and Japanese workers for a minimum day wage of $1.50. In the Imperial
Valley the Filipino Labor Union led the strikes of 1933–34, which
also included a large number of Mexican workers. As a result of
the union's militancy, the Imperial Valley witnessed some of the
worst violence by white vigilante mobs and law enforcement.[53]

Filipinos and Mexicans also struck in the lettuce fields of Salinas in 1934, where about three thousand workers participated, as
well as Guadalupe, Lompoc, and Oceano that same year.[54] Other interethnic strikes occurred in Alameda, Santa Clara, Solano
County, Sacramento, San Mateo County, and Hayward between
1932 and 1934. In San Diego County numerous strikes involved
both Mexicans and Filipinos. Mexican and Filipino celery workers
struck against Japanese and white growers throughout the county. The Regional Labor Board was responsible for dealing with
the situation. These included two major strikes in 1933 and 1936.
The strike in 1936 included the Filipino Labor Union, the Mexican
Union of Laborers, and the Field Workers of San Diego County.[55]
Another successful interethnic strike in Salinas led by the Filipino
Labor Union in 1936 paved the way for union recognition and an
AFL charter as Field Workers Local No. 30326.[56]

By 1938 various Filipino labor organizations across the West
Coast voted to form the Filipino Agricultural Laborers Association.
However, because Filipinos knew the value of interethnic organizing with their Mexicans allies, they decided to change their name
to the Federated Agricultural Laborers Association, which invited
not only Mexicans, but other ethnic groups into the fold. The Association struck against the asparagus industry in 1939, winning a
significant victory. By 1940 its membership exceeded thirty thousand, making it one of the largest interethnic unions of its time.[57]

The militant tactics of Filipinos and their successful organizing
and interethnic unionism with Mexicans and other groups from

1927 to 1940 proved that they were not a docile and incompetent group, as the growers believed them to be, but a powerful force to be reckoned with.[58] As a result of their interethnic unions, both Filipinos and Mexicans won some of their greatest gains, such as higher wages, better working conditions, and union recognition.[59] But when economic crisis hit the United States in the 1930s the public responded to those gains with hostility and violence.

The Backlash

The perceived threat of Filipino and Mexican radicalism and the increasing numbers of Filipino and Mexican immigrants who kept pouring into the U.S. mainland during the early twentieth century did not go unnoticed by nativist and xenophobic whites. Fear of another "yellow peril" and "brown invasion," coupled with the economic collapse and insecurity that resulted from the Great Depression in the 1930s, turned American public opinion against both groups.

As a result of their organizing and protesting, a backlash of anti-Filipino and anti-Mexican rhetoric and violence occurred. In addition Filipinos faced violence as a result of sexual competition with white men over white women. Relationships between Filipinos and white women at local dance halls infuriated white men and resulted in anti-Filipino riots throughout the late 1920s and well into the 1930s in the cities of Exeter and Watsonville and in Monterey, Sonoma, and Tulare counties, among other areas.[60] Bombings, shootings and other acts of violence led to at least two reported deaths of Filipino workers, as well as countless injuries. Filipinos were also chased out of several towns.[61] The Mexican threat, however, was based on economic insecurity, since most Mexican men had families with them and did not compete with white men over white women. Legislation targeted both groups.

The passing of the Tydings-McDuffie Act of 1934 and the Filipino Repatriation Act of 1935 were implemented to drastically limit Filipino immigration to the United States and to send Filipino immigrants back to the Philippines.[62] Yet despite overwhelming support among whites for the legislation, only a small number of Filipinos were deported, compared to the number of Mexicans, both immigrant and U.S.-born, who were "repatriated" back to their homeland.[63] Between 1930 and 1940, along with 2,190 Filipinos sent back to the Philippines, an estimated one million Mexicans were repatriated back to Mexico, even if they were U.S. citizens. This repatriation was the result of voluntary, involuntary, and coercive methods, including what the historian Mae M. Ngai calls "deportation parties."[64] The overwhelming numbers of Mexicans who were deported disrupted entire families and communities. Yet Filipino and Mexican laborers continued to fight side by side for social and economic justice, until the bombing of Pearl Harbor on December 7, 1941, which thrust the United States into World War II.

Wartime Efforts and Organizing

The dawn of the U.S. involvement in World War II signaled many changes for both Filipino and Mexican agricultural workers and their communities. Both Filipinos and Mexicans (many of whom identified as Mexican American) volunteered in large numbers to prove their loyalty and help defend U.S. interests abroad. For Filipinos it was also a chance to fight for the release of their homeland from Japanese occupation. An estimated eighty thousand Filipinos in Hawai'i and the continental United States rushed to their local recruiting centers to enlist.[65] Although Filipinos were at first refused the opportunity to fight in the U.S. armed forces, President Franklin D. Roosevelt signed into law a revision of the Selective Service Act, allowing the formation of the 1st and 2nd Filipino Infantry Regiments, U.S. Army (numbering over seven thousand), which participated in the liberation of the Philippines from Japanese occupation, among other campaigns. More than five hundred thousand Mexican Americans served valiantly as well, earning more Medals of Honor than any other ethnic group.[66] Filipinos and Mexicans who did not join the armed forces flocked to defense industries and prime fish cannery positions, which were previously closed off to them due to racial discrimination. With a lack of white manpower in these industries, racial and ethnic minorities as well as women were now filling the labor void.[67] These areas of employment as well as military service were also means to escape the drudgery and confinement of agricultural work. This led to a decline in the number of domestic farmworkers. Farm labor was now being supplemented primarily under a U.S.-Mexican labor agreement known as the bracero program, which lasted until 1964.[68] The program brought in tens of thousands of Mexican nationals to work in the agricultural fields and provide the labor needed to feed both the nation and its soldiers abroad. As a result, Filipino and Mexican militancy in the fields largely subsided until the mid-1960s, when they began to strike together in the grape fields of Delano. Thus began a new chapter in the interethnic unionism of Filipinos, Mexicans, and other ethnic groups in the agricultural fields of California.

Conclusion

This chapter has described the economic and social factors that contributed to the discontent and frustration of Filipinos on Hawai'i's sugar plantations. As a result of low wages and inadequate living and working conditions, Filipinos, like their Japanese predecessors, fought back and used the weapons of labor organizing and the strike to have their demands met. Although their alliance with the Japanese was fragile, Filipinos in Hawai'i gained valuable learning experiences in interethnic labor organizing for the purposes of numerical strength, class solidarity, and interethnic cooperation. Although they were initially primarily in unskilled occupations, Filipinos slowly gained positions in skilled labor. With the various sugar strikes throughout the Hawaiian Islands during the 1920s, many Filipinos were blacklisted from working on other plantations, thus providing them with a reason to seek employment on the U.S. mainland. This factor, as well as the opportunity to earn higher wages, led them to migrate from Hawai'i to California.[69] Others were deported and/or exiled from Hawai'i for being labor "agitators."

The militancy and determination of the Filipinos proved too

much for the HSPA in Hawai'i. Once in California, Filipinos utilized the knowledge and experiences they gained in working with
the Japanese to obtaining skilled labor positions. Similarly they applied their previous interethnic labor organizing experiences to their
new environment, forming coalitions with Mexicans and other ethnic groups to combat racial oppression and injustice in the fields.
With the formation of interethnic unions, Filipinos and Mexicans
also proved that they were not the docile labor force that California growers expected. Indeed by using their militancy and strike
methods, Filipinos and Mexicans caused a lot of turmoil in the
agricultural fields of California. It was through these actions that
they were able to have their demands met.

Throughout the 1930s both Filipinos and Mexicans continued
to fight, yet became the scapegoats for America's economic crisis
during the Great Depression. As a result both Mexicans and Filipinos were targeted for repatriation back to their homelands. After
World War II and the ending of the bracero program in 1964, Filipinos began another wave of interethnic unionism and organizing
with Mexicans in the mid-1960s and 1970s. The initial strike began in the grape fields of Delano in 1965, where Filipinos had organized in the late 1950s under the Agricultural Workers Organizing Committee. The Filipino labor leader Larry Itliong convinced
César Chávez and the National Farm Workers Association to join
them.[70] In August 1966 the two unions united under a larger coalition of Filipino, Mexican, and other farmworkers. Under the leadership of César Chávez, Larry Itliong, Dolores Huerta, Philip Vera
Cruz, Pete Velasco, and Andy Imutan, among others, they formed
the United Farm Workers Organizing Committee, which later became the United Farm Workers. Their combined efforts against the
grape growers became, as the authors Craig Scharlin and Lilia V.
Villanueva noted, "the most successful chapter in the long history of the farm labor struggles in California."[71] Yet this chapter in
U.S. labor history was but one thread in an intricate web of labor
organizing that linked Hawai'i and California to the labor struggles of Filipinos and their counterparts in both locales.

By showing that they were not a powerless and docile labor force, both Filipinos and Mexicans brought attention to their plight and continued to fight for a better life, not only for themselves, but for their families and future generations in the United States. Their early organizing efforts are a legacy marked by their resistance to racial oppression and marginalization in the workplace and in the larger society. Although Filipinos formed interethnic unions with various ethnic groups in Hawai'i and California from the 1920s through the 1960s, their struggle for social and economic justice did not end. As the Filipino labor leader Pablo Manlapit so eloquently put it, "The keynote of Americanism, for the laborer, is the opportunity to advance — to better his condition. It is one of the cherished American ideals that each generation shall stand in advance of the preceding one, better physically, mentally, and spiritually. And America demands for her workers this opportunity for development."[72]

The experiences of Filipinos in labor organizing with the Japanese in Hawai'i and Mexicans in California were a means to secure a place socially and economically in their adopted country, since the majority of them decided to settle in the United States. Moreover, their progressive thinking and philosophy laid the foundation for future labor and social movements, which utilized interethnic solidarity and organizing. Thus their story is one example of how various ethnic groups came together under the common bond of social and economic justice and fought to have their voices heard. Their victories, although short-lived, gave them hope that a better tomorrow was just beyond the horizon.[73]

Notes

I would like to thank Marivel Danielson, Seline Szkupinski Quiroga, Kelly F. Jackson, Django Paris, and Camilla Fojas for reading previous drafts of this chapter and providing insightful comments throughout the revising process.

1. For more on Pablo Manlapit, see Melinda Tria Kerkvliet, *Unbending Cane: Pablo Manlapit, a Filipino Labor Leader in Hawai'i* (Honolulu:

University of Hawai'i Press, 2002); Melinda Tria Kerkvliet, "Interpret-ing Pablo Manlapit," *Social Process in Hawai'i* 37 (1996): 1–25; Melin-da Tria Kerkvliet, "Pablo Manlapit's Fight for Justice," *Social Process in Hawai'i* 33 (1991): 153–88.

2. HSPA, list of workers discharged as "agitators," n.d., Hawaiian Sugar Plantation Archives, Hawaiian-Pacific Collection, University of Hawai'i at Mānoa. Subsequent sources will be cited as HSPA Archives. See also Melinda Tria Kerkvliet, *For Justice and a Square Deal: Biog-raphy of Pablo Manlapit, Filipino Labor Leader in Hawaii* (Honolulu: Filipino American National Historical Society of Hawai'i, 2000), 30; Kerkvliet, "Interpreting Pablo Manlapit," 10–11.

3. Kerkvliet, "Interpreting Pablo Manlapit," 10–11; Thelma Buch-doldt, *Filipinos in Alaska, 1788–1958* (Anchorage: Aboriginal Press, 1991); Ronald Takaki, *Strangers from a Different Shore: A History of Asian Americans* (Boston: Little, Brown, 1998), 316–20; Chris Friday, *Organizing Asian American Labor: The Pacific Coast Canned Salm-on Industry, 1870–1942* (Philadelphia: Temple University Press, 1994).

4. For more on Mexican labor organizing in California, see Juan Gó-mez-Quiñones, *Mexican American Labor, 1790–1990* (Albuquerque: Uni-versity of New Mexico Press, 1994); Zaragosa Vargas, *Labor Rights Are Civil Rights: Mexican American Workers in Twentieth-Century Ameri-ca* (Princeton NJ: Princeton University Press, 2005); Stephen J. Pitti, *The Devil in Silicon Valley: Northern California, Race, and Mexican Amer-icans* (Princeton NJ: Princeton University Press, 2003); Camille Guérin-Gonzales, *Mexican Workers and American Dreams: Immigration, Re-patriation, and California Farm Labor, 1900–1939* (New Brunswick NJ: Rutgers University Press, 1994); Devra Weber, *Dark Sweat, White Gold: California Farm Workers, Cotton, and the New Deal* (Berkeley: Univer-sity of California Press, 1994); Gilbert G. González, *Labor and Commu-nity: Mexican Citrus Worker Villages in a Southern California County, 1900–1950* (Chicago: University of Illinois Press, 1994).

5. Although Filipinos also worked on pineapple plantations, the Ha-waiian sugar industry was the main employer of laborers from the Phil-ippines. Ronald Takaki, *Pau Hana: Plantation Life and Labor in Ha-waii* (Honolulu: University of Hawai'i Press, 1983), 18–20. See also Carol A. Maclennan, "Hawaii Turns to Sugar: The Rise of Plantation Cen-ters, 1860–1880," *Hawaiian Journal of History* 31 (1997): 97; John

Liu, "Race, Ethnicity, and the Sugar Plantation System: Asian Labor in Hawaii, 1850–1900," in *Labor Immigration under Capitalism: Asian Workers in the United States before World War II*, ed. Lucie Cheng and Edna Bonacich (Berkeley: University of California Press, 1984), 186–93.

6. Maclennan, "Hawaii Turns to Sugar," 97–99; Takaki, *Pau Hana*, 16–18; Edward D. Beechert, *Working in Hawaii: A Labor History* (Honolulu: University of Hawai'i Press, 1985), 16–39.

7. Takaki, *Pau Hana*, 18–20.

8. Miriam Sharma, "Labor Migration and Class Formation among the Filipinos in Hawai'i, 1906–1946," in *Labor Immigration under Capitalism: Asian Workers in the United States before World War II*, ed. Lucie Cheng and Edna Bonacich (Berkeley: University of California Press, 1984), 581–82; and Beechert, *Working in Hawaii*, 183–84.

9. See Takaki, *Strangers from a Different Shore*, 202–10, 331–32; Paul Spickard, *Almost All Aliens: Immigration, Race, and Colonialism in American History and Identity* (New York: Routledge, 2007), 164–65, 255, 273–79.

10. See Ruben R. Alcantara, *Sakada: Filipino Adaptation in Hawai'i* (Washington DC: University Press of America, 1981), vii; Bruno Lasker, *Filipino Immigration to the Continental United States and to Hawai'i* (Chicago: University of Chicago Press, 1931), 31; Sucheng Chan, *Asian Americans: An Interpretive History* (Boston: Twayne, 1991), 16–18.

11. Bureau of Labor and Statistics, Hawaiian Sugar Planters' Association, "Statement of Laborers on Hawaiian Sugar Plantations for the Month of August, 1927," HSPA Archives.

12. HSPA, correspondence to Lihue Plantation Co., September 9, 1927; HSPA, 8-Month Health Survey, n.d., HSPA Archives; Beechert, *Working in Hawaii*, 161–76.

13. Kerkvliet, "Pablo Manlapit's Fight for Justice," 155.

14. HSPA correspondence to all plantation managers concerning Manlapit, May 29, 1928, HSPA Archives.

15. Kerkvliet, "Pablo Manlapit's Fight for Justice," 155–56; Takaki, *Pau Hana*, 166–67.

16. Masayo Umezawa Duus, *The Japanese Conspiracy: The Oahu Sugar Strike of 1920* (Berkeley: University of California Press, 1999), 47–48.

17. Takaki, *Pau Hana*, 174; Duus, *The Japanese Conspiracy*, 47–66.

18. The bonus system was based on a turnout rate that the workers

produced per ton of sugar cane, as well as a profit-sharing bonus that was based on the market price of sugar. For more on this, see Allen W. T. Bottomley, *A Statement Concerning the Sugar Industry in Hawai'i: Labor Conditions on Hawaiian Plantations; Filipino Laborers There-on, and the Alleged Filipino "Strike" of 1924* (Honolulu: Advertiser Press, 1924), 36–37; Beechert, *Working in Hawaii*, 216.

19. For more on this strike, see John E. Reinecke, *The Filipino Piecemeal Sugar Strike of 1924–1925* (Honolulu: Social Science Research Institute, University of Hawai'i Press, 1996); Beechert, *Working in Hawaii*, 219.

20. In order to discuss the causes of the Hanapēpē Massacre, a little background information must be provided on the Filipino workers who were striking. On the sugar plantations there were two distinct groups of Filipinos from different regions in the Philippines: Ilocanos and Visayans. The preexisting Ilocano-Visayan ethnic tension likely started the altercation. According to eyewitnesses and oral interviews that were conducted, Visayan workers were reportedly striking, and Ilocano workers were persuaded not to join them. The Japanese also did not strike with the Filipinos, but offered other forms of support. When two Ilocano workers came within the boundaries of the strike camp, the Visayans abducted them and held them as prisoners. The police came to release the prisoners, and after heated words between the strikers and police, shots were fired. No one knows who fired the first shot, but gunfire and stabbings occurred, which left twenty dead (sixteen strikers and four police). See the following oral interviews conducted by the Ethnic Studies Oral History Project, Hawaiian-Pacific Collections, University of Hawai'i at Mānoa, collected in *The 1924 Filipino Strike on Kauai*, vols. 1 and 2 (Honolulu: University of Hawai'i, 1979), 2:78–85, 1:469–70, 1:506–30, 1:695–772: Isabel Ganada, October 18, 1978; Lindsay Anton Faye, December 9, 1978; Charles Fern, December 14, 1978, and May 16, 1979; and Agapito Bakiano, December 7, 1978. Subsequent sources from this collection are cited as oral interviews. See also Beechert, *Working in Hawaii*, 216–32; Michi Kodama-Nishimoto, Warren S. Nishimoto, and Cynthia A. Oshiro, *Hanahana: An Oral History Anthology of Hawai'i's Working People* (Honolulu: Center for Oral History, 1984), 10–13.

21. Oral interview with Gregario Oroc, December 5, 1978, 2:792–95; oral interview with Charles Fern, May 16, 1979, 2:523; oral interview with anonymous housewife, October 31, 1978, 2:770–71; oral interview

with Lindsay Anton Faye, December 9, 1979, 2:470; Tiffany Hill, "A Massacre Forgotten," *Honolulu Magazine*, January 2010, http://www .honolulumagazine.com/Honolulu-Magazine/January-2010/A-Massa cre-Forgotten (accessed February 5, 2010).

22. Oral interview with Charles Fern, May 16, 1979, 2:527–28.

23. Oral interview with Charles Fern, May 16, 1979, 2:526; oral interview with Junzo Kojiri, August 17, 1978, 2:579; Beechert, *Working in Hawaii*, 222.

24. Bottomley, *A Statement Concerning the Sugar Industry in Hawai'i*, 18–20, 26–27.

25. HSPA, letter to all plantation managers concerning the wage rates of plantation workers, January 29, 1934, HSPA Archives; HSPA, correspondence to all plantations, November 24, 1933, HSPA Archives; Bottomley, *A Statement Concerning the Sugar Industry in Hawai'i*, 30, 30–37, 3–5, 40–41.

26. Bottomley, *A Statement Concerning the Sugar Industry in Hawai'i*, 39.

27. Kodama-Nishimoto, Nishimoto, and Oshiro, *Hanahana*, 110.

28. Beechert, *Working in Hawaii*, 224.

29. Filipino worker monthly work record indicating days worked 1919–34, n.d., HSPA Archives.

30. Takaki, *Pau Hana*, 55. Bangos were small metal tags that workers wore around their neck, which had their identification number stamped on them. As a result workers were often referred to by their number rather than their name, especially when they collected their wages. See Takaki, *Pau Hana*, 81.

31. Paul R. Spickard, *Japanese Americans: The Formation and Transformations of an Ethnic Group* (New York: Twayne, 1996), 23.

32. Will J. French, *Facts about Filipino Immigration into California: Special Bulletin No. 3* (San Francisco: State of California Department of Industrial Relations, 1930), 11–13.

33. "Report Reveals Heavy Movement out of Hawai'i to Points on Mainland," *Honolulu Star Bulletin*, August 31, 1929, and "300 Filipinos Sign for Jobs in California," *Honolulu Star Bulletin*, May 16, 1950, University Archives and Manuscripts, Romanzo Adams Social Research Laboratory Collection, Clippings, A1979:042b, Box 2, Series 4, File C-24, University of Hawai'i at Mānoa.

34. Per an executive order signed by President Theodore Roosevelt in 1907 (under the influence of Hawaiian sugar plantation owners), Japanese holding passports from Hawai'i were prohibited from remigrating to the U.S. mainland. The 1924 National Origins Act also prohibited Japanese immigration to the United States. This limited their opportunities to leave Hawai'i to make more money in the continental United States. See Chan, *Asian Americans*, 37.

35. French, *Facts about Filipino Immigration into California*, 15, 46; Carey McWilliams, *Brothers under the Skin* (Boston: Little, Brown, 1964), 235–37; Chan, *Asian Americans*, 16–18.

36. Takaki, *Strangers from a Different Shore*, 59–60, 347–50; H. Brett Melendy, "California's Discrimination against Filipinos, 1927–1935," in *Racism in California: A Reader in the History of Oppression*, ed. Roger Daniels and Spencer C. Olin Jr. (New York: Macmillan, 1972), 141–51; Barbara Posadas, *The Filipino Americans* (Westport CT: Greenwood Press, 1999), 15.

37. Takaki, *Pau Hana*, 51–52; Takaki, *Strangers from a Different Shore*, 320.

38. For Filipinos in the Pacific Northwest, see Friday, *Organizing Asian American Labor*; Takaki, *Strangers from a Different Shore*, 316–18; Paul S. Taylor and Tom Vasey, *California Farm Labor*, Bureau of Research and Statistics, Federal Writers' Project, January 1937, 15, Folder 2-24, Box 9, Carey McWilliams Papers.

39. The Filipino Oral History Project, *Voices: A Filipino American Oral History* (Stockton CA: Filipino Oral History Project, 1984), 14–18; Ronald Takaki, *In the Heart of Filipino America: Immigrants from the Pacific Isles* (New York: Chelsea House, 1995), 39–40; Fred Cordova, *Filipinos: Forgotten Asian Americans. A Pictorial Essay, 1763–1963* (Dubuque IA: Kendall/Hunt, 1983), 43.

40. HSPA, correspondence to Lihue Plantation Co. concerning the actions of Pablo Manlapit in California and his letters to plantation workers in Hawai'i, May 29, 1928, HSPA Archives.

41. Although the Filipino Labor Union in California was formed in 1934 and the Filipino Agricultural Laborers Association in 1938, Pablo Manlapit is credited for introducing the idea of the Filipino labor union to Filipino field workers in California in the late 1920s. He urged them to organize in Stockton and other areas of California. It is not known

to what extent Manlapit influenced the formation of the Filipino Agricultural Laborers Association. See Stuart Jamieson, *Labor Unionism in American Agriculture*, U.S. Department of Labor Bulletin No. 836 (Washington DC: U.S. Government Printing Office, 1945), 129, 151; Howard DeWitt, *Violence in the Fields: California Farm Labor Unionization during the Great Depression* (Saratoga CA: Century Twenty One, 1980), 80; Kerkvliet, "Pablo Manlapit's Fight for Justice," 162; Kerkvliet, *Unbending Cane*, 63–69.

42. Takaki, *Strangers from a Different Shore*, 198. For more on the Oxnard sugar beet strike, see Tomás Almaguer, "Racial Domination and Class Conflict in Capitalist Agriculture: The Oxnard Sugar Beet Workers' Strike of 1903," *Labor History* 25 (1984): 325–50; Richard Steven Street, *Beasts of the Field: A Narrative History of California's Farmworkers, 1769–1913* (Stanford: Stanford University Press, 2004), 440–69; Gómez-Quiñones, *Mexican American Labor*, 76–77.

43. See Almaguer, "Racial Domination and Class Conflict in Capitalist Agriculture," 325–50; Street, *Beasts of the Field*, 440–69; Gómez-Quiñones, *Mexican American Labor*, 76–77.

44. Gómez-Quiñones, *Mexican American Labor*, 132–33.

45. Jamieson, *Labor Unionism in American Agriculture*, 74.

46. Jamieson, *Labor Unionism in American Agriculture*, 129; Linda C. Majka and Theo J. Majka, *Farm Workers, Agribusiness and the State* (Philadelphia: Temple University Press, 1982), 65; DeWitt, *Violence in the Fields*, 16; Takaki, *Strangers from Different Shores*, 198–200, 321.

47. French, *Facts about Filipino Immigration into California*, 66.

48. By "skilled labor" I mean that Filipinos were very productive and efficient in the cutting and harvesting process of certain crops without waste and destruction, such as asparagus, melons, strawberries, and lettuce. Since Filipinos worked easily in small groups, or labor gangs, they were preferred among many growers. See Jamieson, *Labor Unionism in American Agriculture*, 74–75; French, *Facts about Filipino Immigration into California*, 71; DeWitt, *Violence in the Fields*, 11–12; "An Open Letter to the People of Salinas Valley," *Philippines Mail*, March 17, 1933, in Alex S. Fabros and Annalissa Herbert, eds., *The Filipino American Newspaper Collection: Extracts from 1906–1953* (Fresno CA: Filipino American Research Project, 1994), 97, 156.

49. Jamieson, *Labor Unionism in American Agriculture*, 74;

McWilliams, *Brothers under the Skin*, 239–40; Ernesto Galarza, *Farm Workers and Agribusiness in California, 1947–1960* (Notre Dame IN: University of Notre Dame Press, 1977), 199; Sonia Emily Wallovits, "The Filipinos in California" (MA thesis, University of Southern California, 1966), 28–29; Roberto V. Vallangca, *Pinoy: The First Wave, 1898–1941* (San Francisco: Strawberry Hill Press, 1977), 23; DeWitt, *Violence in the Fields*, 101.

50. The Communist Party wanted to organize elements of the working class that were untouched by the AFL and its "craft-conscious" conservatism. These included unskilled and semiskilled workers in industries such as agriculture, mining, and textiles. Thus the Communist Party set out to organize migratory seasonal farmworkers. Under its Trade Union Unity League, the Party established a new farm labor organization, the Cannery and Agricultural Workers Industrial Union, in 1930. For more on this, see Jamieson, *Labor Unionism in American Agriculture*, 19–20; DeWitt, *Violence in the Fields*, 49–69; Majka and Majka, *Farm Workers, Agribusiness and the State*, 65–69.

51. Jamieson, *Labor Unionism in American Agriculture*, 75.

52. Gómez-Quiñones, *Mexican American Labor*, 131.

53. "More Valley Vigilante Violence," *Open Forum*, April 7, 1934, 1–4, Folder 2-20 (Imperial Valley), Box 8, Carey McWilliams Papers, University of California, Los Angeles, Special Collections; Chester S. Williams, "Imperial Valley Prepares for War," *World Tomorrow*, April 26, 1934, 199–201; Jamieson, *Labor Unionism in American Agriculture*, 107–10; Gilbert G. González, *Mexican Consuls and Labor Organizing: Imperial Politics in the American West* (Austin: University of Texas Press, 1999), 159–96.

54. Federal Writers' Project, "California Agriculture," in *Oriental Labor Unions and Strikes* (Oakland CA: Federal Writers' Project, n.d.), 24; Jamieson, *Labor Unionism in American Agriculture*, 107–10; "Orderly Strike of 2000 Field Workers Awakens Admiration," *Philippines Mail*, August 27, 1934, in Fabros and Herbert, *The Filipino American Newspaper Collection*, 120; Carey McWilliams, *Factories in the Field: The Story of Migratory Farm Labor in California* (Boston: Little, Brown, 1939), 133.

55. "Report from the Regional Labor Board regarding new cases filed during week of June 8, 1935," Box 14, Folder: New Cases Filed, and "Agreement between Japanese Celery and Vegetable Growers in San Diego

County and Workers, July 6, 1934," Box 14, Folder 5460-45 (Labor Agreements), Record Group 25, Records of the National Labor Relations Board, National Archives Record Administration, Laguna Niguel. For the 1933 strike, see "Agitators Urge Wage Raise for Field Workers," *Chula Vista Star News*, January 6, 1933; "Accord Reached for Settlement of Pickers' Row," *San Diego Union*, February 23, 1936.

56. Takaki, *Strangers from a Different Shore*, 323.

57. Larry R. Salomon, *Roots of Justice: Stories of Organizing Communities of Color* (Berkeley: Chardon Press, 1998), 19.

58. Jamieson, *Labor Unionism in American Agriculture*, 77–132; DeWitt, *Violence in the Fields*, 95–96.

59. Jamieson, *Labor Unionism in American Agriculture*, 132.

60. French, *Facts about Filipino Immigration into California*, 73; "Race Trouble Is Threatening Sonoma County Also," *Philippines Mail*, September 17, 1934, and "Watsonville's Problem, Its Causes and Solution," *Three Star* 2, no. 13 (1930): 1, in Fabros and Herbert, *The Filipino American Newspaper Collection*, 156, 163–64; Majka and Majka, *Farm Workers, Agribusiness and the State*, 65; DeWitt, *Violence in the Fields*, 16.

61. The two reported deaths were Aristo Lampky and Fermin Tobera. See "Valley Bomb Blast Injures Four Filipinos," *San Diego Tribune*, December 9, 1930; "Valley Filipinos Near Panic; One Dies from Blast," *San Diego Tribune*, December 10, 1930; "Bomb Outrage at Imperial, California," *Filipino Nation*, January 1931, 21–27; Howard De Witt, "The Watsonville Anti-Filipino Riot of 1930: A Case Study of the Great Depression and Ethnic Conflict in California," *Southern California Quarterly* 61, no. 3 (1979): 291–301; Howard De Witt, *Anti-Filipino Movements in California: A History, Bibliography and Study Guide* (San Francisco: R and E Research Associates, 1976), 50–52; "Reimbursement Bill," *Filipino Nation*, March 1930, 7.

62. The Tydings-McDuffie Act of 1934 promised the Philippines independence after ten years. Until then it would be recognized as a commonwealth and not a U.S. territory. The status of Filipinos changed from national to alien. The act restricted immigration from the Philippines to fifty persons per year, which dramatically stifled the growth of the Filipino community in the United States. The Filipino Repatriation Act of 1935 provided federal funds for the transport of those Filipinos who

voluntarily left the United States to go back to the Philippines. See Posadas, *The Filipino Americans*, 23–24; Takaki, *Strangers from a Different Shore*, 331–32; DeWitt, *Violence in the Fields*, 22.

63. The homeland of U.S.-born Mexican Americans is, of course, the United States. In the San Diego area Mexicans were also repatriated. See "Survey of Alien Mexicans to Aid in Repatriation," *San Diego Union*, August 10, 1934; "Filipinos Expected to Be Repatriated," *San Diego Union*, March 8, 1936.

64. Yen Le Espiritu, *Filipino American Lives* (Philadelphia: Temple University Press, 1995), 13–14; Francisco E. Balderrama and Raymond Rodriguez, *Decade of Betrayal: Mexican Repatriation in the 1930s* (Albuquerque: University of New Mexico Press, 1995), 120–22; Mae M. Ngai, *Impossible Subjects: Illegal Aliens and the Making of Modern America* (Princeton NJ: Princeton University Press, 2004), 122–23; Adelaida Castillo-Tsuchida, "Filipino Migrants in San Diego, 1900–1946" (MA thesis, University of San Diego, 1979); "165 Filipinos Leave for Home," *Philippines Mail*, November 29, 1937, in Fabros and Herbert, *The Filipino American Newspaper Collection*, 171–72.

65. Filipinos Ditoy, Hawaii brochure, *Philippine Islands War Relief Fund, Iti National War Fund*, 1945, HSPA Archives. For more on Filipino and Mexican participation during World War II, see Ronald Takaki, *Democracy and Race: Asian Americans and World War II* (New York: Chelsea House, 1989), 27–37; Crouchett, *Filipinos in California*, 46; Maggie Rivas-Rodriguez, ed., *Mexican Americans and World War II* (Austin: University of Texas Press, 2005).

66. See Alex S. Fabros, "California's Filipino Infantry," http://www .militarymuseum.org/Filipino.html (accessed January 12, 2007); Rivas-Rodriguez, *Mexican Americans and World War II*.

67. By "white manpower" I mean positions that were exclusively for white males prior to World War II.

68. For more on the bracero program, see Ernesto Galarza, *Merchants of Labor: The Mexican Bracero Story. An Account of the Managed Migration of Mexican Farm Workers in California, 1942–1964* (Charlotte NC: McNally & Loftin, 1964); Roger L. Jungmeyer, "The Bracero Program, 1942–1951: Mexican Contract Labor in the United States" (PhD diss., University of Missouri-Columbia, 1988).

69. Statistical data show that Filipinos earned substantially more money

from certain crops, such as asparagus, in California as opposed to Hawai'i, despite what HSPA reports claimed. For more on this, see French, *Facts about Filipino Immigration into California*, 71.

70. Salomon, *Roots of Justice*, 19.

71. Craig Scharlin and Lilia V. Villanueva, *Philip Vera Cruz: A Personal History of Filipino Immigrants and the Farmworkers Movement* (Seattle: University of Washington Press, 2000), xxv.

72. Pablo Manlapit eventually went back to Hawai'i, only to be charged with misconduct and deported again, this time to the Philippines, where he remained from 1934 until his death on April 15, 1969. See Kerkvliet, "Pablo Manlapit's Fight for Justice," 157–64; and Kerkvliet, *Unbending Cane*.

73. In regard to notes 13 and 17: Despite Pablo Manlapit's efforts at creating an interethnic coaltion between Filipino and Japanese sugar plantation workers in Hawai'i, the reality was that the Japanese community was divided over the issue. Not only was the coalition fragile, it ended up being a failure because of the lack of cooperation between both groups. Filipinos, however, brought those experiences of interethnic organizing with them to California. Seeing the potential that could exist with Mexican workers, they utilized those tools and were more successful. I would like to thank Jonathan Okamura for providing me with recent information written by Ruben Alcantara regarding this relationship. For more on this, see http://scholarspace.manoa.hawaii.edu/handle/10125/17651 (accessed November 16, 2011).

Part 3
The American Pacific

Chapter 7

Spectacles of Citizenship
Native Hawaiian Sovereignty Gets a Makeover

Maile Arvin

In October 2006 the Japanese real estate tycoon Genshiro Kawamoto announced that he would "give away" multimillion-dollar houses in a rich Oʻahu suburb to eight "deserving" Native Hawaiian families.[1] He solicited Native Hawaiian families' stories of hardship, and in response received more than three thousand letters. Kawamoto's actions were accompanied by a certain kind of welfare spotlight that popular media has turned on Native Hawaiians in recent years. His stated motivation was pure altruism, as the *New York Times* reported: "He said it gave him great joy to provide places to live to hard-working people who had fallen on tough times, which is why he chose Native Hawaiians."[2] Soon after Kawamoto's announcement, the *New York Times* also published an article on homelessness in Hawaiʻi. The article announced that thousands of predominantly Native Hawaiian homeless were living in tents on beaches, a long-overlooked fact that became a local and national news story as complaints from beach and park visitors increased. Honolulu's city park director Lester Chang commented, "I think all communities have to deal with this situation, but Hawaiʻi is unique because it's an island. . . . There's no place to push them off to."[3]

While Chang's comment classically reveals local officials'

annoyance with the "homeless problem" and their lack of concern about the underlying causes, it also encapsulates the rhetoric
of Hawai'i's island singularity when compared with the rest of the
United States. Today Hawai'i's distinction is being put to use in another market besides tourism. Socioeconomically disadvantaged
Native Hawaiians are conveniently placed to become the new causes
of so-called philanthropists and network executives alike, fueled
by the hyperbole of reality television's tropes about exotic locales,
stiff competition, and riveting authenticity. Of course, Native Hawaiians, though statistically overrepresented, are not the only ones
among Hawai'i's growing homeless population. However, they are
often represented as the most culturally distinct; for the purposes of Kawamoto's "giveaways," for example, the Native Hawaiian
homeless were singled out as likely having the "best" stories. Native Hawaiian arts, language, epistemology, and more have certainly seen a renaissance since the 1970s, and this all continues to be a
significant source of pride for Native Hawaiians. Yet in the reigning multicultural discourse of the late twentieth and early twenty-
first century, this cultural difference is simultaneously lauded and
depoliticized by mainstream discourse. To the American and Japanese mass media and tourism industries, the recognition of Native Hawaiian cultural difference has always been marketable. In
this essay I argue that Native Hawaiian socioeconomic difference
is also increasingly represented in popular media, often in spectacular displays of philanthropy, in ways that position Native Hawaiians as "good citizens" who work hard in the American immigrant tradition to pull themselves up by their bootstraps. Such
narratives require critical attention because they use the rhetoric of
multiculturalism to depoliticize and deny Native Hawaiians' status as a historically colonized, indigenous people.

Native Hawaiians are thus continuously saddled with the burden
of performing their cultural and socioeconomic difference while at
the same time performing good American citizenship. When these
simultaneous performances are carried out successfully, from the
spectator's perspective, the response can be like Kawamoto's: it

gave him great joy to help people who have fallen on hard times. When some part of the performance is not as convincing, usually the failure to demonstrate good citizenship by, for example, not maintaining a job and housing and thereby becoming a taxpayer's "problem," the response is more likely to be the impatient, dehumanizing retort of Lester Chang, the city park director. Echoing the central problem of American settler colonialism assessed by Fredrick Jackson Turner in 1893 as he pondered the significance of the western frontier's close, Chang laments the lack of further unsettled lands: there is nowhere to push the Native or homeless off to.[4]

Into this sociopolitical scene in Hawai'i, critical projects of Native Hawaiian sovereignty thus emerge on a stage fraught with contentions about citizenship and distribution of rights, in the United States as well as any alternative Hawaiian nation. How does one speak as a Native Hawaiian when public discourse writes Native Hawaiians as always doubly "other": as also American, if struggling ones, or as a false minority altogether, opportunistically seizing on distant historical wrongs? This essay therefore seeks to address the ways multiple discourses, each deploying interrelated "economies of looks and looking," to borrow Diana Taylor's definition of spectacle, silence articulations of Native Hawaiian sovereignty that demand land rights.[5]

Specifically, my entry site is another example of what I term "spectacle philanthropy." Echoing the recent home giveaways to Native Hawaiian families by Genshiro Kawamoto, an episode of ABC's *Extreme Makeover: Home Edition*, aired in September 2007, chronicled the experience of a Native Hawaiian family, the Akanas, receiving a mansion. Beyond reading the makeover show against the grain, I question how Native Hawaiians both resist and participate in perpetuating skewed "economies of looks and looking" that produce Native Hawaiians as good American citizens. Accordingly the second half of this essay critically engages the Akaka Bill, a legislative vehicle for the federal recognition of Native Hawaiians, and the debates it has provoked. I argue that the Akaka Bill requires many of the same performances I introduced earlier. For

the proponents of the Akaka Bill, named for Senator Daniel Akaka, the performance of good citizenship along with cultural and
socioeconomic difference should earn Native Hawaiians a settlement package with the United States.

Focusing on how Native Hawaiians are good U.S. citizens simpli-
fies and erases Native Hawaiian indigeneity, especially their unique
claims to the land. Prior to 1893 Native Hawaiians in Hawai'i lived
within their own internationally recognized nation-state. In 1848,
under an act called the Māhele, private landownership was first enacted under King Kamehameha III, who sought to modernize the
country. In 1893 U.S. plantation owners in Hawai'i, frustrated by the
rule of Queen Lili'uokalani, overthrew the Hawaiian government,
and with the support of U.S. naval forces, imprisoned the queen and
began seizing control of the Crown's assets, including land.[6] In the
1993 Apology Resolution, the U.S. Congress officially acknowledged
its role in the 1893 illegal overthrow.[7] Yet neither the Apology Resolution nor the Akaka Bill, introduced in Congress in 2000, substantially addresses how Native Hawaiians will regain their land rights.
Both spectacle philanthropy and compromised government settlements like the Akaka Bill gloss over the legacies of land dispossession — including pervasive homelessness for Native Hawaiians today.
Focusing on their good citizenship also denies the fact that Native
Hawaiians had no meaningful choice in becoming U.S. citizens.

In many ways, then, the Akaka Bill is analogous to the cases of
spectacle philanthropy I examine here. Neutralizing the radical
political thrust of the multifaceted Native Hawaiian sovereignty
movement, the Akaka Bill can be read as another kind of marketable makeover, one that urgently requires critical intervention. I
ultimately argue for understanding the Akaka Bill within a global-historical comparative frame, rather than a solely U.S.-deter-
mined one, as many indigenous and other ethnic nationalist movements have historically urged groups to do. This illuminates many
more transformative possibilities for Native Hawaiians than those
solutions that require settling for the most we can hope for from
"philanthropists," network television shows, or the U.S. Congress.

Extreme Makeovers: Homes, Not Lands

Extreme Makeover's nationally aired show on September 30, 2007, drew on all of the same tropes that Kawamoto did earlier in the year, but the feel-good hype could go even farther in video format. Much of the show was devoted to displaying, in an unabashedly sentimental style, why the Akana family were the perfect recipients of this new wealth. Momi Akana, the family's mother, runs a nonprofit called Keiki 'O Ka 'Äina (literally, "children of the land"), which provides educational programming and other social support to Native Hawaiian families. As the show repeatedly referenced, when Akana started the nonprofit eleven years earlier "she used her food stamps to buy snacks for the center, which she operated out of her home until recently, leaving it in a state of disrepair."[8] The show provided viewers with intimate portraits of the Akana family, which revealed an enduring and humble "aloha spirit," as well as a rapid tour of the Hawaiian Islands as the show's team sought inspiration from the natural landscape as far away from the family's home in urban Kalihi on O'ahu as Volcano National Park on Hawai'i Island.

Viewers claimed that their enjoyment of the show was in its delivery of justice: the good citizen achieving the material rewards of the American dream. The show was publicized in the local newspapers and news channels months before it actually aired, and locals lined up hours early to see the house's unveiling. One of these onlookers was quoted saying, "It gives people hope that if you make the right choice and do the right thing, you'll be rewarded."[9] Thus while *Extreme Makeover* seized on the Akana family as especially deserving Native Hawaiians, the familiar heart of their story is an emphasis on the "pulling yourself up by the bootstraps" narrative, on which the image of the justly rewarded U.S. citizen (especially the hardworking, self-made immigrant citizen) was founded.

That the Akanas are Native Hawaiian is referenced in the introduction to the family, but despite the family's own marking of Hawaiianness in the show's interviews, this becomes ultimately less important than the general sense that they are part of Hawai'i's much lauded "friendly" and multicultural landscape. As often happens with Native Hawaiian issues, the history of particular Native Hawaiians is glossed over as part of the "local" Hawaiian scene that is largely defined by Hawai'i's majority Asian American population. For example, in keeping with the typical narrative of the *Extreme Makeover* series, the key fact that Momi Akana's work particularly serves other Native Hawaiians is less important in the show's portrayal than a simple understanding that she does community welfare work. Why Native Hawaiians require such community welfare programs goes unexamined, and thus viewers—many of whom we can assume know very little of Hawai'i and its history apart from the United States—are left to fill in such gaps themselves or simply ignore such concerns while consuming the feel-good display of the aloha spirit and good citizens receiving their just rewards. Yet average understandings of race or "minorities" in the United States cannot be accurately applied to the Hawaiian context. Reading the Akana family as part of the local multiethnic landscape of Hawai'i misses the historical and contemporary particularities of both Native Hawaiian and Asian American lives.

The incredible scale of the Akana's new 3,500-square-foot house, built in a week using more than four hundred volunteers, also blurred the question of landownership, which the show raised subtly but never directly. The urban plot of land where the family's previous house was located was too small for the crew to build as they wanted to. So while the old house was nevertheless gratuitously demolished, the new one was built on acreage owned by Momi Akana's profit organization. Although the costs of the new house (and a new office building for Keiki 'O Ka 'Āina) were kept secret, the new home's location on land owned by a nonprofit has raised tax complications. The *Honolulu Advertiser* reported on the attorney general's investigation: "The organization is working with the attorney general's office to come up with a lease agreement in which the rents are set at market rates. Under state and federal laws, terms of the lease must be at market rates or they could be considered 'a private benefit,' which could result in significant fines."[10]

Thus *Extreme Makeover* becomes another example of a giveaway that, on closer investigation (as Kawamoto's giveaways were in actual terms limited to a rent-free lease of ten years), is actually not one.[11] Because the Akana family does not own the land beneath their new home, and presumably because the show's producers did not budget for the extremely high price of land in Hawai'i, the family may be required by law to pay rent. Symbolically, paying rent also fits the profile of a good American citizen. In the increasingly pervasive antiwelfare and anti–affirmative action discourses disseminated by political conservatives in the United States, outright gifts of lands and homes would lead to unfair entitlement and laziness among Native Hawaiians. Thus by paying rent or eventually needing to find another place to live, the Akanas and the families assisted by Kawamoto will continue to work hard for their livelihoods, thereby fulfilling their roles as proper American citizens.

In both Kawamoto's giveaways and the *Extreme Makeover* show, the historic loss of land rights for Native Hawaiians was largely skirted both by the philanthropic givers and the media coverage that surrounded each case. The response to the show was overwhelmingly positive, and though Kawamoto's case drew some skepticism, it was largely from Kahala residents (a much wealthier and exclusive neighborhood than the Akana's Kalihi) who complained of Kawamoto's poor upkeep of his properties and suggested this "publicity stunt" was a ploy to further drive down property values in the area.[12] Lee Cataluna, a local playwright and columnist, was one of the few respondents, in her regular *Honolulu Advertiser* column, to focus skepticism of Kawamoto's giveaways on how Native Hawaiians were being represented. She questioned the naming of Kawamoto as a philanthropist to Native Hawaiians: "That title assumes an unpalatable belief: that Native Hawaiians could not manage movin' on up to the East side without an act of charity from a benevolent outsider. . . . Does selecting a handful of low-income, plenty kids Native Hawaiian families to live in his expensive mansions make Kawamoto a friend or foe to the race and to the cause? Is this a hand up, a hand out or an insult?" Cataluna went on to criticize the extent of Kawamoto's charity and point out the misnomer of the "giveaway." Bringing up the omitted issue of land rights through actual property ownership, she referred to the overburdened Department of Hawaiian Home Lands (DHHL): "If Kawamoto truly wants to get Hawaiians back into Kahala, he should give away the houses. Certainly Micah Kane at DHHL would be happy to add Kawamoto's properties to the assets of the homelands."[13]

While Cataluna's column was significant in its attempt to turn the tide of publicity away from a reification of Native Hawaiian neediness being remedied by benevolent outsiders, her gesture toward the Department of Hawaiian Home Lands as a more reputable source for bettering what she characterizes as the Native Hawaiian "cause" can be questioned as well. Indeed as Kēhaulani Kauanui has detailed in her book *Hawaiian Blood*, the Hawaiian Homestead Commission Act that created the DHHL in 1920 as a federal project of rehabilitation of Native Hawaiians is shot through with many of the same contradictions as the examples of spectacle philanthropy I have discussed.[14] Instead of granting Native Hawaiians land for the exercise of indigenous sovereign rights (as the United States did for some Native American groups on the U.S. mainland), or granting individuals the land in fee simple (as the 1862 Homestead Act did for white Americans seeking to move west from the Northeast), the Homestead Act leased homesteads to Kānaka Maoli for ninety-nine years at a time. Then, as today, there was no way to ever officially own a Hawaiian homestead. Instead as an effect of the de facto "ward of the state" relationship Native Hawaiians came to have with the United States, the land is continually held in trust by the state and federal governments.

Kauanui thus persuasively argues that, in lieu of returning land to Native Hawaiians, the Homestead Act "returned" Native Hawaiians, who in the early twentieth century were increasingly making up the burgeoning population of Honolulu's slums, to "remote lands with poor soil and with little water or infrastructure for homesteading by Kanaka Maoli."[15] Like the isolated cases of the giveaways described above, homesteading did (and continues to do) little to move Kānaka Maoli toward broad socioeconomic equality with white settlers. As Kauanui argues, the Homestead Act instead "institutionalized a form of racial segregation for 'native Hawaiian' lessees who occupied the allotted territories that make up Hawaiian Home Lands on the margins of society."[16]

My point here is not to disparage the very real significance of Hawaiian homesteads to Kanaka Maoli families that lease them—indeed, as Lee Cataluna points out, these homesteads are often treasured, as the number of homesteads available falls drastically short of the large numbers of Kānaka Maoli who often wait decades to receive them. Nor do I doubt the significance of the new homes to the families who have received them from Kawamoto or *Extreme Makeover*. My own reaction to the Akanas' experience, as for many other Native Hawaiians I spoke to about it, was pride, especially because it enabled Keiki 'O Ka 'Āina to expand its programming in exciting ways for the Kanaka Maoli community. My point is simply that transformative social justice for Kanaka Maoli as a collective will require, as a basic starting point, land rights rather than questionably philanthropic leases. This will also require understanding of Kanaka Maoli as indigenous people rather than victims in need of rehabilitation and charity, with a history that cannot be flattened into the multicultural image of the United States as a nation of immigrants. These acknowledgments in conjunction with a discussion of land rights are what could shift the power in the existing spectacle made of Native Hawaiians' poor socioeconomic status toward more equitable "economies of looks and looking" in which Native Hawaiians have more say over both their representations and their rights.

Accordingly the representations of Native Hawaiians conjured by *Extreme Makeover* and Kawamoto beg further questioning and intervention. How is it that the Native Hawaiian objects of these spectacular philanthropy cases were successfully portrayed as special *and* ordinary; as distinct culturally, economically, and physically *and* simultaneously all-American; as needy *and* deserving of extravagance? When we look at other representations of Native Hawaiians in national media, such as those created by conservative politicians who argue that Native Hawaiians do not deserve "special treatment," we find the same racialized binaries but deployed in a wholly different polemical field. The same binaries rigidly enforced can no longer be transcended, and thus the category "Native Hawaiian" becomes untenable and, in some eyes, broken entirely: the trope of the vanishing Native is deployed to disprove Kanaka Maoli authenticity altogether.

Citizenship and the Akaka Bill

On October 24, 2007, the Akaka Bill passed in the U.S. House of Representatives, sparking a familiar round of backlash against the possible federal recognition of Native Hawaiians as indigenous people with the right to self-governance. In the *Washington Post*, for example, the conservative pundit George Will published a column likening Native Hawaiians to Nazis, ostensibly because the bill would allow the new governing entity to decide, as the Nazis decided who were Jews, the potentially racially exclusive criteria for its new Native Hawaiian membership.[17] As the ethnic studies scholar Denise da Silva would say, conservative critiques of the Akaka Bill discursively deploy racialized strategies of both obliteration (i.e., the belief that colonialism has either killed or whitened through miscegenation every Native) and engulfment (i.e., the purported potential for every race to become American).[18] The assumption is always that authentic Native Hawaiians have long since ceased to exist, and even if they do exist, it is their own failing for not yet having chosen to assimilate.

Arguments like Will's have circulated with the Akaka Bill since its introduction to Congress in 2000 and are likely to continue. As it has for nearly a decade now, the Akaka Bill stalled in the Senate after its passage in the House in 2007. Senator Akaka has consistently responded to such attacks with a paradoxical insistence on Native Hawaiians as true-blue Americans. In a November 2007 editorial published in the *Washington Times*, Akaka and one of

Hawai'i's representatives, Neil Abercrombie, responded to George Will's attack: "The Akaka bill doesn't divide Americans. Today's Native Hawaiians are proud citizens of the United States. They work hard. They raise families. They pay taxes. And they have been front and center in the ranks of our military for decades. . . . Until recently, the measure was never partisan in the House. . . . We hope it will not be partisan in the Senate. It has never been partisan in Hawaii."[19]

Here the incontrovertible truth of Native Hawaiians working hard, raising families, and paying taxes is used to place them as good American citizens. The legal scholar Nan Seuffert has argued, with a focus on the settler colonial context of New Zealand, that good citizenship is "the fulfillment of dual individual and national interests, sometimes overlapping."[20] Similarly Akaka and Abercrombie focus only on an image of Native Hawaiians fulfilling their lives in harmony with their duties as U.S. citizens. Erased are the many Kānaka Maoli who do not consider themselves U.S. citizens and view the Akaka Bill as another legislative act (in line with Hawai'i's annexation in 1898 and statehood in 1959) by the U.S. government that assumes, without substantial recourse, Kanaka Maoli consent to American hegemony.

Understanding how the Akaka Bill would recognize and foster "good citizenship" for Native Hawaiians is somewhat difficult to grasp, especially with a sole focus on the text of the bill itself. Nevertheless it is important to see what the bill says and, just as important, does not say, to understand how it has become an unavoidable referent in the contemporary Native Hawaiian political sphere today.

First introduced to Congress in 2000 by Senator Daniel Akaka, the legislation was officially labeled a process determining "Native Hawaiian federal recognition" and claimed "to express the policy of the United States regarding the United States' relationship with Native Hawaiians."[21] The background and purpose of the bill is framed by an overview of Hawaiian history before and after Euro-American colonial contact, with particular reference to the

1993 Apology Resolution.[22] The Apology includes an important
disclaimer: "Nothing in this Joint Resolution is intended to serve
as a settlement of any claims against the United States."[23] This acknowledgment without an immediate attempt at rectification was
nonetheless something of a victory for Native Hawaiians, coming
on the heels of many rallies in 1993 commemorating and reinvig-
orating the resistance that never died out during the one hundred
years since Hawai'i's overthrow. Many Kanaka Maoli scholars
and activists recognized it as a starting point toward justice.[24] Although the Akaka Bill also includes the disclaimer "Nothing in
this Act is intended to serve as a settlement of any claims against
the United States" (amended in the 2009 version to add "or to affect the rights of the Native Hawaiian people under international law"), it does ostensibly pick up where the Apology Resolution
left off. It is precisely the terms on which the Akaka Bill seems to
be a settlement of claims that make the legislation unacceptable to
many, and require a closer examination.

The content of the Akaka Bill is largely an outline of bureaucratic offices that the legislation would establish. These include an
office of special trustee for Native Hawaiian affairs in the Department of the Interior, a Native Hawaiian interagency task force composed primarily of officials from "each Federal agency that establishes or implements policies that affect Native Hawaiians," and a
Native Hawaiian interim governing council "for the organization
of a Native Hawaiian Governing Body."[25] The major task of the
interim governing council would be to establish a roll delineating
the "adult members of the Native Hawaiian community who wish
to participate in the reorganization of a Native Hawaiian governing body." While the legislation is careful to state that the proposed
governing body will eventually be granted the right to establish its
own criteria for Native Hawaiian membership, the initial roll includes those who can prove they are

> (A) the adult members of the Native Hawaiian community who wish
> to become members of a Native Hawaiian governing body and who

are the lineal descendents of the aboriginal, indigenous, native people who resided in the islands that now comprise the State of Hawaii on January, 1, 1893, and who exercised sovereignty in the Hawaiian archipelago, including the area that now constitutes the State of Hawaii, as evidenced by (but not limited to) —

i. genealogical records;

ii. Native Hawaiian kupuna (elders) verification or affidavits;

iii. church or census records; or

iv. government birth or death certificates or other vital statistics records; and

(B) the children of the adult members listed on the roll prepared under this subsection.[26]

What is notable here is that the Akaka Bill attempts to sidestep issues of blood quantum that the federal government itself helped to establish in previous acts, especially the Hawaiian Homestead Commission Act of 1920, which limited leases to Native Hawaiians with verifiable 50 percent or more Native Hawaiian blood.[27] Legacies from blood quantum policies have produced contentious racial and gendered divides and are the subject of battles in and outside of courts in the Native Hawaiian community. The Akaka Bill thus does not specify a minimum "fraction" of belonging, but it does require some verifiable genealogical link. It limits initial membership in the Native Hawaiian governing body to "the lineal descendents of the aboriginal, indigenous, native people" residing in Hawai'i at the time of the 1893 overthrow. However, simply because it remains linked to definitions of "aboriginal, indigenous, native" (no matter how loosely defined, in contrast to blood quantum restrictions), the Akaka Bill has drawn consistent attacks from the Republican Right, alleging that the creation of "race-based" governments in the United States is fundamentally unconstitutional. The bill's supporters point opponents to the existence of Native American governments as precedents, but to no avail.

The other main conservative argument against the Akaka Bill is that it will allow casino development by Native Hawaiians in

Hawai'i, under the same federal laws that allow gaming for Native American tribes. This is an argument used by politicians such as Arnold Schwarzenegger, who boosted his election campaign to become governor of California by proclaiming that he would not pander to "Indian casino tribes play[ing] money politics in Sacramento."[28] Locally the gambling threat was deployed along two fronts: first, there was fear that the Akaka Bill would legalize gambling in Hawai'i but limit gambling rights to Native Hawaiians; second, there was fear that a new casino market would compete with established tourism venues in Hawai'i. This line of opposition led the legislation to be revised in 2006 with a clause pointedly outlawing casinos: "Nothing in this Act shall be construed to authorize the Native Hawaiian governing entity to conduct gaming activities under the authority of the Indian Gaming Regulatory Act."[29]

This change did little to quell Republican opposition. However, likely because of the drastically changed power dynamics in Congress after the 2008 election, this clause was initially dropped in a subsequent version of the bill. An editorial in the *Honolulu Star-Bulletin* suggested that dropping the clause was key to Native Hawaiians achieving justice. Tellingly, however, the *Star-Bulletin*'s support of gaming rights for Native Hawaiians locates the exercise of those rights outside the state: "Tribes received nearly $30 billion in casino revenue in 2006, according to the National Indian Gaming Association. The Akaka Bill could provide a lucrative source of revenue to Hawaiians by opening casinos in mainland states that allow gambling. The federal regulatory act does not allow such activity by tribes in states, including Hawaii, where gambling is illegal and should remain that way."[30]

Justice for Native Hawaiians curiously requires fueling, rather than making efforts to reverse, the Native Hawaiian diaspora to the mainland United States by positing establishment of casinos in the states where it is legal as Hawaiians' best opportunity. This vision for Native Hawaiians' future contrasts seriously with most Kanaka Maoli epistemologies that rely on a connection with (not necessarily ownership of) the land of the Hawaiian Islands, an epistemology that Noenoe Silva, among many others, refers to as *aloha ʻāina* (literally, "love of or care for the land").[31] The vision of outsourcing Native Hawaiian casinos also requires Kānaka Maoli to further participate in American settler colonialism by quite directly settling in Native American lands and competing with Native American casinos. The back-and-forth nature of the gambling issue reemerged when the bill's reintroduction to Congress in March 2009 included the text of the 2006 ban, thus making the issue of casinos in Hawaiʻi or the U.S. mainland moot once again.[32]

A key point on which the Akaka Bill has consistently remained silent is in fact the issue of land rights in Hawaiʻi, which, like Native American reservations or the land rights given to Alaska Native corporations, could provide a more meaningful base for sustaining Native Hawaiian communities. Haunani-Kay Trask addressed this oversight, which she saw replicated in debates on the bill and is not reflective of the concerns of a broad Native Hawaiian community:

> Hawaiians need to be included in the federal policy on recognized native nations on our own terms. . . .
>
> What Hawaiians need is power: the power to reclaim ceded lands,[33] all entitlements that accompany them, and substantive recognition as a self-governing nation.
>
> In other words, Hawaiians need sovereignty on our own land base in our own country run by our own elected representatives. We do not need the latest version of a paper nation railroaded by the congressional delegation and their hand-picked Hawaiian collaborators. Hawaiians must oppose the current Akaka bill. If passed, it will be the death knell of any native claim to land and self-government.[34]

Trask represents one of the many radical Kanaka Maoli sovereignty leaders who advocate rejecting not just the Akaka Bill as proposed but the very terms on which the Akaka Bill rests. She argues instead for "recognized native nations on our own terms," which can be addressed by federal policy but not as a tokenized "paper nation" that enacts no substantive changes to Native Hawaiian communities. Trask and one of the groups she is associated with,

Ka Lāhui Hawai'i, argue that the proper venue for Native Hawaiian recognition is at the international, not the U.S. national, level.[35] Similarly I argue that the frame for shaping scholarship and
political practice for Kānaka Maoli must extend beyond a U.S.-
centered frame in order to undiscipline the colonial order that too
easily becomes totalizing.

Situating Native Hawaiians Globally and Historically

Hawai'i has been overdetermined by a history and ongoing presence of U.S. settler colonialism to the extent that, as the intricacies of the Akaka Bill demonstrate, Native Hawaiian political and
cultural subjectivities are constantly shaped in relation to, or in
distinction from, American ones. A central problem in analyzing
these subject formations emerges from this same overdetermina-
tion. In the extensive history of violent epistemological and material shifts enacted variously by business interests, culturally driv-
en ideologies, and governmental policies, all shaped in and by the
United States, the United States remains a seemingly unshakeable
referent. This creates U.S.-determined temporal and geographical
boundaries that make it difficult to assess the situation of Native
Hawaiians within the interrelated processes of global capitalism
that continue to shape Hawai'i and the United States in drastically uneven ways. As Cedric Robinson writes, limiting a study's perspective to national boundaries of time and space mistakes the "*ordering* of things," chronologically or spatially, for the autonomous
"*order* of things."[36] How can these bounded frames be unlearned
and, in a meaningful and lasting sense, undisciplined?

Tracking the aggregation of a global black radical tradition, Robinson's answer was to understand that the "institution of American slave labor could not be effectively conceptualized as a thing
in and of itself." Instead he situated slavery as "a particular historical development for world capitalism."[37] For him, this approach
reflected not only macroprocesses at the level of finance capital
and international political battles, but the "lived legacies" of black
people. More recently Denise da Silva has formulated a broader

critical intervention into all studies of race, nation, and culture by
positing a framework of global-historical analysis:

> Throughout the twentieth century, under the rule of the principle of
> nationality, I contend, both former European colonial powers and the
> others of Europe (on the American continent, in the colonies of Asia
> and Africa, and in other areas never under official colonial subjec-
> tion) deployed the historical signifier (the nation) and the global sig-
> nifiers (the racial and the cultural) to write their particular version of
> the subject of transcendental poesis. Neither the citizen, the "individ-
> ual," . . . nor the national subject . . . can describe them because the
> political things inhabiting the contemporary global configuration are
> global/historical subjects.[38]

Crucially Silva emphasizes that the impact of such a global-historical approach beyond only national or universal "human" frames
is not to produce and celebrate "better historicity" but to use historical materialism toward a "critique of modern thought, a de-
lineation of a social ontology that more productively challenges
both the *scene of regulation* . . . and the *scene of representation*."[39]

In relation to my own study, the Akaka Bill is styled on the scene
of regulation in the sense that it argues for regulatory adjustments:
formal, legal, and bureaucratic justice (its own "self-government"
and thus its own national-historic signifier). This is a call for better
historicity (that is, in this case, recognition and redress of past injustice), which is not unique to supporters of the Akaka Bill, though
other Native Hawaiian claims have radically different conceptions
of just what "better historicity" would require. However, this project also heavily depends on logics developed on the scene of representation—a proclaimed need for Native Hawaiian culture and
race to find a place at the First World table. Thus the Akaka Bill's
ultimate goal of providing Native Hawaiians with a national-historic signifier (Native Hawaiian self-government) is inextricable
from the goal of reformatting Native Hawaiian racial and cultural signifiers so they can finally inhabit the transcendental, trans-
parent subjectivity that has been wielded against them for so long.

To take seriously Silva's critique requires more than attention to the pitfalls of the formal, macropolitical processes in which Native Hawaiians and the Akaka Bill are imbricated. It also requires tracking how racialized and multicultural projects are used, in ways both obvious and subtle and by white and Asian settlers as much as Native Hawaiians themselves.

Understanding the Akaka Bill and representations of Native Hawaiians as objects in need of rehabilitation or makeovers thus requires an account of the global neoliberalism developed in the late twentieth century. As nation-states have increasingly cut funding to public social programs, privatization has made former rights, to things like affordable health care and education, privileges available only to a select few. A nonprofit industrial complex has also arisen under neoliberalism, and the available state and private funds for nonprofit projects often force nonprofits to depoliticize their goals.[40] Again one must prove good citizenship, even if the programs are part of the new nonprofit "shadow state" rather than the nation-state directly.[41] The price of such a structure is that projects that directly critique the nation-state or model themselves in ways other than as good citizens must struggle to survive. Neoliberalism has created and substantially structured the projects of nonprofits like the Council for Native Hawaiian Advancement (one of the Akaka Bill's main supporters) through the employment of global and historical signifiers, including racial, cultural, and gendered signifiers in addition to the national ones. The impacts of such policies, illumined by this comparative global frame, are poised to reconfigure not only Native Hawaiian lives and identities, but also broader understandings of both citizenship and indigeneity, and thus require further study.

Alternative Models of Kanaka Maoli Citizenship

It is important not to overstate what may seem like the totalizing force of the Akaka Bill in shaping the sphere of Kanaka Maoli politics. Notably the concerns that have determined the shape of the bill's content—state recognition, casino rights, and racial battles over membership—are not at the forefront of, or anywhere mentioned in, the organizing goals of many Kanaka Maoli groups dedicated to political and social change. Judy Rohrer, in a critical discussion of the *Rice v. Cayetano* lawsuit, argues, "Precontact Kānaka Maoli did not think in terms of race and certainly never asked to be 'raced.'"[42] She sees an untangling of the mess caused by the race-baiting tactics of those like George Will and blood quantum issues as vital to the survival of Native Hawaiians. "A primary goal of decolonization," Rohrer asserts, "is (re)discovering community-based definitions of one's group and trying to make a place for them in neo- or post-colonial societies."[43] I would argue that redefining one's group (e.g., substantially overturning what Kauanui calls the "bloody mess" of blood quantum politics) must be a project that works in tandem with redefining the goals of a community's political praxis. While this essay does not pretend to have the blueprints to achieve such broad redefinitions, I end by looking at some of the ways Native Hawaiian political action has historically oriented and continues to orient itself by goals that go far beyond state recognition. I will focus on two historically significant Kanaka Maoli organizations: Kōkua Hawai'i (operating in the 1960s and 1970s) and Ka Lāhui Hawai'i (at its most visible in the 1980s and 1990s). The first positioned itself on a very local level (though it drew inspiration from Native and ethnic national movements in the mainland United States); the latter positioned itself strategically on an international scale. I argue that each provides important orientations for contemporary Kanaka Maoli political movements opposed to the Akaka Bill.

Haunani-Kay Trask cites the formation of the Kōkua Kalama Committee in 1970 as "Hawaiian history . . . being made. . . . By 1980, activists would look back and see in Kalama Valley the first land struggle of modern Hawaiian resistance."[44] The Committee was formed to protest the development of high-cost subdivisions in Kalama Valley, for which developers bulldozed the farm houses of many Native Hawaiian (and non-Native) residents. Although the protests were ultimately unsuccessful in stopping the development of Kalama Valley, the Kōkua Kalama Committee had succeeded in drawing much support and attention to their cause.⁴⁵ This spurred them to reorganize into a broader structure named Kōkua Hawai'i in 1971. With the goal of leading anti-eviction and other land rights struggles across the state, Kōkua Hawai'i was inspired by and modeled after the political strategies used by the Black Panthers in the mainland United States.

Fighting institutional racism even among Native Hawaiian organizations was a key component of Kōkua Hawai'i's plan, as Bishop Estate (a wealthy nonprofit charitable trust founded on the assets of the Native Hawaiian Princess Bernice Pauahi Bishop) officially owned the land that Native Hawaiians were being evicted from. Though the group was inspired by the Black Panthers, the particular manifestation of institutional racism and colonial legacies in Hawai'i centered on issues of land and environmental rights. Kōkua Hawai'i published a full-page ad detailing their plan of action in the *Honolulu Advertiser* in 1971:

> 1. We must save our farm lands to grow food. We must stop the developers who want to pour concrete over everything.
> 2. We must stop people from moving here until we can first take care of our own local people's needs.
> 3. We must take care of our air, land, and water. If we kill water, nature will kill us.
> 4. We must get back our land from the few big landholders that have almost all of it. It was stolen from us in the first place.
> 5. We must use our land to house and feed our people and learn to rely on ourselves to do it—not on the mainland.
> 6. As a start, we demand that Kalama Valley be saved for the local people and that the tourist and high-income development planned by Bishop Estate and Kaiser-Aetna be stopped.⁴⁶

There is no vagueness or possible overture of compromise in the demands Kōkua Hawai'i states here: land must be returned; land must be used to feed and house our people; local communities must become self-sustaining. Also the emphasis on environmental issues and local people's needs are not limited to the good of Native Hawaiians. Rather it is clear from their publishing their manifesto in the *Honolulu Advertiser* that forwarding the cause of Native Hawaiian land rights is best for the entire Hawai'i community. The use of the term "locals," encompassing both Native Hawaiians and non-Native longtime residents of Hawai'i, as a collective identity in organizing like this changed slowly later in the 1970s. Trask notes that under this shift "the rights of 'locals' were not thereby opposed. But Hawaiians' historic and cultural claims to the land as the *first* and *original* claimants were increasingly seen, at least by Hawaiians, as primary."[47]

This ethos of pushing Native Hawaiian demands to the forefront of political organizing, also modeled after the Native and ethnic nationalist movements in the mainland United States, would come to shape other seminal Native Hawaiian political actions, such as the 1976 occupation of Kaho'olawe, the smallest of the eight major islands in the Hawaiian chain. The U.S. military had used Kaho'olawe as a site for bombing target practice since 1941, directly denigrating the religious and cultural significance of the land to Native Hawaiians. In 1990 the military finally responded to the continued protests by ending bombing, although struggles against the military there and elsewhere around the state continue forcefully today.

Ka Lāhui Hawai'i (literally, "the Hawaiian nation"), whose membership included many who had participated in Kōkua Hawai'i, was founded in 1987 by a large group of Kānaka Maoli, including activist-scholars such as Mililani Trask. Ka Lāhui became well-known in the early 1990s for taking part in several events that energized the sovereignty movement around 1993, the year marking the hundredth anniversary of Hawai'i's overthrow by American businessmen. Ka Lāhui enrolled eighteen thousand Kanaka Maoli citizens into a government "generally based on the American democratic model with four branches: executive, legislative, judicial, and Ali'i Nui (High Chiefs). The latter have no voting power, but merely advise on matters of traditional protocol."[48] Proposing a

"Nation within a Nation" relationship that consciously draws parallels with the relationship between many Native American nations and the United States, Ka Lāhui sees itself as seating a government in exile and on this basis attends UN meetings to advocate for Native Hawaiians.

Certainly the institutional conditions of possibility for Ka Lāhui Hawai'i's emergence can be located within U.S.-determined structures, just like the Akaka Bill; the United Nations can often do little against the power of the United States. Yet the political program of Ka Lāhui is positioned quite differently from the Akaka Bill and links more directly to the international indigenous movement, described well by Ronald Niezen. To Niezen, the emergent international indigenous movement is a process in which "indigenism involves reinvigoration of the comfort and color of local traditions with the safety-in-numbers effect of a global movement." He goes on to note, "The most common goals of indigenous peoples are not so much individual-oriented racial equality and liberation within a national framework as the affirmation of their collective rights, recognition of their sovereignty, and emancipation through the exercise of power."[49]

This framework of international indigenous solidarity and the strategic leveraging of international coalitions to critique nation-state policies that damage indigenous rights is precisely what Ka Lāhui Hawai'i adopted in the 1990s to increase their visibility. For example, in 1993 Ka Lāhui was instrumental in convening an International People's Tribunal (Ka Ho'okolokolonui Kanaka Maoli), which operated in the tradition of the Russell Tribunal, organized in 1966 to investigate American war crimes in Vietnam by the philosophers Bertrand Russell and Jean-Paul Sartre. The findings by the Kanaka Maoli Tribunal Komike (Committee), for whom the judges were drawn internationally and represented a variety of indigenous activists and scholars, indicted the United States on several counts, including acts of genocide and ethnocide against the Kanaka Maoli.[50] It was in part due to Ka Lāhui Hawai'i's actions in the early 1990s that the U.S. Congress in 1993 issued its formal Apology

Resolution for the overthrow of the Hawaiian monarchy in 1893.

My point in summarily reviewing the political history of the Native Hawaiian sovereignty movement is not to characterize it in full but to suggest that the issues most salient to Native Hawaiian communities have changed very little over the past fifty years: land and environmental rights, community sustainability over development of the tourism industry, self-organized political structures, and international indigenous solidarity. Though the Apology Resolution has signaled little material improvement in the relationship of the United States to Native Hawaiians, and in fact is part of the reason for the Akaka Bill, it was a legal concession that the Kanaka Maoli community had fought for. The Akaka Bill, as a largely top-down strategy aimed at the settlement of Kanaka Maoli claims, is quite a different matter. Today many Kanaka Maoli groups continue to orient themselves by the importance of issues such as land rights, and they value the political traditions of recent history, in addition to (and perhaps inseparable from) the richly lived cultural traditions of Kanaka Maoli. Lisa Kahaleole Hall writes, "In Hawaiian metaphorical terms, we face *forward* toward the past; it does not lie behind us. Far from being inherently regressive, a call to reclaim tradition can open new/old ways of being."[51] Hall's elegant description is a reconfiguration of time and ontoepistemology that is a powerful rebuke to the "ward of the state" subjectivities instituted by both the Akaka Bill and the spectacle philanthropy projects with which this essay opened.

As the examples from Kōkua Hawai'i and Ka Lāhui Hawai'i demonstrate, Kānaka Maoli approach citizenship and nation in multiple ways. These processes make Kanaka Maoli identity much more complex than the representation of Native Hawaiians as good American citizens that is continually advanced by Senator Akaka and other Akaka Bill supporters. Many proponents of the Akaka Bill argue that pursuing a Native Hawaiian self-governing entity at the federal level does not exclude other Kānaka Maoli from pursuing further political action at the international level, such as at the United Nations. Yet critics of the bill argue that once settlements are made with the U.S. government, revising such legislation, especially in regard to land rights, will be difficult. Such arguments are rarely given full respect, however, since the increasingly powerful Council for Native Hawaiian Advancement (funded generously by the government and private sponsors such as the Bank of Hawai'i) lobbies for the Akaka Bill, purporting to be *the* voice of all Native Hawaiians. In Hawai'i's nonprofit industrial complex, other Kanaka Maoli organizations that advance models of sovereignty that are more critical of the United States fail to receive similar funding, and thus their voices go unheard, and the Akaka Bill is presented as the only viable option for Native Hawaiians' future.

This essay does not attempt to summarize the many other approaches to citizenship beyond the historical review I have offered, but I would argue that the growing body of indigenous scholarship today, and especially for this essay Audra Simpson's inquires of citizenship in Kahnawake Mohawk communities, suggests further productive possibilities for both political practice and scholarship in Kanaka Maoli communities. For even when grounded in legal definitions, Simpson reads Kahnawake "citizenships" on the U.S.-Canadian border and beyond as always extending beyond the legal to constitute a "relentless discursive and living practice that takes on different forms in the everyday life of community."[52] This is a gesture not only toward the importance of present everyday practices of Kahnawake; these forms are not necessarily fixed but expect to creatively adapt as current and future challenges require.

For Simpson, the people of Kahnawake's self-recognition are shaped by historical legal and cultural understandings of "who they are" as much as "who they would like to be," which requires a complex and contradictory existence that is never only "resistant" nor only "acquiescent" to institutional power.[53] Native nationhood in this account is never exactly fixed because for Native people, "remaining who they are" requires a "relentless" practice of negotiating the often damaging notions of what the state would like them to be. For Kanaka Maoli, I have argued, the damaging "economies of looks and looking" instituted by the discourses of good citizenship embedded in both philanthropic home giveaways and the Akaka Bill do require a relentless practice of "remaining who they are." No matter the fate of the Akaka Bill (which many claim is riper than ever for passage under President Obama's administration), Kānaka Maoli will continue to be more than the totalizing picture of victimized citizenry that congressmen and television shows may find easy to present. Kanaka Maoli history and future encompass a much more complex existence that will always be harder to completely and irrevocably overthrow, or in newer terms, "make over," than the discourse of mainstream accounts would have us believe.

Notes

In different versions, this essay was presented at the "Post-colonial" Futures in a Not-Yet Postcolonial World Conference at the Ethnic Studies Department of the University of California at San Diego (March 2008) and the Native American Indigenous Studies Conference at the University of Georgia in Athens (April 2008). Many thanks to Michael Lujan Bevacqua, Vince Diaz, Ross Frank, Dan Talaupapa McMullin, Angie Morrill, Denise Ferreira da Silva, and especially Audra Simpson, who have provided helpful comments on this essay at its different stages. Rudy Guevarra and Camilla Fojas also provided crucial guidance and feedback in revising this essay. All errors remain my own.

1. I use both "Native Hawaiian" and "Kanaka Maoli" in this essay to refer to the indigenous people of Hawai'i. "Kanaka Maoli" is a Hawaiian-language term for Native Hawaiian. I use the terms interchangeably, but generally the former is used by media and by state, federal, and other institutions, and the latter is more frequently used as a self-identification by activists, cultural practitioners, and scholars. As Noenoe Silva explains, "Kanaka" means "person, people, but also Hawaiian; Kānaka is [the] plural form, Kanaka is singular and the category." Kanaka Maoli means "real person or people, i.e., native." See Noenoe Silva, *Aloha Betrayed: Native Hawaiian Resistance to American Colonialism* (Durham NC: Duke University Press, 2004), 238.

2. Evelyn Nieves, "Giveaway in Honolulu Raises Eyebrows as It Lifts Spirits," *New York Times*, April 1, 2007.

3. Janis Magin, "For 1,000 or More Homeless in Hawaii, Beaches Are the Best Option," *New York Times*, December 5, 2006.

4. Frederick Jackson Turner, "The Significance of the Frontier in American History," in *The Frontier in American History* (New York: H. Holt, 1920), 1–38.

5. Diana Taylor, *The Archive and the Repertoire: Performing Cultural Memory in the Americas* (Durham NC: Duke University Press, 2003), 13.

6. For more on these historic events, see Lilikalā Kameʻeleihiwa, *Native Land and Foreign Desires* (Honolulu: Bishop Museum Press, 1992); Jonathan Osorio, *Dismembering Lāhui: A History of the Hawaiian Nation to 1887* (Honolulu: University of Hawaiʻi Press, 2002).

7. U.S. Congress, *To Acknowledge the 100th Anniversary of the Jan. 17, 1893 Overthrow of the Kingdom of Hawaii . . .* , Public Law 103-150, 103rd Cong., 2nd sess., November 23, 1993.

8. Katherine Nichols, "Kalihi Family Getting Home 'Makeover,'" *Honolulu Star-Bulletin*, June 7, 2007.

9. Katherine Nichols, "Miracle of 'Makeover' Moves Many: The Akana Family's Emotional Return Caps a Week of Activity," *Honolulu Star-Bulletin*, June 14, 2007.

10. Rod Ohira, "Hawaii Family Celebrates 'Extreme Makeover' Blessing as Show Airs Nationwide," *Honolulu Advertiser*, October 1, 2007.

11. Nieves, "Giveaway in Honolulu Raises Eyebrows"; Lee Cataluna, "Rock Pools in Kahala for Kanaka," *Honolulu Advertiser*, March 25, 2007.

12. Curtis Lum, "Welcome to Kahala," *Honolulu Advertiser*, March 23, 2007.

13. Cataluna, "Rock Pools in Kahala for Kanaka."

14. J. Kēhaulani Kauanui, *Hawaiian Blood: Colonialism and the Politics of Sovereignty and Indigeneity* (Durham NC: Duke University Press, 2008).

15. Kauanui, *Hawaiian Blood*, 119.

16. Kauanui, *Hawaiian Blood*, 87.

17. George Will, "Social Engineers in Paradise," *Washington Post*, November 29, 2007.

18. Denise Ferreira da Silva, *Towards a Global Idea of Race* (Minneapolis: University of Minnesota Press, 2007).

19. Daniel Akaka and Neil Abercrombie, "Native Hawaiians, Proud Citizens," *Washington Times*, November 1, 2007.

20. Nan Seuffert, *Jurisprudence of National Identity: Kaleidoscopes of Imperialism and Globalisation from Aotearoa New Zealand* (Hampshire, England: Ashgate, 2006), 16–17.

21. U.S. Congress, Joint Hearing, Senate Committee on Indian Affairs and House of Representatives Committee on Resources, *To Express the Policy of the United States Regarding the United States' Relationship with Native Hawaiians*, S. HRG 106-753, 1, 106th Cong., 2nd sess., August 28, 2000.

22. U.S. Congress, Senate Committee on Indian Affairs, *Expressing the Policy of the United States Regarding the United States' Relationship with Native Hawaiians . . .* , Report 108-85, 1–34, 108th Cong., 1st sess., June 27, 2003.

23. U.S. Congress, *To Acknowledge the 100th Anniversary.*

24. Ward Churchill, Sharon Venne, and Lilikala Kame'eleihiwa, eds., *Islands in Captivity: The International Tribunal on the Rights of Indigenous Hawaiians* (Cambridge MA: South End Press, 2004).

25. U.S. Congress, *To Express the Policy of the United States*, 1.

26. U.S. Congress, *To Express the Policy of the United States*, 21–22.

27. Kauanui, *Hawaiian Blood.*

28. Associated Press, "Analysis of New Arnold Schwarzenegger Ads," September 23, 2003, quoted in Kevin Bruyneel, *The Third Space of Sovereignty: The Postcolonial Politics of U.S. Indigenous Relations* (Minneapolis: University of Minnesota Press, 2007), 191.

29. 25 USC 2701 et seq.; U.S. Congress, Senate, *Native Hawaiian Government Reorganization Act of 2006*, S3064, 109th Cong., 2nd sess., May 26, 2006.

30. "Pass Sovereignty Bill Restored to Original," editorial, *Honolulu Star-Bulletin*, February 8, 2009.

31. N. Silva, *Aloha Betrayed.*

32. Gordon Pang, "Gambling Ban Made Clear in Native Hawaiian Recognition Bill," *Honolulu Advertiser*, March 26, 2009.

33. "Ceded" lands (which many prefer to call "seized" lands) are those 1.8 million acres in Hawai'i formerly owned by the Hawaiian monarchy and since the overthrow held in trust by the U.S. and state governments.

34. Haunani-Kay Trask, "Pro, Con Articles on Akaka Bill Fail to Address Land Issues," *Honolulu Advertiser*, May 2, 2004.

35. Haunani-Kay Trask, *From a Native Daughter: Colonialism and Sovereignty in Hawai'i* (Honolulu: University of Hawai'i Press, 1999).

36. Cedric Robinson, *Black Marxism: The Making of the Black Radical Tradition* (Chapel Hill: University of North Carolina Press, 2000), 177.

37. Robinson, *Black Marxism*, 177.

38. D. Silva, *Towards a Global Idea of Race*, 181.

39. D. Silva, *Towards a Global Idea of Race*, 187.

40. Incite! Women of Color against Violence, eds., *The Revolution Will Not Be Funded: Beyond the Non-profit Industrial Complex* (Cambridge MA: South End Press, 2005).

41. Incite! Women of Color against Violence, *The Revolution Will Not Be Funded*.

42. *Rice v. Cayetano* (U.S. Supreme Court, 2000) was a landmark case that ultimately declared unconstitutional the previously accepted practice of allowing only Native Hawaiians to vote for the trustees of the Office of Hawaiian Affairs. The plaintiff in the case, Harold Rice, a white resident of Hawai'i, sued the state over the Native Hawaiian–only voting policy, successfully claiming the policy violated the equal protection clause of the Fourteenth Amendment and the Fifteenth Amendment of the U.S. Constitution. Judy Rohrer, "'Got Race?' The Production of Haole and the Distortion of Indigeneity in the Rice Decision," *Contemporary Pacific* 18, no. 1 (2006): 9.

43. Rohrer, "'Got Race?'" 10.

44. Haunani-Kay Trask, "The Birth of the Modern Hawaiian Movement: Kalama Valley, O'ahu," *Hawaiian Journal of History* 12 (1987): 127.

45. Trask, *From a Native Daughter*, 67.

46. Quoted in Trask, "The Birth of the Modern Hawaiian Movement," 149.

47. Trask, *From a Native Daughter*, 67.

48. Lilikalā Kame'eleihiwa, "The Hawaiian Sovereignty Movement," in Churchill, Venne, and Kame'eleihiwa, *Islands in Captivity*, xx.

49. Ronald Niezen, *The Origins of Indigenism: Human Rights and the Politics of Identity* (Berkeley: University of California Press, 2008), 13, 18.

50. Churchill, Venne, and Kame'eleihiwa, *Islands in Captivity*.

51. Lisa Kahaleole Hall, "Strategies of Erasure: U.S. Colonialism and Native Hawaiian Feminism," *American Quarterly* 60, no. 2 (2008): 279.

52. Audra Simpson, "To the Reserve and Back Again: Kahnawake Mohawk Narratives of Self, Home and Nation" (PhD diss., McGill University, 2003), 53.

53. Simpson, "To the Reserve and Back Again," 54.

Chapter 8

From Captain Cook to Captain Kirk, or,
From Colonial Exploration to Indigenous Exploitation
Issues of Hawaiian Land, Identity, and
Nationhood in a "Postethnic" World

ku'ualoha ho'omanawanui

"Eia Hawai'i, he moku, he kanaka, ke kanaka nui o Hawai'i ē"
(Behold Hawai'i, an island, a man, a great chief is Hawai'i indeed).[1]
Thus begins an ancient *oli* (chant) from the sixteenth century equating Hawaiian identity with that of the *'āina* (land) itself. It reflects
a well-known *'ōlelo no'eau* (proverb) proclaiming in part, *he ali'i
ka 'āina*—the *land* is the chief.[2] For Kanaka Maoli (Native Hawaiians), the connection between our *'āina* and us is a primary cultural concept we continue to embrace.[3] One example is found in the
lyrics of popular *mele* (songs) in which we proudly proclaim, "He
Hawai'i au, mau a mau" (I am Hawaiian forever).[4] In a 2004 address at the Kamehameha Schools Research Conference on Hawaiian well-being, the *kumu hula* (dance master) and scholar Pualani
Kanaka'ole Kanahele emphasized this point, saying, "Every day I
am reminded that I am who I am because of my participation with
others around me, whether seen or unseen. I have two convictions
in life. . . . One . . . is that I am Hawaiian. The other . . . is that I
am this land and this land is me. There is a correlation."[5]

This essay addresses specific challenges to Kanaka Maoli identity and nationhood in relation to our *'āina* used by haole (Amer-European) and Asian settler society.[6] Central to this argument are issues of identity, as non-Native ethnic groups in Hawai'i and beyond

(including Asian, white, and other groups) insist on claiming an indigenized identity through the use of such terms as *kama'āina*, "local," "hapa," and "Hawaiian at heart." I argue that this insistence on an indigenized identity is a continuation of the erasure of the Native that began during initial exploration and claims on the islands by explorers and colonizers. This erasure continues today in both real and imagined worlds, when Hawai'i and Hawaiians are represented in many media, from cyberspace to animated film. Furthermore this strategy of "becoming Native" is a twofold process. On one hand, it is a real-life interpolation of the "gone Native" trope first established in the minds of white British and later American society through the journals of explorers such as the British captain James Cook and furthered through the genre of explorative science fiction narratives, of which *Star Trek* and its central hero figure, Capt. James T. Kirk, is a highly visible representative. This fantasy of exploration, adventure, discovery, and settlement (both temporary and permanent) where the explorer or settler transforms his or her identity into that of indigenized "local" by taking on markers of the real indigenous people is a purposeful tool used to erase indigenous identity and, by extension, of nullifying indigenous claims to land and nationhood. Such erasure prompts the following central questions: Are indigenous claims to identity, land, and nationhood still relevant in today's transglobal world? Is there a possibility for immigrant and settler groups to support indigenous claims to land, nationhood, and identity? What are the problems and issues between indigenous, Pacific, and American identities — ethnic, cultural, national, and individual? How does land and governance relate to this?

Mai ka Pō (Origins)

Hawaiian *mo'olelo* (story and history) include etiological knowledge explaining our *kanaka* origins. The Kumulipo, a Hawaiian cosmogonic genealogy, ties our human lineage to primordial ancestors. The genealogy of Papahānaumoku (Earth Mother) and Wā kea (Sky Father) describes the birth of Hāloa (Long Breath), the first

Kanaka Maoli, as the younger brother of Hāloa-naka-lau-kapali-li (Hāloa of the Quivering Leaf), the first *kalo* (taro) plant. Other moʻolelo describe *akua* (gods) and *ʻaumākua* (family guardian spirits), which simultaneously embody and inhabit nature as ancestors. Pele, the Hawaiian volcano goddess, whose name means "lava," is the ʻāina and creator of ʻāina to whom Kanaka Maoli today trace their ancestry. Hawaiian words for people are related to words for land, demonstrating the close relationship between the two in our culture: *makaʻāinana* (steward of the land), *kamaʻāina* (child born on the land), and *kupa* (sprouting from the land). *Kupa ʻai au* (Native-born who is long attached to the place) literally means "Native eating a long time from the land."[7]

The Logic of Elimination and Identity Theft

In his work on settler colonialism, Patrick Wolfe identifies the settler-colonial tendency of dispossessing Natives as "the logic of elimination."[8] Strategies of elimination of the Hawaiian Native include physical removal from the land, appropriation and erasure of indigenous identity, and reinscription of ʻāina through the rhetoric of development. Physical removal and dispossession of Kanaka Maoli from ʻāina is beyond the focus of this chapter because it is the most obvious and therefore most thoroughly addressed aspect of elimination. I would, however, like to at least acknowledge the incredible damage done to Kanaka Maoli by legal and other moves of dispossession, beginning with the 1848 Māhele, followed by the establishment of leasehold land in the 1950s, land "reform" beginning in the 1970s, mandatory lease-to-fee conversions in the 1990s, military confiscation and occupation of lands from the 1940s to the present (Kahoʻolawe, Makua, Waikāne, Nōhili, Pōhakuloa, etc.), and in the name of science (Mauna Kea), redevelopment (Kakaako, Sand Island) and even "preservation" (Hanauma Bay, Kahana Valley, Northwest Hawaiian islands). It is also important to acknowledge that physical removal includes death in violent conflicts between Natives and settlers, as well as from settler-introduced diseases, which devastated the Kanaka Maoli population throughout the nineteenth century.[9] However, I want to focus on the appropriation and erasure of indigenous identity, another settler strategy of elimination, which is not as easily recognized as such.

Strategies of Elimination in Hawai'i: Now We Are All Haole?

Indigenous Hawaiian identity is appropriated and erased in multiple ways by settler colonialism. Most recognized is the quantification of blood in the legal system (legislation of identity through blood quantum). This issue is meticulously addressed in J. Kehaulani Kauanui's *Hawaiian Blood: Colonialism and the Politics of Sovereignty and Indigeneity*, which examines, in part, the argument of how "blood racialization constructs Hawaiian identity as measurable and dilutable" and how this affects claims to Kanaka Maoli land and nationhood.[10] The neoliberal discourse of multiculturalism grants equality to all regardless of ethnic, cultural, or other differences, which settlers evoke in their claiming of an indigenous Hawaiian identity. The concluding section of Gavan Daws's problematic history of Hawai'i, *Shoal of Time*, which discusses the period of Hawai'i's history leading up to statehood, is titled "Now We Are All Haole," suggesting that once Hawai'i became a U.S. state, 'Ōiwi indigeneity ceased to exist, or to matter. Ironically a speech on the topic given prior to the publication of the book was titled "Now We Are All Hawaiian," suggesting that everyone who lives in Hawai'i has a claim to indigenous status. This confusion is evident throughout the history of settler colonialism in Hawai'i, with settler confusion, or *huikau*, being cast onto Native Hawaiians as well.[11] Most insidious is the appropriation of Kanaka Hawai'i terms of identity by settlers, notably *kama'āina* (child of the land), "Hawaiian at heart," and "hapa" (mixed blood).

The Kama'āina Anti-Conquest

Kama'āina literally means "child [kama] of the land ['āina]." More specifically it referred to Kanaka Maoli who were native to a particular 'āina or location.[12] Today kama'āina discounts are common in Hawai'i as an advertising and marketing tool to promote everything from restaurant patronage to museum access. Business entities from employment assistance (kamaainajobs.com) to child care (Kamaaina Kids) to pest control (Kamaaina Termite and Pest) also appropriate the name, evoking a "local" sense of place tied to Hawaiian land and culture, even when their businesses have no real connection to either. In Hawai'i the slogan of the national fast-food conglomerate Pizza Hut is "Your *kama'aina* Pizza Hut," and KFC markets "kama'aina chicken" meal deals.[13] Throughout the cyber galaxy, sites encourage the adoption of kama'āina identity with ease. On the popular social networking site Facebook, for example, one can take a quick ten-question quiz to determine one's kama'āina status. Successfully answering inane questions such as "Can you name the eight Hawaiian island?" grants appropriated, indigenized status to anyone who knows how to Google.

Houston Wood traces the "the rhetoric of the kama'āina anti-conquest" back to the arrival of American Calvinist missionaries in 1819 and their "rhetoric of revulsion," which "labeled even the simplest of Native acts as 'depraved.' The worse this rhetoric could make Hawaiians seem, the more the missionaries could present themselves as courageous, righteous, and worthy of . . . continued . . . support." A few generations later, descendants of these same missionaries "led a movement to replace the rhetoric of revulsion with a rhetoric that emphasized the need to preserve many of the same cultural practices the missionaries had so doggedly opposed." In effect this meant that the newly minted haole "kama'ā ina" now became the preservers and practitioners of Hawaiian traditions. As a consequence Kanaka Maoli were essentialized, and the "increasingly frequent use of the rhetoric of race by American and Asian settler expansion helped disguise their violent displacement of Kanaka Maoli" in the eighteenth and nineteenth centuries and into the present.[14] This functioned, to borrow Mary Louise Pratt's term, as an "anti-conquest." Pratt recognized that the anti-conquest rhetoric employs "strategies of representation whereby European bourgeois subjects seek to secure their innocence in the same moment as they assert European hegemony,"[15] a practice that became entrenched in Hawaiʻi beginning in the nineteenth century and still flourishes today. One way this occurs is through the use of the word *kamaʻāina*.

The successful integration of settler society's appropriation of Hawaiian identity and simultaneous erasure of actual indigeneity is evident in the use of the term in dominant discourse, including its incorporation in American reference sources such as dictionaries. For example, Merriam-Webster's online dictionary defines *kamaʻāina* as "one who has lived in Hawaiʻi a long time."[16] Merriam-Webster sites 1903 as the date of first use, which supports Wood's research into the use of the term in the early 1900s beginning with the Honolulu-based magazine *Paradise of the Pacific*. The magazine, founded in 1888, rarely used the term *kamaʻāina* until around the 1930s, when "kamaʻāina referred to Caucasians who had lived long in the islands, or who claimed to know much about 'island ways,'" the result being that "many of these newly self-named kamaʻāina were now even asserting they knew more about 'authentic' Hawaiian culture than did Kanaka Maoli themselves." This sentiment underpins the revolting "Hawaiian at heart" adage, which asserts, in essence, that although one is not ethnically Hawaiian or genealogically linked (to circumvent Western race-based arguments) to the ʻāina through the *moʻokūʻauhau* (genealogy) of Hāloa, one can still identify with such deep, ʻāina-rooted cultural experience and practice because one "feels" it. As in claiming a kamaʻāina identity, settlers often assert being Hawaiian at heart: "Suggesting they are intimate with the Kanaka Maoli experience, . . . [they] rarely [if at all] embrace the reciprocal claim that [Kanaka Maoli] are 'Caucasians or haole at heart' and so to be accepted as living representations of authentic Euroamerican traditions [as] Kanaka Maoli 'blood' supposedly restricts such Native achievements."[17] Not that Kanaka Maoli would claim with any enthusiasm to be a "settler colonialist or haole at heart." Rather they would be labeled confused, mentally incapacitated, or a sellout, the result of what Jonathan Kamakawiwoʻole Osorio recognizes as huikau in an essay on Hawaiian identity.[18]

Wood continues, "The rhetoric of the kamaʻāina anti-conquest not only includes claims that Native Hawaiian primitiveness necessitates Native servitude, but it also maintains that Hawaiians are personally fulfilled by serving whites." This Amer-European-centric notion is the beginning of the construction of the idea of "aloha" and thus "aloha spirit" being "at the core of the Hawaiian's innate [essentialized] nature." It is this construction of "natural aloha" and a "naturally giving" nature that "helped colonizing whites explain to themselves, to visitors, and to Hawaiians as well why Polynesians should be expected to give freely their natural resources, land and labor to [the] kamaʻāina [settlers]. Hawaiians then and now who do not yield their nation and lives with smiles are accused of being 'bad' Hawaiians."[19]

Statehood factors into the kamaʻāina anti-conquest as well, because it "encouraged and increased emphasis on the mostly kamaʻāina-invented claim that 'giving to others' is the core Native Hawaiian cultural value" that underpins the commercial capitalism of tourism. It also provided an opportunity for Americans of Japanese ancestry to transform into kamaʻāina too: "[While] whites still dominated the media, higher education, foundations, and major corporate boardrooms, . . . island-born Japanese Americans were now the single most influential group in shaping public discourse on all aspects of island life, including discussions of Native Hawaiians. In general, these new discussions perpetuated the tropes of the older kamaʻāina anti-conquest rhetoric. Now, however, it is as often kamaʻāina Asians as kamaʻāina Caucasians who claim to 'become Polynesian' while dancing the hula or while fishing at ancient Native Hawaiian fishing spots."[20]

What is ignored in this appropriation of Kanaka Maoli identity is that the term heavily suggests that in order to be acquainted or familiar with the land, one must be of the land, implying a *kuleana* (responsibility) and moʻokūʻauhau to that land, not as property owner, agriculturalist, speculator, or tourist, but as *ʻohana* (family). Writing about indigenous sovereignty, Sharon Venne discusses the use of the term "indigenous" to describe the status of

Native American identity and relationship to the land: "Early in the
work at the United Nations, Indigenous Peoples decided to identify ourselves as Indigenous—from the land or of the land. This
word works for the Peoples who come from the lands. . . . While
our Indigenous languages give us our names for ourselves, these
names are not readily translated. Indigenous Peoples decided that
'native,' 'aboriginal,' 'Indian,' 'heathen,' 'pagan' and many other
names would no longer apply to [us]. These names were given to
us by the colonizers who occupy our lands. We must continue to
retake our position as subjects of laws rather than as objects."[21]
By defining "indigenous" as being "from the land or of the land,"
Venne is essentially describing the term *kama'āina*, although defining the concept in an indigenous rather than settler way. It is
not just being born in a location, as haole and Asian settlers argue.
Rather it recognizes the genealogical connection that is inherent in
an indigenous worldview. This is a key point because as much as
settlers want to claim such status, they will not and cannot claim
a genealogy to Hāloa, or ancestry to Papahānaumoku and Wākea,
generally preferring to acknowledge origins from other faith systems, particular Judeo-Christianity.

A high-profile example is President Barak Obama. Obama has expressed pride in being born and at least partially raised in Hawai'i.
He has acknowledged that the islands' multicultural society influenced him in many ways. The construction of Obama as kama'āina
began long before his election, and gleefully continues today, promoted by settler society in Hawai'i, who claim him as their own.
Numerous examples of this abound, beginning with the now famous 2008 photo of a fit and confident "local" boy turned successful presidential candidate bodysurfing at Sandy Beach.[22] On
the national level, the photo offered an unusual twist on presidential candidates demonstrating physical fitness, a youthful, exciting,
dangerous, and exotic twist on the obligatory jog through a local
park. But it was read differently in Hawai'i, where it was viewed
as more than just a confident and fit president demonstrating his
athletic skills. Instead it purposefully connected the president to a

specific locale notorious for its treacherous shore break and body-breaking abilities. The photo depicts Obama as a kama'āina local boy demonstrating his street cred, if you will, not only by being in the know regarding where the locals surf, but demonstrating his knowledge of the 'āina by successfully interacting with and conquering it. Moreover Obama's successful mastery of the wave is understood as mastery over an incredibly difficult place, garnering a higher level of respect than if he were at a safer location, such as Kalama at Kailua beach. The president has since been prominently featured on the Go Hawai'i website, which promotes itself as "Hawaii's official tourism site." An entire section of the site is dedicated to his 2008 family visit back to the islands, prominently featuring Hawai'i Visitors Bureau photo ops, such as the president eating Waiola Shave Ice with his daughters, golfing with friends, and visiting Pearl Harbor and the Pali lookout. To make sure viewers, including prospective tourists, understand the significance of Obama's connection to the islands, the site features a section titled "Kamaaina: Local at Heart." The caption reads, "The Hawaiian word *kamaaina* means someone who is native born or who has lived in Hawaii for some time. When Barak Obama returns to Hawaii with his family, he comes as a kamaaina, a local who knows where to go, where to eat, and what to do."[23]

The website also describes the traditional, indigenous cultural practice of aloha, often appropriated in settler rhetorics, such as tourism, where "the spirit of aloha" epitomizes the commodification of indigenous identity and cultural practice. In settler hands, aloha, the aloha spirit, and "Aloha [as] The Spirit of Obama" are all conflated, as in Obama's oft-quoted line, "What's best in me, and what's best in my message, is consistent with this tradition of Hawaii." Referencing Hawai'i's "plantation days" as the triumph of Hawai'i's being a multicultural paradise, the site nowhere acknowledges Kanaka Maoli. Our long history of resistance to such settler theft of land and identity is glossed over on the site, which states, "It is this *culture of acceptance and aloha* that has had a profound effect on Barak Obama and will continue to influence him in the future."[24]

This conveyance of identity is rampant from the local to the national. For example, in a commentary discussing universal health care in *ā Ka Leo*, the student newspaper of the University of Hawaiʻi at Mānoa, Lisa Cushing concluded, "We can only hope now that, *as a kamaʻaina*, Obama will pay attention to and learn from the mistakes that doomed the Keiki Care program in order to ensure that similar mistakes are not made with his new health care reforms."[25]

Another example comes from a Hawaiʻi hotel marketing campaign. Cecilia Brown, the sales and marketing services manager of Hotel Renew in Waikīkī, writes on the company's website:

> As a *kamaʻaina* long time resident or native Hawaiian, President Obama's experiences and stepping stones in this vibrant, multicultural blend significantly impacted his perspective and his fresh approach to rebuilding our nation.
>
> As America sees our new president break new ground each day in office, Hotel guests have thoroughly enjoyed this fun, informal tour . . . to walk in Barack Obama's footsteps and gain insight into what made Barack Obama the man, the *kamaʻaina* and the president he is today.[26]

On the national level, the Asian American writer Maxine Hong Kingston has also anointed Obama with kamaʻāina status. In an article for the *Huffington Post* posted in 2008 she writes, "[Obama] showed them the ʻaina — people said to one another, 'He's a local boy.' The newspapers declared, 'Obama's a local boy.' . . . Among the people of Hawaiʻi, it's an honor . . . to be dubbed local boy [and] kamaʻaina, child of the land."[27] Hong Kingston thus launches a vigorous discussion between multiple Hawaiʻi settlers as to who has the right to name and claim kamaʻāina identity.

The first respondent to Hong Kingston wrote, "Governor Linda Lingle [of Hawaiʻi] has been campaigning in Nevada and Colorado saying that Obama is NOT kamaʻaina. And I'm very puzzled. Is she implying that Barack *did not live in Hawaii long enough*?"[28] In her *Honolulu Advertiser* column, Lee Cataluna addressed Lingle's attack on Obama, saying, "Since when does the governor's office issue and revoke local status and kamaʻaina cred? Obama was born here and graduated from high school here. Lingle did neither. Does she really want to open up that debate? . . . Let's hope the governor doesn't feel that way about *everyone who calls Hawai'i home.* Lots of folks will have to turn in their kama'aina cards."[29] Here Cataluna incorrectly equates being kama'āina with Hawaiian residency. Regardless of intention, no one involved in the larger discussion has the kuleana to bestow such status on a former resident whose tenure here is as a third-generation member of a nonindigenous family who benefited from Hawai'i's indigenous people's being displaced and their lands opened up to outsiders through the processes of settler colonialism.

Even more problematic is an advertisement for an Obama T-shirt I came across in March 2009 on a trip home to Kaua'i. The image depicts Obama in a Hawaiian *mahi'ole* (feathered helmet) and *ahu'ula* (feathered cape), both sacred symbols of Hawaiian royalty. The caption reads, "I kū i ka lani Obama," which is open to multiple translations, including "Held in the highest esteem Obama," "Standing in the heavens Obama" (referencing chiefly rank), and "Commander in Chief Obama" (my translations). The maile lei that surrounds Obama's profile is a particularly Kaua'i symbol, and lei are often given to people held in high esteem and on special occasions. It is difficult to tell if Obama's face is transposed over that of a Hawaiian chief, or if the chiefly symbols denoting the highest royal rank are transposed onto an image of Obama; either placement is problematic. The image and text, in my reading, transcend the kama'āina argument and bestow a chiefly, indigenous identity on the president, elevating him as a supposed symbol of Hawaiian nationhood. Moreover the image is located in Anahola, a primarily Native Hawaiian community, which supports a large Department of Hawaiian Homelands homestead population, thus further layering the implied indigeneity, erasing the line between indigenous and settler.

Obama's election as the first nonwhite president of the United States has caused some political pundits on the national level to proclaim the beginning of a "postethnic" era in U.S. history, and in Hawaiʻi his presidency is being hailed as the ultimate kamaʻāina achievement. Yet for Native Hawaiian nationalists, this celebration is problematic for several reasons, including the continued erasure and lack of recognition of Hawaiian political claims for land, nation, and even identity. Claim to a local or kamaʻāina identity erases indigenous identity and, by extension, indigenous claims to our ʻāina. A fight that has been quietly brewing within Hawaiʻi for some time has now very publicly breached our shores, expanding to a national level: Obama's alleged native or kamaʻāina status, combined with his powerful political position at the helm of the warship called U.S. Empire and his relationship with Senators Inouye and Akaka and support of the Akaka Bill have once again brought us to the brink of defeat by settler colonial strategies to eliminate us from our land and identity.

This strand of settler rhetoric is commonly seen in settler capitalism and industries such as tourism. Over the past few years the Polynesian Cultural Center, located in Lāʻie, Oʻahu, and run by the Mormon Church, has been running a series of advertisements for this cultural amusement park, which plays on this conflated identity of settler as native. In one ad the caption reads, "Inside every mainlander is a native trying to get out," implying that settlers (mainlanders) are really Natives whose indigeneity has been encased in the trappings of modernity, and if given a chance, the indigenous, exotic, fire-eating savage can be unleashed. In the side photos, a topless, bare-chested (and fit) Polynesian male is undertaking a brave, masculine task: "eating" fire. A white male looks on with admiration in the background; a white female is smiling, entertained. Another white man, in shorts and a T-shirt, climbs a coconut tree. Tourists and Polynesian Native engage in cultural activities in picture-perfect harmony, perpetuating the dominant Western narrative of "natural" aloha, and also suggesting shared culture and "aloha for all." In between, a presumably Māori male (indicated by a *moko*, or traditional Māori face tattoo), peers out from the foliage in a somewhat menacing, somewhat exotic, enticing way, both observer and subject.

In another ad the caption reads, "A single visit will change you. Just ask Steve, an accountant from Cincinnati." This ad also features a bare-chested Polynesian man sporting a moko and holding a *taiaha* (ceremonial spear), his tongue extended in a *pukana* (a Māori word that describes staring wildly, dilating the eyes, and sticking out the tongue, done by both genders as a means of intimidation), standing in a recognizable *haka* (a Māori dance, often performed with rhythmic chant and vigorous movement to intimidate the opposition, traditionally used in confrontation or war) pose. The ad implies that this is Steve, who has come home to the Pacific to practice his ancestral Māori culture. However, a more accurate reading of this ad speaks to Steve's being a white settler who "goes native" when he ventures into the Pacific, represented by the Polynesian Cultural Center. Cincinnati, which promotes itself as "the Queen City," symbolizes Middle America, and accounting is a respectable professional position. Altogether the ad presents a bland, middle-class existence transformed by the "gone native" fantasy first described in the journals of the British explorer Capt. James Cook in the 1700s upon his explorations in the Pacific, and later appearing in modern science fiction space exploration narratives such as *Star Trek* and fictional heroes such as Capt. James T. Kirk. Thus the ad feeds the fantasy of the "average American" white male, who yearns for adventure and exploration in exotic, far-off lands, where his perceived superiority and authority allow him the privilege of becoming the Native, effectively erasing the identity of actual Natives.

Writing/Righting Hapa Identity

Kanaka Maoli identity has not only been stolen and appropriated by settlers on our own ʻāina. It is happening away from our shores as well, through the appropriation of the Hawaiian term "hapa" by North American Asian settlers with tenuous—if any—ties to Hawaiʻi. Unlike *kamaʻāina*, a word with deep roots in Hawaiian culture, the term "hapa" to describe mixed ethnic identity originated in the 1800s when Kanaka Maoli began having children

with non-Hawaiians. The word is a Hawaiianization of the English
word "half"; its denotative meaning is "portion, fragment, part,
fraction, installment; to be partial, less; of mixed blood, person of
mixed blood."[30] Initially it meant one who was half-Hawaiian and
half-haole, hence the term "hapa haole." As Kanaka Maoli continued having children with people of multiple ethnicities, the word
took on the larger meaning of one with mixed blood, heritage, or
ancestry, one who is bi- or multiracial. But because the term originated in a Kanaka Maoli cultural context, it has always been understood that part of that ancestry is Kanaka Maoli. The earliest
definition of the term is found in Lorrin Andrews's 1865 *A Dictionary of Hawaiian Language*, which defines "hapa" as "to dimin-
ish, make less; an indefinite part of a thing; a few; a small part."[31]
The lack of reference to mixed ancestry in 1865 provides some insight into the evolution of the term to mean mixed Hawaiian heritage. The word appeared in print soon after the Hawaiian-language
newspapers began to be published in the 1830s; the first reference
to "hapa haole" as mixed ancestry is found in *Ke Kumu Hawaii*
(December 5, 1838), although no definition of the term was provided.[32] The first definition of "hapa haole" appeared in *Hoku o
ka Pakipika* (1861). The article "Olelo Paipai" (Words of support)
refers to a person of mixed Hawaiian ancestry as a "hapa kanaka, a he hapa haole" (half-Hawaiian and half-white) (*Ka Hoku o
ka Pakipika*, October 3, 1861).[33] A similar definition is provided in
Kuokoa on April 30, 1864, and January 12, 1865, where a "keiki
hapa haole, hapa Hawaii" (half-white, half-Hawaiian child) is described. Here again, as with the "Eia Hawai'i" chant from previous centuries, the word for a person of Hawaiian ethnicity is the
same as the word for Hawai'i, the 'āina.

Although interethnic relationships had been ongoing since the
arrival of the first haole in the late eighteenth century, a specific
term to describe the offspring of such unions does not appear to be
codified until the later part of the nineteenth century, when "hapa"
as an ethnic descriptor began to be used more extensively, describing Kanaka Maoli with significant social status. One example is

Princess Kaʻiulani (1865–99), the daughter of Princess Miriam Likelike (sister to Queen Liliʻuokalani) and a Scottish businessman and one-time governor of Oʻahu, Archibald Cleghorn. This is not to imply that only Kanaka Maoli of higher social status were referenced this way, nor that Kanaka Maoli did not wrestle with the place of hapa Hawaiians within Hawaiian society, as demonstrated in newspaper articles of the day.[34] In fact in the election campaign for Mōʻī in 1882, Kalākaua was successful in casting doubt on Emma's credibility as a ruler because of her hapa lineage and moʻokūʻauhau. An exploration of the evolution of hapa identity within Kanaka Maoli society has recently begun, with Brandon Ledward's 2007 dissertation and a recent article in *Hūlili* journal.[35]

In the past decade or so, however, the meaning of this word, which originally connoted indigenous heritage, has been removed from an indigenous context altogether and utilized abroad (outside of Hawaiʻi) by Asians and haole to define their mixed ancestry, many of whom have absolutely no ties to Hawaiʻi whatsoever. "Hapa" has become en vogue among younger, educated Asian Americans, even when they have no ancestral ties to Asian settlers in Hawaiʻi, or to Hawaiʻi itself. I make this distinction because Asian settlers in Hawaiʻi, specifically those with plantation ties to the islands (particularly Chinese, Japanese, Korean, and Filipino), can at least account for their exposure to and sometimes intermixing with Hawaiian culture and language. Thus their use of the term, though also problematic, has a historical and cultural context of lived experience within an environment of multiple negotiations between cultures such as Kanaka Maoli, some Asian, and perhaps to a lesser degree haole, Portuguese, and some Hispanic (primarily Mexican *paniolo* or cowboys and Puerto Rican sugar plantation immigrants) and other cultures.

Ignorant of Hawaiian language and culture, as well as beneficiaries of settler colonialism, these mixed-heritage Asians not only claim hapa identity, but have redefined the language and term to suit their own identity crisis and psychological needs. From academic scholarship to cyberspace, mixed-blood Asians define the term "hapa" as referring to *"anyone* part *Asian or Pacific Island-er* and, generally, part Caucasian."[36] In the context of settler colonialism, indigenous Hawaiian genealogy is no longer necessary for hapa identity. This extends from pop culture usage such as how "hapa" is defined on urbandictionary.com, to scholarship and research in academic institutions.

An entry on Asian American families in the *International Encyclopedia of Marriage and Family* (2002) by Susan Matoba Adler acknowledges a Hawaiʻi-based origin of the term, although she inaccurately defines "hapa" as "mixed race Asian American."[37] In a research report on Asian American acculturation the psychologist William Liu and his coauthors make a similar assertion, defining "hapa" as "half Asian and half non-Asian."[38] Kimberly Powell picks up on these definitions in an article discussing her foray into Japanese taiko drumming. When another woman in the group mistakes her for hapa, she provides the following footnote: "In this context, she was referring to *hapa* as someone who is of partial Asian or Pacific Islander racial/ethnic heritage. Of Hawaiian origins, the term has traditionally referred to portion or half, as in half-White, half-Hawaiian. *Sometimes used in a derogatory manner, it has more recently been used more generally to describe ethnic or racial mix.*"[39]

The perpetuated misuse of the term is problematic in other ways, such as the reference to its being derogatory. This false definition is used elsewhere, as on the website of Seaweed Productions, which also notes that "hapa," "once a derogatory label . . . has since been embraced as a term of pride by many whose mixed racial heritage includes *Asian or Pacific Island descent.*"[40] I have found no evidence that Kanaka Maoli describe the term as negative, although *being* hapa has its own set of negotiations depending on time period, ethnic mixing, and other social, political, and cultural factors. Moreover the term does not need rescuing by Asian Americans, as it is a dynamic descriptor of ethnic heritage that is alive and evolving within the Hawaiian community.

The *pake-haole* (Chinese Caucasian) artist Kip Fulbeck incorrectly calls the term "Hawaiian slang" to describe "someone whose mixed racial heritage includes *Asian or Pacific Islander ancestry*" in his book *Part Asian, 100% Hapa*, which, as one reviewer noted, is a "photo album of the twenty-first-century global village" of people of mixed ethnic background. Inaccurately defining a Hawaiian-language term is again problematic, but so is the confused romanticism and subversive racism that goes along with the rest of the description of the project, in which the same reviewer states, "Fulbeck's simply composed portraits are profoundly evocative. Each person's ethnic background *reads like a poem hinting at dramatic journeys and improbable love*: Japanese, French, Chinese, Irish, Swedish, Sioux, Thai, Mexican, Irish, and Native American (Yaqui). And their pithy handwritten personal statements are *wry and wicked, sweet and tangy*."[41]

Hapa in Cyberspace

With the explosion of the Internet and social networking over the past decade, the problem of Asian Americans misappropriating a Kanaka Maoli identity with the use of the term "hapa" has sparked intense debates and a Native Hawaiian backlash across the World Wide Web. One of many sites that acknowledges the term's Hawaiian origins but goes on to define the term as referring to "individuals who are part Hawaiian *or* part Asian" is Hapa Culture, a commercial site that sells various products. Again, when did indigenous Kanaka Maoli identity become conflated with Asian ancestry? The site, like many others, takes it a step further and extends the definition, stating, "At Hapa Culture, we like to embrace the term as a broader and more inclusive concept by involving *any mix of cultural influences*."[42] In actuality it is a storefront to showcase Berkeley culture with an Asian-haole twist.

Despite its claims of multiculturalism and alleged inclusion of Hawaiian identity, there are no Kanaka Maoli (or indigenous Pacific) representations in products featured on the site. For example, in a section on books, fiction writers such as Amy Tan, Jhumpa Lahiri, and Gish Jen are listed, but no Hawaiian or Pacific authors (and I'm being generous in including Pacific here, utilizing the site's own definition of "hapa" as including Pacific Islanders). In the nonfiction section, books such as Fulbeck's *100% Hapa, Good Luck Life: The Essential Guide to Chinese American Celebrations and Culture* by Rosemary Gong, *Western Influence on Japanese Art: The Akita Ranga Art School* by Hiroko Johnson, and even *Dreams of My Father: A Story of Race and Inheritance* by Barak Obama are offered, but there are no representations of Hawaiian or Pacific literature. The children and teens book section includes Sandra Cisneros's *The House on Mango Street*, Oliver Chin's *The Year of the Pig*, and Tajuna Desai Hidier's *Born Confused*.

Likewise their film section includes titles such as *Crash, Lost in Translation, Map of the Human Heart, Bend It Like Beckham, Mulan* (seriously—she's hapa? Since when?), *My Big Fat Greek Wedding, The Joy Luck Club* (again), and *Rabbit Proof Fence*. But no Hawaiʻi or Pacific Islander representation. It is not even worth discussing the pathetic lack of music selections. Although a great deal of vibrant music from Hawaiʻi and the Pacific exists and is easily found online, the music section is represented by the sole "Hawaiian" group Hapa and a handful of local Berkeley bands.

How does a site that boasts its celebration of multicultural diversity—including Kanaka Maoli, whose word (and identity) they appropriate—forget Kanaka Maoli? Many examples of Kanaka Maoli and Pacific books, DVDs, and music are easily available on the web. Books include Lurline Wailana McGregor's *Between the Deep Blue Sea and Me* (2008); Brandy Nalani McDougall's *The Salt Wind, Ka Makani Paʻakai* (2008); Matthew Kaleialiʻi Kaʻōpio's *Written in the Sky* (2005); Haunani-Kay Trask's *Light in a Crevice Never Seen* (1994), *Night Is a Sharkskin Drum* (2002), and *From a Native Daughter* (1993); and *ʻOiwi: A Native Hawaiian Journal* from Kuleana "Oiwi Press" (four volumes now available). Among DVDs are *Samoan Wedding* (2007), *The Ride* (2006), *Beyond Paradise* (2003), *Whale Rider* (2003), and *Once Were Warriors* (1995). Contemporary Hawaiian and Pacific music such as O-shen, King Kapisi, Nesian Mystic, Che Fu, Fiji, and many, many others are widely available. Clearly it is not simply a matter of access (or lack thereof) to Hawaiʻi and Pacific resources. Rather it appears that multiethnic Asian Internet sites such as Hapa Culture have a different agenda than accurate representation of Hawaiians and Pacific Islanders in its claim of multicultural hapa representation.

These sites represent the cyberspace variant of settler elimination of the Native Wolfe describes, even in otherwise respected academic arenas. For example, Cornell University boasts a Hapa Club, which defines "hapa" in a manner similar to the examples already provided. Its website states, "'Hapa' is often used to describe *a person of mixed Asian ancestry*; however, we feel that this definition is incorrect and too narrow. Cornell Hapa has joined other groups in promoting 'Hapa' as a term encompassing *all* racially mixed people."[43]

This extension of mixed ancestry, excluding Hawaiians, is found elsewhere on the Internet referenced in other ways. For example, type "hapa" into a Google search and www.hapas.com is one site that will pop up. Click on it, and you are greeted with the message, "This site have [*sic*] been moved to www.mixedasians.com." On her website Real Hapas (www.realhapas.com), Lani Robbins says the web address was changed due to criticism of how "hapa" was being misappropriated. Despite the name change, however, the site describes itself as "relating to the eurasian, biracial, multiracial, amerasian, mixed asian, blasian, hafu, half asian, and hapa. The site provides a place to discuss and share information on the racial and ethnic diversity found in the *partial asian and pacific islander heritage*."[44] It is somewhat ironic and certainly infuriating that Asian settlers in particular, who are well aware of racism and oppression, appropriate for their own purposes a word to describe a mixed ethnic identity they have no relationship with, one stolen from an indigenous group, with no thought or care as to how this impacts Kanaka Maoli. This callous ignorance demonstrates several ways settler colonialism works in such insidious ways. First, Asian settlers born, raised, or residing on the North American continent are there because those lands were cleared of their indigenous populations through settler colonialism, opening up space for the importation of labor (physical and intellectual). Because white racism has created poor socioeconomic conditions for some Asian Americans, there is little thought of the even worse conditions suffered by Native Americans. Second, most of the Asian Americans who claim hapa as their own identity are educated within the dominant Western system; for example, "hapa" clubs and social groups are prominently featured on university campuses from Cornell to the University of California, Berkeley.

Third, for most Asian Americans, English is the dominant language. There is an identity gap between foreign-born parents or ancestors and their U.S.-born children, as well as an identity gap between a parent of one ethnic background and a parent of another (or others). English terms such as "mixed blood," "bi-" or "multiracial/ethnic," and "half-breed" and concepts of hybridity come across as harsh, derogatory, or racist. Because Asian America comprises many different ethnic cultures that sometimes have more than one language (for example, Mandarin and Cantonese are Chinese languages; Tagalog, Ilocano, and Visayan are languages and cultures of the Philippines) choosing a term from one of those languages to represent the whole is problematic. Appropriating "hapa" to cover all Asian ethnicities and combinations appears to be an attractive way out of this dilemma.

However, I believe there are other reasons "hapa" has become so popular with Asian Americans. First, as settlers, there is no (kuleana) consciousness of the effect of their appropriation of an indigenous Hawaiian word, because, having bought into American values and wanting to be a part of dominant society, they have no consciousness of the indigenous. Second, they have bought into the Western narrative of Hawaiʻi and the Pacific as desirable and exotic; thus to claim a hapa identity is to claim a positively marketed exotic status, one that is hip and trendy, casting aside a highly racialized, stereotyped, negative, colonial image of the "Yellow Peril" and adopting an equally exotic, although positively tragic image of the beautiful, languid, desirable, attractive, tragically dying Noble Savage.

Other Appropriations of Hapa

Several years ago a Filipina student born and raised in California wrote a paper for my English 100 course in which she confessed to allowing others to identify her as hapa—Hawaiian and Filipino—even though she was not Hawaiian nor from Hawai'i. She wrote that this was common among her California peers, who were accustomed to the negative racialization of their Chinese, Japanese, Filipino, or Korean heritage in California, where Asian Americans are still a numerical minority. In states like California and Arizona, being racialized as Asian or Hispanic by the dominant white society is problematic for many. By adopting or allowing themselves to be recognized as hapa, which implies an ethnic Hawaiian heritage, Asian settlers are able to put a more positive, romanticized, exoticized spin on their identity, feeling better about themselves in the process, even when this identity is fake and contrived.

In an interview with National Public Radio, Kristen Lee, who uses the word "hapa" to describe her Asian American identity, describes a similar experience:

> I'm a quarter Chinese and . . . Swedish. From my appearance, people assume I am Asian, but how could a quarter . . . define who I am? . . . I flaunt all of my cultural mix but so many people want me to pick a label. So if I have to choose, I'd choose "hapa." *It means half Asian and half another race. It's actually Hawaiian slang that I picked up in college. It's meant to be slightly derogatory* but I embrace it as a source of empowerment.
>
> When I studied [in Hawai'i], I was viewed *as a local* because . . . my racial features fit the *Hawaiian* template. I have almond-shaped eyes, fine dark hair and olive skin. . . . I was a confident and proud hapa in Hawaii, but when I came back to Michigan, my predominantly white peers still saw me as a model minority statistic, exotic foreigner and a token Asian in the classroom.[45]

Lee's conflation of indigenous and settler identities is problematic, as is her incorporation of a food metaphor that invites another kind of consumption by evoking cannibalism. This represents the dominant Western narrative of the exotic, unknowable "Other," the untamable, dangerous savagery these hapa-wannabes profess they are trying to escape.

This desire to be misrepresented as hapa and associated with Hawaiʻi still occurs. When discussing issues of ethnicity and cultural identification, mixed Asians born in North America or Hawaiʻi gleefully boast about their hapa heritage in class and in their writing. They are shocked and confused by Hawaiian resistance to their appropriation of the term to describe themselves, often citing how accepted it is "back home," and admitting part of their interest in attending college in Hawaiʻi was to experience the "freedom" of a hapa identity not easily available beyond Hawaiʻi's shores. Their attitude is only reinforced through lived experience and popular culture, with hit TV shows like *Hawaii 5-0* (CBS, 2010) featuring glamorous haole and Asian actors (Alex O'Laughlin, Scott Caan, Daniel Dae Kim, Grace Park) standing in for Native Hawaiians.[46]

The use of the term "hapa" in the many contexts outlined above actually elucidates a second layer of Asian settler colonialism that extends beyond Haunani-Kay Trask's definition and Hawaiʻi's shores. Trask discusses the problems of Asian settler colonialism in Hawaiʻi in a recent essay, in which she argues that the preferred term "local" to describe Hawaiʻi-born Asians "is . . . a particularly celebrated American gloss for settler." Asian settlers in Hawaiʻi prefer the term "local," Trask assets, because "they greatly outnumber us. They claim Hawaiʻi as their own, denying indigenous history, their long collaboration in our continued dispossession, and the benefits therefrom."[47] Asian settler colonialism in Hawaiʻi, I assert, includes Asians on the U.S. continent, who may not lay direct claim to Hawaiian land but certainly lay claim to Hawaiian identity through their appropriation of the term "hapa."

Tammy Conard-Salvo, director of the Writing Lab at Purdue University, maintains a personal website, Hapa Stories, which she describes as "a collection of my stories . . . on what it means for me to be a multiracial Asian-American." Conard-Salvo identifies herself as a hapa woman of Korean, Native American, and Caucasian ancestry. In viewing her site, I came across a page titled "In Defense of My Use of the Term 'Hapa'":

Recently . . . I received some very surprising email from . . . people in Hawaii who challenged my usage and definition of the word "hapa." Their emails challenged my own adoption of the term to describe my own identity, telling me that not only had I misappropriated the term, I was not a hapa at all.

I admit I was taken aback by these email messages, even though it's not the first time I've heard of Hawaiian groups trying to defend the word. *They see it as a hijacking.* . . . *I see it as an evolution of the word*, like all words. . . . It still seems strange that they would object to my usage of the word . . . when *Kip Fulbeck and Hapa Issues Forum and Mavin* are . . . just a few examples of groups embracing hapa *as a term for biracial and multiracial Asian-Americans.*

These Hawaiian groups want to reclaim what was originally a Hawaiian word *and keep it in its purest form.* As someone who deals with language and writing every day, I know that language itself cannot be kept pure. . . . *The ugly truth is that many of these linguistic alterations happen as a result of colonialism* or even simple borrowing of concepts.

Does this mean that these Hawaiian groups do not have a legitimate claim to the word hapa or that anyone, myself included, can simply use the word willy-nilly *because it's a neat way to describe one's ethnic and cultural identity?* I do think that these groups have a point, and their goal to educate others about the origins of the word is a noble and valuable one. *Nevertheless, I don't believe that I am simply adopting a trendy word because I cannot find or create a better way to describe myself.*

When I first heard about the word hapa, I was intrigued. I did not realize that people who *shared my ethnic background, who were part-Asian*, used *such a precise term.* They didn't have to . . . call themselves *biracial or multiracial.* They weren't *generically Asian-American. They also didn't have to call themselves half-anything.* These individuals — members of college campus organizations, scholars, artists, etc. — call themselves hapa because it describes who they are, who I am.

So while I completely understand why these individuals would try to correct me in my usage of the word hapa, I respectfully disagree with their assessment and *will not cease and desist.* I will continue to describe myself as hapa and *only hope that this experience will establish a dialog about language, change, and identity.*[48]

Conard-Salvo describes the misappropriation of the term "hapa" by people with no linguistic or cultural connection to the word as an "evolution," connoting something scientific and inevitable. As a beneficiary (and confessed misappropriater) of the term, she unconsciously elevates herself as an Asian settler to a status above indigenous Kanaka Maoli, then backtracks, evoking a generic Native American heritage later in her essay in her defense, trying to demonstrate her understanding of what such hijacking of culture feels like. Yet throughout the piece, including her opening description, she continuously refers to her Asian — not Native American — identity, leaving the impression that although she is comfortable enough to evoke her indigenous heritage, she doesn't incorporate it into her argument, in essence pushing against it, choosing a mainstream settler colonial platform on which to stand and position herself.

Next she argues that her right to use the term is based on Asian and other settlers who are also misappropriating the term, using the rather juvenile excuse that it is okay to do something wrong because everyone else is doing it (never mind the old adage "Two wrongs don't make a right"). Her assertion that Hawaiians want to "keep the word in the purest form" is also problematic, because it frames the discussion in a linguistic rather than cultural paradigm. Kanaka Maoli want to reclaim a stolen identity, not keep a word with nineteenth-century (i.e., not very old or "pure") origins in a state that has already changed — as noted throughout this essay and elsewhere (including in Conard-Salvo's own essay). For Asian Americans and others to recognize that indigenous Hawaiians have had our identity misappropriated by them is to accept their role in our elimination. This may be something that settlers desire to be true, but in reality it is not true at this historical moment or for the foreseeable future. By asserting our indigenous rights against the theft of cultural objects—including language—we demonstrate our resistance to colonization and our insistence on our own survival against the onslaught of colonial oppression, to engage in the world on our terms, not be silenced by the colonizer.

Like other settlers, Conard-Salvo does not see her use of the term "hapa" as being trendy or because of an inability to come up with another word. I disagree. I assert that as with other aspects of cultural objects that have been misappropriated and commodified, the term "hapa" in an Asian settler context has suffered the same fate, hence the plethora of websites and commercial capitalism that market this misappropriation in the glossy and lucrative packaging of multicultural celebration. I for one find it incredible that with the many beautiful, rich, and diverse languages around the world, and those represented by the varied and diverse Asian American communities alone, there isn't a single term that can be adopted, created, or applied to the concept of mixed Asian and white heritage. Moreover because English is the primary language unifying all the cultures represented in this diverse and multicultural mix, why not find or create something from that? Conard-Salvo is incorrect to say that "hapa" is a "precise" term that is the only one, like Cinderella's glass slipper, that fits. This is particularly ironic when she states that by using this term, Asian Americans don't have to call themselves half or biracial, because this is the *original* meaning of the word—*from English.* So how is the Hawaiianization of the English word "half" more "precise" a term than the original?

Why do ethnically mixed Asians continue to perpetuate these myths? Some possibilities include their ignorance of Hawaiian language and culture and *kaona* (metaphoric values or nuances of meaning); their conflations of "hapa" with *ho'ohaole*, a Hawaiian term meaning "to act or behave as Amer-Europeans," which is not the same thing as appropriating someone else's cultural identity; and their acceptance of settler colonialism's romanticized (but false) exoticism of some ethnic groups (Polynesians) over others (Asians).

"Yellow Peril" versus "the Nobel Savage" and the
Romance of the "Fatal Impact" Theory

I believe the misappropriation of the term "hapa" by Asian settlers
is, as Conard-Salvo confesses, part of the "ugly truth" about colonialism. What multiethnic Asian settlers are trying to appropriate
is a positive exoticized image of the hapa haole hula girl, the light-
skinned (but not too light), royalty-descended, hip-swaying, beautiful, sweet-smelling, lei-bedecked hula maiden who is the envy and
desire of the Western colonizer. It is a way to push away from negative racist stereotypes of Asians by the colonizer, to protect against
the hurt of negative and sometimes cruel experiences of bigotry,
hate, and ignorance perpetrated by white American society. By embracing the image of the beautiful, desirable Polynesian as crafted by the Hawaiian Visitors Bureau, Asian settlers are trying to
shed the image of one colonially imposed and inaccurate identity
for another, meaning that the hapa experience for Kanaka Maoli
and others has been at times equally as painful, if not more so, for
various reasons. There is a forgetting, or an ignorance, of the pain
and suffering Kanaka Maoli have endured throughout the colonization process, beginning with the theft of our lands and continuing through the theft of our identity.

In a bizarre twist of fallacious logic, Conard-Salvo contends that
if Kanaka Maoli want our word back, then she wants the word
"kimchi" back. She writes, "If people are really concerned about
what's pure and who owns what, here is my response: give me back
my kimchi. Kimchi, a 'pure' Korean food, is now part of Hawaiian cuisine, a regular menu item at local restaurants, an option on
various plate lunch combinations. If you demand that I give you
back the word hapa, give me back my kimchi."[49]

Like Asian settlers in Hawai'i, Conard-Salvo conflates Kanaka
Maoli experiences with Asian ones. She also fails to recognize, as
is the goal of settler colonialism, that a difference exists between
the displaced Native, who had no choice in being removed from the
'āina or removed from positions of political, social, and economic

power, and the Asians and others imported as indentured servants to work the sugar plantations of the haole oligarchy. Hawai'i's modern multicultural society is built upon the 'āina of displaced and eliminated Natives and the backs of imported labor, both suffering the effects of colonialism to differing degrees. While imported laborers and others to whom Hawai'i was opened up because of foreign political and economic control eventually carved out a place for themselves and became a new wave of settler colonialism, all was done at the expense of the indigenous kanaka, displaced to make room for others, not by our invitation or choice. Thus Kanaka Maoli did not steal kimchi from Koreans; it was imported to our shores with Korean laborers on the plantation, a situation beyond Kanaka Maoli control. These Korean laborers, like all others imported to work on the sugar plantations, lived, worked, and died on lands that had previously been occupied by Kanaka Maoli, lands Kanaka Maoli were dispossessed of by settler colonialism. There is a huge difference between that situation, where kimchi was one food item incorporated into the multicultural "plate lunch," and the purposeful theft of a Hawaiian word to misrepresent an identity that is suggestively Hawaiian. Moreover the two are not analogous, as "hapa" is being applied to something it wasn't meant to be, while kimchi—on every plate lunch and restaurant menu in Hawai'i—is, well, kimchi (or kimchee, depending on the lunch wagon or restaurant). The only exception I've experienced thus far is at Alan Wong's Pineapple Room restaurant (in Macy's at the Ala Moana Shopping Center), which boasts (a very delicious) "Kimchee Reuben Sandwich," a pastrami and swiss on rye with kimchee described as "Asian Sauerkraut."[50] I leave it up to Conard-Salvo and Wong to untangle the restaurant's creative culinary description, if they so choose.

In her essay Conard-Salvo defends her position by evoking the misappropriation of the term by other Asian American groups, such as the Hapa Issues Forum and Mavin, questioning whether it was right for them to revise their definitions of the word, to which her response is no. She continues, "Using a word that evolved because of a colonialist experience seems fitting, so perhaps it isn't a mis-appropriation at all. Of course, the Hawaiians will disagree, and I wish them well in their quest to reclaim all that is theirs and theirs alone."[51] The "colonialist experience" she cites in her defense firm-ly places her within the realm of settler colonialism, participating in the elimination of the Native on a personal level, by a personal choice. By identifying with mainstream settler society, Asian set-tlers buy into the concept of the elimination of the Native, wheth-er they realize it or not.

The positively exoticized image of hapa is everywhere and is worthy of a complete discussion in itself. Needless to say, if Asian settlers are so intent on utilizing Hawaiian terms to describe their own identity, I suggest not stealing or inventing one. Here's one I offer for adoption: *kōlea*. Not to be confused with *Kōlea*, the Ha-waiian word for "Korean," *kōlea* is defined as the "Pacific gold-en plover (*Pluvialis dominica*), a migratory bird which comes to Hawaiʻi about the end of August and leaves early in May for Siberia and Alaska." Those conversant in the kaona of Hawaiian language may find this amusing, so perhaps I should disclose the figurative definition as well. Metaphorically the term *kōlea* also functions as "a scornful reference to foreigners who come to Hawaii and be-come prosperous, and then leave with their wealth, just as the plo-ver arrives thin in the fall each year, fattens up, and leaves; a less common figurative reference is *to one who claims friendship or kinship that does not exist*."[52] Given the circumstances of multieth-nic Asians stealing Kanaka Maoli identity, perhaps this Hawaiian term is more fitting, as it more accurately describes what they are doing in misappropriating this term. It was originally applied to haole, as was the term "hapa" (i.e., hapa haole). It was also effec-tively applied to the provisional government, which was composed of American and European haole instrumental in overthrowing Queen Liliʻuokalani in 1893 and for annexing the stolen ʻāina and government to the United States, a recognized illegal act that is the reason for the 1993 Apology Bill signed by President Bill Clinton. But Theodore Kelsey, a haole expert in Hawaiian language, says the term can be used to describe all foreigners and is thus applicable to Asian settlers. After all, if Conard-Salvo and the others she cites in her defense can explain to Hawaiians how our language fits their identity, then by all means, here's another expression for their fragile, confused repertoire.

Kanaka Maoli have various responses to the misappropriation of the Hawaiian term "hapa" by multiethnic Asians based in North America. Some are surprised the term has been "transplanted" to the continental United States and wonder why anyone would want to use a word from a language and culture they are not a part of to describe themselves, as Ledward discusses in his dissertation. Many others, like myself, are offended by this practice for myriad reasons, including the misappropriation of our heritage language and cultural identity. There are several websites, forums, and discussion boards administered by Kanaka Maoli that have taken on the kuleana to address this issue. The first, Real Hapas, was created by Lana Robbins in 2004.[53] On the site, Robbins discloses her *hapa maoli* (indigenous hapa) status and response to our collective identity theft, stating, "As someone of English, Chinese, Hawaiian, and Portuguese descent I was shocked that so many mixed Asians were unknowingly and/or unwittingly disrespecting the Hawaiian culture . . . thus disrespecting its people." In an introduction explaining the purpose of the site, "The REAL Hapa: Hawaiian Hapa," Robbins writes:

> Around 2002, I noticed that many people of mixed Asian descent were disrespecting Hawaiians and part of our culture by misusing and misappropriating the Hawaiian word "hapa." It became evident at Alvin Soltis' [hapa.com] that there was an assault and an attack on . . . our Hawaiian culture. . . . It became my personal mission to ensure that I do what I can to protect this gift that our kupuna gave to us which future Hawaiian children should . . . have as well. This is one of many ways that I . . . protect this gift as well as other gifts from our kupuna such as the iwi (or "bones") that all Hawaiians share.

Robbins is quite strong in her position against multiethnic Asians and others misappropriating a hapa identity. She describes "hapa" as a word Hawaiians used to describe themselves "until nisei began to rape their language." She continues, "Today's rape of the Hawaiian language also implies that the Hawaiian language means nothing and thus the Hawaiian people are nothing. Thus we are now exposing this rape and it's about time." The "bottom line," she says, is that "the misuse and misappropriation of the word 'hapa' *must* end." In staking an indigenous position of protection of language and culture, Robbins cites "possible legal means" to accomplish this through the Native American Languages Act of 1990 and the United Nations' "Rights of Indigenous Peoples."

Since the website went online Robbins has unapologetically stood her ground, a courageous, difficult position since Kanaka Maoli are so marginalized, overpowered, and underrepresented. The only site representing a Hawaiian hapa perspective, Real Hapa has been hacked and disabled at least once (in 2005) and has received much criticism, presumably by non–Kanaka Maoli, which Robbins acknowledges on the website: "Many people have opposed the viewpoints expressed on this website. However we will not stop until people start respecting the Hawaiian culture and its people. So far many have written into us expressing anger, bitterness, and/or surprise. . . . This website is about protecting and preserving part of our culture. . . . I dedicate this website to all Hawaiian children, young and old, who are descendants of Wakea and Papa." Robbins is adamant in her defense of Kanaka genealogy, language, and culture, evoking a well-known ʻōlelo noʻeau (proverb), *i ka ʻōlelo ke ola, i ka ʻolelo ka make*, "in the word/language is life, in the word/language is death," meaning that great care must be taken in choosing words because of the power they hold, a foundational tenant of Hawaiian cultural practice and worldview.

Despite the insistence of some mixed Asian Americans like Conard-Salvo to cling to the term "hapa" and misappropriate it for their own self-interest, it is also encouraging that others are demonstrating a more educated, sympathetic response. In an essay originally published in the online magazine *Hyphen* in 2007, Wei Ming Dariotis discusses how she decided to give up the word to describe her mixed-Asian heritage, understanding that the use of the word was "a question of power":

> Who has the power or right to use language? Native Hawaiians, in addition to all of the other ways that their sovereignty has been abrogated, lost for many years the right to their own language through oppressive English-language education. Given this history and given the contemporary social and political reality (and realty—as in real estate) of Hawaiian, the appropriation of this one word has a significance deeper than many Asian Americans are willing to recognize. To have this symbolic word used by Asians, particularly by Japanese Americans, as though it is their own, seems to symbolically mirror the way Native Hawaiian land was first taken by European Americans, and is now owned by European Americans, Japanese and Japanese Americans and other Asian American ethnic groups that numerically and economically dominate Native Hawaiians in their own land.[54]

With this recognition of language and power, Dariotis concludes that moving away from using "hapa" as "a shorthand for Asian Americans of mixed heritage" will be "a steep uphill struggle."[55] But it is also an important step to right/write the injustices that its continued use perpetuates against Kanaka Maoli.

Haʻina ʻia mai ana ka puana (Conclusion): Fatal Impact?

In the 1960s the anthropologist Alan Moorehead popularized the "fatal impact" theory, which proposes that Native Pacific populations haven't recovered (and theoretically can't recover) from the initial Western contact.[56] This trope of the dying Native also supports white, Western superiority and patriarchal dominance, which has cast the West as hero and the Native as tragic figure. At the end of *An Act of War* (1993), the groundbreaking, award-winning documentary detailing the overthrow of the Hawaiian Kingdom in 1893, the narrator states, "And what has been the result of becoming a part of America? Our children were punished for speaking our native language, taught to be ashamed of our culture, our names, our skin. Our home became Americans' playground, their battleground, their 50th state, their real estate. And in our own homeland, we are the homeless, we are the poor, we have the shortest life expectancy, we are the uneducated, we fill the prisons. But, after more than a century of dispossession, we are still here."[57] The death of Kanaka Maoli has been predicted for over a century. But we are still here. Kalākaua proclaimed *ho'oulu lāhui*: increase, reinvigorate, perpetuate the Hawaiian people. We have begun to flourish again not only in number, but in political and cultural consciousness. We are survivors.

As our *kūpuna* (ancestors) remind us, land is necessary for life. Therefore, Wolfe argues, "contests for land can be . . . [and] often are—contests for life"—not just physical existence, but also way of life, cultural practice.[58] Thus the adoption of a "kuleana consciousness" or acceptance of responsibility is a first step to reconciliation with Kanaka Maoli and the abandonment of settler colonialism's practice of appropriating indigenous identity.

Kuleana is a Hawaiian term that means both one's rights and one's responsibilities. We all have multidimensional and simultaneous kuleana at any given moment based on our positionality. As Kanaka Maoli, it is our kuleana to continue the fight for our culture, 'āina, nation, identity, to follow the path so clearly set by our ancestors. But kuleana to correct the wrongs of the past that are perpetuated in the present, with the intent to change the future, is not ours alone. As we are *nā kupa o ka 'āina* (the natives of the land), the movement of resistance is not just resistance to colonialism, which puts all the responsibility on our shoulders and suggests a perpetual victimization, but also insistence in claiming our own power and right to demand action. We insist on perpetuating our *lāhui* (nation), reclaiming our land, holding on to and defining our identity, practicing our culture. In other work I have identified this as a kuleana consciousness, a specific recognition of responsibility and a call to act (*ma ka hana ka 'ike, ma ka hana ka mana*—"in action is knowledge, in action is spiritual power"). Moreover this kuleana consciousness extends to all. Settler colonialism benefits settlers and is bent on eliminating the Native.

Settlers and others with new insights, having heard this story, can adopt a form of kuleana consciousness. What is settlers' kuleana to Hawai'i? What is settlers' kuleana to Kanaka Maoli? One aspect of settler kuleana is to embrace the truth of history and place and stop stealing Kanaka Maoli identity and claiming a false indigeneity. Settlers should speak up against other settlers, such as the continental-based mixed-blood Asians who insist on their right to be identity thieves.

Identity is not only stolen from individuals. There are myriad ways settler colonialism undermines us every day. One example cited earlier is the use of Hawaiian names for businesses. Another is through the use of indigenous cultural motifs for logos and sports teams, something particularly upsetting in Native American cultures, who have protested the name of the Washington Redskins and other sports teams. During the June Jones era of University of Hawai'i football in the 1990s, the Rainbows bowed to peer pressure and capitalism and Jones changed the name, color scheme, and logo of the team; overnight the green and white Rainbows became the black and green Warriors, with the new Polynesian tapa-patterned "H" logo designed by Kurt Ozaki, a Kapa'a High School alum (and Asian settler). The UH mascot also underwent several transformations, from a cartoonish foam warrior sarcastically dubbed the "Marshmallow Man," to a Hawaiian warrior buffed out in foam padding with airbrushed muscles sporting a *malo* (loincloth), ahu'ula, and mahi'ole, symbols of Hawaiian *ali'i* (chiefly) status, to a live Pacific Islander, Vili Fehoko, whose wild sideline antics play into the Western narrative of the slightly comical, slightly dangerous, untrustworthy, and savage Pacific Native. As part of this pseudo-indigenized identity of the premier Western-based academic institution in the state, a Māori pregame haka (traditional Māori dance) was implemented, which, under protest from Māori, Kanaka Maoli, and others, was replaced by a *ha'a* (traditional Hawaiian dance form). These settler sports invite players and their fans to don fake representations of indigenous identity—one with a tomahawk and feathers adorning their helmets,

the other with tattoo-inspired motifs adorning theirs—to literally "go native" in a controlled, colonial paradigm.

In all of these examples and more, settlers have had many opportunities to exercise kuleana toward Kanaka Maoli and resist
their participation in these tokenized representations because of
their positions of power in the creation of such images. Jones, a
settler, proposed the changes to the football logo and mascot with
the intent of making money; her proposal was protested by Kanaka Maoli but supported by a vast array of haole and Asian settlers
in the University of Hawaiʻi system and the general community.
Similarly the committee that decided on the final images for the
state quarter that was forwarded to the U.S. Mint also collaborat-
ed in the promotion of these images in a way that tokenizes the au-
thentically indigenous as a gloss for all living on Hawaiian ʻāina.

What does identity theft have to do with nationhood in Hawaiʻi?
Discussing sovereignty (or nationhood) in an indigenous, Native
American context, Venne stresses:

> Our Elders and leadership never sold lands at the time of the Treaty.
> We could never sell, surrender, cede our lands to the colonizers. These
> lands and territories were given to us by the Creator. The land makes
> us. . . . To sell or give up the lands is to give up ourselves. If Indige-
> nous Peoples give up the lands, then what happens to the future gener-
> ations? They will have nothing to live with and care for. They would be
> lost people. It is not possible for us to sell [the land]. . . . We know the
> laws given to us by the Creator. It is an obligation. It is a duty. It is the
> future of our children's children. We cannot like the non-indigenous
> people who make rules and regulations and change them when they
> don't like the rule or regulation. We were given the laws by the Creator.
> We have to live the laws. This is sovereignty of Indigenous Peoples.[59]

This argument is applicable to a Kanaka Maoli context in our quest
to regain political sovereignty and be recognized by the U.S. government, the fight to regain control of ceded lands to prevent the
state government from transferring or selling lands that rightfully
do not belong to the state, but to Kanaka Maoli.

Throughout 2009 the State of Hawai'i celebrated fifty years of statehood, which began on August 12, 1959. In late 2008 the 50th Anniversary of Statehood Commission began running print, television, and radio ads featuring Hawai'i residents of all ethnic backgrounds waxing poetic on the benefits and joys of statehood. As the state settles into fifty years of American democracy, Native Hawaiian claims of land, identity, and nationhood are steadily being eroded under intense pressures of social and political assimilation.

Thus because of heightened settler aggression Kanaka Maoli claims to land, identity, and nationhood are as appropriate and necessary as they ever were, as we continue to heed the words of our ancestors, including the thought encapsulated by Kalālaua, to ho'oulu lāhui, increase, perpetuate, and invigorate the Hawaiian people and, by extension, our 'āina and our nation. Osorio reminds us, "There are certain things that cannot be taken . . . only . . . surrendered. . . . As a people, we are knowledgeable about the things taken but not always conscious of the things we have not surrendered."[60] Kanaka Maoli are conscious of what has been taken and kept from us—our 'āina, our identity, and our nation. Yet we have not and do not surrender to these truths of our colonial history. The master narrative of exploration, exploitation, and the rights of settlers to colonize our lands and appropriate our identities has plagued Kanaka Maoli as it has other indigenous peoples for at least two centuries. If nothing else, we persevere in our fight to reclaim all of these for ourselves and future generations, to assert a *mo'olelo kū'ē*, a counternarrative to settler colonialism, to continue to proclaim with pride, *he Hawai'i mau a mau*—I am Hawaiian forever, *kūpa'a mā hope o ka 'āina*, and to stand firmly upon our land confident in this knowledge.

Notes

1. Kamahualani, "Eia Hawaii," in *Account of the Polynesian Race*, ed. Abraham Fornander (Rutland VT: Charles E. Tuttle, 1973), 10, my translation.

2. Mary Kawena Pukui, *'Ōlelo No'eau, Hawaiian Proverbs and Poetical Sayings* (Honolulu: Bishop Museum Press, 1986), 62.

3. The terms "Kanaka Maoli," "Kanaka," "Kanaka ʻŌiwi," "Kanaka Hawaiʻi," "Native Hawaiian," and "Hawaiian" are synonyms and are used interchangeably throughout this chapter. They refer to the indigenous population of the Hawaiian islands prior to Western intrusion in 1778, and their descendants.

4. The mele "Kulaiwi" by Larry Lindsey Kimura includes the line "He Hawaiʻi au mau a mau." The mele "He Hawaiʻi Au" by Ron Rocha, Peter Moon, and Alice Nāmakelua is self-explanatory in the title. Lyrics are available at Huapala's website, www.huapala.org.

5. Pualani Kanakaʻole Kanahele, "I Am This Land and This Land Is Me," *Hūlili, Multidisciplinary Research on Hawaiian Well-Being* 2, no. 1 (2005): 23.

6. "Amer-European" is a term used by the Native American literary scholar Jace Weaver to describe white Americans of European ancestry. Although synonymous with "Euroamerican," a more well-known term, "'Amer-European' connotes something very different. They are Europeans who happen to live in America." The term "reflects the difference in worldview between the two peoples, Native and non-Native. Born of and shaped by a different continent, Amer-Europeans . . . never truly belong here, no matter how many generations they may dwell here." Jace Weaver, *That the People Might Live: Native American Literatures and Native American Community* (New York: Oxford University Press, 1997), xiii–ix.

7. Samuel H. Elbert and Mary Kawena Pukui, *Hawaiian Dictionary*, rev. ed. (Honolulu: University of Hawaiʻi Press, 1986), 184.

8. Patrick Wolfe, "Settler Colonialism and the Elimination of the Native," *Journal of Genocide Research* 8, no. 4 (2006): 387.

9. An excellent resource is David Stannard's *Before the Horror: The Population of Hawaiʻi on the Eve of Western Contact* (Honolulu: Social Science Research Institute, University of Hawaiʻi Press, 1989).

10. J. Kehaulani Kauanui, *Hawaiian Blood: Colonialism and the Politics of Sovereignty and Indigeneity* (Durham NC: Duke University Press, 2008), 3.

11. Jonathan K. Osorio, "On Being Hawaiian," *Hūlili: Multidisciplinary Research on Hawaiian Well-being* 3, no. 1 (2006): 19.

12. Elbert and Pukui, *Hawaiian Dictionary*, 124.

13. Pizza Hut Hawaiʻi website, www.pizzahuthawaii.com; KFC television commercial, November 29, 2010.

14. Houston Wood, *Displacing Natives: the Rhetorical Production of Hawai'i* (Lanham MD: Rowman & Littlefield, 1999), 37, 45, 40.

15. Mary Louise Pratt quoted in Wood, *Displacing Natives*, 40.

16. Merriam-Webster online, s.v. "kamaaina," http://mw1.merriam -webster.com/dictionary/kamaaina (accessed April 10, 2009).

17. Wood, *Displacing Natives*, 41, 42.

18. Osorio, "On Being Hawaiian," 19. This is not to say that Hawaiians have not been accused of being ho'ohaole (acting Amer-European), euphemistically referred to as being a "coconut" (brown on the outside, white on the inside). But acting a particular way and being or claiming a particular identity are two different things.

19. Wood, *Displacing Natives*, 43, 44–45.

20. Wood, *Displacing Natives*, 49, 50.

21. Sharon H. Venne, "What Is the Meaning of Sovereignty?" *Indigenous Women's Network Magazine*, June 18, 2007, www.indigenous women.org.

22. The indigenous term for this area is Awāwamalu ("Shaded Valley"), which is not commonly used.

23. http://www.gohawaii.com/statewide/guidebook/barack -obama-hawaii.

24. http://www.gohawaii.com/statewide/guidebook/barack -obama-hawaii.

25. Lisa Cushing, "Obama's Universal Health Care Plan Must Learn from Hawaii's Failures," *Ka Leo o Hawaii*, November 24, 2008, http:// www.kaleo.org/2.13229/obama-s-universal-health-care-plan-must-learn -from-hawai-i-s-failures-1.1790224, my emphasis.

26. Cecelia Brown, "Unofficial Guide to Barak Obama's Hawaii," Hotel Renew, www.hotelrenew.com/images/pdf/unofficial-obama-guide -orientation.doc.

27. Maxine Hong Kingston, "Obama on Oahu," *Huffington Post*, www. huffingtonpost.com/maxine-hong-kingston/obama-on-oahu_b_139417 .html.

28. Hong Kingston, "Obama on Oahu."

29. Lee Cataluna, "Is Lingle Losing Her Local Cred?" *Honolulu Advertiser*, October 17, 2008, http://the.honoluluadvertiser.com/article/2008/ Oct/17/ln/hawaii810170338.html.

30. Elbert and Pukui, *Hawaiian Dictionary*, 58.

31. Lorrin Andrews, *A Dictionary of the Hawaiian Language* (Honolulu: Island Heritage, 2003), 151.

32. An article titled "Pinao Kuhihewa" (Blurred error in judgment) begins with a common salutation addressing an audience from one end of the island to the other: "Mai Hawaii a Kauai, maloko hoi o keia mau mea a pau, na kane na wahine a me na kamalii, na'lii kamaniha a me na konohiki auhau hoopunipuni, na haole a me na hapa haole" (From Hawai'i island to Kaua'i, outside of all of these things, the men, the women and the children, the uncivilized chiefs and the lying government officials, the whites and the part-whites). *Ke Kumu Hawaii*, buke 4, pepa 14, December 5, 1838, my translation.

33. "Kanaka" generically translates to "human," but in particular contexts, such as in the Hawaiian-language newspaper of the time, it also means someone of Hawaiian ancestry, "Hawaiian." Elbert and Pukui, *Hawaiian Dictionary*, 127.

34. For example, *Ka Manawa*, 1895.

35. Brandon Ledward, "Inseparably Hapa, the Making and Unmaking of a Hawaiian Monolith" (PhD diss., University of Hawai'i at Mānoa, 2007) provides an excellent insight into the history of the word "hapa" in different social, cultural, and even literary settings. More recent literary work by hapa Hawaiian writers include that of Kahi Brooks, Kehaulani Kauanui, Naomi Losch, Puanani Burgess, Kaimalino Andrade, and Matthew Kaleiali'i Ka'ōpio, just to name a few.

36. *Urban Dictionary*, s.v. "hapa," www.urbandictionary.com (accessed 20 April 2009), my emphasis.

37. Susan Matoba Adler, "Asian American Families," in *International Encyclopedia of Marriage and Families*, ed. James J. Ponsetti (New York: Macmillan, 2002), 7.

38. William M. Liu et al., "Understanding the Function of Acculturation and Prejudicial Attitudes among Asian Americans," *Cultural Diversity and Ethnic Minority Psychology* 5, no. 4 (2008): 320.

39. Kimberly Powell, "Drumming against the Quiet: The Sounds of Asian American Identity in an Amorphous Landscape," *Qualitative Inquiry* 14 (2008): 901n922, http://qix.sagepub.com/cgi/content/ab stract/14/6/901, my emphasis.

40. www.seaweedproductions.com/hapa, my emphasis. For original citation, see Kip Fulbeck, *Part Asian, 100% Hapa* (San Francisco: Chronicle Books, 2006).

41. Excerpt from Booklist review of Kip Fulbeck's *Part Asian, 100% Hapa* by Donna Seaman, American Library Association, can be found at http://www.amazon.com/Part-Asian-100-Hapa-Fulbeck/dp/0811849597, my emphasis.

42. www.hapaculture.com, my emphasis.

43. Cornell University Hapa Club, website inactive.

44. www.mixedasians.com, my emphasis.

45. Kristen Lee, "Multi-Culturalism Explained in One Word: Hapa," *Tell Me More*, National Public Radio, broadcast transcript and audio file, April 18, 2009, http://www.npr.org/templates/story/story.php?storyId=93690045, my emphasis.

46. While neither Kim nor Park is Hawaiian, it is implied in the story line that their characters, Chin Ho Kelly and Kono Kalakaua, are. In the original series, Kelly was played by Kam Fong Chun, who was ethnically Chinese, and Kalakaua by Gilbert "Zulu" Kauahi, who was ethnically Hawaiian. There was no relationship between them in the original series, but in the 2010 remake Kelly and Kalakaua are cousins.

47. Haunani-Kay Trask, "Settlers of Color and 'Immigrant' Hegemony: 'Locals' in Hawai'i," in *Asian Settler Colonialism, from Local Governance to the Habits of Everyday Life in Hawai'i*, ed. Candace Fujikane and Jonathan Okamura (Honolulu: University of Hawai'i Press, 2008), 46.

48. www.hapastories.com, my emphasis.

49. www.hapastories.com.

50. http://www.alanwongs.com/pineapple-room-menu-lunch.

51. www.hapastories.com.

52. Elbert and Pukui, *Hawaiian Dictionary*, 162, my emphasis.

53. The website has not been online since April 2009, although in an e-mail exchange the webmaster assured me the site was undergoing maintenance and would be online again soon (April 29, 2009). In the meantime, I was able to access some web content saved on other websites and retrieve site information from cached and archival sources.

54. Wei Ming Dariotis, "Hapa: The Word of Power," *Hyphen Magazine*, December 3, 2007; www.mixedheritagecenter.org.

55. Dariotis, "Hapa."

56. Alan Moorehead, *The Fatal Impact: An Account of the Invasion of the South Pacific, 1767–1840* (New York: Penguin, 1966).

57. *An Act of War: The Overthrow of the Hawaiian Nation*, video

produced by Na Maka o ka Aina, unpublished transcript of film documentary written by Haunani-Kay Trask and Lilikala Kameeleihiwa, 1993, 30.

58. Wolfe, "Settler Colonialism," 387.

59. Sharon Venne, "What Is Sovereignty?" www.indigenouswomen.org.

60. Osorio, "On Being Hawaiian," 23.

Chapter 9

Re-archiving Asian Settler Colonialism in a Time of Hawaiian Decolonization, or, Two Walks along Kamehameha Highway

Bianca Isaki

In 1893 the U.S. military aided the overthrow of the last monarch of the Kingdom of Hawai'i, Queen Lili'uokalani. A white-dominated oligarchy governed the Hawaiian Republic from 1894 until 1900, when it became a U.S. territorial government. This historic wrong was formally recognized in the 1993 "Apology Bill," when President Bill Clinton signed a joint resolution that acknowledged U.S. complicity in the aftermath of the 1893 overthrow.[1] Despite an official recognition of the truth of Hawai'i's settler colonial origins, Hawaiians continue to struggle for a land base and political independence.[2]

Since the late 1960s Hawaiians have renewed a push past U.S. frameworks to re-archive their histories as Native national subjects.[3] Foregrounding the illegal overthrow of the Hawaiian Kingdom, they refract struggles for citizen equality into claims to national self-determination, entitlements to "ceded" lands, and, most fundamentally, Hawai'i's eccentricity to U.S. legal jurisdiction.[4] As Hawaiians decolonize *these* histories, Asian settlers cannot have a history of becoming U.S. citizens in Hawai'i anymore. This essay begins to unravel what this might mean.

The 1993 Apology signals a shift in settler colonial historicity.[5] The usual pattern of settler colonial history reasons away the constitutive violence on which the colonial state is founded, claiming that Hawaiian Natives never constituted a nation and therefore the United States never overthrew a legitimate government. But the United States is not denying or forgetting the overthrow of the Hawaiian Kingdom. If we follow Foucault's wisdom—that truth is produced as a certain organization of power—then we need to understand how power displaces even what it *recognizes* truth onto a time-lag between a past and the present.[6] Here the Apology acts as a time machine; it poses as scenario in which today's U.S. leaders can affirm that they would not visit the same violence on Hawaiians as their forefathers did in 1893.

Crucially feelings function as placeholders, holding a present colonial order in place. This way of displacing wrongdoing, or at least keeping it at a distance, cites contrition as our new difference from the authors of past injustice, the effect of which is to reconfirm the justice of colonial authority as itself a resource for trumping a violent colonial past. Tropes of reconciliation, healing, and optimism for a nation that knows better *now* condition a communal insensitivity to the threat that belies the promise held out by Clinton's Apology. After the Apology, Hawai'i remains within the United States, but supposedly with higher hopes for reclaiming U.S. justice.

Following Foucault, I ask: how can truth be made not to matter? Or: how is truth deferred to mattering outside of the actual space and time of living? Further—and this is my focus: how are national temporalities lived by Asian settlers managed in order to maintain Hawai'i as a settler colony? To answer these questions, which are mostly questions about the affective forms that U.S. imperialism takes, I consider the conjoining of Asian settler intergenerational family time and U.S. imperialist histories within new affective registers of settler colonialism.

Asian Settler Colonial Histories in Hawai'i

In 1894 an abusive *luna* (foreman) on Hawai'i's Kahuku plantation badly beat a Japanese worker. The other workers went on strike and walked to Honolulu. The record of the 1894 trek is drawn from Roland Kotani's oft-cited *The Japanese of Hawaii: A Century of Struggle*: "Setting off on a 38-mile trek from Kahuku to Honolulu, more than 200 strikers walked all day and all night. Slipping and sliding on Nuuanu [*sic*] Pali trails on wooden clogs or in their bare feet in the darkness and rain, the weary marchers reached Honolulu about midnight. In the morning, they presented their grievances to Goro Narita, Japanese charge d'affaires to the Hawaiian Republic. As a reward for their efforts, they were arrested by the police, fined $5 each and forced to walk back to the Kahuku Plantation."[7]

These workers trod trails that are now the double-lane Kamehameha Highway. From Kahuku, at the northeastern tip of O'ahu, Hawai'i, the highway skirts the shore until it intersects with the Pali road, which cuts across the Ko'olau Mountains and leads into downtown Honolulu. More than a century later my grandmother, Thelma Shigemitsu, and I walked along a stretch of the Kamehameha Highway in Kahuku. Usually these two events would be set in complementary stories of our grandparents' struggle and intergenerational intimacy. This essay instead contextualizes these Asian settler "walks" within the historical and ongoing project of Native Hawaiian decolonization in Hawai'i.

Asian settlement in Hawai'i begins with the approximately three hundred thousand plantation laborers who arrived between 1850 and 1920.[8] Asian settlers' historical disenfranchisement and atypicality as colonizers make it difficult to acknowledge how they have contributed to colonization. They did not come for the recognizably colonial reasons of conquering or Christian conversion. Viewed by planters as mere "supplies" that could be mistreated with impunity, early Asian migrant plantation workers and later their descendants fought back by claiming equality as citizens and collective labor rights.[9] Asian settler colonialism is the future of past practices of land theft and political control through which descendants of migrant plantation laborers moved into a middle class and U.S. citizenship in Hawai'i. Yet these are not the only practices of settler colonialism, nor are they only in the past.

Doubtless decolonization must mean the return of land and the right of self-determination to Hawaiians most of all. In furtherance of that project, I wonder about the ways that *affective* practices that are supposed to mean the most to and about us—like having a history, being part of a family, striving for justice, remembering a community, passing on a heritage and wanting a home—are part of a settler colonial apparatus in Hawai'i. Typically, because these practices don't look particularly harmful nor are necessarily carried out by an intending subject, they are made to compete, to seem irrelevant or even trivializing to decolonial projects.

The story that is usually told about Asian settlers' movement from Hawai'i's plantation era (1890s–1959) to the colonial present is not the story of colonization. In this usual story they left the plantation, fought in "the good war," and were elected into office under a banner of U.S. patriotism, racial equality, and workers' rights. Plantations were crucial arenas of labor organizing, patriotism, and community formation that contributed to the emergence of a markedly Asian, multiracial local ruling class in the 1950s. Yet once in power, members of this new class notoriously exploited their elected positions as legislators and landowners to capitalize on post–World War II tourism-driven land development and an expanding U.S. defense industry in Hawai'i.[10] Asian settlers' upward mobility and "racial equality" after statehood (1959) are achieved through complicity with Hawaiian national dispossession. Decolonizing history must involve re-archiving structures that obscure the historical formation of Asian settler colonialism under U.S. capitalism.

Among other things, re-archiving colonial narratives requires attending to the making of U.S. citizens from Asian settlers who were hard workers, meritocratic subjects, and self-sacrificing patriots. Newly archived in Hawaiian Hawai'i, these figures record practices whereby Asian settlers affirm a history of becoming U.S. citizens in Hawai'i. This affirmation is important because it signals agency—achieved historically and in the present—in Hawai'i and the United States. Remaining in Hawai'i merely because one's family migrated here generations ago underexplains the agency of those earlier migrants and our own in the present. Kotani's Japanese laborers did not come to Hawai'i as mere accidents of economic and political conditions. Nor do Asian settlers continue to reside out of inertia. Settlement involves stickier, complex attachments to a settler colonial apparatus that must be reckoned with to meet the demands of the Hawaiian decolonizing struggle.

Nation Times and Family Time

To no longer have a U.S. history means losing "national time."[11] Partly the Hegelian march toward state perfection, national time is mainly the coordinated spatial-temporal simultaneity of the nation-state that holds a polity together. As much as it is a category of political community, the nation exists through the management of temporalities that mark it as itself a historical event. Declarations were written and delivered, wars were waged, and holidays were inaugurated and commemorated in order to create a polity that would move through time together. National time is an everyday enactment through which the nation is realized by directing the rhythms of lived lives, the insistence that histories begin at the moment of Western "contact," the grammar through which we talk about "our boys" fighting in Afghanistan, in addition to the formal structures of governance. In Hawai'i the nation erupts in daily encounters with ubiquitous military discounts in commercial venues and the H3 highway, which was designed explicitly to channel people and things between two major military bases on O'ahu.

Over time and in a territory, the nation-state manages movement within and across boundaries, monopolizing violence, enforcing laws, and policing populations. These orchestrations are carried out in the name of a nation supposedly embodied in a people that live nearby, obey a common authority, and span time together. The political theorist Michael Shapiro notes that "national times" impose coherence onto "what is actually a series of fragmentary and arbitrary conditions of historical assemblage."[12] U.S. history nationalizes what are otherwise diverse ways of being in history. Delaminating Asian settler pasts from national time thus require a way of assembling these pasts that Kotani fails to offer.

Kotani's book is an invaluable historical document. However, it also archives the worker-trekkers' moment of class struggle as a colonial backstory to the citizen-becoming of Japanese settlers. Here colonial power enjoins a confirmation of our present distance from the past suffering of this documented scene of nineteenth-century protest as "evidence of progress under U.S. capitalism."[13] We know they were going somewhere better because, supposedly, that is where we are now. This timeline is a political practice; its script puts feelings, memory, and narrative literacy into a chronology that is adapted into a colonized present. The workers' frustrated struggle to access public justice is told in terms that intone indignation.[14] "Strike," "protest," "all day and all night," a ruthless "overseer," and the suffering implicit in a seventy-six-mile hike—thirty-eight miles each way—accomplished in substandard footwear animates this moment with the momentum of imminent social transformation. Our very indignation at this injustice is scripted as evidence that their past suffering can be redeemed in a present that has, implicitly, progressed toward racial equality under U.S. capitalism.

This phrasing of progress as evidence of distance and difference from past injustice is also the device used by Clinton's Apology. Here affective registers trade on the appeal of institutional recognition, which, among other things, relieves marginalized groups from the experience of being a social contradiction.[15] Judith Butler schematizes this dynamic: "The appeal to the state is at once an appeal to a fantasy already institutionalized by the state, and a leave-taking from existing social complexity in the hope of becoming 'socially coherent' at last."[16] This desire for relief is read retroactively (for example, after citizenship is achieved), as an occasion to reinvest optimism for the United States.

Problematically stories of Asian settler labor struggle and oppression have been enlisted into the work of maintaining Hawai'i as a U.S. settler colony. This is the settler colonial labor of making selves intelligible as market segments, emotionally appropriate citizens, and, in my examples, living receptacles that absorb colonial contradictions in ways that let a colonial order live on. To be clear, I'm reporting, not interpreting. Hawai'i's plantation worker heritage has been institutionalized in living museums, public school textbooks, talk-story sessions, community organizations, and various memorials. While there is no seamless line that connects a collective desire to remember suffering and tribulation as part of one's history to a larger generalizable desire to "belong" to a U.S. history, this is a considerable industry built up around the tendency of the connection. What makes these institutions colonial is an often invoked and carefully managed equation between a history of struggle and an earned claim to Hawai'i.[17] Asian settler class experience is calculated in an index of deserving that converts having a history of adversity into a political calculus that, problematically, sees "hard work" as struggles for legitimacy conferred by the healing space of the U.S. nation. This logic banks on a moral economy of merit—of earning a place in Hawai'i—that tenses against Hawaiian accounts of being dispossessed of that place by a settler colonial order, in which Asian settlers play no small part.

In Hawai'i's settler colony, appeals to home and history are never out of the orbit of contests over land and right of occupation. Asian settler affects serve a settler colonial order when they mimic, and thus come to supplant, indigenous relationships to land. My grandmother's home in Kahuku and the meritorious suffering of Japanese plantation workers in 1894 Kahuku function as claims to (Hawaiian) land. They produce Hawai'i as an object of Asian settler affection, an object that can be owned and operated by settlers.

An Asian settler history cannot create a claim to an indigenous relationship with Hawai'i. History must instead be another political space for archiving existences with uncertain, but material, positions in a colonial landscape—like walks along the road. The 1894 thirty-eight-mile trek and my grandmother's walk in 2004 expand in the slowed-down tempos of emotion, memory, and, implicitly, intellect—because as we're thinking it through, we're taking time to do so. My effort to sync the diverse times in the two walks of my title seeks to specify the integration of affective labor into colonial reproduction.

Affects are the material of emotion and memory, which have effects, particularly on the production of self-awareness, of ways of being in time. The plantation era is full of selves that exist in times that are not directed *only* toward U.S. citizenship: plantation work schedules, the weekly tempos of washing and ironing days, being someone's daughter or grandmother, being absorbed in a fantasy, and the story of one's life. In these moments different (non-U.S.-directed) selves might break out from what is intimate and definitive about Asian settler pasts in Hawai'i.

My claim to have watched my grandmother reconnect to the landscape traffics closely in national discourses of subject-making through blood and belonging. I exploit this proximity to outline the ways that feelings for family and history shade into settler colonial nationalism. Within and against the national time of the protestors, the second Kahuku-based trek—the walk I shared with my grandmother in 2004—traverses a pathway between remembered and present Kahuku in family time. These moments are not linked by an empty progression through time, but by a history that is alive to the biopolitical management of familial sexuality as a dimension of settler colonial citizenship.

Shigemitsu's Walk

On March 12, 2004, Thelma Shigemitsu was walking alone along the Kahuku stretch of Kamehameha Highway. Her head nodded thoughtfully over the houses that stood at attention to this road, which bisects the town. She seemed oblivious to my presence as I trailed her meanderings in the shoulder lane. Before Shigemitsu's memory, or even before the memory of her grandmother, Kahuku was not centered around the highway. Before settler times, the center was a fish pond, Kukio, which was surrounded by a large Hawaiian settlement.[18]

Witnessing her movements was watching memory reconnect to landscape. She remembered Kahuku to me in stories ordered by the landmarks as they came into view, saying things like "Obasan's house was just over here, by a big mango tree . . . or maybe a little ways over." But her stories were invisible to me. They resided in the stark spaces before us and her lingering over a house yard that had held family reunion attendees, an avenue crowded with playmates during after school hours, and my eighty-four-year-old grandmother in a slip dress climbing a mulberry tree to sit on the rooftop at night. I see modest lawns, simple houses, an empty lot that she assures me was the commercial center of the town, fading highway paint, dried-out flowerbeds, a dirt road made impassable by overgrowth, and a billboard promising a new housing subdivision development, Kuaʻuli Estates.

My affectively intoned narration imbues this scene with the sentimental cadences common in genres of family storytelling. Indeed Shigemitsu's affective attachments to a past Kahuku are part of reproductive kinship (kin attachments based on a biological line of reproduction) and a structure of feeling for community, nation, and family, as well as heteronormative networks of obligation, care, futurity, and identity self-extension through blood. My grandmother was sharing stories of her experience of Kahuku's plantation era with me as we trudged along Kamehameha Highway. Crucially her desire to pass on experience, and my receptivity to that inheritance, are part of the historical motion of settler colonialism. Her shared experience becomes family property through colonial media: the discourses, histories, and institutional arrangements that make her claims to Kahuku meaningful and allow me to accept these claims as extensions of my own identity.

I underscore two closely related kinds of time in this scenario: capitalist family time and intergenerational memory. By "underscore," I don't mean "celebrate." Colonialism and capital coordinate to Asian settler family affects in sync with U.S. national time. When they keep this time, Shigemitsu's memories of a past Kahuku, and my feelings for her and her past, become substrates of a settler colonial heritage in which Hawaiʻi can be affectively available to settlers. This is a Hawaiʻi accessed through an experience of community, work, and family that is heavily coded by values that America claims for itself.

In the usual family record, reproductive kinship retains its weighty sexual, national, and gendered role as an indelible marker of socio-cultural being where familial sentiments supposedly mean something human and eternal about one's ability to transcend the self composed by capital and history. This second weary-walking episode maintains a time that is intimate and familial as well as historically material to colonial capitalism.

Subjective understanding isn't only what holds each kind of time together. Formally family time is an eddy in shifting late capitalist regimes created by a work schedule that harbors a sentimental heart in the domestic haven. Reproductive kinship synchronizes promises of emotional fulfillment with investments in complicit forms of authority, such as capital inheritance and the state's overlapping duties to patriarchy and private property. The interplay between national and capitalist temporalities that compose family time has ambivalent effects, although it almost always shores up U.S. settler hegemony. This shoring up happens when feelings for family coordinate with settler colonial national reproduction. U.S. citizenship legitimates subjects, like grandparents, who cabin sex within the reproductive couple form. Asian settlers' claims to Hawai'i as their family home invoke this sexual structure of national authority, and through family, colonialism entwines physical being and national territoriality. Yet these are not inevitably entwined. Kinship's flesh-and-blood patrilineality compels *reading* the experience of familiality as a way of belonging to the (settler colonial) nation. The very need for an interpretive apparatus suggests the variability of reading the reproductive family's works for the (settler colonial) nation-state. Pedagogies of U.S. citizenship proceed from public education, property inheritance, and military veterans' benefits, educating citizens about what their kinship identities meant to the nation.[19] These lessons teach citizens to make familial being bear the meaning of attachments to a U.S.-occupied Hawai'i.

Even if national family forms have discontinuous meanings across historical contexts, they almost always situate one's familial being within institutions of capital, colonialism, and the liberal state. The modern nation-state borrows forms of authority from the family to compile governance techniques (patriarchy, capitalism, and citizenship) that offer a conceptual frame for what is colonial about settler kinship. I'm referring to an art of government that manages a population through national values, conventions, and familial kin-relation networks that figuratively root settler colonists.[20] Motherhood, family values, home, generations of residence, and filiation are also common entries in the nation's conventional primers of kin identity.

Sentimental figures of home, family, "honest" labor, and intimately suffered racism that riddle Asian settler history achieve their affective values because of their currency in a settler colonial order. That is, a settler colonial context produces the putatively private meanings of being part of a family and the workforce that "built" Hawai'i, as well as Shigemitsu's Kahuku town, as claims to belonging to a place and time. Understood as a process of home making in a U.S. Hawai'i, Shigemitsu's felt place-based attachments to Kahuku, and my historical extension through them, are made into a rooted, intergenerational heritage that competes with accounts of Hawaiian displacement from land.

Kinship's privileged relationship with natural birth allies with the state to install citizenship into the meaning and matter of one's physical being—a notion of citizenship by birthplace and blood.[21] Convergent institutions of *jus soli* and *jus sanguinis* citizenship facilitate the nation's capacity to poach a narrative birth from the terrain of reproductive kinship.[22] Problematically the collaboration with naturalness tends to make reproductive kinship opaque to interrogation. How, for instance, does my kin relationship to my grandmother *not* naturally fit into a national story of familial belonging? Family's fitness as an alternative scaffolding for Asian settler historicity is at stake in this question.

Another reading of the family story in my grandmother's highway-walking scene may offer this alternative scaffold for an Asian

settler historical subject. Such a subject seems possible in a negotiation with the heteronormative, patriarchal, and classist limits of
reproductive kinship that expands the realm of acting outside of
the person history has set one up to be.

Family timelines are smaller and episodic and tend to be insensi-
tive to the grandiosity that characterizes the nation's official history. Attention to the time of family allows historical space for Asian
settler subjects as more than misplaced in a decolonizing present.
While identified within them, Shigemitsu's feelings for a Kahuku
home sit at a remove from colonial state heritage-making projects
or public pronouncements that Hawai'i belongs to everyone, especially "Americans." I'm proposing a context in which her feelings and mine would not be forced into an equation between place-
based modes of being-historical and a claim to that place.

Sensation, Historicity, and Colonialism

I have made much of my grandmother lost in a moment, as an intergenerational transmission of cultural memory. She's giving herself, and me, a history by weaving together a plantation town past
with an embodied present. Shigemitsu wasn't quite proclaiming
her history as a claim to Kahuku-land, which, not incidentally,
has recently been released to private developers by the James T.
Campbell Estate, one of the original white capitalist dynasties of
Hawai'i's plantation era. However, her remembering and feeling
are doing the work of synthesizing self and history by connecting
to lands that are under Native contest and reproducing them for
family memory.[23] That this can now be considered *colonizing* work
owes much to its insertion into structures of heteronormative kinship and a U.S.-authored notion of good community.

In this sense, decolonization means parsing convergent processes that turn family being into evidence that Hawai'i is part of an
(Asian) American history. One such process is sensation, the naming of a sense as a feeling, the insertion of that name into systems
of social intelligibility, and then the matching of meaning with a
truth claim. Diffracting emotions, experience, and memory over

the distance of this relay can slow down their conversion into the sites of political meaning.

Karen Kosasa and Stanley Tomita offer one articulation of sensation and colonial temporality: "Only Hawaiians can fully understand the destruction of their culture; as settlers we have been *too busy* benefiting from colonial practices."[24] Importantly they emphasize that being "too busy" is a political act insofar as it describes a competition for resources of time, labor, and attention. Undoing this sense of time's scarcity—being too busy—suggests that decolonization involves a shift in sensation. This undoing means reinstalling sensations that thicken attachments to settler colonial regimes, particularly those sensations that feel immediate and natural. The idea is that undoing (not just historicizing) affective, corporeal, felt dimensions of attachments that keep us engrossed in broken political systems, like a U.S.-occupied Hawai'i, might allow us to remake those attachments.

Bodily sensations are historical writings. Elizabeth Freeman explains how. In the United States workers experienced the modern temporalities engendered by industrialization in affective terms: "The nineteenth century's celebrated sentimental heart, experienced by its owner as the bearer of archaic or recalcitrant sensations, was the laboring body's double, the flip side of the coin of industrialization. Mourning and romance, empathy and affection, even 'family time,' were not segmented into clock time, and in this sense, they countered 'work time,' even if they were also a dialectical product of it."[25] Read within this rubric, Shigemitsu's time to herself could be a countertempo, an outside to domestic labor engendered by the waged working day. Here opposing a capitalist regime is not the same as decolonization. The slow time of feeling is both engendered through off-the-clock time and an integral component of the sentimental domestic sphere. Further, sentimental settler nostalgia is more often a mode of colonial complicity whereby the nation fulfills its role in organizing familial selves into citizens. The national value of the normal family utilizes family feeling, an aftereffect of the family wage, to site "America" in the goodness that governs domestic units (filiation, industrious housekeeping, breadwinning, monogamy, etc.).

Like the set of bodily sensations that are rendered new at the cusp of modern industrialization, vestiges of a Fordist apparatus triangulate the time of family feeling in Shigemitsu's walk into new structures of sentimental attachments to U.S. settler colonialism.[26] While Shigemitsu is taking time for herself, the space produced in its difference from her usual care work is meeting up with a mechanism whereby it enacts another kind of work for forces that maintain Hawai'i as a U.S. state. In this way her walk is recruited into deeply meaningful attachments to a colonial regime. The whole process is nearly seamless because, in Marxist terms, the labor is not felt to be alienated.

Family memories *can* be aggressively sentimental claims to belonging, but not always. This other time can occur in moments that show what is *un*inevitable about family. When family is not working for the settler colonial nation or capital, it might hold a viable decolonizing story of an Asian settler subject. *Un*inevitably entwined with U.S. national time, reproductive kinship's invaginated space of capital time might be used to interrogate Asian settler affects in ways that do not sync with national history. Detaching Shigemitsu's walk, and my presence in it, from nation-making narratives may give us another space in time that doesn't compete, or at least competes differently, with Hawaiian histories. Such a space contrasts with Kotani's version, which competes with accounts of colonialism by positing Japanese Americans as a later line of "immigrants, beginning with the first Polynesian settlers."[27]

Family time, as Shigemitsu shows me, is not only the rhythms of social and physical reproduction. They are also times taken *out* from the present. I made that moment of watching her walk around into an image for cultural memory. But I didn't just see a claim to cultural heritage in Kahuku through her; I also saw her departing from her care-worker self. Her meandering along the highway was striking because, for once, I did not see her in a scene of "activity towards reproducing life . . . to making it or oneself *better*."[28]

For perhaps the first time in my adult life, I saw her *not* engaged in reproductive labor. She's an older sister, wife, five-time mother, eight-time grandmother, and four-time great-grandmother. So it was odd to see this woman, whose body was perpetually connected to shopping bags or bent in attention to others' appetites, weightlessly wandering forward. It seemed I witnessed her taking a leave of absence from herself, a leave-taking from her personality.

Shigemitsu's meanderings might instead offer a figure for thinking about the aleatory dimension of settler lifeworlds in ways that can disturb the ways they are "unknowingly . . . a part" of the business of maintaining a colonized Hawai'i.[29] "Families," Michael Shapiro argues, "are the ('often arbitrary') after-effects of political and economic forces."[30] Likewise I'm suggesting that the time Shigemitsu takes out for familial remembering and the intergenerational resonances of her acts might be an eddy, moving contrary to the direction of the main current of a history that produces it. Not inevitably tied to the reproduction of the national settler community, family time might pace a countertempo to Asian settler history's synchronicity with U.S. settler colonialism. Insofar as Shigemitsu's memory event stops the binding of family time with heteronormative nationality, her nostalgia for Kahuku, her feelings and my presence to that past, might run contrary to a case for a U.S. Hawai'i. That is, instead of falling toward genres of "growing-up local" storytelling (that tend to configure Hawai'i only as an Asian settler home), her story might insert uncertainties about the care worker who fostered that growing up.

A decolonized history must be a place patient with uncertain moments. At the same time that it organizes real pasts, decolonized histories are spaces within which subjects gestate, fantasize, hope, and otherwise reorient a seemingly established sense of being in history.[31] This is the staging of Shigemitsu's walk at a conjuncture of affect, experience, and modes of production. Her remembering self suggests what is *changeable* about subjects in relation to history. In this scene transgression does not comport with intention-driven resistance, but in the course of remembering, Shigemitsu's feelings for *this* plantation place instruct us about the ambivalence of identity. At that moment her identity is ambivalent because it is a respite from who she "is." That she was unaware of the processes that I am proposing is important. Agency is something other than awareness here. Action was neither unthinking nor "synonymous with agency in the tactical or effectual sense dedicated to self-negation or self-extension."[32] She was not *trying* to extend herself, but was taking a "small vacation" at "sites of episodic intermissions from personality."[33] Seeking respite suggests coping rather than conscious resistance, and it is precisely this point in the process where familiality mimics the rhythms of sociohistorical awareness. This is the seduction of kinship's protocols, which can offer a respite from the need to assert oneself socially or guard against unbelonging.

Insofar as hers are a respite from a care worker identity, Shigemitsu's movements show how feelings can be temporal contexts. Remembering took up time; it created a "moment of negative density" in which she wasn't saturated with activities of reproducing her usual self.[34] This slowed-down time *might* be a pace that lets reproducing one's historicity disengage from hegemonic versions of what that history is supposed to mean: to slow down a near-automatic attachment of sensation to feeling, feeling to social meaning, and from there embedding that deep meaning into a national attachment. She *acted this way* in the course of remembering something and thus took a momentary departure from who she is now by renarrating what was *then*. In this pause she posited the possibility that reconstituting feelings for our pasts can become ways of inhabiting Hawai'i differently from what our personal and national histories have usually predicted for us. It may not matter whether she was aware of her difference from herself. Slowing down may allow denaturalizing seemingly opaque processes of feeling through which identities attach to certain, particularly national, versions of history.

Conclusion

Asian settlers in Hawai'i cannot have an "American" history anymore. Parsed into different times, nationality appears an uninevitable process whereby diverse senses of being in time are interpreted as attachments to that nation's version of history. I mean to introduce uncertainty about feelings that invest us in histories and, crucially, allow us to be present to decolonizing struggles. Pluralizing the points in this relay between sensation, hegemony, and interpretation undermines the idea that having a long, hard history in Hawai'i exempts one from settler colonial complicities. My reading of Kotani's history cautions against holding a history of progress under U.S. capitalism too tightly. I look to a possibility for loosening this grip in another walking episode, a familial pathway between past and present Hawai'i. While Kahuku's protesting plantation workers have been incorporated into a past that progresses within a U.S. national history, Shigemitsu's storytelling inhabits both the future history of these trekkers and a colonial present. That colonial present approaches what we're left with when history falls away from national narration. These leftovers are important because they fill the distance from U.S. history that a decolonizing Hawai'i demands.

Heeding Berlant's caution that "shifts in affective atmosphere are not equal to changing the world," I conclude by pointing to limits that inhere in my approach to decolonizing Asian settler histories.[35] That is, I close by making a problem out of my project. This project offers a nuanced view of colonial power, deeply historicized and patiently attentive to singularity and its eruption in strange and unexpected places that are supposed to mean the most to and about us — like feelings, grandmothers, and intergenerational connectivity. But my work calls for more research, teaching, and understanding — scholarly activities that may risk the assumption that taking the time to know more will make a better political world. In other words, does my approach imbue decolonization with too much quietude? Does tracking subjects in the shape of their feelings about family, nation, and history shake up their attachments to colonial orders? Or does it merely redescribe the reasons people remain attached to colonialism?

There are ways of valorizing people who can be lost in a moment as cultivated selves who can flourish amid dehumanizing and impersonal economic forces.[36] It might be that the time taken to feel something remains a mute oasis around which capital time flows, uninterrupted. Thus the event remains structured by, enfolded within, and complicit with political, economic, and historical components of colonization. If this is the case, Shigemitsu's walk does nothing but while away an afternoon in the course of colonial business as usual. We might ask, Is hers a break from colonial capitalist circuits, or a way of living in them?

In light of these uncertainties, I much prefer Haunani-Kay Trask's analysis, which straddles academic and activist roles and resolves into direct prescriptions. Don't come to Hawai'i and donate your car, money, or legal expertise, and don't show up to vote for Native Hawaiian initiatives.[37] Money and body-count matter when you're talking about the genocidal impulses of U.S. colonialism. Put plainly, I've presented a complex way of archiving Asian settler pasts that works within the limits of knowledge production. Nevertheless I want to close by pointing to those limits as an asymptotic relationship between academic inquiries and the time of activist struggle, which will be the test of what any history will mean in the long run.

Notes

1. In *Hawai'i v. The Office of Hawaiian Affairs et al.* (2009), No. 07-1372, the U.S. Supreme Court decided that the Apology does "not [use] the kind of language Congress uses to create substantive rights, especially rights enforceable against the cosovereign States."

2. In Hawai'i, "Hawaiian" implicitly refers to the Native peoples of Hawai'i. Out of recognition of the space from which I write, I retain this convention.

3. Haunani-Kay Trask, "The Birth of the Modern Hawaiian Movement: Kalama Valley, O'ahu," *Hawaiian Journal of History* 21 (1987): 126–53; Bob Nakata, "The Struggles of the Waiahole-Waikane Community Association," in "The Ethnic Studies Story: Politics and Social Movements in Hawai'i," ed. Ibrahim G. Aoudé, special issue, *Social Process in Hawai'i* 30 (1999): 60–73.

4. In 1898, 1.4 million acres of lands were ceded to the U.S. federal government upon annexation and then to the State of Hawai'i in 1959, when Hawai'i became a U.S. state. Another 180,000 acres is currently held in trust by the State of Hawai'i under the Department of Hawaiian Homelands.

5. Patrick Wolfe, *Settler Colonialism and the Transformation of Anthropology: The Politics and Poetics of an Ethnographic Event* (New York: Continuum International, 1999), 2.

6. Michel Foucault, *Power/Knowledge: Selected Interviews and Other Writings, 1972–1977*, ed. and trans. Colin Gordon (New York: Pantheon Books, 1980).

7. Roland Kotani, *The Japanese of Hawaii: A Century of Struggle*, the Official Program Booklet of the Oahu Kanyaku Imin Centennial Committee (Honolulu: Hawaii Hochi, 1985), 43.

8. Ronald Takaki, *Pau Hana: Plantation Life and Labor in Hawaii 1835–1920* (Honolulu: University of Hawai'i Press, 1983), 132.

9. Takaki, *Pau Hana*.

10. George Cooper and Gavan Daws, *Land and Power in Hawaii: The Democratic Years* (Honolulu: Benchmark Books, 1985).

11. Michael J. Shapiro, "National Times and Other Times: Re-Thinking Citizenship," *Cultural Studies* 14, no. 1 (2000): 79–98.

12. Shapiro, "National Times and Other Times," 80.

13. Gayatri Chakravorty Spivak, *A Critique of Postcolonial Reason: Toward a History of the Vanishing Present* (Cambridge MA: Harvard University Press, 1999), 199.

14. Because these plantation laborers were bound by private contracts, strikes were illegal. These workers welcomed the Organic Act (1900), which effectively annexed Hawai'i, because it also ended the contract labor system. Takaki, *Pau Hana*, 148.

15. This is "racist love," which happens when a marginalized group falsely claims a racial identity on the premise that such a reductive misrecognition is still more than none. See Lisa Kahaleole Hall, "'Hawaiian at Heart' and Other Fictions," *Contemporary Pacific* 17, no. 2 (2005): 404–13.

16. Judith Butler, "Is Kinship Always Already Heterosexual?" in *Left Legalism/Left Critique*, ed. Wendy Brown and Janet Halley (Durham NC: Duke University Press, 2002), 243.

17. Preserving a "plantation heritage" is part of the institutional mandate of organizations like the Kahuku Village Association, the Hawai'i Plantation Village, and the Hawai'i Japanese Cultural Center. Pat Pitzer, "Kahuku: The Preservation of a Plucky Plantation Town," *Honolulu Magazine* 12, no. 3 (1977), www.hawaiiplantationvillage.org; "Hawaii's Plantation Village: Living History Museum and Botanical Garden at Waipahu Cultural Garden Park," www.hawaiiplantationvillage.org.

18. Elspeth P. Sterling and Catherine P. Summers, "Kukio Pond: Site 262," in *Sites of Oahu* (Honolulu: Bishop Museum Press, 1978).

19. Jacqueline Stevens, *Reproducing the State* (Princeton NJ: Princeton University Press, 1999), 35.

20. Michel Foucault, "Governmentality," in *The Foucault Effect: Studies in Governmentality*, ed. Graham Burchell, Colin Gordon, and Peter Miller (Chicago: University of Chicago Press, 1991), 92.

21. Lauren Berlant, *The Anatomy of National Fantasy: Hawthorne, Utopia and Everyday Life* (Chicago: University of Chicago Press, 1991), 20.

22. Stevens, *Reproducing the State*.

23. Kahuku town abuts ceded lands, which are used by the Kahuku Military Training Area.

24. Karen K. Kosasa and Stan Tomita, "Whose Vision, 2000," *Amerasia Journal* 26, no. 2 (2000): xii, emphasis mine.

25. Elizabeth Freeman, "Turn the Beat Around: Sadomasochism, Temporality, History," *Differences: A Journal of Feminist Cultural Studies* 19, no. 1 (2008): 33.

26. Among other things, Fordism is the scientific management of household consumption and factory production. In this circuit, the domestic household is a haven in a heartless world.

27. Franklin Odo and Kazuko Sinoto, *A Pictorial History of the Japanese in Hawai'i* (Honolulu: Bishop Museum Press, 1985), 11.

28. Lauren Berlant, "Slow Death (Sovereignty, Obesity, Lateral Agency)," *Critical Inquiry* 33, no. 4 (2007): 778–79.

29. Candace Fujikane and Jonathan Okamura, eds., *Asian Settler Colonialism: From Local Governance to the Habits of Everyday Life* (Honolulu: University of Hawai'i Press, 2008), 20.

30. Shapiro, "National Times and Other Times," 87.

31. I'm paraphrasing Berlant's argument about fantasy and feeling historical. Lauren Berlant, "Intuitionists: History and the Affective Event," *American Literary History* 20, no. 4 (2008): 845–60.

32. Berlant, "Slow Death," 778–79.

33. Berlant, "Slow Death," 778–79.

34. Lauren Berlant, "Two Girls, Fat and Thin," in *Regarding Sedgwick: Essays on Queer Culture and Critical Theory*, ed. Stephen M. Barber and David L. Clark (New York: Routledge, 2002), 85.

35. Lauren Berlant, "Cruel Optimism: On Marx, Loss and the Senses," *New Formations* 63, no. 1 (2008): 49.

36. Berlant, "Cruel Optimism," 40.

37. Haunani-Kay Trask, Cynthia Franklin, and Laura E. Lyons, "Land, Leadership, and Nation: Haunani-Kay Trask on the Testimonial Uses of Life Writing in Hawai'i," *Biography* 27, no. 1 (2004): 242.

Chapter 10

Multitasking Mediators
Intracolonial Leadership in Filipino and Puerto Rican
Communities in Hawai'i, 1900–1928

JoAnna Poblete

In 1901 Florentin Souza served as a labor liaison for Puerto Ricans at multiple sugar plantations on the east side of the Island of Hawai'i. He also worked as a manager for the Hawaiian Business Agency in Hilo, where he handled real estate transactions, finance collection, accounting, and general commission projects in the region. During the 1924–25 labor strike in Hawai'i, Flaviano M. Santa Ana spoke on behalf of Filipino laborers at the Ola'a plantation on the east side of the Island of Hawai'i. In addition to his role as a community representative, Santa Ana worked as a member of the plantation special police, a unit of armed men paid by the plantation to maintain order during strike times. His conflicting responsibilities as labor spokesperson and plantation security became further complicated by his position as a Protestant minister. How did these two people come to fill these multiple roles? The larger political-legal context of their regions of origin directly impacted the paths of both Santa Ana and Souza.

After the War of 1898 and the subsequent Treaty of Paris, the U.S. government gained possession and authority over the Spanish colonies of Puerto Rico, the Philippines, and Guam.[1] In 1904 the U.S. Supreme Court ruled that the people from these former Spanish colonies were not aliens of the United States, but the justices refused to rule on whether they were citizens of the United States, stating, "We are not required to discuss [whether] . . . the cession of Porto Rico accomplished the naturalization of its people; or . . . that a citizen of Porto Rico, under the act of 1900, is necessarily a citizen of the United States."[2] The Court's unwillingness to determine the citizenship of these populations resulted in an ambiguous political-legal status. Unlike foreigners, Puerto Ricans and Filipinos were fully subject to U.S. rule. Yet unlike citizens, they did not have full constitutional protections.[3]

Neither citizens nor foreigners, Filipinos and Puerto Ricans also did not have independent government officials representing them.[4] Foreign laborers in Hawai'i had consuls general residing in Honolulu with official power and local influence to resolve their daily issues within a week or two. Citizens had locally elected government representatives to address their concerns. Puerto Ricans and Filipinos did not have local official leadership in the Hawaiian Islands due to their ambiguous status as wards of the United States.[5] The absence of permanent government representatives made Puerto Ricans and Filipinos heavily reliant on community leaders, like Souza and Santa Ana, to deal with their everyday affairs. While foreign migrants also worked with neighborhood mediators, U.S. colonials were dependent on these unofficial community leaders for services that foreign consuls general usually handled.[6] Souza and Santa Ana became two of the best options for local leadership in the Puerto Rican and Filipino labor community on the Island of Hawai'i. Literate and fluent in both English and the workers' dialect, these men were two of just a handful of individuals who could explain employer and government expectations to these non-English-speaking groups of migrant workers. These factors resulted in Souza and Santa Ana handling multiple, contradictory responsibilities in the Islands.

Overall nongovernmental Filipino and Puerto Rican ethnic mediators played a greater role in the daily lives of intracolonials than in the lives of foreigners or citizens in the Territory of Hawai'i. Although Lisa Rose Mar has demonstrated the importance of labor brokers for Chinese immigrants in Canada, scholars of immigration and labor often do not discuss the importance of community ethnic mediators in much detail.[7] Instead recent scholarship on migrant labor has focused on issues of citizenship, state control, and transnationalism.[8] This essay demonstrates how community ethnic mediators were among the few trusted leaders for Filipino and Puerto Rican intracolonials living thousands of miles away from their home regions.

Despite their legally identical classification by the Treaty of Paris and the Supreme Court, Filipinos and Puerto Ricans have generally not been analyzed together in academic scholarship. The sociologists Julian Go and Lanny Thompson have conducted the most recent studies of both groups, focusing on the political impact of U.S. colonialism in each region.[9] Continuing their efforts to compare Filipino and Puerto Rican experiences, I have developed the category of *U.S. colonial*.[10] This overarching term can be applied to all groups who have come under some form of U.S. authority, including American Indians, Chicanos in the Southwest, Native Tejanos, Alaska Natives, Native Hawaiians, Puerto Ricans, Filipinos, Chamorros in the Northern Marianas and Guam, American Sāmoans, and U.S. Virgin Islanders. Such dependents, or wards of the United States, have historically existed as a result of U.S. expansionism or the extension of U.S. authority over areas beyond its official borders. Starting with the removal of American Indians in the nineteenth century and continuing in the twenty-first century with U.S. presence in areas like American Sāmoa and the U.S. Virgin Islands, the U.S. government has repeatedly taken charge of regions outside its jurisdiction. Even though the specific political-legal relationship of each U.S. colonial group with the United States has varied, they all occupied positions subordinate to the interests of the U.S. federal government. The concept of U.S. colonials emphasizes the imperial status of each group and calls attention to the impact of U.S. authority in their daily lives. The consequent regulation and treatment of U.S. colonials fundamentally differed from those of foreigners and citizens.

To develop an understanding of general U.S. colonial experiences, I explore the migration and labor histories of Filipinos and Puerto Ricans. As wards of the United States, Filipinos and Puerto Ricans were partially protected by the U.S. Constitution and fully subject to U.S. authority. This in-between political legal status enabled them to move freely within the U.S. Empire, despite the strict anti-immigration legislation of the period.[11] Both groups migrated to the U.S. Territory of Hawai'i to work on sugar plantations in the first half of the twentieth century. As colonized people living in a second colonized place, a status I call *intracolonial*, Filipinos and Puerto Ricans lived five thousand miles from the center of imperial power in Washington DC and the same distance from their home regions.

The concept of intracoloniality is a new direction for scholarship on U.S. colonialism. Scholars such as Frederick Cooper, Amy Kaplan, and Ann Laura Stoler have examined the impact of the colonizer in the colonized region, the influence of colonization on the culture of the metropole, and the impact of colonialism on the identity of the colonized.[12] Building on these works, my analysis examines the complications involved in moving from a colonial home region to another area of the same empire. Such intracolonial mobility resulted in a local leadership vacuum. Without long-term local official government representatives to champion their issues, Puerto Ricans and Filipinos in Hawai'i relied on informal ethnic mediators. Local community members like Souza and Santa Ana became multitasking leaders for Puerto Rican and Filipino intracolonials because they could speak their native language and help negotiate regional policies, daily issues, and moments of crisis.

Other scholars have studied the various ways U.S. imperialism has impacted the individual regions of Puerto Rico and the Philippines. Alfred McCoy and Francisco Scarano's expansive anthology, *The Colonial Crucible*, brought together studies of U.S. colonialism in Puerto Rico and the Philippines, as well as other imperial locations like Cuba and Hawai'i. The essays in this collection, however, generally focus on one area at a time.[13] To add to these studies about government policies and identity politics, I discuss the influences of intracolonial mobility on more than one group of U.S. colonials in the same time and place to demonstrate both the similarities and differences in their experiences.

Outside Hawai'i few people learn about the history of Puerto Rican migration to and labor in the Islands. Filipinos, in contrast, are seen as almost synonymous with plantation labor in Hawai'i, with close to one hundred community organizations in the Islands. Such discrepancies in contemporary Filipino and Puerto Rican visibility in Hawai'i are directly linked to each group's differential access to local mediators who could fill the leadership gaps that were products of their in-between political-legal status as U.S. colonials in a second colonized space.

Between 1912 and 1933 the Filipino community in Hawai'i had access to Filipino union organizers, temporary labor commissioners from the Philippines, and between 1923 and 1933 a resident labor commissioner.[14] Puerto Ricans, in contrast, had access to only a few private labor agents and unofficial charismatic individuals. Without as many local advocates to publicize their issues and struggles, Puerto Ricans became an invisible population in the political, social, economic, and religious life of Hawai'i. Despite efforts by the Puerto Rican community to increase knowledge about their role in Hawai'i, the invisibility of their experiences and history continues today.[15]

To understand the similar impact that intracolonial status had on both Puerto Ricans and Filipinos, this chapter focuses on how unofficial mediators for each group could access and straddle the worlds of both intracolonial workers and Anglo sugar plantation management more effectively than temporary government or union representatives. Despite the differences in the amount of local leadership available for Filipinos and Puerto Ricans, both Santa Ana and Souza became important advocates and mediators for them *and* sugar plantation management at the same time and place.

Becoming Mediators

In 1901 Florentin Souza lobbied to obtain the position of labor liaison for Puerto Ricans at multiple plantations on the east side of

the Island of Hawai'i. On his own volition he contacted the Pepeekeo, Hakalau, and Ola'a plantations, offering his "services for
all matters in connection with Porto-Rican laborers," saying, "I
wish to help the Plantations to keep them."[16] As a manager for the
Hawaiian Business Agency in Hilo, Souza was familiar with both
U.S. business practices and Puerto Rican culture. He was also fluent in Spanish and English. According to Claudio Lomnitz-Adler,
power brokers built ties "between the locality and state and private
institutions."[17] These go-betweens had special access to or knowledge of political, social, and/or economic power structures. Their
monopolization of certain values and processes became essential
to their positions as influential multitasking community mediators.
Souza's own broad skill set positioned him to become a powerful
mediator for both Puerto Rican workers and local sugar management in the Islands. In fact many Puerto Ricans approached him
for help. Souza stated, "Knowing their country, their habits and
their language, the Porto Ricans have found their way to me, with
a great variety of requests."[18] These Latino intracolonials viewed
Souza as a trustworthy compatriot and believed he would assist
them with their work issues. He identified the need for leadership
in this Latino community and actively worked to fill this vacuum.

Filipinos at the Ola'a plantation were also looking for an ethnic
leader. In 1915 Leon Foronda wrote the Protestant Church leadership in the Islands, known as the Hawaiian Evangelical Association (HEA): "No doubt you inderstand that what the Filipinos need
in Hawaii is a leader, and we need one bad in Pahoa and Olaa . . .
for who would want to sell his country or misrepresent his country."[19] Intracolonials at this location believed a Filipino minister
would be a loyal and much needed advocate for them. Protestant
Filipinos at Ola'a also wanted a pastor they could relate to: someone who looked like them, spoke like them, and came from the
same culture. Appeals like Foronda's encouraged the HEA to start
employing Filipino ethnic ministers. In 1917 the HEA Board of
Trustees sent Flaviano Santa Ana to the Ola'a plantation to help
all Filipinos, Protestant or not. Thus both Santa Ana and Souza

started working for intracolonials in Hawai'i in response to direct requests for local assistance and leadership from the Filipinos and Puerto Ricans themselves.

The leadership gap among intracolonials in Hawai'i also meant the sugar industry had no official representative they could communicate with to manage Filipino and Puerto Rican issues. Without a local government leader with whom he could work, A. J. Watt, the Ola'a plantation manager from 1922 to 1938, hired Santa Ana to help with the plantation's daily interactions with the non-English-speaking Filipino workers. Watt gave Santa Ana free housing, a partial salary, and free household amenities. He also supplied Santa Ana's church with land at very low rent, offered discounted prices on construction lumber, and gave monetary donations for other needs.[20] In return Santa Ana was responsible for addressing any and all Filipino issues that came to the plantation manager. He acted as a translator for the plantation office, met Filipino laborers upon arrival, and helped them get settled. He also distributed letters from the Philippines to workers in the camps, delivered contract cards for the plantation, and disseminated plantation communications to workers. Due to the intracolonial leadership vacuum in the Islands, Watt depended on Santa Ana for his knowledge, connections, and influence over the plantation's main source of labor: Filipinos.

Plantation management also worked closely with Protestant ethnic ministers like Santa Ana because they were part of the HEA, the powerful pro-plantation and pro-colonial religious institution in Hawai'i. Historically, Protestant missionaries in Hawai'i functioned as a significant part of the U.S. colonial project in the Islands.[21] Plantation owners and management knew these ethnic ministers were supervised by and subject to the directions of pro-business Anglo religious leaders. Affiliation with the HEA gave Santa Ana legitimacy and access to Filipinos on private plantation land.

Plantation managers on the east side of the Island of Hawai'i also relied on Souza for help with intracolonials in the Puerto Rican community. F. B. McStocker, the Ola'a plantation manager

from 1899 to 1904, acknowledged that an interpreter was needed for his interactions with Puerto Ricans. He knew poor translation could lead to frequent labor disputes, stating, "If we wish to
avoid misunderstanding and consequently trouble, an intelligent
interpreter of their needs medical and otherwise is required."[22]
Administrators sought an educated individual to help them maintain a stable and amiable Puerto Rican labor force on their plantations, and Souza happily pursued and filled this potentially profitable leadership position.

As an independent contractor, Souza charged plantation managers a flat rate of $25 for handling all Puerto Rican issues in commu-
nities with fewer than one hundred laborers. Since the sugar industry highly valued a stable labor force, and Puerto Rican laborers had
a tendency to move from plantation to plantation when they were
unhappy, he felt justified in charging 35 cents for each laborer who
worked steadily on plantations with more than one hundred laborers. Working on three different plantations on the east side of the
Island of Hawai'i, Souza earned about $137 per month from these
fees. This salary was $117 more than the monthly earnings of an
average Puerto Rican field laborer who completed back-breaking
agricultural labor six days a week for ten hours a day. In addition
to these payments from the sugar industry, Souza also charged the
workers when he obtained jobs on their behalf. In this way the leadership vacuum in the Puerto Rican intracolonial community helped
Souza create an extremely profitable niche for himself in the Islands.

As employees of the plantation, Souza's and Santa Ana's opinions and recommendations were more influential than those of other community mediators, such as union leaders, who did not have
any direct affiliation with the sugar industry. In fact labor organizers were often closely monitored and harassed by plantation administrators and local police. Filipino workers also did not trust
the temporary labor commissioners from the Philippines. These
representatives usually associated closely with the sugar planters
during their visits. Santa Ana and Souza, in contrast, had the trust
and support of both workers and plantation managers.

Without a permanent government representative for Filipinos and Puerto Ricans in the region, laborers and administrators needed local mediators to help them interact with each other. Both groups relied on Souza and Santa Ana for daily assistance. This labor agent and this Protestant ethnic minister consequently occupied particularly powerful multitasking broker positions on the east side of the Island of Hawai'i.

Services Provided

Due to the lack of permanent official local government representatives for intracolonials in Hawai'i, Santa Ana and Souza addressed a wide variety of issues. Santa Ana provided the Filipino community at the Ola'a plantation with both religious services and practical assistance on a daily basis. He conducted Sunday worship, Sunday school, prayer meetings, religious interviews, and other religious activities. He also developed a women's group, children's Bible study, and choir. In addition to church-related activities, he helped Filipino intracolonials with a wide range of nonreligious activities such as mediating domestic disputes and financial issues, providing transport to the hospital, and interpreting and writing work-related and personal communications on behalf of laborers. Santa Ana helped about ten people a week, or 405 people in a fourteen-month period. He spent twenty weeks bringing sick people to the hospital, eighteen weeks helping people apply for return passage back to the Philippines, eighteen requesting plantation jobs for Filipinos, fourteen addressing the personal troubles of individuals, and seven dealing with plantation-related issues.[23] Without any permanent official leadership in the Islands, about 40 percent of the one thousand Filipinos at the Ola'a plantation went to Santa Ana for help with secular issues. They relied on him to negotiate with plantation managers, file a variety of paperwork, and assist them with their personal needs.

Souza also facilitated communication between Puerto Rican laborers and plantation leadership about a variety of labor and personal issues. Puerto Rican workers in Hawai'i wanted to make sure they received comparable and fair wages. They greatly despised being insulted by their work supervisors. Souza also found that Puerto Ricans wanted "medical attention . . . and better employment," and he wrote, "I have helped them in both matters."[24] For example, in August 1901 Souza wrote McStocker about his investigation of twelve workers who had abandoned the Mountain View camp. He believed these men stopped working for one of two reasons: either one of the laborers incorrectly translated information for the rest of the work gang or the field overseer (*luna*) was mistreating the workers. Souza stated that the impromptu translator in the work group told the others that "the luna called one of them 'S-of-a-B' and moved as if to strike him."[25] This man also told his fellow workers that the non-Spanish-speaking luna disliked all of them and planned to fire them at some point. Since Puerto Ricans often refused to stay at plantations where they were treated poorly, these laborers abandoned their work to avoid further abuse and perhaps show solidarity for their compatriot. Souza spoke to them and promised to get them a new Spanish-speaking luna if they promised to return to work. He also explained the misunderstanding to McStocker and requested a new supervisor who could speak Spanish to oversee this work gang. Souza linguistically and conceptually translated the issues of Puerto Rican workers to the plantation management, helping McStocker comprehend the actions of the laborers. He helped the Puerto Ricans understand their new job environment and the employers understand the perspective of their new laborers. He facilitated the clear communication of expectations and perspectives of both employees and employers to each other.

Souza's and Santa Ana's ability to straddle both the non-English-speaking world of U.S. colonial workers and the English-speaking realm of Anglo leadership in Hawai'i combined with the gap in local leadership for Puerto Rican and Filipino intracolonials to place them in powerful positions in the Islands. Their ability and willingness to assist plantations in the management of intracolonials led to their employment and acceptance within the sugar industry.

Cooperation with plantations also gave them access to workers on private plantations. Daily contact with workers provided Santa Ana and Souza with special insight intro the attitudes and needs in the Filipino and Puerto Rican communities on the east side of the Island of Hawai'i.

Intracolonial laborers relied on Souza and Santa Ana to appropriately translate and submit their issues to plantation management. Anglo leadership also relied on these two men to maintain stability among the Puerto Rican and Filipino workers. Since other local mediators did not have direct relationships with the plantation managers, they did not have the same kind of access or influence over plantation administrators and policies. Santa Ana and Souza consequently provided crucial daily assistance for both intracolonials and sugar plantation management in Hawai'i.

Mediator Motivations

While they both provided essential services for workers and employers, Souza's and Santa Ana's reasons for involvement in the intracolonial communities were quite different. Souza readily admitted his profit-oriented motivations to fill the Puerto Rican leadership vacuum in the Hawaiian Islands. In a letter to the Pepeekeo plantation manager, he wrote, "I must be frank in saying that I also wish to do some thing for myself and I feel sure of my influence with these people."[26] Because four-fifths of his monthly commission for labor mediation was dependent on the number of Puerto Ricans who remained on each plantation, Souza had extreme self-interest in keeping Puerto Ricans happy, or at least steady workers.

To this end, Souza created the Porto Rican Association. Generally mutual benefit societies required a nominal yearly membership fee in return for burial services and other types of financial aid during times of crisis.[27] Souza acknowledged that he used this association as a way to get Puerto Ricans to stay on their assigned plantation: "I have told every one of them, that if they leave your plantation, I will never give them any assistance, and that they will also lose all their rights to the protection of the 'Porto-Rican' Association, which object is to better their condition in every way, providing that they obey the instructions of the Association. This has so far had the very best influence to make them stay in one place. They all want to be registered in the Association and have it as their protection in case of any trouble. As I have the sole management and control of the Association and I only send those registered in it."[28]

Puerto Ricans relied on Souza for protection through the Porto Rican Association, but he also used this organization to create a more stable, hence more profitable workforce. He saw the vulnerability of the Puerto Ricans and their great need for a Spanish-speaking leader or organization to look after their own interests, and he capitalized on that need to obtain members. Once workers became part of this group, Souza used their desire for local protection and advocacy as a way to control their movement. Puerto Rican laborers likely felt they had few options other than to follow Souza's directions. Not able to communicate on their own to non-Spanish-speaking Anglo leaders in Hawai'i, they submitted to Souza's control in exchange for a source of leadership support, guidance, knowledge, and assistance.[29] Puerto Ricans in Hawai'i were consequently subject to Souza's personal profit motivations.

As a revenue-oriented labor agent, Souza felt no obligation to remain loyal to the Puerto Rican intracolonials. In fact his devotion fluctuated with changes in the most profitable means to make money. In February 1901 he explored the possibilities for recruitment of another labor group. He told McStocker, "[Mexicans are] very good laborers from South California, they are of a much better class than the Porto-Ricans. . . . They could be brought direct to Hilo and at much less expense than the Porto-Ricans. I would very much like to have you to make an experiment, because I am sure that they would give you entire satisfaction."[30] He likely recommended this group because he wanted a monopoly on this particular labor source. To promote his recruitment proposal, Souza willingly criticized Puerto Rican intracolonials. As a profit-motivated local leader, he could never be fully trusted or relied upon.

In fact his focus on generating as large an income as possible also

led him to offer non-ethnic-related services to plantation management. Travel to Hilo at the turn of the twentieth century required
the costly use of horses or hours of walking. Souza told plantation
managers he was willing to conduct business in town on their behalf: "Outside of Porto-Rican affairs, you may have some other
errands to which I could attend and as to the salary, I would accept whatever you would consider right."[31] Souza hoped the trust
he had built as a Puerto Rican labor agent would pave the way for
plantation managers to rely on him for a variety of other services.
He wanted to become the go-to guy for sugar industry leaders and
gain additional sources for income.

Although Souza was not a devoted advocate for Puerto Rican
workers, he also was not a pawn of the plantations. He did not care
about the sugar industry's efforts to keep workers at one plantation
for the duration of their three-year work agreements. When plantation managers complained that Souza employed laborers who still
had debt at other plantations, Souza defended himself by stating
that Puerto Ricans came to him and he had no way of knowing
their prior work or debt history. He claimed it was not his job, responsibility, or business to obtain that kind of information. When
hiring workers, he did not bother to check their background. He
focused only on plantation labor needs and warm bodies to fill job
vacancies. He did not favor plantation policies over worker rights.
He just acted in the most profitable way.

Souza, however, did not fill these roles for long. When Puerto Rican labor recruitment ended in 1901, this group became less
central to the plantation workforce, and sugar plantations stopped
paying Souza for his services. Without monetary compensation, he
immediately ended his work as a labor agent. Looking for a more
stable and long-term financial prospect in Hawai'i, he decided to
hire a group of more than one hundred dissatisfied Puerto Ricans
who did not want to return to their original plantations to start
his own sugar-growing business in December 1901. Plantations
contracted with independent farmers to cultivate additional sugar
cane. The farmers were paid after the harvest based on the total

weight of cane supplied. Souza financed the costs of planting and managed the workers in return for a percentage of the total pay-out at harvest time. In this way he continued to profit from Puer-to Rican labor and the sugar industry.

But Souza's move away from general labor mediation among mul-tiple plantations left a huge gap in leadership for the other Puerto Ricans he worked with in Hawai'i. Spanish-speaking Puerto Ri-cans still needed interpreters and local leaders to champion their issues. After Souza's change in career path, the Puerto Rican U.S. colonial community lost a leader who could effectively access and communicate with Anglo leadership on their behalf.

Santa Ana, on the other hand, was motivated to work with Fil-ipino intracolonials by his sense of moral duty and obligation to serve his community, the HEA, the Protestant Church, and God. He focused on providing the best services for Filipinos at Ola'a, with hopes to also convert them to Protestantism.[32] In one weekly re-port to the HEA he wrote, "My work now is going house to h[o]use every afternoon, doing personal work."[33] To free up more time for one-on-one work with Filipinos, Santa Ana reduced the number of open-air meetings he conducted, a standard among evangelists at that time. He changed his HEA-prescribed daily routine to reflect and accommodate the needs of the local intracolonial community.

Despite his efforts to meet the secular and religious needs of Filipinos at Ola'a, they started to disapprove of Santa Ana's work for the plantation. According to Santa Ana, "All the strikers and the strike leaders are against [the] Filipino Pastor, and they call us a Plantation Cat."[34] Protesters believed someone who worked for the plantation could not also work for the interests of laborers. The HEA also questioned Santa Ana's multiple roles at the Ola'a plantation and asked him to solely focus on his religious responsi-bilities. While Santa Ana stopped helping the plantation in 1924, he still assisted the Filipino community with many of the same is-sues as before. As the best source of intracolonial leadership in the area, he continued to bring sick people to the hospital, medi-ate personal troubles, such as domestic disputes and money issues, file applications for return passage, and submit requests for jobs or other plantation-related issues. Regardless of HEA directives to provide only religious aid, Santa Ana prioritized and served the daily personal and work requests of his Filipino community. When the HEA found out he had not stopped his nonreligious activities at Ola'a and that he had no plans to stop doing such work, the organization transferred him to another island and another plantation.[35] The HEA then assigned a new Filipino minister to the Ola'a plantation.

Over the course of the first half of the twentieth century, the Filipino community in the Islands also gained access to local labor organizers, temporary labor commissioners, and a resident labor commissioner. In contrast, Puerto Ricans never obtained a dedicated local official representative to address their issues or handle their complaints, thus they had fewer sources of advocacy and assistance with Anglo leadership. Ironically Puerto Ricans' permanent settlement in the Islands made the presence of local leaders *more* important to them. Filipino laborers, in contrast, often moved back and forth between Hawai'i and the Philippines after the end of their three-year work contracts.[36]

Shifts in Political-Legal Status

Even though Puerto Ricans attained U.S. citizenship in 1917, they were not entitled to, or granted, full membership in the United States. They could not vote at the federal level, and their political relationship with the United States could be revoked at any time by an act of Congress. Local representation for Puerto Ricans in Hawai'i, who were indefinite dependents of the United States, was low on the priority list of the U.S. colonial government. The limited amount of mediators for Puerto Ricans in the Islands meant there were fewer people who could effectively advocate for this group on plantations, in politics, and in the general social community in Hawai'i.

Filipinos, in contrast, continued to obtain local leaders during this period because the U.S. government promised them eventual independence. Early on during U.S. rule in the Philippines, Filipinos became categorized as future aliens who would someday become independent foreigners. This policy was formally established by the Philippine Organic Act, also known as the Philippine Bill of 1902. This temporary act created a Philippine civil government supervised by the U.S. federal government. Eventual sovereignty was confirmed by the 1934 Tydings-McDuffie Act, which promised Philippine independence in ten years. Throughout the twentieth century U.S. officials increasingly transitioned the mediation of Filipino issues from Anglo administrators to Philippine leaders as part of the training for self-rule, or the Filipinization process.[37] This shift from colonization to eventual independence did not occur for Puerto Rico.

In fact Puerto Rico became a commonwealth of the United States in 1935, an imperial status that continues today. As a result of this prolonged subordinate status to the United States, Puerto Ricans in Hawai'i constantly struggled to obtain fair representation and positive acknowledgment in the Islands throughout the twentieth century.[38] Despite gaining U.S. citizenship, Puerto Ricans in Hawai'i faced resistance from local government officials over their efforts to register to vote. They also continued to be stereotyped as lazy and violent. Without local community leaders like Souza, who had the trust and attention of plantation management, Puerto Ricans lost a rare and important source of advocacy and assistance in Hawai'i. Such absences contributed to the lack of attention to Puerto Rican issues in the Islands throughout the twentieth century and the consequent invisibility of these intracolonials and their history in the Pacific.

Conclusion

This comparative study of Filipino and Puerto Rican intracolonial experiences in Hawai'i can provide insights into the shared experiences of past, current, and future wards of the United States. A detailed study of Souza's and Santa Ana's activities contributes to an understanding of the critical role that local community leaders played in the lives of colonized people living and working in a second colonized space. A leadership vacuum existed for all intracolonials. Unofficial local ethnic leaders like Santa Ana and Souza consequently played essential roles in mediating the daily issues of Filipinos and Puerto Ricans in the Islands. These leaders also provided important services for the Hawaiian sugar planters. Santa Ana and Souza worked hard to balance the needs that multiple sectors had for their services and assistance.

Other groups have traveled intracolonially, especially to Hawaiʻi, in the twentieth century. Many American Sāmoans were encouraged to relocate to the Islands by the Mormon community there, and were also attracted by the prospects for a better quality of life and more job opportunities.[39] Chamorros from Guam also compose a significant population in Hawaiʻi.[40] These intracolonial groups, like Filipinos and Puerto Ricans, relied on local ethnic community mediators, such as church leaders, to help them with everyday living and work issues in the Islands.

The in-between political-legal status of all U.S. intracolonials significantly impacts the kind of representatives each group has access to and can rely on for daily assistance. As wards of the United States, colonials have faced and continue to face unique leadership gaps that foreigners and citizens do not experience. With this knowledge, we can acknowledge the existence of U.S. colonials and start to identify commonalities among them across time periods, cultures, and regions. This study also highlights alternative forms of colonial interactions that need more attention and analysis. Research should look beyond the colony and metropole to investigate the complications intracolonials experience living and working in liminal or in-between spaces of empire.

Notes

1. The United States also gained influence over Cuba after the War of 1898. While the Treaty of Paris gave Cuba independence, U.S. troops remained on the island for several years, establishing social and economic structures in the region. The United States also pressured Cubans to

include the Platt Amendment in their 1903 Cuban Constitution. This amendment gave the United States extraordinary land rights and authority over Cuban foreign relations until it was repealed in 1934.

2. *Gonzales v. Williams*, No. 225, 192 U.S. 1, 12. For more detailed discussions of this case, see Christina Duffy Burnett, "'They Say I Am Not an American . . .': The Noncitizen National and the Law of American Empire," *Virginia Journal of International Law* 48, no. 659 (2008): 659–718; Sam Erman, "Meanings of Citizenship in the U.S. Empire: Puerto Rico, Isabel Gonzalez, and the Supreme Court, 1898 to 1905," *Journal of American Ethnic History* 27, no. 4 (2008): 5–33.

3. There was a differential application of constitutional rights to territories and their inhabitants, such as no right to a jury trial, adjusted tariff laws, and lack of federal representation. See Bartholomew H. Sparrow, *The Insular Cases and the Emergence of American Empire: Landmark Law Cases and American Society* (Lawrence: University Press of Kansas, 2006). Puerto Ricans gained U.S. citizenship in 1917, but such status did not result in much change in their treatment in the Territory of Hawai'i. They could access higher paying government jobs, but most local government officials and members of the public looked down on this population. A general ignorance of Puerto Ricans' citizenship status was prevalent in Hawai'i throughout the twentieth century.

4. They had resident commissioners in Washington DC and eventually elected local officials in their home regions. As colonial subjects, however, these leaders were closely monitored and regulated by the U.S. federal government.

5. Filipinos did have access to a resident labor commissioner in 1923, but this position existed for only nine years. The Filipino community in Hawai'i quickly developed distrust of this official and resisted cooperation with him. They even tried to remove him from office several times during his tenure.

6. Chinese, Japanese, Hawaiian, Portuguese, and Spanish-speaking labor groups also had Protestant ethnic ministers in the Islands. However, these workers could and did go to their consuls general, or locally elected representatives in the case of Hawaiians, to obtain secular forms of assistance.

7. Lisa Rose Mar, *Brokering Belonging: Chinese in Canada's Exclusion Era, 1885–1945* (New York: Oxford University Press, 2010).

8. Examples of such work can be found in David Gutierrez and Pierrette Hondagneu-Sotelo, eds., "Nation and Migration: Past and Future," special issue, *American Quarterly* 60, no. 3 (2008).

9. See Julian Go, *American Empire and the Politics of Meaning: Elite Political Cultures in the Philippines and Puerto Rico during U.S. Colonialism* (Durham NC: Duke University Press, 2008); Lanny Thompson, "The Imperial Republic: A Comparison of the Insular Territories under U.S. Dominion after 1898," *Pacific Historical Review* 71, no. 4 (2002): 535–74. Additional comparative work by Faye Caronan Chen is included in this anthology.

10. Historically Filipinos have been categorized as U.S. nationals. Puerto Ricans were classified as citizens of Puerto Rico until they became U.S. citizens in 1917.

11. The Chinese Exclusion Acts of the 1880s prohibited Chinese laborers, or anyone of this nationality suspected of becoming a public ward, from entering the United States. The Gentleman's Agreement of 1907 halted the entry of Japanese laborers to the United States. The 1924 National Origins Act reduced immigration quotas to 2 percent of a country's foreign-born residents living in the United States in 1890. Since Western Europeans composed the majority of foreign-born peoples that year, this legislation effectively ended the immigration of non–Western Europeans into the United States until 1965.

12. Frederick Cooper, *Colonialism in Question: Theory, Knowledge, History* (Berkeley: University of California Press, 2005); Frederick Cooper and Ann Laura Stoler, *Tensions of Empire: Colonial Cultures in a Bourgeois World* (Berkeley: University of California Press, 1997); Amy Kaplan, *The Anarchy of Empire in the Making of U.S. Culture* (Cambridge MA: Harvard University Press, 2002).

13. For example, the four essays in the section on police, prisons, and law enforcement either focused on Puerto Rico or the Philippines. See Alfred W. McCoy and Francisco A. Scarano, eds., *The Colonial Crucible: Empire in the Making of the Modern American State* (Madison: University of Wisconsin Press, 2009).

14. Pablo Manlapit, Carl Damaso, Francisco Carbonel, Manuel Fagel, and Emigdio Milanio were some of the notable Filipino labor organizers in Hawai'i. Temporary labor commissioners from the Philippines traveled to Hawai'i in 1912, 1919, and 1920. Cayetano Ligot was the resident labor commissioner in Hawai'i from 1923 to 1933.

15. Puerto Ricans in Hawai'i developed community groups beginning in 1931. See Norma Carr, "The Puerto Ricans in Hawaii: 1900–1958" (PhD diss., University of Hawai'i, 1989), chapter 6. Puerto Ricans also held their centennial celebration of migration to the islands in 2000.

16. F. Souza to H. Deacon, June 28, 1901, Hawaiian Sugar Planters' Association (HSPA) Archives, Puna Sugar Company (PSC) 17/6, Sundry Letters, June to September 1901, Hawaiian/Pacific Collection, Hamilton Library, University of Hawai'i at Mānoa.

17. Claudio Lomnitz-Adler, *Deep Mexico, Silent Mexico: An Anthropology of Nationalism* (Minneapolis: University of Minnesota Press, 2001), xv.

18. Florentin Souza to F. B. McStocker, July 17, 1901, HSPA Archives, PSC 17/6, Sundry Letters, June to September 1901, 1.

19. Leon Foronda to Vincente Lionson, March 25, 1915, Hawaiian Evangelical Association (HEA) Archives, Filipino Department, Filipino Evangelist, T. F. Anderson, Hilo and Puna 1914–1917, Hawaiian Mission Children's Society Library, Mission Houses Museum, Honolulu.

20. For details of this arrangement, see HSPA Archives, PSC 23/8, Sundry Letters, 1923.

21. For background information on missionaries to Hawai'i, see Mark Edward Gallagher, "No More a Christian Nation: The Protestant Church in Territorial Hawai'i, 1898–1919" (PhD diss., University of Hawai'i, 1983); Patricia Grimshaw, *Paths of Duty: American Missionary Wives in Nineteenth-Century Hawaii* (Honolulu: University of Hawai'i Press, 1989); Mary Zwiep, *Pilgrim Path: The First Company of Women Missionaries to Hawaii* (Madison: University of Wisconsin Press, 1991).

22. F. B. McStocker to B. F. Dillingham Co., July 5, 1901, HSPA Archives, PSC 2/1, B. F. Dillingham, 1.

23. Statistics were averaged from forty-seven weekly reports filed by Santa Ana from October 1924 to December 1925. F. M. Santa Ana, Weekly Report, Reverend Santa Ana, 1920, 1924, 1925, HEA Archives. While the majority of Filipinos at the plantations were Catholic, priests from that denomination did not have the same kind of cordial relationships with both plantation managers and workers as Santa Ana.

24. F. Souza to F. B. McStocker, July 17, 1901, HSPA Archives, PSC 17/6, Sundry Letters, June to September 1901, 1.

25. F. Souza to F. B. McStocker, August 1, 1901, HSPA Archives, PSC 17/6, Sundry Letters, June to September 1901.

26. F. Souza to H. Deacon, June 28, 1901, HSPA Archives, PSC 17/6, Sundry Letters, June to September 1901. Souza's attitude is similar to that of the labor agents who managed Filipino laborers in Alaska. See Chris Friday, *Organizing Asian American Labor: The Pacific Coast Canned-Salmon Industry, 1870–1942* (Philadelphia: Temple University Press, 1994); Dorothy Fujita-Rony, *American Workers, Colonial Power: Philippine Seattle and the Transpacific West, 1919–1941* (Berkeley: University of California Press, 2003).

27. For more information on mutual benefit societies, see David T. Beito, *From Mutual Aid to the Welfare State: Fraternal Societies and Social Services, 1890–1967* (Chapel Hill: University of North Carolina Press, 2000).

28. F. Souza to F. B. McStocker, August 4, 1901, HSPA Archives, PSC 17/6, Sundry Letters, June to September 1901, 1.

29. In my forthcoming book I discuss how another labor mediator, Alberto Minvielle, started to work in the region in the summer of 1901. While he was also paid by the plantation, he lived alongside Puerto Rican workers and formed close relationships beyond the strict business transactions typical of Souza's style.

30. F. Souza to F. B. McStocker, February 13, 1901, HSPA Archives, PSC 7/17, Sundry Letters, June to September 1901.

31. F. Souza to F. B. McStocker, October 7, 1901, HSPA Archives, PSC 17/6, Sundry Letters, June to September 1901.

32. Santa Ana provided nonreligious services to Filipinos whether or not they were Protestants. In my forthcoming book I discuss the complications involved in the interactions between the predominantly Catholic Filipino community and Santa Ana, who always tried to convert them.

33. F. M. Santa Ana, Weekly Report, July 13 to July 19, 1925, HEA Archives, Reverend Santa Ana, 1920, 1924, 1925.

34. Santa Ana to Schenck, July 21 1924, HEA Archives, Reverend Santa Ana, 1920, 1924, 1925.

35. Santa Ana was relocated to the Waipahu plantation on Oʻahu, where he continued to serve Filipino interests for the rest of his career. Even today he is fondly remembered as a leader of the Filipino community in that area. Personal interview with Helen Nagtalon-Miller, Kaneohe, Oʻahu, February 22, 2003.

36. In my forthcoming book I discuss a program set up by the HSPA

to pay for travel back to the Philippines after the completion of three-year work contracts. This program greatly facilitated the flow of Filipino plantation workers between Hawai'i and the Philippines. Such a program did not exist for any other labor group in Hawai'i.

37. For more information on Filipinization, or tutelary colonialism, see Go, *American Empire and the Politics of Meaning*.

38. For an extended history of Puerto Rican life in Hawai'i, see Carr, "Puerto Ricans in Hawaii"; Iris Lopez, "Borinkis and Chop Suey: Puerto Rican Identity in Hawaii, 1900 to 2000," in *The Puerto Rican Diaspora: Historical Perspectives*, ed. Carmen Teresa Whalen and Victor Vazquez-Hernandez (Philadelphia: Temple University Press, 2005); Milton N. Silva and Blase Camacho Souza, "The Puerto Ricans of Hawaii: On Becoming Hawaii's People," *Journal of Contemporary Puerto Rican Thought* 1, no. 1 (1982): 29–39.

39. Compared to overpopulation and lack of employment in their home region, moving to Hawai'i seemed like an improvement to circumstances in American Sāmoa. Hokulani K. Aikau, "Polynesian Pioneers: Twentieth Century Religious Racial Formations and Migration in Hawai'i" (PhD diss., University of Michigan, 2005); Robert W. Franco, *Samoans in Hawaii: A Demographic Profile* (Honolulu: East-West Population Institute, 1987).

40. See Faye Untalan Munoz, "An Exploratory Study of Island Migration: Chamorros of Guam" (PhD diss., University of California at Los Angeles, 1979).

Part 4

Crossroads of American Migration

Chapter 11

The "Yellow Peril" in the United States and Peru
A Transnational History of Japanese
Exclusion, 1920s–World War II

Erika Lee

The day before the U.S. Congress passed the 1924 Immigration Act, which excluded Asian immigrants and tied immigrant admissions to quotas based on national origin, the *San Francisco Examiner* made the following suggestion: "If world is to avoid war, every nation must exclude Japanese like U.S." As a long-time advocate for the exclusion of Asian immigrants to the United States, the *Examiner* believed that unrestricted Japanese immigration would lead to an inevitable race war between the United States and Japan. It saw in the 1924 Immigration Act an immigration policy solution that would work not only for the United States, but for other nations as well. Until the day when the exclusion of Japanese became a universal policy, however, the newspaper worried that the "yellow peril" of Japanese immigration would not be easily contained. "Where are Japan's overflowing millions to go?" it asked.[1]

The answer was Latin America, specifically Peru and Brazil. By 1928 the United States and Canada were both closed to Japanese immigration. But migration abroad had become an important economic lifeline for many Japanese families, and migration to Latin America was actively promoted by the Japanese government.[2] As the Japanese population grew in Latin American countries, so did anti-Japanese sentiment and hostility. By the 1930s Peru and

Brazil had passed restrictive immigration policies and other laws that curbed the rights of Japanese residents. The *San Francisco Examiner*'s suggestion "that every nation must exclude Japanese" was closer to becoming translated into policy.

This chapter begins with a few questions: How should we interpret these U.S. and Latin American histories of race and immigration policy? Are they products of national processes alone? Or might we understand them as part of transnational interactions of race across the Americas? The historiographies of Asian migration to the Americas have primarily focused on single nations.[3] Histories of race relations and law are similarly understood within national frameworks, dependent as they are on specific population demographics and histories as well as political contexts and legal systems. But as the 1924 headline from the *San Francisco Examiner* illustrates, the "problem" of Japanese immigration was considered within transnational, even global contexts during the 1920s and 1930s.

This chapter explores the ways anti-Japanese racism and immigration restriction in North and South America were part of a larger interconnected history of Asians in the Americas. Asians first arrived in the Americas in the seventeenth century. Over the past four hundred years they have migrated and remigrated throughout the region and have maintained transnational networks and ties spanning the Pacific and throughout the Americas. Asians also became targets of some of the first national laws that excluded immigrants on the basis of race and victims of state-sanctioned violence, expulsion, and incarceration. A hemispheric Asian American history explores these movements and links in order to better understand Asian diasporic communities and to revise existing nation-centered historical narratives of the Americas.[4]

Japanese immigration to the United States and Peru was a particularly important chapter in the interconnected history of Asians in the Americas. The United States was the favored destination for most Japanese migrants from the very beginning of the migration period in 1868 to the U.S. declaration of war against Japan in 1941.

Peru was the first Latin American country to establish diplomatic relations with Japan (1873), and it received the largest number of Japanese immigrants within Spanish America, especially after the United States barred Japanese immigrants altogether in 1924.[5] Moreover Peru's history of Japanese migration and anti-Japanese sentiment was structurally more similar to North American patterns, and it was the first country to participate in U.S. hemispheric security efforts by interning Japanese civilians during World War II.

Viewed from a comparative, transnational perspective, the anti-Japanese campaigns and policies of the 1920s and 1930s reveal how the construction of race is tied to *transnational* flows of people across borders, *national* processes of nation building, and *international* relations between nation-states.[6] As Howard Winant has explained through the concept of the "globality of race," national ideas about racial difference and systems of racial ordering were in fact highly interactive and transnational processes. The United States and Peru developed their own understandings of immigration and race in nation-specific contexts, transnational connections and comparisons, and U.S.-Peruvian international relations.[7]

In the Americas Asian migration and exclusion was shaped by what I call "hemispheric Orientalism," anti-Asian racism that moved across national boundaries and contributed to an unparalleled transnational conversation about race, migration, and national and hemispheric security in the late nineteenth and early twentieth century. The United States and Peru understood Japanese immigration within a larger global landscape that focused on the "yellow peril"—the alleged threat that both Japan and Japanese immigration posed to the West. The shared "problem" of Japanese immigration also became part of the constellation of U.S.-Latin American and U.S.-Peruvian encounters that was shaped by growing U.S. hegemony in the region during the first half of the twentieth century.[8] Both led to parallel, and sometimes intersecting, processes of race making, immigration restriction, and nation building that would eventually lead the two countries to cooperate in the internment of both Japanese Americans and Japanese Peruvians in U.S. camps during World War II.

Global Anxieties about Race and the "Yellow Peril" in the United States

From the late nineteenth century until the beginning of World War II, nearly 340,000 Japanese, mostly young male laborers, arrived in the United States. They were recruited to work on the sugar plantations on the Hawaiian Islands or as laborers on railroads and in mines, lumber mills, fish canneries, farms, and orchards throughout the Pacific Coast states on the U.S. mainland. But Japanese did not remain laborers forever. They became independent farmers just as West Coast agriculture exploded with the development of irrigation and a distribution system that carried produce across the nation in refrigerator cars for the first time.

By the early twentieth century the economic success and increased numbers of Japanese immigrants in the United States sparked an organized movement to exclude Japanese immigration. Labor unions, farmers, and politicians charged the Japanese with unfairly taking away jobs from white workers, crowding out white farmers, and being an unassimilable alien race. Mass rallies decried further Japanese immigration, West Coast newspapers ran headlines describing the "Japanese invasion" of the United States, and the Asiatic Exclusion League formed to push Congress for changes in the country's immigration laws. After the League successfully lobbied the San Francisco School Board to remove all Japanese schoolchildren from the city's public schools and place them in the segregated Oriental Public School, the localized anti-Japanese campaign on the West Coast turned into a major international incident. Japan protested the discrimination against its citizens, and U.S. President Theodore Roosevelt became involved. To calm exclusionists, the president issued an executive order preventing the entry of Japanese laborers from Hawai'i, Mexico, and Canada to the continental United States. He then negotiated a diplomatic agreement, known as the Gentlemen's Agreement, whereby the Japanese government voluntarily agreed to stop issuing passports to Japanese laborers bound for the United States. In exchange the president successfully convinced the San Francisco School Board to revoke its order segregating Japanese schoolchildren from the general school population.

Almost simultaneously Canada too entered into a brokered Gentlemen's Agreement with Japan. Both policies largely curtailed Japanese immigration to North America. The impact was greatest in the United States, which had been the destination of most Japanese immigrants to North America. In 1908 9,544 Japanese had entered the United States; in the following year only 2,432 did. Japanese did not stop coming altogether, however. A loophole in the law still allowed Japanese immigrants already in the United States to sponsor their family members' entry into the country. Merchants, diplomats, students, visitors, and returning U.S. residents could also continue to come or reenter the United States. Indeed 120,000 Japanese, many of them the "picture brides" of U.S. residents, arrived in the United States until the 1924 Immigration Act stopped Japanese immigration altogether.[9]

The continuation of Japanese immigration to the United States fueled a resurgence in anti-Japanese sentiment in the country during the 1920s. But this time domestic U.S. concerns about Japanese immigration were also shaped by larger global anxieties about race. Beginning in the early twentieth century, a wide range of writers described the vulnerability of the white race as the "colored races" grew in power and number around the globe.[10] "Oriental" hordes overwhelming the West and threatening white supremacy were a particularly popular topic. A common denominator in "yellow peril" discourse was fear of the changing relationship between Europe and Asia, a relationship that was becoming "more intimate and equal" through migration and trade. With China in decline and Chinese immigrants excluded from the United States and many other countries by the early twentieth century, the main focus of the yellow peril was Japan, a rising military power, and the migrants it sent abroad.[11]

These fears were best articulated in 1920, in the best-selling book *The Rising Tide of Color against White World Supremacy* by the U.S. eugenicist Lothrop Stoddard. Stoddard described in dramatic, sensationalist terms the threat emanating from Japan: the peril of arms (military expansion), the peril of markets (economic competition), and the peril of migration. Japan's economic and military rise to world power status represented the first peril to the white world because Japan's thirst for expansionism could not be contained within the "yellow man's lands" of Asia, Stoddard claimed. However, it was the peril of migration that was the most dangerous, according to Stoddard, for it was the "greatest external problem which face[d] the white world." Moreover, he continued ominously, it was "already upon us." Stoddard thus conflated global anxieties over the "rising tide of color" with the very specific threat of Japanese migration to North and South America.[12]

Stoddard's articulation of the yellow peril—the alleged threat that Japanese immigration and expansionism posed to the Western world—gave strength to existing campaigns to exclude Japanese immigrants from the United States and Canada in the early twentieth century. In the United States anxieties over massive immigration, racial amalgamation, and new imperial responsibilities shaped Americans' response to yellow peril discourses and politics. Opponents of Japanese immigration in the United States first focused on the dramatic growth of the Japanese community. In 1924 V. S. McClatchy, a leader of the anti-Japanese movement in California, warned an audience at the Lions Club of San Francisco that the state's Japanese population had "quadrupled within the past fifteen years," and that the growth of this "unassimilable population" presented nothing less than "a deadly menace to the nation."[13]

Second was the problem of economic competition between Japanese and whites. Japanese farmers experienced enormous success in the fertile California delta region and helped to develop the state's massive agricultural industry. In 1905 Japanese leased, contracted, or owned 62,000 acres of farmland in the state; by 1920 that figure was over 458,000.[14] Japanese success in agriculture sparked a great deal of resentment among white Californians. The *San Francisco Examiner* bemoaned the spectacle of "thousands

of acres of our richest and most productive farmlands" being under the control of "an unassimilable race."[15] U.S. Senator James D.
Phelan told a newspaper in 1907 that the Japanese occupied "valleys in California by lease or purchase of land to the exclusion of
. . . whites." If the "silent invasion" was not checked by the federal government, he predicted, the "fairest state in the union [would
turn] into a Japanese colony."[16]

For many anti-Japanese activists, the demographic and economic
factors relating to Japanese immigration were overshadowed by the
pure racial threat that Japanese immigrants allegedly posed to the
country. Social scientists, politicians, and ordinary citizens alike
claimed that an "immigrant invasion" from Japan could never be
absorbed. Rather it would only add to existing racial strife that included the continued subjugation of African Americans, the exclusion and restriction of Asian, Mexican, and southern and eastern
European immigrants, and the incorporation of colonized peoples
abroad.[17] Others claimed that the Japanese were "less assimila-
ble and more dangerous than any other peoples . . . [because] they
never cease being Japanese."[18] The threat of racial miscegenation
was also a consistent fear. The writer Montaville Flowers was concerned that because Japanese and other "Orientals" were excep-
tionally "fertile races," their ability to reproduce would lead to the
eradication of the white race. Flowers also believed that the children of mixed-race unions inherited all of the inferior characteristics of each race, making them deficient and dangerous.[19]

Third, Japanese immigrants were suspected of being the advance
guard of an expansionist Japan intent on conquering the West. The
writer Homer Lea argued that Japanese immigrants in Hawai'i were
the first installment of soldiers ready to seize control of the islands.
Lea also claimed that a similar imperialist invasion was well under
way in California, where Japanese constituted "more than one-sev-
enth" of all male adults of military age.[20] U.S. Senator Phelan of California echoed the warning, stating that the Pacific Coast "would be
an easy prey in case of attack" because Japanese immigrants in California were not peaceful settlers, but the "enemy within our gates."[21]

By the end of World War I the anti-Japanese movement in the United States had entered a new phase that was more national in scope, appealed to both the working and middle class, and focused on both the national and the international threat of Japanese migrants and an expansionist Japan.[22] Agitation against Japanese immigration led directly to changes in immigration policy. The U.S. Immigration Act of 1924 established quotas based on national origin and denied admission to all aliens who were "ineligible for citizenship" (i.e. those to whom naturalization was denied). As existing nationality laws excluded Asian immigrants from naturalization, this provision was aimed at Japanese, the only Asian group not previously excluded. After decades of activism by anti-Japanese activists, the gates to the United States were finally barred to Japanese immigrants.[23] In 1928 Canada also amended its diplomatic agreement with Japan, and Japanese immigration to that country slowed to a trickle.[24]

Japanese Migration to Latin America

With North America now closed, Japanese migrants looked instead to Latin America. Small groups of Japanese had settled in Peru, Mexico, Chile, Bolivia, Argentina, and Brazil beginning in the late nineteenth and early twentieth century, but large-scale Japanese migration did not occur until after the passage of the 1924 Immigration Act in the United States.[25] General immigration policies of Latin American countries encouraged the migration of laborers to replace freed African slaves in the development of new commercial crops. The preference was for white immigrants from Europe, but Asian immigrants found no real barriers to their admission until the 1930s.[26] In Japan migration to Latin America was heavily promoted. In 1924 the *Japan Times and Weekly* reported that Latin America had "large regions which have much the same climatic conditions as are found in Japan . . . , broad lands which invite the agriculturist, . . . growing industries which would like to employ Japanese workmen, . . . vast natural resources which beckon to Japanese capital."[27] The Japanese government also became actively involved in emigration matters. In an attempt to avoid the anti-Japanese agitation that had characterized the North American response to Japanese laborers, the government centralized emigration under the Kaigai Kogyo Kaisha (Overseas Development Corporation) and sent mostly settlers and capitalists to Latin America, especially to Brazil.[28] Japanese migrants to Latin America expressed regret that they could not enter the United States or Canada as their relatives had done in earlier years, but they increasingly viewed Latin America as a suitable alternative. Seiichi Higashide, who arrived in Peru in 1930, explained, "Aside from the United States, Peru had the next largest number of Japanese immigrants who had found success."[29]

Statistics kept by the Japanese Foreign Office on departures to Latin America illustrate the dramatic shift in Japanese migration from North to South America that occurred in the 1920s. In 1905 only 2.6 percent (346) of Japanese migrants worldwide went to Latin America, all to Mexico. In 1908, after the U.S. and Canadian governments had barred the entry of Japanese laborers, 35 percent (10,447) of all Japanese migrants went to Latin America, with 2,880 going to Peru alone. Japanese migration ebbed and flowed in the intervening years, especially before and after World War I. In 1924 4,474 Japanese went to Latin America, 34 percent of the total migration worldwide. In 1925, after the United States had passed its Immigration Act, 6,111 Japanese were destined for Latin America, 57 percent of the total worldwide Japanese migration for that year. In 1930 and 1934 15,477 and 23,625 Japanese migrated to Latin America, 71 percent and 84 percent, respectively, of all Japanese migration globally.

In all years the vast majority headed to Brazil, reflecting the Japanese government's new system of controlled emigration to that country. But Peru's Japanese population also increased dramatically.[30] Before World War II the Japanese community in Peru was largest in 1934, when the population was an estimated 20,385. The vast majority were poor young men between the ages of twenty and forty-five who had been farmers or farm laborers in Japan and had little education or formal training. Over time the numbers of women and children arriving in Peru also increased. The newcomers were concentrated in either the Chancay Valley growing cotton or, more commonly, in urban commerce in Lima.[31] Community organizations and Japanese-language newspapers and schools all grew in number to serve the newcomers and their families, and in the 1920s and 1930s Peru's Japanese community was growing and thriving.[32]

"El Peligro Amarillo" in Peru: Race, Economics, Colonization, and Anti-Japanese Laws

With the increased numbers of Japanese immigrants to Latin America came an accompanying new debate over Japanese immigration and its impact on Peru. Anti-Japanese sentiment came from many sectors of Peruvian society. The country's leading business organizations, such as the National Agrarian Society, the National Industrial Society, and the Lima Chamber of Commerce, were all passionate critics of Japanese immigration and the economic competition that Japanese immigrants allegedly posed.[33] Labor unions also consistently rallied behind the cause of ending Asian immigration after World War I, and a wide range of news media contributed to the anti-Japanese movement, including mainstream daily newspapers like *La Prensa* and *El Comercio*, the labor movement's *El Obrero Textil*, and smaller newspapers such as *La Crónica* and *Mundo Grafico*. Echoing Lothrop Stoddard's warning of the "rising tide of color," *El Comercio* and *La Prensa* warned of "the rising tide of yellow immigrants" in Peru.[34] Newspapers routinely published stories on what they called "la invasión de los japoneses" that were similar to those found in West Coast papers in the United States.[35] During the 1930s *La Prensa* led the media's anti-Japanese crusade with a long-running column on "la infiltración japonesa" edited by Peruvian politicians and intellectuals such as Dr. Guillermo Salinas Cossío, Carlos Moreyra y Paz-Soldán, and José Manuel Ramírez Gonzáles.[36] Within a few years newspapers regularly referred to "el peligro japonés" (the Japanese peril) and "el peligro amarillo" (the "yellow peril").[37]

The anti-Japanese movement enjoyed broad political support from both the working and the middle class. Anti-Japanese legislation was passed by three different governments in the 1920s and 1930s and was an important issue for Luis Sánchez Cerro's fascist party, the Unión Revolucionaria (Revolutionary Union Party), and the emerging Alianza Popular Revolucionaria Americana (American Popular Revolutionary Alliance), the largest political party in contemporary Peru.[38]

Race was one of the primary factors contributing to the anti-Japanese campaign in Peru, especially in the capital city of Lima, where the vast majority of Japanese in the country (87 percent in 1930 and 82 percent in 1940) lived. In the early decades of the twentieth century the city underwent great demographic change. The city's population almost doubled between 1898 and 1920, growing from more than 113,000 to almost 224,000. Moreover internal migration dramatically altered the racial and ethnic composition of the city. While *blancos* (people of European descent and/or high socioeconomic status) remained the political, economic, and social elite, the city was becoming more mestizo (mixed race) and indigenous. By 1931 over half of all Limeños (residents of Lima) were mestizos and Indians. European immigrant communities, which had been welcomed by the city's *blanca* elite in the early 1900s and had played a prominent role in the city's economy, were slowly moving out of the city. By the 1920s the Japanese constituted the single largest immigrant community. As Jun Kodani points out, the Japanese were probably "the major *foreign* element" in many Lima neighborhoods which were becoming less white and more indigenous.[39]

The growing numbers of Japanese in the rapidly changing city of Lima were increasingly seen as a menace. As in the United States, the presence of Japanese immigrants in Peru was considered against the backdrop of Peru's existing struggles with race and national identity. In the early twentieth century the Peruvian state was dominated by *criollos* (the white descendants of the Spanish colonizers) and other Europeans. Although they were a distinct minority

(10 percent) in an indigenous (47 percent) and mestizo (40 percent) country with a small population of Asians and blacks (3 percent), the white elite dominated Peruvian politics, academia, society, and culture. Prominent Peruvian intellectuals and public figures regularly articulated a racial hierarchy that placed all nonwhites far below whites.[40] They expressed concerns about the supposed racial inferiority of the nonwhite population and their potential to disrupt national state-building projects. Like many others throughout Latin America in the late nineteenth and early twentieth century, Peruvian elites sought to absorb or assimilate the "barbarous races" of blacks and Indians. A variety of state policies tried to address the country's "Indian problem" by preparing them for their eventual entry into the labor market as an underclass of laborers or farmers.[41]

At the same time many important Peruvian intellectuals promoted "constructive miscegenation" as an alternative to the country's racial problems, and populist national projects promoting both *mestizaje* (racial mixing) and *indigenismo* (indigenous culture) emerged in the late nineteenth and early twentieth century throughout Latin America.[42] *Blanqueamiento* (whitening) of the population was a particularly popular ideology advocated by Peru's white elites, who also insisted that Peru was "European" and "occidental" with a "racially homogeneous" (i.e., white) population even though descendants of Europeans were clearly a small minority of the population.[43] Intellectuals and academics agreed that if Peru were to welcome immigrants, it should be those from "compatible races," as the philosopher Javier Prado explained in 1909. They believed that state policies promoting the immigration of Europeans would help solve the Peruvian racial predicament, for European capital investment and culture were equated with national progress and prosperity.[44] In an attempt to attract European immigrants, the Peruvian government passed "white preference laws" in 1873 and 1906 that subsidized European and U.S. immigrants exclusively.[45]

To the distress of people like Professor Victor J. Guevara, however,

Europeans preferred to migrate to Argentina, Chile, and Brazil. By the 1920s the "incompatible" race of Japanese constituted the largest immigrant group in Lima, and tensions increased. Like the Japanese in Canada and the United States, the Japanese in Peru suffered from an anti-Asian, anti-Chinese sentiment and history that considered the Chinese—and all other Asians—to be racially distinct peoples.[46] Almost one hundred thousand Chinese coolie laborers had been brought to Peru to work in the guano mines between 1849 and 1874. Viewed as cheap laborers, they faced much discrimination and strong public opposition. After Japanese began arriving in the country, both groups were referred to by a common racial terminology, such as *la raza denigrante* (denigrated race), *los amarillos* (yellow race), or *asiaticos* (Asiatics), all of which were derogatory and set Asians apart from the other peoples in Peru. Japanese merchants were derided as *chinos de la esquina* (street-corner Chinese). As the labor newspaper *El Obrero Textil* explained to its readers in 1919, "[These] Chinese and Japanese . . . both constitute the same plague with different names."[47] *Acción*, the Unión Revolucionaria's newspaper, added, "The yellow element cannot compare biologically to the European element, that is the white race."[48]

According to most opponents of Japanese immigration, the gravest problem was that the Japanese were an unassimilable race and culture, "the most difficult to assimilate."[49] Echoing similar concerns coming from the United States, writers and politicians such as the former Peruvian president Francisco García Calderón argued that the Japanese were not absorbed into the nation and were thus a danger to the nation.[50] In 1907 a Peruvian congressman warned that the Japanese were "an alien race dissimilar in habits, morals, and process of thought."[51] Professor Victor J. Guevara added, "[The Japanese are] not susceptible to assimilation and incorporation into the nation, as are other foreigners. . . . [They] maintain themselves in this indissoluble state [with their own Japanese-language newspapers, festivals, clubs, and schools,] "in which they teach love not of Peru, but of the Empire, geographically distant, but which reigns in the heart of the Japanese encamped in the soil of the New World."[52]

Such sentiments coming from broad sectors of society greatly impacted how Peruvians viewed the Japanese in their midst. The numerous Japanese societies, schools, and newspapers all aroused a great deal of suspicion and fear. Peruvians believed that the Japanese were reluctant to integrate into their society. As Kodani observes, the Japanese community in Lima began to be seen as a *colonia* (colony) that was distinctive, distant from, and potentially threatening to indigenous society, rather than another immigrant community.[53] The Japanese were perceived to be a "stand-offish and organized foreign group," "people who do not speak Castilian, do not profess the Catholic faith, do not attempt to participate in the social and intellectual life of the country, and send their money away." Ordinary Peruvians regarded them with misgiving and distrust. Thus, like their counterparts in the United States, Peruvian elites and ordinary citizens worried about the effects that unassimilable foreigners and "exotics" would have on a country already saddled with problems stemming from its racially diverse (and inferior) peoples. The assimilation of blacks, Chinese, and indigenous peoples was still an ongoing project. From the point of view of many Peruvians, Japanese immigrants were an additional and more threatening problem for Peru.[54] The journalist Alejandro Cruz Montero opined, "If the Indian is a problem, the Japanese is a danger."[55]

The charge that Japanese immigrants competed unfairly with Peruvians for jobs and in commerce was the second most common argument in the anti-Japanese campaign. As in the United States and Canada, Asian immigrant workers and their use by industrialists to break strikes and undercut native workers were greatly resented. Peruvian labor unions had organized against Chinese immigrants in the late nineteenth century. During World War I, when workers suffered from rising inflation, stagnant wages, and unemployment, an increase in anti-Japanese sentiment mobilized the labor movement. In 1917 Lima's main labor union established the Anti-Asian

Association. Its newspaper, *La Hoja Amarilla* (Yellow page), urged the Peruvian government to end "yellow immigration."[56]

By the 1920s and 1930s Japanese were increasingly entering the urban commercial sector and replacing European immigrant business owners, especially Italians. Anti-Japanese sentiment began to focus less on Japanese being used as cheap labor and more on Japanese merchants being a "degenerate and harmful plague upon the people."[57] The labor newspaper *El Obrero Textil* argued that the Japanese threatened the working poor because their businesses competed with the street vending, peddling, and other small commercial activities traditionally done by workingmen's wives, sisters, and children. Japanese immigrants, the paper implied, threatened entire Peruvian families.[58]

Peruvian discontent over the concentration of Japanese in successful sectors of the economy reached a high point during the global depression in the 1930s.[59] Exports had fallen sharply and decreased in value, trade had plateaued, and Peruvians, especially the working poor, faced growing unemployment rates and reduced wages. Between 1931 and 1933 the number of unemployed had risen from 13,202 to 20,619. About 45 percent of these were based in the Lima-Callao area. Those who did have jobs found their wages slashed by 50 percent.[60] In contrast, the Japanese seemed to be expanding their commercial success into new areas that competed with and caused discontent among the native population. Japanese were buying land in the fertile Chancay valley; expanding their control over the profitable cotton industry; increasing their shares in the fruit, flower, and truck gardening sectors; dominating the ownership of urban grocery stores, small restaurants, bars, coffee shops, barber shops, jewelry stores, and *bazares* (discount stores); and moving into the manufacturing industries, such as clothing, candy, and bakery products. Once laborers, the Japanese had become employers, landowners, business owners, and "middle-man minorities."[61] Increasingly they were labeled "monopolists" who excluded Peruvians and exploited the workers they employed.[62] In this context, the fascist Unión Revolucionaria made Asian immigration a central issue in its movement and drew on the discontent of the urban middle class, who suffered from unemployment and competition from Japanese businesses. It organized an anti-Asian society in 1934 and called for the expulsion of Japanese immigrants and economic boycotts of Japanese stores in the name of "Peruvianizing" the economy.[63]

Another source of economic anxiety was Peru's trade imbalance, including with Japan, during the 1930s. The foreign domination of key sectors of the Peruvian economy during the 1930s engendered intense nationalism and xenophobia against all foreigners. But Peruvians consistently expressed the most anxiety over the increase of trade with Japan and the existence of Japanese companies in the country. Japanese-Peruvian trade, which consisted mostly of exporting raw materials from Peru and importing textiles and manufactured goods from Japan, was never very large, and it paled in comparison to Peru's trade with the United States and European nations. But its rapid increase in the 1930s alarmed Peruvians.[64] Moreover the threat of Japanese commercial investment in the country was conflated with the economic success of Japanese immigrants residing in Peru. In 1930 and 1931 many Japanese stores were burned or looted, and the Japanese Peruvian community became targets of a hate campaign.[65] In 1935 the influential Asociación de Comercio e Industrias de Arequipa (Association of Commerce and Industry of Arequipa) published a message to the president calling for protection from both Japanese immigration and commercial infiltration by Japan.[66]

By the 1930s Japanese immigrants and foreign investment were no longer viewed as a threat only to the Peruvian working class. Increasingly they were regarded as a danger to the entire "welfare and progress of the nation and all its people."[67] Peru joined the rest of the world in watching with fear and dread the growing Japanese military expansion in East Asia. In 1931 Japan invaded Inner (Chinese) Manchuria and created the Japanese-controlled puppet state of Manchukuo. After the international community condemned this action, Japan resigned from the League of Nations in 1933.

Japan invaded China in 1937, and the second Sino-Japanese War began. Japan formed the Axis Pact with Germany and Italy on September 27, 1940. As Lima newspapers covered these developments, Peruvians became even more exposed to the fear that Japanese immigration and Japanese control of the Peruvian economy would eventually lead to the military occupation of South America's western regions.[68]

The topic of Japan as a "world menace" and the Japanese immigrant community in Peru as a "sinister conspirator" and "advance guard" was regularly covered in the daily Peruvian press and in other publications.[69] Francisco García Calderón predicted in 1911 that "the Japanese would invade Western America and convert the Pacific into a vast closed sea, closed to foreign ambitions . . . peopled by Japanese colonies."[70] Writing in 1939, Victor Guevara claimed that Japanese immigration was one of the four *grandes cuestiones nacionales* (great national questions) facing the country. Japanese immigrants, he argued, were foreign bodies invading the Peruvian nation, and Lima was turning into a launching base for a Japanese invasion of Peru.[71] One writer to *La Prensa* opined, "Whomever controls the land controls the purse; and whomever controls the purse, controls the country." *La Prensa* editors themselves warned that "after the [Japanese] merchant comes the soldier." Julio González Tello and Manuel González Tello ominously warned their readers, "The day will come when every Peruvian is servant of a Japanese."[72]

Such anxiety over Japanese immigration resulted in the passage of a series of anti-Japanese laws in Peru during the 1930s.[73] Three types of laws were passed by three different governments led by Augusto Leguía (1919–30), Luis Sanchez Cerro (1930–33), and Oscar Benavides (1933–39). The first were laws designed to restrict Japanese immigration. The Peruvian government under Leguía excluded Chinese immigration in 1922 and passed another bill that prohibited Japanese agricultural contract labor the next year. Thereafter only Japanese immigrants who had been invited to migrate by family members already residing in Peru could enter

the country.[74] Peru's 1936 immigration law was passed in direct reaction to the U.S. Immigration Act of 1924 and Brazil's Immigration Act of 1934, both of which restricted Japanese immigration.
The Peruvian government feared that with both North America
and Brazil closed to Japanese immigration, the numbers coming
to Peru would increase dramatically. Both the Peruvian and Brazilian immigration laws included quota amendments and racial
restrictions modeled on U.S. laws.[75] Peru's law established an immigration quota of sixteen thousand per nation, which was approximately 0.2 of 1 percent of Peru's total population. It also specifically barred the immigration of "racial groups."[76] As the number
of Japanese in Peru in 1930 (10,385) was already above the quota, the law effectively closed off immigration from Japan. Like the
laws in the United States and Brazil, Peru's policy was designed to
protect the "racial homogeneity" of the Peruvian people. It made
no explicit reference to the Japanese in order to avoid formal or explicit racial discrimination of them. However, as the author of the
law, Minister of Foreign Affairs Alberto Ulloa, made clear, the law
was designed to specifically address "the seriousness of the Japanese menace."[77]

   The second group of laws curbed the rights of Japanese immigrants already in the country. The 1936 immigration law contained
a provision that dictated that only 20 percent of employees in all
businesses and professions could be foreigners and that 80 percent
had to be native Peruvians. The so-called 80 percent law clearly
targeted Japanese businesses, which primarily relied on family labor or hired fellow Japanese.[78] Another provision in the 1936 law
affected foreign residents of Peru who returned home after a visit to their native land. After 1936 they could return to Peru only
within the established quotas. Because Japanese often traveled back
and forth to Japan for education and for other reasons, this policy was meant to target them.[79] During General Oscar Benavides's
six-year military dictatorship (1933–39), a new constitution was
enacted that required foreigners to renounce their dual citizenship.
Later the government also denied aliens the right to be naturalized

altogether. In 1937 Decree Law 8526 suspended birthright citizenship to children of resident foreigners in the country if the birth had occurred before June 26, 1936. A series of laws passed in 1940 made Peruvian citizenship even more restrictive. Second-generation Peruvians who left Peru for their immigrant parents' homelands to live, study, or undergo military training before they reached adulthood automatically lost their Peruvian citizenship. A law passed in September 1940 declared that sons of foreigners, even if born in Peru, were during their minority to be considered the same nationality as their father. And a November 29, 1940, law targeted Japanese institutions and the press by requiring all foreign newspapers in Lima that printed in other than roman type to publish a parallel translation of the text in Spanish. Again, because Japanese were the largest foreign group in the country at the time, all of these laws were clearly aimed at them.[80]

The remaining anti-Japanese laws were designed to place barriers on Japanese trade. In 1930 the 1924 Treaty of Commerce and Amity between Peru and Japan was renounced. In 1934 Peru limited the importation of textiles. The next year it broke the trade agreement with Japan and placed further quotas on textile imports, and in 1936 a new law limited the number of businesses and certain manual trades that could be Japanese-owned and made it illegal to transfer business ownership.[81]

The twin goals of Peru's anti-Japanese movement—ending Japanese immigration and imposing restrictions on Japanese commercial activities—were achieved by 1936. However, anti-Japanese agitation did not completely end. Lima's newspapers continued to publicize sensational stories linking Japanese immigrants to subversive activities that threatened Peru and Peruvian sovereignty.[82] When false rumors circulated throughout the city that firearms had been found in Japanese haciendas, anti-Japanese sentiment erupted into violence on May 13, 1940.[83] An anti-Japanese demonstration organized for that day quickly developed into a full-scale riot. Roving bands of people assaulted Japanese-owned businesses in the city, breaking down doors and attacking shops with clubs. Rioting led to massive looting, often while police looked on. It was not until May 14 that Peruvian troops finally had the situation under control, but almost all Japanese-owned shops had already been destroyed. In the end 620 households reported riot losses, totaling at least $1.64 million. Scores of individuals were injured, and ten Japanese were killed in the violence.[84]

"Yellow Peril" Connections across the Americas

The Lima riots of 1940 were a manifestation of local anti-Japanese politics and violence. Like the laws directed toward Japanese immigrants to and Japanese residents in Peru, the riots and the larger anti-Japanese campaign were rooted in unique local, regional, and national demographic and political contexts. Yet the yellow peril discourse and the ways it was employed in Peru were strikingly similar to campaigns elsewhere in the Americas. In the United States, Canada, and Peru, the argument that Japanese, like the Chinese before them, were cheap laborers who threatened the economic livelihood of native workers evolved into arguments that Japanese farmers and business owners were unfairly competing with the native middle class. Moreover their alleged inability and unwillingness to assimilate into mainstream society made them dangerous to the larger society in all three countries. As Japan expanded its empire in East Asia, sensationalist claims of Japanese invasions of the west coast of both North and South America were made in a wide range of media and circulated throughout the hemisphere. Lothrop Stoddard's *The Rising Tide of Color* was reprinted in *La Prensa* and other daily newspapers as part of a focus on the dangers of Japanese immigration.[85] The activist V. S. McClatchy in California self-published his anti-Japanese pamphlets in Spanish so that they could be more easily disseminated in Mexico and Spanish-speaking Latin America.[86]

The U.S. and Peruvian governments viewed the threat of the yellow peril in distinct ways and in the context of their own vantage points on U.S.–Latin American relations. The transnational lens through which Peruvians interpreted Japanese migration and expansionism was based on Peru's complicated and unequal relationship with the United States and how it defined itself and its interest vis-à-vis that relationship. As Fernando Coronil reminds us, encounters between the United States and Latin America were complex interactions between unequal social actors that involved cooperation, subjection, and resistance.[87] Increasingly, both Americans and Peruvians understood that the yellow peril in one country or even on one continent could not be separated from the yellow peril throughout the Americas. When politicians and intellectuals in both countries expressed the belief that the U.S. example and U.S. assistance would be Peru's best defense against the Japanese menace, they reflected and reinforced the hegemony of the United States in Latin America.

To many Peruvians, the most immediate peril was the *peligro yanqui* (Yankee peril) rather than the *peligro amarillo* (yellow peril).[88] The United States continued to expand its economic dominance in the region, and by the mid-1930s was Peru's major creditor and controlled most of the largest corporations.[89] However, the rising power of Japan became a source of growing anxiety. Former president García Calderón astutely recognized that in the context of the larger struggle between the United States and Japan for dominance in the Pacific, Latin America was essentially stuck between a rock and a hard place: "We are then face to face with a struggle of races, a clash of irreconcilable interests." Should war occur, Latin America would be greatly affected, he explained.[90]

Some Latin Americans looked to Japan as a counterweight or ally against the growing hegemony of the United States.[91] Both Manuel Ugarte of Argentina and Francisco García Calderón of Peru observed that a friendly alliance with Japan would free Latin America from U.S. influence. On the other hand, García Calderón also realized that a Japanese threat to U.S. interests in the region would not be tolerated by the Anglo-Saxons. The Monroe Doctrine would propel the United States to "protect" Latin America against the "menace of the East," he predicted. He eventually concluded that as much as he liked the idea of checking U.S. influence in the region, the prospect of a Japanese invasion of South America would prove disastrous for Peru. "Japanese hegemony would not be a mere change of tutelage for the nations of America," he wrote. "The Japanese civilization would weigh too heavily upon the Latin democracies, mixed as they are. . . . In the conflict between half-breed America and stoic Japan, the former would lose both its autonomy and its traditions." Moreover García Calderón explained that "in spite of essential differences," the peoples of Latin America and the United States had more in common with each other, including, Christianity and a "coherent, European, occidental civilization," than they had with Japan. There might be some "obscure fraternity between the Japanese and the American Indians," but the "ruling race, the dominant type of Spanish origin, which imposes the civilization of the white man upon America, is hostile to the entire invading East." Japanese rule of Latin America would thus be disastrous, García Calderón concluded, for Japanese dominance in the country would mean the end of the Peruvian people.[92] For García Calderón, the shared problem of Japanese immigration had revealed commonalities between Peru and the United States, and he and others claimed whiteness (rather than mestizaje) and kinship to the United States through the act of distancing Peru from Japan and Japanese. As they did so, the peligro yanqui was erased, but the peligro amarillo remained in place.

With this common ground established, Peruvian journalists, politicians, and citizens turned their attention northward to better understand the danger that faced them. What plagued Peru was also destroying other countries in the Americas, García Calderón observed in 1911: "The terrible yellow peril . . . has been felt in America from Vancouver and California down to Chile." If anything, he thought, the threat was most serious in Peru: "The Japanese emigrate to Canada, there to establish a base for the invasion of the United States; they do the same in Mexico, and settle even in Chile; but Peru is the favourite soil of these imperialistic adventurers."[93]

Peruvian politicians and the media also paid close attention to the passage of the 1924 Immigration Act in the United States. Just days after it had been made into law, *El Comercio* praised the actions of the U.S. government to "create an ethnic amalgam" from the "best currents of European blood" through its national origins quotas and its exclusion of Japanese immigrants. "Is there any country who can claim the right to disturb this admirable task?" the editors asked. "No. The law of exclusion is a given." Similarly in 1934 the fascist newspaper *Acción* praised the United States for its "admirable foresight" in excluding all "inferior races" such as the Chinese and Japanese.[94] In the 1930s the mainstream press continued to suggest that Peru emulate U.S. immigration restrictions. In 1934 Pedro Icochea held up the "United States of North America" as an example of how to "impede successive yellow immigration." "We don't see a reason why Peru doesn't follow such a laudable example," he concluded.[95]

Following the U.S. example was not a simple matter for Peru, however. As an imperial nation and a growing world power the United States could risk facing the wrath of the Japanese government, but Peru lacked the same status. By the 1920s the exclusion of Japanese immigrants was unquestionably desirable to most Peruvians, but Peruvian diplomats and politicians had to consider how Peru would protect itself in case of an attack by a vengeful Japan. Increasingly they looked to the United States, calling attention to the Japanese infiltration of their country.[96] Jorge M. Corbacho, a member of the Peruvian Congress, impressed upon the participants at the 1919 Pan American Commercial Conference in Washington DC that the Japanese "penetration" of Peru was a serious issue. He passionately described the invasion of Japanese goods and peoples into his country and pleaded for a "more intimate commercial relationship with the United States." He argued that the threat of Japanese expansion into Latin America was a danger to the white race in general. "Sixty million of the yellow race," he claimed (grossly exaggerating the number of Japanese in South America), "are engaged in preparing the commercial, industrial, and financial bankruptcy of the people of the white race in the southern half of the American continent." If not stopped,

Peru would soon be part of the Japanese Empire, he warned. But Corbacho had an answer: tragedy could be averted through Pan-American solidarity and a closer relationship between the peoples of Latin America and the United States.[97]

Ordinary Peruvians also began to call upon the United States for assistance with the yellow peril from Japan. In 1938 a self-described Peruvian "workingman" wrote a long letter to a prominent American based in Lima in the hopes that his detailed warning of Japanese activities on the Peruvian coast would be brought to the attention of the U.S. delegates at the Pan-American Conference held in Lima in December. The Japanese were "multiplying" in the "most astonishing way," he reported, and Peruvian workers were suffering from misery and unemployment "forced upon [them] by the Japanese monster." He added that the Japanese were staging military maneuvers and concluded with this dire statement: "Peru belongs to the Japanese and not to the Peruvians." The United States, he felt, should protect its interests. "It behooves the United States, more than any other nation, to take action in Peru."[98]

Such rhetoric translated into real policy considerations after the 1924 Immigration Act was passed in the United States. Records indicate that Peruvian diplomats and politicians initiated conversations with the U.S. government about the possibility of U.S. protection should Peru decide to exclude Japanese immigrants as well. In Kobe, Japan, Peruvian Consul José B. Goyburu Elias asked U.S. Consul E. R. Dickover what might happen should Peru also prohibit the further entry of Japanese immigrants. If the Japanese government threatened Peru, what action would the U.S. government take, he asked. Almost at the same time, the U.S. diplomat Wallace Thompson met with President Leguía to discuss the 1924 Immigration Act and Japanese-Peruvian relations. Although the Japanese were unpopular and unwanted in Peru, Leguía explained, their exclusion would mean war, unless the United States pledged its support. Leguía also hinted at "joint action by west coast South American governments against the Japanese" if the United States would support them. U.S. diplomats in Lima wrote back to Washington

DC, "The question of further Asiatic immigration to South America, and especially to Peru, will depend largely on the action taken by the Government of the United States."[99] By the 1930s, then, the shared problem of Japanese immigration had helped Peruvians to further identify with the United States and encouraged them to look directly for U.S. assistance and support against the yellow peril.

Just as Peruvians viewed the yellow peril in the context of U.S.-Peruvian relations, Americans also viewed the developments in Latin America as part of the larger question of the role of the United States in the region.[100] In the late nineteenth century the United States had begun to institutionalize its rising claim to hegemony in the western hemisphere as first laid out in the Monroe Doctrine of 1823. U.S.-led Pan-American solidarity, which sought to preserve peace within the hemisphere and aid in commercial development and integration, eventually led to more forceful claims of direct interference and expansion under President Theodore Roosevelt. By the 1930s President Franklin Roosevelt's noninterventionist "good neighbor" policy treated Latin American nations as sovereign entities and equal partners. However, this policy was, as Peter Smith explains, "not so much a departure from past practice as an adaptation and extension of it." The United States continued to exert its hegemony in Latin America, albeit by employing economic strength and diplomatic pressure. It also deployed an ideological argument promoting a "western hemisphere idea" that defined the Americas as a "culturally unified, ideologically unique, and politically superior" realm of the globe that was best protected by the United States. At the Pan-American conferences throughout the 1930s U.S. efforts consistently defined the need for inter-American solidarity and cooperation. By the end of the decade the groundwork for future U.S. intervention in the region had been laid. At the Pan-American Conference in Panama in 1939 the United States sponsored a resolution that clearly declared its right and intention to fight against extrahemispheric ideologies and threats.[101]

It was in this larger context of changing U.S.-Latin American relations and growing U.S. hegemony in the Americas that the

United States interpreted Japanese migration to Latin America as a threat to both U.S. sovereignty and hemispheric security. The overall concern in the United States was that while North America had done its part to close the gates to the Japanese "menace," South America still remained open and vulnerable to Japanese expansion from within and abroad. Some of the leading yellow peril ideologues in the United States had warned of Japan's interest in Latin America since the early 1900s.[102] As early as 1908 U.S. officials listened closely to German intelligence reports that there were thousands of Japanese in Mexico, Peru, and Chile.[103] Beginning with World War I and intensifying in the 1930s, anti-Asian activists, Latin American scholars, and exiled Latin American leftists kept up a steady stream of sensationalist publications describing the threat of the yellow peril in the region. Writing in U.S. publications ranging from domestic home magazines to foreign policy journals, these writers warned of the "Japanese spearhead in the Americas," the "acute Japanese problem in South America," and "Japan's penetration of Latin America."[104]

Edward Alsworth Ross and G. Charles Hodges, for example, predicted that twenty or thirty million Orientals would be found in Latin America by the end of the twentieth century and would "forever end the dream of European immigration to the region."[105] The anti-Asian activist V. S. McClatchy told the U.S. State Department in 1921 that the Japanese already occupied many districts in the nitrate ports of Peru and had secured control of many lines of business. "In Lima, nearly every market stall is kept by Japanese and the Lima newspapers have called on the Government to protect the Peruvian people who are rapidly being displaced," he reported.[106]

To these Americans, the presence of Japanese immigrants in Latin America was a sign of an imminent Japanese invasion of the United States.[107] U.S. relations with both Japan and Mexico were deteriorating in the first two decades of the twentieth century. Anti-Japanese discrimination in the United States greatly affronted Japan, causing a serious break in relations. The situation was even worse with Mexico, for President Woodrow Wilson refused to recognize the newly established government of Victoriano Huerta in 1913. With its relations with both countries at a low point, the United States feared a Japanese-Mexican alliance that would threaten U.S. sovereignty. The *Chicago Herald and Examiner* reported that the Japanese were shipping arms to Mexico under the headline "Japs in U.S. Invasion Plot," and a U.S. Senate Foreign Relations Committee investigation uncovered an alleged plot by the Japanese to reclaim the U.S. Southwest by invading the country from Mexico.[108] The writer H. M. Hyndman argued that the Japanese had settled colonists within striking distance of the Panama Canal, had secured a naval base in Ecuador's Galapagos Islands, and were scouting out good landing spots on the Mexican coasts. The Japanese Empire, assisted by its "reservist colonists in America's Pacific possessions," would be ready to strike in case of war and thus posed a serious menace, he claimed.[109] U.S. attention was focused on the potential threat of Japanese communities and actions in Mexico, Brazil, and Peru, but many agreed that "Japan's strongest hold [was] on Peru."[110]

Peruvians also fed U.S. fears about the Japanese presence in the country. In 1927 an unnamed Peruvian sent information to the U.S. consul general in Peru about a Japanese company that had obtained a long-term lease for a barren site of land south of Pisco. The site, the informant suggested, would make "an ideal landing field for aircraft."[111] The prize-winning author Ciro Alegría also wrote on the Japanese problem for U.S. audiences. Alegría, who was dedicated to social reform and to improving the welfare of Peru's indigenous peoples, was well known to U.S. readers through his 1941 novel about an Andean indigenous community, *El mundo es ancho y ajeno* (*Broad and Alien Is the World*), which had been read widely in the United States. Forced into exile for his oppositional politics, Alegría cowrote an article in English titled "Japanese Spearhead in the Americas" that was published in the journal *Free World* in 1942. In an appeal to Pan-Americanism, he wrote to the "American reader, North and South," to report that the Japanese in Peru were organized into a "powerful fifth column" that constituted a "sharp spearhead pointed right at the heart of American democracy." The Japanese hid their real numbers, monopolized Peruvian agriculture and commerce, and were secretly training their young men for an impending military takeover. The journal's editors felt fortunate to be the first to present "authentic, first-hand information on Japan's preparation for an attack on the Americas."[112]

But it was the U.S. eugenicist Lothrop Stoddard who articulated the magnitude of the threat in Latin America most effectively. Japan, he argued, had "glimpsed in Latin America precious avenues to that racial expansion which is the key-note of Japanese foreign policy." Since 1914 the west coast of South America had been "flooded with Japanese goods, merchants, commercial missions, and financial agents seeking concessions of every kind." This was not just a problem for Latin America, he warned; it was a problem for the white race in general. "To allow the whole tropic belt clear round the world to pass into Asiatic hands would practically spell white race-suicide," he declared. Should "Asiatic colonization" succeed in Latin America, Japan would be able to use the region's "incalculable resources" and rise to world dominance. The entire "political, economic, and eventually the racial balance of power in the world" would be overturned in favor of Asia.[113]

The problem was that Latin America, what Stoddard referred to as "mongrel-ruled tropical America," could not stand alone. The United States and other white nations could not count on Latin America's ability to withstand the onslaught because it was racially weak, mongrel "red man's lands." "Virile" and ambitious "yellow Asia," Stoddard predicted, would take advantage of the mestizo or "half-caste" peoples of Latin America.[114] Edward Ross and G. Charles Hodges argued that Latin American nations were not strong enough militarily or diplomatically to block either Japanese military advances on the region or the Japanese immigrants who worked on behalf of the empire. All of these authors believed that the fate of Latin America lay in the hands of the United States as the only power in the western hemisphere strong enough to check

the Japanese flood. They also believed that Latin American leaders were right to beseech the United States to "back them up in
discriminating against Asiatic immigrants." They argued that the
United States had the right to intervene under the Monroe Doctrine.[115] To Stoddard, it was the white world's "race duty" to reso-
lutely oppose Asian invasions of both "white race-areas" (United
States, Canada, Australia) and other "non-Asiatic regions" inhabited by the "really inferior races" (Latin America).[116]

These sensationalist publications did several things. By identifying Latin America as the next target for Japanese expansion, they
confirmed the U.S. claim that the Japanese yellow peril was global. They also contributed to the new argument that Mexico and
Central and South America were weak links in U.S. national and
hemispheric security. And when these writers claimed that Latin America was not capable of fighting a Japanese conquest, they
helped justify further U.S. dominance in the region.[117]

Such shared attitudes about the menace of Japanese immigration
and the need for action in both the United States and Peru during
the 1930s foreshadowed the discussion of anti-Japanese policies
that would benefit both countries. Anxious about growing Japanese economic competition at the expense of the United States, the
U.S. government encouraged Latin American countries to take measures against Japanese economic expansion during the Pan-American conferences held between 1920 and 1940.[118] U.S. involvement
in World War II led to more draconian measures by both countries,
including the coordinated internment of Japanese Peruvians in the
United States during World War II. As soon as the United States
declared war with Japan after the attack on Pearl Harbor, Peru, a
U.S. ally, ended its diplomatic relations with Japan. The Japanese in
Peru became de facto "enemy aliens." In the eyes of Foreign Minister Alberto Ulloa, the Japanese community in Peru posed a national security threat. Peru was a "political and spiritual natural
ally of the great nation of the north," he claimed, but the twenty
thousand Japanese in Peru were an "active or virtual provocation
against the United States and against Peru." Ulloa's ideal solution

was to end all Japanese immigration to Peru, decrease the number of existing residents, and prevent Japanese from opening or operating businesses or acquiring land:"[They should] disappear completely from our country to return to theirs or to direct themselves to nearby lands of their more natural influence. Only when we have succeeded will we have consolidated an important aspect of the independence of Peru."[119]

With the aid of the United States, anti-Japanese measures were enacted in Peru. Shortly after the attack on Pearl Harbor on December 7, 1941, Peruvian government officials worked with the U.S. government to establish a blacklist of commercial enterprises owned or operated by persons of German, Japanese, or Italian ancestry or nationality. These businesses were subject to boycott and/or expropriation without compensation. As the U.S. State Department acknowledged in 1945, the primary targets of the blacklist were Japanese business owners in Lima.[120] Japanese community institutions were disbanded, and Japanese-language publications and meetings were prohibited on the claim that they constituted espionage activities.[121] In 1942 the United States invited Latin American countries to intern their dangerous enemy aliens.[122] Twelve countries deported some or all of their internees to the United States for custody. Peru offered to send *all* of its Japanese, an estimated twenty thousand people. The United States ultimately declined Peru's offer due to a lack of available transportation.[123] In the end 2,118 Japanese were sent to the United States from Latin America; 80 percent were from Peru alone, and they included Peruvian citizens by naturalization or birth.[124] The internees were meant to be exchanged for U.S. civilians interned in Japan, but the exchange never happened. Stripped of their passports en route to the United States, Japanese Peruvians were charged with being "illegal aliens" who entered the United States without proper visas and were deported or repatriated. More than nine hundred Japanese Latin Americans were deported to war-devastated Japan during and after the war. More than 350 remained in the United States and fought deportation in the courts. Eventually about one hundred were able to return to Latin America.[125]

Conclusion

Asians have a long and diverse history in the Americas. They immigrated under different circumstances and lived and worked in various locales in North America, Latin America, and the Caribbean, but their worlds and the policies that regulated their movements and lives were often interconnected. Thus the history of Asians in the Americas cannot be told from one national vantage point or one field of study (i.e., U.S. history, Asian American studies, Latin American studies, or Asian studies) alone. Rather only a comparative, transnational, and hemispheric perspective can put these fields in conversation with each other. When we are able to fully understand the complexity and dynamism of this interconnected world in motion, the history of Asians in the Americas becomes part of a larger global history of race, migration, and empire.

Japanese first migrated to North America, especially Hawai'i and the U.S. mainland, in the late nineteenth century. But once the United States and Canada closed their doors to Japanese immigration, migrants turned south, to Latin America. Conceptions of Japanese as a yellow peril and their immigration as an invasion followed them south as global anxieties about race, the "rising tide of color," and Japanese expansionism resonated throughout North and South America. These discourses circulated across national borders, were deployed in regional and national politics, and then circulated back out again. As the anti-Japanese campaign in Peru intensified in the 1930s, writers, politicians, intellectuals, and others increasingly looked to the United States for support, and the anti-Japanese laws passed during that decade were conceived of in a global environment in which the law of exclusion was becoming commonplace. As news of Japanese expansion in Asia spread around the world, the Peruvian government increasingly warmed to the idea of relying on U.S. protection. Similarly politicians and pundits in the United States looked south and saw a yellow peril that could easily cross borders into the United States and threaten the security of the entire hemisphere. Both perspectives were

inextricably related to growing U.S. hegemony in the region. During World War II the transnational lens through which both countries viewed the problem of Japanese immigration became translated into coordinated internment policies in the name of national
and hemispheric security.

Asians in the Americas were situated at the crossroads of their
Asian homelands, with which they maintained strong economic,
familial, and cultural ties; the Pacific, which they crossed and re-
crossed on their transnational journeys; and the Americas, where
they lived, worked, and became part of communities even as their
rights were curtailed and they faced exclusionary legislation. The
Asian Americas they inhabited was a world in motion in which people, racial ideologies, and policies moved and interacted with each
other *across* national borders instead of solely *within* them. Their
histories must be told across the varied spaces in which they lived.

Notes

1. *San Francisco Examiner*, May 25, 1924; Jules Becker, *The Course of
Exclusion, 1882–1924: San Francisco Newspaper Coverage of the Chi-
nese and Japanese in the United States* (San Francisco: Mellen Research
University Press, 1991), 192.

2. Eiichiro Azuma, "Historical Overview of Japanese Emigration,
1868–2000," in *Encyclopedia of Japanese Descendants in the Americas:
An Illustrated History of the Nikkei*, ed. Akemi Kikumura-Yano (Walnut Creek CA: Alta Mira Press, 2002), 33; Ayumi Takenaka, "The Japanese in Peru: History of Immigration, Settlement, and Racialization,"
Latin American Perspectives 136 31, no. 3 (2004): 78–79.

3. Examples include Roger Daniels, *The Politics of Prejudice: The Anti-Japanese Movement in California and the Struggle for Japanese Exclusion* (Berkeley: University of California Press, 1962); W. Peter Ward,
*White Canada Forever: Popular Attitudes and Public Policy toward Ori-
entals in British Columbia* (Montreal: McGill-Queen's University Press,
1978); Patricia Roy, *A White Man's Province: British Columbia Politicians
and Chinese and Japanese Immigrants, 1858–1914* (Vancouver: University of British Columbia Press, 1989) and *The Oriental Question: Con-
solidating a White Man's Province, 1914–1941* (Vancouver: University

of British Columbia Press, 2003); Daniel Masterson and Sakaya Funada-Classen, *The Japanese in Latin America* (Urbana: University of Illinois Press, 2004); C. Harvey Gardiner, *The Japanese and Peru, 1873–1973* (Albuquerque: University of New Mexico Press, 1975).

4. A hemispheric American history examines the shared histories and legacies of diverse indigenous societies, European colonialism, slavery, mass migration, and nation-state building in the Americas as well as the transnational flows, networks, and communities connecting the Americas to the rest of the world. The United States is decentered as a primary site of inquiry, but its hegemonic role in the region is not. A hemispheric Asian American history compares and connects not only the experiences of Asians in the United States and Latin America—the most common reference points in the new hemispheric American studies—but also Canada and the Pacific World, two other sites to which Asians migrated and/or retained strong ties. On new hemispheric and transnational perspectives of the Americas, see Sandhya Shukla and Heidi Tinsman, eds., *Imaging Our Americas: Toward a Transnationl Frame* (Durham NC: Duke University Press, 2007).

5. Brazil received the largest number of Japanese immigrants in all of Latin America. The centralized and government-controlled pattern of Japanese migration to that country contrasted sharply with the loosely regulated labor migration to the United States, Canada, and Peru.

6. On comparative and transnational approaches, see Micol Seigel, "Beyond Compare: Comparative Method after the Transnational Turn," *Radical History Review* 91 (Winter 2005): 62–90; Sanjeev Khagram and Peggy Levitt, "Constructing Transnational Studies," in *The Transnational Studies Reader*, ed. Sanjeev Khagram and Peggy Levitt (New York: Routledge, 2008), 1–18.

7. Howard Winant, *The World Is a Ghetto: Race and Democracy since World War II* (New York: Basic Books, 2002), 143. On the interactive process of race making, see also Henry Yu, "How Tiger Woods Lost His Stripes: Post-Nationalist American Studies as a History of Race, Migration, and the Commodification of Culture," in *Post-Nationalist American Studies*, ed. John Carlos Rowe (Berkeley: University of California Press, 2000), 224.

8. Gilbert Joseph has described how U.S. networks, exchanges, behaviors, discourses, and meanings were received, contested, and appropriated

in Latin America in what he calls "foreign-local encounters" between the United States and Latin America. See Gilbert M. Joseph, "Close Encounters: Toward a New Cultural History of U.S.-Latin American Relations," in *Close Encounters of Empire: Writing the Cultural History of U.S.-Latin American Relations*, ed. Gilbert M. Joseph, Catherine C. Legrand, and Ricardo D. Salvatore (Durham NC: Duke University Press, 1998), 5, 15.

9. Daniels, *Politics of Prejudice*, 20–21, 25–26, 32, 41–44; Asiatic Exclusion League, *Proceedings of the First International Convention: First International Convention of the Asiatic Exclusion League of North America* (San Francisco: Asiatic Exclusion League, 1908), 68; Erika Lee and Judy Yung, *Angel Island: Immigrant Gateway to America* (New York: Oxford University Press, 2010), 115–16.

10. See, for example, Charles Henry Pearson, *National Life and Character: A Forecast* (London: Macmillan, 1894).

11. Richard Austin Thompson, *The Yellow Peril, 1890–1924* (1957; repr., New York: Arno Press, 1978), 37; Gary Okihiro, *Margins and Mainstreams: Asians in American History and Culture* (Seattle: University of Washington Press, 1994), 137. Early "yellow peril" works include Homer Lea, *The Valor of Ignorance: The Inevitable Japanese-American War* (New York: Harper and Brothers, 1909); James Francis Abbot, *Japanese Expansion and American Policies* (New York: Macmillan, 1916).

12. Lothrop Stoddard, *The Rising Tide of Color against White World Supremacy* (New York: Charles Scriber's Sons, 1926), 17–53, 229, 241–49, 48–49, 251.

13. *San Francisco Examiner*, February 27, 1924, cited in Becker, *The Course of Exclusion*, 191.

14. Eiichiro Azuma, *Between Two Empires: Race, History, and Transnationalism in Japanese America* (New York: Oxford University Press, 2005), 62–65.

15. *San Francisco Examiner*, January 21, 1924, cited in Becker, *The Course of Exclusion*, 189.

16. Dylan Yeats, "Documenting Exclusion and the Logic of Difference," in *Yellow Peril: Collecting Xenophobia* (New York: Asian/Pacific/American Institute, New York University, 2007), 22.

17. Jesse Frederick Steiner, *The Japanese Invasion: A Study in the Psychology of Inter-Racial Contacts* (Chicago: A. C. McClurg, 1917), v–vi, 197, 209; Okihiro, *Margins and Mainstreams*, 134.

18. Daniels, *The Politics of Prejudice*, 99.

19. Thompson, *The Yellow Peril*, 29–36; Montaville Flowers, *The Japanese Conquest of American Opinion* (New York: George H. Doran, 1917), 202, 216, 222–24; Okhiro, *Margins and Mainstreams*, 133.

20. Lea, *The Valor of Ignorance*, 249–51, 343.

21. Daniels, *The Politics of Prejudice*, 70.

22. Daniels, *The Politics of Prejudice*, 65, 106.

23. The 1924 Immigration Act expanded the quotas that had been set by the Quota Act of 1921. It established temporary quotas that were allocated to each European country at 2 percent of the number of foreign-born of each nationality in the 1890 census. Under this formula, 85 percent of the quotas went to northern and western European nations. No restrictions were based on immigration from the western hemisphere. Permanent immigration quotas went into effect in 1929 and stayed in place until 1952. Mae M. Ngai, "The Architecture of Race in American Immigration Law: A Reexamination of the Immigration Act of 1924," *Journal of American History* 86, no. 1 (1999): 67.

24. Ward, *White Canada Forever*, 131–33.

25. From 1899 to 1908, 155,772 Japanese immigrants arrived in Canada and the United States. During the same years only 18,203 Japanese migrated to Latin American countries. Masterson and Funada-Classen, *The Japanese in Latin America*, 11.

26. Gardiner, *The Japanese and Peru*, 23; J. F. Normano and Antonello Gerbi, *The Japanese in South America: An Introductory Survey with Special Reference to Peru* (New York: John Day Col, 1943), 5–7; Fred J. Rippy, "The Japanese in Latin America," *Inter-American Economic Affairs* 8, no. 1 (1949): 52.

27. Rippy, "The Japanese in Latin America," 54–55; Takenaka, "The Japanese in Peru," 77.

28. Emigration was a vital aspect of Japan's modernization campaign. Azuma, "Historical Overview of Japanese Emigration, 1868–2000," 37, 39; Normano and Gerbi, *The Japanese in South America*, 3–4, 24, 45, 47–49; J. F. Normano, "Japanese Emigration to Latin America," *Genus*, May 1938, 48.

29. Seiichi Higashide, *Adios to Tears: The Memoirs of a Japanese-Peruvian Internee in U.S. Concentration Camps* (Seattle: University of Washington Press, 2000), 35.

30. Normano, "Japanese Emigration to Latin America," 55–56; Normano and Gerbi, *The Japanese in South America*, 6; Gardiner, *The Japanese and Peru*, 38.

31. Takenaka, "The Japanese in Peru," 80, 84; Masterson and Funada-Classen, *The Japanese in Latin America*, 64–65, 70.

32. Gardiner, *The Japanese and Peru*, 72–78; Jun Kodani, "The Japanese Peruvians of Lima and Anti-Japanese Agitation, 1900–1940" (MA thesis, University of California, Berkeley, 1984), 23–24, 55; Normano and Gerbi, *The Japanese in South America*, 83.

33. Orazio Ciccarelli, "Peru's Anti-Japanese Campaign in the 1930s: Economic Dependency and Abortive Nationalism," *Canadian Review of Studies in Nationalism* 5 (1981–82): 122–24.

34. Kodani, "The Japanese Peruvians," 12, 66, 65.

35. See, for example, "La invasión de los japoneses en el Perú," *El Buen Humor* (Lima), November 18, 1933, and November 19, 1933; "La protección contra la invasión japonesa," *La Prensa* (Lima), December 11, 1934.

36. The series was printed in *La Prensa* beginning on August 21, 1937, and ended October 31, 1937, and included forty-nine articles. Salinas Cossío was the most prominent of these men. He was a professor of aesthetics and art history at the National School of Fine Arts and was the founding president of the Cotton Council of Peru and president of the National Agrarian Society in the 1930s. For information on Cossío, see his obituaries in *El Comercio*, May 7, 1941, and *Universal*, May 7, 1941; Amelia Morimoto, *Los Inmigrantes Japoneses en el Perú* (Lima: Taller de Estudios Andinos, Universidad Nacional Agraria, 1979), 69; Normano and Gerbi, *The Japanese in South America*, 78.

37. See, for example, "El peligro-chino-japonés," *La Prensa*, July 1, 1934; "Los peligros de la inmigración asiática," *El Liberal* (Lima), January 22, 1934; "Sobre el peligro Amarillo," *La Prensa*, August 2, 1934; "Ante el peligro Amarillo," *La Prensa*, August 13, 1934.

38. Tirso Molinari Morales, *El Fascismo en el Peru: La Unión Revolucionaria 1931–36* (Lima: Fondo Editorial de la Facultad de Ciencias Sociales, 2006), 224; Kodani, "The Japanese Peruvians," 72–73; Ciccarelli, "Peru's Anti-Japanese Campaign," 126–27.

39. Kodani, "The Japanese Peruvians," 17, italics original; Normano and Gerbi, *The Japanese in South America*, 8.

40. Takenaka, "The Japanese in Peru," 82–83.

41. Brooke Larson, *Trials of Nation Making: Liberalism, Race, and Ethnicity in the Andes, 1810–1910* (New York: Cambridge University Press, 2004), 60–61nn35–36, 247.

42. On the ways mestizaje came to symbolize elites' "hopes, hatreds, and fears upon the future of the race and nation" in nineteenth-century Latin America, see Brooke Larson, *Cochabamba, 1550–1900: Colonialism and Agrarian Transformation in Bolivia* (Durham NC: Duke University Press, 1998), 377; Marisol de la Cadena, *Indigenous Mestizos: The Politics of Race and Culture in Cuzco, Peru, 1919–1991* (Durham NC: Duke University Press, 2000), 13. On some philosophers' critiques of mestizaje, see Thomas E. Skidmore and Peter H. Smith, *Modern Latin America* (New York: Oxford University Press, 1997), 191.

43. See, for example, the characterization of Peru as "occidental" by former president Francisco García Calderón, *The Rise of Latin America* (London: Unwin, 1911), 330–31; and the description of Peru as a "European country" with a "racially homogeneous" population by former foreign minister Alberto Ulloa in Normano and Gerbi, *The Japanese in South America*, 114.

44. De la Cadena, *Indigenous Mestizos*, 16. See also Victor J. Guevara, *Las Grandes Cuestiones Nacionales: El Petroleo, Los Ferrocarriles, la Inmigración Japonesa, el Problema Moral* (Cuzco, Peru: Biblioteca de la Revista de Filosofia y Derech, 1939), 130–31, 133. Peruvian fascists also maintained the supremacy of Europeans and the desirability of European immigration. Molinari Morales, *El Fascismo en el Peru*, 225–26, 233–34.

45. Takenaka, "The Japanese in Peru," 83.

46. Normano and Gerbi, *The Japanese in South America*, 68, 73.

47. Kodani, "The Japanese Peruvians," 29, 42n6, 31, 42n12; Gardiner, *The Japanese and Peru*, 31; Takenaka, "The Japanese in Peru," 86.

48. *Acción*, April 30, 1934, cited in Molinari Morales, *El Fascismo en el Peru*, 234.

49. Normano and Gerbi, *The Japanese in South America*, 124–25.

50. García Calderón was a lawyer and academic and was president of Peru for a short seven-month period in 1881, during the War of the Pacific with Chile. García Calderón, *Latin America*, 324, 329–30; Gardiner, *The Japanese and Peru*, 65.

51. *American Review of Reviews*, 1907, 622–23, cited in Takenaka, "The Japanese in Peru," 88.

52. Guevara, *Las Grandes Cuestiones Nacionales*, 136.

53. Kodani, "The Japanese Peruvians," 23–24, 55.

54. Normano and Gerbi, *The Japanese in South America*, 114, 122, 125.

55. Gardiner, *The Japanese and Peru*, 68.

56. In 1919 *El Obrero Textil* urged workers to organize a campaign to pressure the Peruvian Congress to adopt Asian exclusion legislation. Kodani, "The Japanese Peruvians," 31; Takenaka, "The Japanese in Peru," 86.

57. Kodani, "The Japanese Peruvians," 2–13, 48, 54, 30.

58. *El Obrero Textil*, March 13, 1920, cited in Kodani, "The Japanese Peruvians," 31, 42n11.

59. Morimoto, *Los Inmigrantes Japoneses en el Perú*, 69.

60. Ciccarelli, "Peru's Anti-Japanese Campaign," 114; Kodani, "The Japanese Peruvians," 50.

61. Japanese migrants chose these businesses because they required little capital and few skills. Small businesses such as these allowed migrants to rely on cheap, nonwage or family labor, could be easily liquidated if the migrant wished to return to Japan, and they relied on Japanese imports of low-cost goods and ethnic associations that offered credit. Takenaka, "The Japanese in Peru," 85–86.

62. Mischia Titiev, "The Japanese Colony in Peru," *Far Eastern Quarterly* 10, no. 3 (1951): 228–29; Gardiner, *The Japanese and Peru*, 64; Peter Blanchard, "Asian Immigrants in Peru, 1899–1923," *NorthSouth* 4 (1979): 66; *La Prensa*, October 1, 1937.

63. See *Acción*, June 17, 1934, and August 7, 1934; Molinari Morales, *El Fascismo en el Peru*, 224–30, 237–38, 240–42. On the general appeal of fascism in Peru, see Orazio Ciccarelli, "Fascism and Politics in Peru during the Benavides Regime, 1933–1939: The Italian Perspective," *Hispanic American Historical Review* 70, no. 3 (1990): 405, 407–8; Adam Andarle, *Los movimientos políticos en el Perú entre las dos guerras mundiales* (Havana: Casa de las Americas, 1985); José Ignacio López Soria, *El pensamiento fascista (1930–1945)* (Lima: Lima Mosca Azul Ed., 1981).

64. Rippy, "The Japanese in Latin America," 61; Gardiner, *The Japanese and Peru*, 60.

65. Ciccarelli, "Peru's Anti-Japanese Campaign," 116.

66. Normano and Gerbi, *The Japanese in South America*, 77.

67. Kodani, "The Japanese Peruvians," 81.

68. Ciccarelli, "Peru's Anti-Japanese Campaign," 117.

69. Normano, "Japanese Emigration," 74.

70. García Calderón, *Latin America*, 324, 329–30; Gardiner, *The Japanese and Peru*, 65.

71. Guevara, *Las Grandes Cuestiones Nacionales*, 129–30, 146, 162, 136.

72. *La Prensa*, August 27, 1937, September 6, 1937, and October 14, 1937.

73. Blanchard, "Asian Immigrants in Peru," 67–70.

74. The pretext behind the contract labor law was that Japanese laborers had abandoned the plantations and so their use as laborers should be ended. More likely the need for contract labor had declined. Takenaka, "The Japanese in Peru," 86; Masterson and Funada-Classen, *The Japanese in Latin America*, 71; Gardiner, *The Japanese and Peru*, 44; Kodani, "The Japanese Peruvians," 65.

75. Brazil's immigration law fixed an annual quota of 2 percent of the number of immigrants from each nation who had arrived in the previous fifty years. Farmers were given preference. The law affected Japan more than any other country. Its annual quota was restricted to 2,845. Masterson and Funada-Classen, *The Japanese in Latin America*, 72; Normano and Gerbi, *The Japanese in South America*, 21–23; Jeffrey Lesser, *Negotiating National Identity: Immigrants, Minorities, and the Struggle for Ethnicity in Brazil* (Durham NC: Duke University Press, 1999), 120.

76. Normano and Gerbi, *The Japanese in South America*, 8, 115; Gardiner, *The Japanese and Peru*, 77, 114–16; Masterson and Funada-Classen, *The Japanese in Latin America*, 72–73; Morimoto, *Los Inmigrantes Japoneses en el Perú*, 70; Takenaka, "The Japanese in Peru," 87.

77. Normano and Gerbi, *The Japanese in South America*, 113–14.

78. The 80 percent law had first been passed as Decree Law 7505 of April 8, 1932. It coincided with parallel attempts in Mexico to require Chinese-owned businesses to hire Mexican employees.

79. Kodani, "The Japanese Peruvians," 76; Gardiner, *The Japanese and Peru*, 114–16.

80. The July 31, 1940, law forfeited the citizenship of *kibei*, Japanese born in Peru but educated in Japan and then returned to Peru. Normano and Gerbi, *The Japanese in South America*, 8, 113, 115–16; Morimoto, *Los Inmigrantes Japoneses en el Perú*, 70, 74; Masterson and Funada-Classen, *The Japanese in Latin America*, 72–73, 152; Edward Barnhart,

"Japanese Internees from Peru," *Pacific Historical Review* 31 (1962): 170; Takenaka, "The Japanese in Peru," 87.

81. The Decree Law of May 10, 1934, limited the importation of textiles. The trade agreement (*tratado de comercio*) was broken on October 15, 1934. The 1935 quotas were put in place in May on the grounds that "foreign" textiles had invaded the Peruvian markets and endangered domestic mills and employment. The decree of June 26, 1936, aimed at stopping the increase of new Japanese-owned small businesses. Gardiner, *The Japanese and Peru*, 50; Morimoto, *Los Inmigrantes Japoneses en el Perú*, 71–72; Normano and Gerbi, *The Japanese in South America*, 117; Takenaka, "The Japanese in Peru," 87.

82. Kodani, "The Japanese Peruvians," 77.

83. Ciro Alegría and Alfredo Saco, "Japanese Spearhead in the Americas, Part 2," *Free World* 2, no. 2 (1942): 181.

84. Higashide, *Adios to Tears*, 105–10; Normano and Gerbi, *The Japanese in South America*, 79; Gardiner, *The Japanese and Peru*, 52–53. Estimates on damages differ. Higashide claims that the Japanese community suffered $600 million in losses. Gardiner, citing official Japanese sources, reports a much lower figure of $1.64 million.

85. Dr. Carlos Enrique Paz Soldan proposed a pro-eugenicist campaign at the Institute of Social Medicine at the University of San Marcos and cited at length Stoddard's book in his article "The Japanese Penetration in Peru," *La Prensa*, September 26, 1937.

86. See, for example, V. S. McClatchy, *La Repuesta De California Al Japon: La Ley De Exclusión No Hiere El Honor Del Japon: Historia De Los Hechos: Contestación a La Edición Especial Del "Japan Times" De Tokio Y a Su Amigable "Mensaje De Japon a América* (San Francisco: Comité Unido de Inmigración de California United States California San Francisco, 1925); V. S. McClatchy, *Los Japoneses En California: Resultados Obtenidos Al Ponerse En Vigor La Ley Sobre Adquisición De Tierras Por Extranjeros* (San Francisco: Comité Unido de Inmigración de California, 1924).

87. Fernando Coronil, preface to *Close Encounters of Empire: Writing the Cultural History of U.S.-Latin American Relations*, ed. Gilbert M. Joseph, Catherine C. Legrand, and Ricardo D. Salvatore (Durham NC: Duke University Press, 1998), ix.

88. Normano and Gerbi, *The Japanese in South America*, 54.

89. Ciccarelli, "Peru's Anti-Japanese Campaign," 115.

90. García Calderón, *The Rise of Latin America*, 323, 325.

91. Normano, "Japanese Emigration," 80–81; Rippy, "The Japanese in Latin America," 55.

92. Manuel Ugarte, *El Porvenir de la América Española: La Raza, la Integridad Territorial y Moral, la Organización Interior* (Ann Arbor: University of Michigan Library, 1920), chapter 8, cited in Rippy, "The Japanese in Latin America," 55–56; García Calderón, *The Rise of Latin America*, 323, 325, 330–31. Fred Rippy notes that Agustín Edwards, a nineteenth-century Chilean politician and businessman, expressed similar sentiments (57n24).

93. García Calderón, *The Rise of Latin America*, 323, 327.

94. *El Comercio*, May 29, 1924, and *Acción*, April 30, 1934, cited in Molinari Morales, *El Fascismo en el Peru*, 233–34.

95. *La Prensa*, November 30, 1934.

96. Normano, "Japanese Emigration," 79.

97. Jorge M. Corbacho, *American Commerce in South America and the Menace of Japan's Expansionist Plans* (Washington DC: Second Pan-American Commercial Conference, 1919), 6, 8; Normano, "Japanese Emigration," 80. Similarly the Peruvian eugenicist Dr. Carlos Enrique Paz Soldán attempted to sound the alarm about the "racial asianation of America" at the seventh Pan-American Conference on the Child in Mexico in 1937. *La Prensa*, October 3, 1937; *Memoria del VII Congreso Panamericano del Niño* (Mexico City: Talleres Graficos de la Nacion, 1937).

98. "Japanese 'Menace' Seen by a Peruvian," *New York Times*, January 22, 1939.

99. Gardiner, *The Japanese and Peru*, 46–47.

100. As Ricardo Salvatore has illustrated, from 1890 to 1930, South America became a common "textual space for the projection of the cultural anxieties" of the United States and its expansive commercial culture and power and "an immense source of 'evidence' for validating theories and propositions." Ricardo Salvatore, "The Enterprise of Knowledge: Representational Machines of Informal Empire," in *Close Encounters of Empire: Writing the Cultural History of U.S.-Latin American Relations*, ed. Gilbert M. Joseph, Catherine C. Legrand, and Ricardo D. Salvatore (Durham NC: Duke University Press, 1998), 93.

101. The Monroe Doctrine declared in 1823 that any foreign efforts

to colonize or interfere with states in the Americas would be viewed by
the United States as an act of aggression. Peter H. Smith, *Talons of the
Eagle: Dynamics of U.S.-Latin American Relations* (New York: Oxford University Press, 2000), 29–30, 36, 63–64 68–69, 75, 80–81, 85.

102. Lea, *The Valor of Ignorance*, 136. Frank McGowan, a member
of the Asiatic Exclusion League in San Francisco, gave a speech in 1910
warning that Japanese immigrants could enter South America and that
this was a threat to the United States. "Proceedings of the Asiatic Exclusion League" (June 1910), in *Proceedings of the Asiatic Exclusion League
1907–1913* (New York: Arno Press, 1977), 41.

103. Thomas A. Bailey, *Theodore Roosevelt and the Japanese-American Crisis* (Gloucester MA: Peter Smith, 1964), 268–69; Ute Mehnert,
"German *Weltpolitik* and the American Two-Front Dilemma: The 'Japanese Peril' in German-American Relations, 1904–1917," *Journal of American History* 84, no. 2 (1996): 1452–55.

104. See, for example, Ciro Alegría and Alfredo Saco, "Japanese Spearhead in the Americas, Part 1," *Free World* 2, no. 1 (1942): 81–84; Alegría
and Saco, "Japanese Spearhead in the Americas, Part 2," 181–84; Genaro Arbaiza, "Acute Japanese Problem in South America," *Current History* 21 (1925): 735–39; Catherine Porter, "Japan's 'Penetration' of Latin America," *Far Eastern Survey* 4, no. 10 (1935): 73–78.

105. Edward A. Ross, *South of Panama* (New York: Century, 1915),
91; G. Charles Hodges, "Japanese Ambitions and Latin America," *Sunset*
37 (October 1916): 16–17, 82–85; Thompson, *The Yellow Peril*, 365–66.

106. V. S. McClatchy, *Japanese Immigration and Colonization: Brief
Prepared for Consideration of the State Department* (San Francisco: R
and E Research Associates, 1921), 63.

107. Jerry García, "Japanese Immigration and Community Development in México, 1897–1940" (PhD diss., Washington State University,
1999), 211.

108. *Chicago Herald and Examiner*, November 25, 1919, and January 5, 14, 20, 1920, cited in Thompson, *The Yellow Peril*, 398; U.S. Senate, Foreign Relations Committee, "Investigation of Mexican Affairs,"
Senate Document no. 285, serials 7665 and 7666, 1205–6, 1304, 66th
Cong., 2nd sess., May 24, 1920; Stoddard, *Rising Tide of Color*, 133–35, cited in Thompson, *The Yellow Peril*, 395–96.

109. H. M. Hyndman, *The Awakening of Asia* (New York: Boni and
Liveright, 1919), 150–51.

110. Carlton Beals, *The Coming Struggle for Latin America* (Philadelphia: J. B. Lippincott, 1938), 43; Stoddard, *Rising Tide of Color*, 133–35; Thompson, *The Yellow Peril*, 395–96; Betty Kirk, "Mexico's War on Hidden Japanese," *Inter-American* 2, no. 1 (1943): 14–16.

111. Gardiner, *The Japanese and Peru*, 66–67.

112. Alegría and Saco, "Japanese Spearhead in the Americas, Part 1," 81–84 and "Part 2," 181–84.

113. Stoddard, *The Rising Tide of Color*, 130–32, 249, 232.

114. Stoddard explained that while Latin America was commonly considered part of the white world, it was racially not "Latin" but "Amerindian or negroid, with a thin Spanish or Portuguese veneer." Stoddard, *The Rising Tide of Color*, 232, 105, 115, 141, 130–32. On the common understanding among early twentieth-century intellectuals and race theorists that miscegenation and political instability led to the undeveloped, immature, and "backward" status of the region, see Salvatore, "The Enterprise of Knowledge," 82–83; Emily S. Rosenberg, "Turning to Culture," in *Close Encounters of Empire: Writing the Cultural History of U.S.-Latin American Relations*, ed. Gilbert M. Joseph, Catherine C. Legrand, and Ricardo D. Salvatore (Durham NC: Duke University Press, 1998), 499–500.

115. Ross, *South of Panama*, 93; Thompson, *The Yellow Peril*, 365–67. Carl Crow, a newspaper journalist who had worked and lived in both China and Japan, also advocated U.S. action under the Monroe Doctrine to check Oriental immigration in Latin America. Carl Crow, *Japan and America* (New York: R. M. McBride, 1916), 188–93, 197–98.

116. Stoddard, *The Rising Tide of Color*, 232.

117. In 1938 the writer Carlton Beals reported that the U.S. Army and Navy intelligence departments believed that "nearly every Jap in Latin America is a slick spy." Beals, *The Coming Struggle for Latin America*, 13.

118. Takenaka, "The Japanese in Peru," 91.

119. Alberto Ulloa, *Posición internacional del Perú* (Lima, Peru: Imprenta Torres Aguirre, 1941), 361, 363.

120. U.S. Department of State, *Papers Relating to the Foreign Relations of the United States*, vol. 9 (1945), cited in Kodani, "The Japanese Peruvians," 78.

121. Takenaka, "The Japanese in Peru," 92.

122. *Personal Justice Denied: Report of the Commission on Wartime*

Relocation and Internment of Civilians (Seattle: University of Washington Press, 1997), 307.

123. Max Friedman, *Nazis and Good Neighbors: The United States Campaign against the Germans of Latin America in World War II* (New York: Cambridge University Press, 2005), 238n19.

124. These included 1,024 men who were considered "dangerous aliens" by Peru and 1,094 "voluntary internees" who were family members seeking to be reunified with their husbands and fathers in the United States. See Barnhart, "Japanese Internees," 172.

125. C. Harvey Gardiner, *Pawns in a Triangle of Hate: The Peruvian Japanese and the United States* (Seattle: University of Washington Press, 1981), 112–31; Higashide, *Adios to Tears*, 179; Masterson and Funada-Classen, *The Japanese in Latin America*, 166, 168.

Chapter 12

Crossing Borders, Locating Home
Ethical Responsibility in Karen Tei Yamashita's
Tropic of Orange

Stella Oh

The U.S.-Mexico border *es una herida abierta* where the Third World grates against the first and bleeds. And before a scab forms it hemorrhages again, the lifeblood of two worlds merging to form a third country—a border culture.—GLORIA ANZALDÚA, *Borderlands/La Frontera: The New Mestiza*

The concept of borderlands has garnered much debate in contemporary U.S. cultural representations.[1] In *Border Matters: Remapping American Cultural Studies*, José Saldívar argues for "changing borderland subjectivities" within the U.S.-Mexican border and points to Karen Tei Yamashita's *Tropic of Orange* (1997) as a border novel that illustrates an "emerging U.S.-Mexico *frontera* imaginary."[2] Saldívar traces how physical and discursive spaces of the U.S.-Mexican border inflect the reality of U.S. cultural productions. By adding an Asian presence to the border, Yamashita complicates Saldívar's notion of an exclusive U.S.-Mexican border. This Asian presence on the border also signals the effects of the process of globalization.

Tracing the changing nature of borderlands, Yamashita examines how borders redefine notions of home and how increased globalization unmoors fixed ethnic, national, and geographic identities.

Globalization necessarily involves movement and deterritorialization, creating new nonterritorial identities and social activities. Globalization also increases our interconnectedness and hastens the process of change that underpins modern society. In this essay, I examine how the characters of Yamashita's text experience national (dis)identification and a sense of "homelessness": Bobby, a Chinese Singaporean Koreatown workaholic; Rafaela, a Mexican mother; Emi, a Japanese American media producer; Gabriel, a Mexican American journalist; Arcangel, a Mexican prophet and fighter; Buzzworm, an African American Vietnam vet, a.k.a. "Angel of Mercy"; and Manzanar, a homeless sansei surgeon conducting symphonies on the freeway. Their multiple positioning inscribes their bodies as material sites for reevaluating concepts of identities based on racial essentialism and nation-states. Yamashita not only criticizes the formation of nations as circumscribed by borders, but more important, creates new modes of cross-cultural and transnational homelands that respond to recent transformations in globalization, exploring the possibility of making new homes while traveling through difference. This journey is exemplified by several passages in the novel: capital flows of poisoned oranges from Brazil to Mexico to California; the organ-smuggling operation from Mexico to the United States; the geopolitical transformation from the Tropic of Cancer to the Tropic of Orange; Arcangel's journey north to fight SUPERNAFTA, an allegorical figure who embodies the neocolonial mechanism of capitalism; Rafaela and Bobby's journey south; and the inaudible symphonies that Manzanar Marukami conducts on the overpass of the Los Angeles Freeway. All these movements signal discourses of displacement as the characters travel different routes searching for their roots.

The Commerce of Humankind

Standing on a freeway overpass in Los Angeles, Manzanar Marukami conducts the "excruciatingly beautiful" traffic of automobiles, their drivers, and the cargo they carry on the serpentine highway, a "great root system, an organic living entity." He "understood the

nature of the truck beast, whose purpose was to transport the great
products of civilization: home and office appliances, steel beams
and turbines, fruits, vegetables, meats, and grain, Coca-Cola and
Sparkeletts, Hollywood sets, this fall's fashions, military hardware,
gasoline, concrete, and garbage. Nothing was more and less important."[3] The highway that carries all the products of "civilization" is "an organic living entity." The route of the highway transforms into a "great root system" that anchors civilization. While
goods and vehicles are made organic, human beings are commodified in the novel. Yamashita reveals this highly ironic situation by
contextualizing the novel within the larger black market trafficking of drugs, human labor, and baby organs.

While the material goods of civilization are made visible, the
people who compose that civilization are rendered invisible. When
a large fire erupts on the freeway, we witness thousands of homeless come out from their encampments under the freeway. As Manzanar continued to conduct, "even he, who knew the dense hidden
community living on the no-man's-land of public property, was surprised by the numbers of people who descended the slopes."[4] The
underpass represents a borderland that Gloria Anzaldúa argues is
inhabited by the prohibited and the forbidden. As a place that is
always in "transition," it draws the lines between "places that are
safe and unsafe, to distinguish *us* from *them*."[5] In order to distinguish *us*, the civilized, from *them*, the undesirable members of society, the homeless are treated as less than human. An LAPD heli-
copter indiscriminately shoots at the homeless encampment in an
effort to get them out of other people's cars. Here property is giv-
en preference over human lives. As the homeless cross borders and
inhabit spaces reserved for normal Americans, they test the limits
of ethical responsibility in modern civilization. As Rey Chow argues in *Ethics after Idealism*, ethical responsibility results in the
relationship between the subject and Other. Chow insists that an
emphasis must be placed on trauma that results from the confrontation between the self and the real, a real that is at once the other
as well as the positive identities through which we try to order our

ourselves and the world we live in. She demonstrates this concern in interrogations of fantasies that structure the self and the other, especially as they are employed in filmic representations. Ethical responsibility between self and other can also be seen in literary works. As when watching a film, readers put themselves in the position of the protagonist while they simultaneously realize that they are separate from the character in the story.[6] However, filmic and literary representations also differ. Whereas film usually leaves little to the imagination, literature tends to offer a more rich and in-depth narrative of a character or scene. Films provide most of the images, while literatures leave those images to the individual imagination of the reader. As such the ethical responsibility between self and other is even more pronounced in works of literature because how the reader envisions the characters and his relationship to them are highly self-reflective of his social location. Yamashita's novel not only challenges how we confront the other but also how we envision and imagine the Other.

Buzzworm's desire to "humanize the homeless" points to this kind of ethical responsibility. With the help of Emi, the Japanese American producer, Buzzworm broadcasts a show depicting the lives of a homeless family living in an abandoned car on the freeway. The family plants a garden in the car's engine: "Now we got a garden goin'. Something we always wanted. Got lettuce in this corner, some baby carrots over here, tomatoes here. A patch like this'll do some good feedin'."[7] Buzzworm also broadcasts a homeless mother and her newborn baby living out of a '64 Impala; the woman "stor[es] baby food and diapers under the trunk hood painted with the calla lilies."[8] The humanity of the homeless on camera is sharply interrupted by gunfire. When the homeless, who represent the other, clash with everyday Americans a violent conflict arises, resulting in the death of Emi.

The forced removal of the undesirable and economically dispossessed homeless mirrors the exclusionary attitudes toward racial and class minorities. In *Tropic of Orange* the homeless and other undesirables such as immigrants constitute the invisible reality of a cosmopolitan city. However, it is a reality that is swept under the cloud of multiculturalism and global commercialism. The figure of Manzanar Marukami embodies this exclusionary policy. Once a respectable surgeon, Manzanar chooses to give up his job and become homeless. His decision directly challenges U.S. exclusionary attitudes toward racial minorities. On February 19, 1942, Franklin D. Roosevelt issued Executive Order 9066, which forced approximately 120,000 people of Japanese ancestry into internment camps. Two-thirds of those interned were American citizens.[9] Their experiences in the camps and the incongruity they encountered between the promise of citizenship and the reality of the camps speak to the inconsistencies in America's policies and its theories of citizenship. The enforced invisibility of Japanese Americans in the public space of the nation stands in ironic counterpoise to the high visibility of surveillance they were subjected to in the camps. Mitsuye Yamada has called Japanese Americans "the visible minority that is invisible."[10] During World War II the American public sought to erase the presence of Japanese Americans from the imagined community of the nation; they excluded them from the public space of the nation by confining them to internment camps, where they would not be visible to the public eye. The character of Manzanar reminds us of the real political and economic issues of the internment as well as the systematic amnesia of this event among the larger American public. The ugly realities of the Japanese American internment were not made known to the public until the civil rights movement of the late 1960s and the publication of several books highlighting the internment, such as Mine Okubo's *Citizen 13660*, Michi Nishiura Weglyn's *Years of Infamy*, and *Personal Justice Denied* by the Commission on Wartime Relocation and Internment of Civilians.[11] It was not until 1988 that the U.S. government issued a formal apology for the internment.

Manzanar takes his name from the place of his birth, Manzanar Concentration Camp in the Owens Valley.[12] His decision to take on the name of an internment camp and his conscious choice to be homeless allude to Japanese Americans' dispossession of their rights as citizens as well as their personal property. His choice to be highly visible as a homeless person conducting traffic on the freeway overpass, refutes the government's and society's attempts to make invisible the histories and persons who are deemed undesirable. By choosing to be homeless rather than a successful surgeon, Manzanar rejects the myth of the model minority placed on Asian Americans and exemplifies a politically conscious Asian America that engages in activism and protest. Through characters such as Buzzworm, Arcangel, and Manzanar, Yamashita attempts to humanize the homeless and to bring to light the cruel histories of exclusion and denial of homelands.

Yamashita challenges notions of who is considered a legitimate inhabitant of national spaces. Japanese American citizens were considered illegitimate Americans; they were removed from their homes, stripped of their property, and denied the right of due process. The contradictions regarding citizenship rights in the United States pertain not only to Japanese Americans, but also to other racial groups throughout America's history. Mexicans were promised citizenship after the United States acquired northern Mexico with the signing of the Treaty of Guadalupe Hidalgo. However, several factors, such as an unfamiliar language and an unfair justice system, prevented Mexicans from retaining and exercising their right of citizenship. By alluding to the histories of the Japanese American internment and the dispossession of Mexican lands,

> *the deportation of 400,000 Mexican*
> *citizens in 1932*
> *coaxing back of 2.2 million*
> *braceros in 1942*
> *only to exile the same 2.2 million*
> *wetbacks in 1953*

Yamashita complicates the idea of migration and home.[13]

Latino and Asian groups share a common experience of immigration. Gail Nomura has outlined how the existence of the U.S.-Mexican border has not only affected Latino borderlands but "impinged upon the lives of Asian Americans by reconceiving the passage of nineteenth-century immigration and naturalization laws against Asians as the Asian American Frontier."[14] The increasing internationalization of U.S. capital has also exploited Asians and Latinos in their countries of origin and stimulated immigration to the United States.[15] Arcangel refers to NAFTA as an instrument of neocolonialism whose notion of progress is rooted in capitalist mechanisms that depend on turning human beings into labor and natural resources into property. Arcangel states,

> *"He [SUPERNAFTA] is only concerned with the*
> *commerce of money and things.*
> *What is this compared to the great*
> *commerce of humankind?*
> *His challenge is doomed to failure."*[16]

Similar to the post-NAFTA developments in Mexico, the rapid industrial growth in China has led to a great migration out of China, including illegal migration. Sebastian Rotella has argued that since 1993 "the cooperation of Chinese snakeheads and Mexican coyotes (people smugglers) has transformed the U.S.-Mexico borderlands into one of the top locations for undocumented Chinese immigration to U.S. Chinatowns."[17] Undocumented Chinese immigration across the U.S.-Mexican border has a long history. As a result of various exclusion acts, including the 1882 Chinese Exclusion Act, many Chinese ships carrying undocumented laborers used a landing point in Baja California nicknamed "Punta China."[18] With sustained attention to human passage, Yamashita argues that home on the borderlands has become, as Saldívar notes, "a paradigm of crossing, resistance, and circulation."[19] Perhaps in an increasingly globalized world, where national identifications are blurred by border crossings and racial identities made indistinct by multiculturalism, consumerism provides the only remaining form of identification.

Molly Wallace explains that "consumerism, in *Tropic of Orange*, replaces nationalism as a form of 'postnational' identification

that can be exported around the world." She argues that economics represents a "new model of cultural globality."[20] What Arcangel calls the "commerce of humankind" reflects how consumerism
has replaced nationalism as a form of postnational identification.[21]
Youngsuk Chae has also noted that border crossing implicitly questions "whether promoting cultural diversity signifies appreciating
differences in race and culture, or whether it is merely a convenient
password for transnationalizing capital serving as an ideological
mouthpiece for globalizing U.S. capitalism."[22] The Japanese American character Emi articulates this concern well. From Emi's perspective, discussions of U.S. multiculturalism are not much different
from the consumption of diverse ethnic commodities. Alluding to
American capitalist expansion beyond national borders, Emi tells
Gabriel, "It's just about money. It's not about good honest people
like you or about whether us Chicanos or Asians get a bum rap
or whether third world countries deserve dictators or whether we
should make the world safe for democracy. It's about selling things:
Reebok, Pepsi, Chevrolet, AllState, Pampers, El Pollo Loco, Le-
vis, Fritos, Larry Parks Esq., Tide, Raid, the Pillsbury Doughboy,
and Famous Amos."[23]

It is not only about "selling things" but also about the people
who make these things and the exploitation that is involved in the
production and reproduction of economic and geopolitical inequalities. Moreover the majority of work under the auspices of NAFTA
and in free trade zones is performed by women of color.[24] Julie Sze
has argued that in *Tropic of Orange*, "women's bodies and labor
are central to the new global economy and are targeted by acts of
symbolic and actual violence. Yamashita's text reveals that women
of color, along with transportation networks, embody how production and consumption work through the flow of goods, garbage,
and people in an era of intensified 'free trade.'"[25] Sze argues that it
is no accident that of the seven primary characters in the novel, the
two women, Rafaela and Emi, are the only ones to suffer graphic
bodily violence. Women of color are the primary consumers and
producers of the toxicity of our postindustrial society and stand

in the front lines of the battles over trade and ethical responsibility. In addition there are a growing number of Asian women who travel to foreign lands for work, leaving their family behind.[26] This "commerce of humanity" is exhibited not only in the exploitation of labor through global institutions such as transnational corporations and NAFTA, but also in the local (mis)management of labor and consumption.

In *Tropic of Orange* Bobby emigrates to the United States looking for work and a better life. He is "Chinese from Singapore with a Vietnam name speaking like a Mexican living in Koreatown." Making his new home in Los Angeles, Bobby is preoccupied with work: "Ever since he's been here, never stopped working. Always working." He works "washing dishes," "chopping vegetables," "cleaning floors," "cooking hamburgers," "painting walls," "laying brick," "digging ditches," "sweeping trash," "fixing pipes," "pumping toilets," "scrubbing urinals," "washing clothes," because he has "got rent to pay. Got dreams. Got hope." His wife, Rafaela, tells him that "people like him doing all the work. Couldn't he see that? . . . She kept talking, saying we're not wanted here. Nobody respects our work." Although Rafaela and Bobby possess a plethora of goods—a "32[-inch] Sony KV32V25 stereo TV with picture-in-picture and the Panasonic PUS4670 Super VHS VCR, the Sony Super ESP CD player, the AT&T 9100 cordless phone, the furniture, the clothing, the two-door Frigidaire with the icemaker, the Maytag super-capacity washer and gas dryer, the Sharp Carousel R1471 microwave"—what they experience most is not their economic identity but their social invisibility in the United States.[27] Bobby, Rafaela, and an army of nighttime janitors are an unseen workforce symptomatic of the invisible nature of cheap immigrant labor. They and others like them left their native countries to make a new home in the United States. However, being employed and acquiring American material goods do not offer them a home. Rafaela ultimately leaves all of the material furnishings of her house in Los Angeles and returns to her native Mexico looking for something more.

American Express: Mi Casa/Su Casa

The interlacing of characters signals a heteroglossic notion of home
that exceeds ethnic and national borders and definitions by drawing
on the interconnectedness of different types of discourses. The last
chapter of Yamashita's novel is titled "American Express: Mi Casa/
Su Casa." As this title suggests, the bridge between "my home" and
"your home" is linked by American Express. Wallace has argued
that this title suggests "a more democratic promise of hybridity"
in which consuming American brand-names offers an acquisition
of American identity.[28] By purchasing American goods with an
American Express credit card, one can quickly assume an American identity. Bobby's cousin easily crosses the border because her
consumption of American goods offers her a passing American
identity that is not scrutinized by border patrol officers:

> Bobby takes the little cuz to a T.J. [Tijuana] beauty shop. Get rid of
> the pigtails. Get rid of the Chinagirl look. Get a cut looking like Ra-
> faela. That's it. Now get her a T-shirt and some jeans and some tennis
> shoes. Jeans say Levi's. Shoes say Nike. T-shirt says Malibu. That's
> it. Border's nothing but desks and lines of people on linoleum floors.
> Bobby's in line like one more tourist. He's got the cuz holding a new
> Barbie doll in a box, like she bought it cheap in T.J. Official eyeballs
> Bobby's passport and waves them through. That's it. Two celestials
> without a plan. Drag themselves through the slit jus' like Americanos.
> Just like Visa cards.[29]

However, American identity is not constructed merely through
the consumption of American brand-name goods. By titling her
last chapter "American Express: Mi Casa/Su Casa," Yamashita critiques American consumerism and the ethically questionable practice of the commerce of humankind. When Bobby is faced with the
prospect of having to pay $10,000 to smuggle his cousin across the
U.S.-Mexican border, he recalls that years before he paid $4,000
to get Rafaela across that same border. Bobby, who works all day
at menial jobs, barely making ends meet, critiques the profitable
and ethically questionable business of transporting people across

the border: "Goddamn lawyers. Goddamn smugglers. Goddamn border."[30] Yamashita likens the transaction at the border in which Bobby and his cousin "drag themselves through the slit jus' like Americanos" to a transaction of goods purchased with Visa cards. However, the Visa card here signals more than the financial credit with which one purchases goods.

Yamashita is very conscious of the amount of credit individuals like Bobby, his cousin, Rafaela, Manzanar, Buzzworm, and Arcangel have in American society. Those who are poor and belong to communities of color possess very little cultural capital and credibility regardless of how much American name-brand material they possess. Material goods do not offer these characters cultural and national belonging. As Arcangel crosses the border, he is stopped and questioned by Immigration and Naturalization Services: "Where is your Visa?" "Your passport?" "Where did you learn to speak English?" He replies, "At Harvard at the School of Business. I was there at the same time as Carlos Salinas de Gortari. Then at Stanford University in Economics with Henrique Cardoso. Also at Columbia University with Fidel Castro; I did my thesis in political theory there, you see. And finally at Annapolis; what I studied there is a secret."[31]

By referring to Annapolis, home to the U.S. Naval Academy, and political leaders from Mexico, Brazil, and Cuba, Arcangel comments on the "secret" relationship between Latin American countries and the United States that engendered decades of economic disparity and interdependence. Arcangel, whose age remains a mystery, serves as a repository for five hundred years of Mexico's colonial history, from "the halls of Montezuma" to the Treaty of Guadalupe Hidalgo, the "braceros in 1942," the implementation of NAFTA, the importing of "all the people who do the work of machines," and Mexican agricultural goods like "the corn and the bananas, the coffee and the sugar cane." The visa that allows migrants to come to the United States legally also commodifies human beings into "machines" of labor. The border is a place where

Everything and everybody got in lines—
citizens and aliens—
the great undocumented foment,
the Third World War,
the gliding wings of a dream.[32]

The lines of *"citizens and aliens"* at the INS checkpoint at the U.S.-Mexican border point to the economic and political ties between the two countries.

This connection is also reinforced in the novel through "the strands of the line extended from two ends of the orange, reaching out . . . and across the land." In his nostalgic attempt to find his roots, Gabriel purchases a home in Mexico and plants one tree each year. He brings a navel orange tree from Riverside that "may be the descendent of the original trees first brought to California from Brazil in 1873 and planted by L. C. Tibbetts." Yamashita links the colonial legacy of the orange tree with the imperialist history between the United States and Mexico. She writes, "[Gabriel] had taken pains to plant the tree as a marker—to mark the Tropic of Cancer." This orange, which replaces the Tropic of Cancer with the Tropic of Orange, is a key symbol in the novel. Rafaela asks, "Gabriel, what is the Tropic of Cancer? I mean I know what it is, but what *is* it?" He answers, "A line. An imaginary line."[33] As the orange from the South replaces the Tropic of Cancer, the imaginary line that divides and defines what is north of the equator begins to change. The borders between the United States and Mexico and their cultures and populations undergo constant change.[34] As the orange travels with Arcangel in his journey north to Los Angeles to fight SUPERNAFTA, we witness a shift in the geography of the landscape: "The grid was changing."[35]

Home and an Imaginary Line

The "imaginary line" of the orange seems to magically pull the landscape as it travels north. This imaginary line also links together the Babel of voices of the various characters who are on the fringes of society, searching for their roots. In the end all of them metaphorically come home. Bobby and Rafaela are reunited; Gabriel leaves his "homeland—East L.A." and goes to Mexico, to his nostalgic home he "had so long yearned," to follow a story lead; Emi recognizes her grandfather Manzanar before her tragic death; and Arcangel, a.k.a. El Gran Mojado, the "Great Wetback," goes home to the "second largest city of Mexico, also known as Los Angeles," to challenge SUPERNAFTA to a fight and reclaim his homeland. The character of Buzzworm also "finally went home. Grandma's house down Fifth and Jefferson was still intact. Took a bath. Took a nap. Swept the porch out. Watered the palms. . . . Grow there; grow here too." Although these characters are uprooted from their houses, homelands, families, and histories, they all desire to "grow there; grow here too."[36]

In *Borderlands*, Anzaldúa writes, "Every step forward is *travesia*, a crossing. I am again an alien in new territory. And again, and again. But if I escape conscious awareness, escape 'knowing,' I won't be moving. Knowledge makes me more aware, it makes me more conscious. 'Knowing' is painful because after 'it' happens I can't stay in the same place and be comfortable. I am no longer the same person I was before."[37] Yamashita's *Tropic of Orange* offers new spaces of belonging that emerge from the intersections of conflicts and disassociations associated with border crossings. As such her characters and the spaces they inhabit make us feel uncomfortable. These spaces created by imaginary lines are home, "this thin edge of / barbwire."[38]

Yamashita conceptualizes a mode of identification in which there is a desire for a return to a mythic home and the difficulty of such homecoming. For all of the characters except Bobby and Rafaela, their journeys end in disconnection. Buzzworm literally "pulled the plug" from his Walkman, which he listened to throughout the novel. Manzanar Marukami, who heard the "greatest orchestra on Earth" in the movement of cars and people, suddenly "heard nothing" as the spray of bullets fatally wounded Emi, his granddaughter.[39] Gabriel is thousands of miles away in Mexico when his girlfriend Emi is shot. Arcangel is mortally wounded in the end, and so is his nemesis, SUPERNAFTA. The only characters who form and retain connections are Rafaela, Bobby, and Sol. Similar to her plot in *Through the Arc of the Rainforest*, Yamashita privileges the interracial family unit.[40]

Sol is the irrepressible life urge, the sun-child of a biracial and transnational family. In his name Yamashita employs the imagery of the sun and the sunflower. Like the orange, the sunflower has a long colonial history: it was a North American flower cultivated by Native Americans, brought to Europe by Spanish colonizers around 1500, and in the eighteenth century became popular in Russia. A hybrid version was brought to North America from Russia in the nineteenth century. Both the orange and the sunflower gesture to how the legacy of colonialism and conquest has shaped borders and homelands, "a border made plain by the sun itself."[41]

In the last chapter, Sol enters the wrestling match between SUPERNAFTA and Arcangel, a.k.a. El Gran Mojado, perched on Arcangel's shoulders. Sol's entry into this match between men who represent the first world and the third world signals other possibilities that draw from "the lifeblood of two worlds [and] merg[e] to form a third country—a border culture."[42] As a biracial child of Chinese and Mexican descent, a bilingual child who understands English and Spanish, who travels between Mexico and Los Angeles, Sol represents the mixture and interdependence of several cultures, languages, and borders. The simultaneous deaths of both SUPERNAFTA and El Gran Mojado point to the increasingly symbiotic relationship between the United States and Mexico and the border they share. Rafaela feeds the orange to the dying Gran Mojado and cuts the hemispheric line that the orange had delineated throughout the novel. In the end Bobby is left holding on to its two ends, asking, "What are these goddamn lines anyway? What do they connect? What do they divide? He gropes forward, inching nearer. Anybody looking sees his arms open wide like he's flying. Like he's flying forward to embrace. Don't nobody know he's hanging on to these invisible bungy cords. That's when he lets go.

Let's the lines slither around his wrists, past his palms, through his fingers. Let go. Go figure. Embrace. That's it."[43]

Tropic of Orange is a blend of postmodern fiction and magical realism that is keenly attuned to the materialities of U.S. capital and the borders that separate as well as connect us in an increasingly globalizing world. Yamashita offers a critique not only of border politics that exist with NAFTA and other forms of free trade or illegal markets, but also interrogates the discourses of homelands and nation-states that these borders are supposed to define. However, she chooses to end her novel with "Embrace. That's it," reinforcing the notion of human touch and affection amid material consumptions of goods and peoples that dominate discussions on globalization. She signals an ethical responsibility between self and other in this embrace. In an increasingly globalized world, space between nations grows closer with travel, and information is shared more rapidly with advances in technology. Yet the distance between people and the ethical relationships and responsibilities between them grow further apart. By highlighting the commerce of humankind in her novel, Yamashita interrogates the structures of global capital as it produces and reproduces economic and geopolitical inequalities and renders those, like the homeless, invisible. Like Buzzworm, who broadcasts the lives of the homeless to humanize them, Yamashita also broadcasts the lives of those marginalized in the community. *Tropic of Orange* leaves us questioning our own ethics of responsibility as readers who imagine and relate to the characters of Buzzworm, Manzanar Marukami, Arcangel, Rafaela, Bobby, and Sol—characters that exist in the literary work but also remind us of similar individuals on the margins of our real society.

Notes

1. Gloria Anzaldúa, *Borderlands/La Frontera: The New Mestiza* (San Francisco: Aunt Lute Books, 1987), 3.

2. José David Saldívar, *Border Matters: Remapping American Cultural Studies* (Berkeley: University of California Press, 1997), x, xii; Karen Tei Yamashita, *Tropic of Orange* (Minneapolis MN: Coffee House Press, 1997).

3. Yamashita, *Tropic of Orange*, 33, 37, 120.

4. Yamashita, *Tropic of Orange*, 121.

5. Anzaldúa, *Borderlands/La Frontera*, 3.

6. Rey Chow, *Ethics after Idealism* (Bloomington: Indiana University Press, 1998), 35.

7. Yamashita, *Tropic of Orange*, 43, 191.

8. Yamashita, *Tropic of Orange*, 215.

9. Japanese Americans on the West Coast were sent to one of ten internment camps: Amache, Colorado; Gila River, Arizona; Heart Mountain, Wyoming; Jerome, Arkansas; Manzanar, California; Minidoka, Idaho; Poston, Arizona; Rohwer, Arizona; Topaz, Utah; and Tule Lake, California. While the camps were hastily being built by government contractors, Japanese Americans were sent to assembly centers that served as temporary camps in Mayer, Arizona; Portland, Oregon; Puyallup, Washington; and Fresno, Marysville, Merced, Pinedale, Pomona, Sacramento, Salinas, Santa Anita, Stockton, Tanforan, Tulare, Tulare, and Manzanar, California. Manzanar was converted to a relocation camp on June 1, 1942. In addition to the assembly centers and relocation camps under the supervision of the War Relocation Authority, there were also U.S. Department of Justice camps, which housed Japanese aliens considered "dangerous persons" (and in some cases their families), in Crystal City, Texas; Seagoville, Texas; Kooskia, Idaho; Santa Fe, New Mexico; and Ft. Missoula, Montana. Those detained in these camps were mostly Japanese American community leaders, fishermen, and newspaper men. Roger Daniels, Sandra Taylor, and Harry Kitano, eds., *Japanese Americans: From Relocation to Redress* (Salt Lake City: University of Utah Press, 1986).

10. Mitsuye Yamada, "Invisibility Is an Unnatural Disaster," in *This Bridge Called My Back: Writings by Radical Women of Color*, ed. Cherríe L. Moraga and Gloria E. Anzaldúa (Berkeley: Third Women Press, 2002), 35.

11. Mine Okubo, *Citizen 13660* (Seattle: University of Washington Press, 1946); Michi Nishiura Weglyn, *Years of Infamy* (Seattle: University of Washington Press, 1976); Commission on Wartime Relocation and Internment of Civilians, *Personal Justice Denied* (Washington DC: U.S. Government Printing Office, 1983).

12. Yamashita, *Tropic of Orange*, 110.

13. Yamashita, *Tropic of Orange*, 198.

14. Claudia Sadowski-Smith cites Gail Nomura in her essay "The U.S.-Mexico Borderlands Write Back: Cross-Cultural Transnationalism in Contemporary U.S. Women of Color Fiction," *Arizona Quarterly* 57, no. 1 (2001): 103.

15. Edward J. W. Park, *Probationary Americans: Contemporary Immigration Policies and the Shaping of Asian American Communities* (New York: Routledge, 2005); Jae Junn and Kerry L. Haynie, eds., *New Race Politics in America: Understanding Minority and Immigrant Politics* (New York: Cambridge University Press, 2008); David Diaz and Marta Lopez-Garza, eds., *Asian and Latino Immigrants in a Restructuring Economy: The Metamorphosis of Southern California* (Stanford: Stanford University Press, 2001).

16. Yamashita, *Tropic of Orange*, 133–34.

17. Sebastian Rotella, *Twilight on the Line: Underworlds and Politics at the U.S.-Mexico Border* (New York: Norton, 1998), 72–73.

18. Peter Kwong, *Forbidden Workers: Illegal Chinese Immigrants and American Labor* (New York: New Press 1997), 77.

19. Saldívar, *Border Matters*, xiii.

20. Molly Wallace, "Tropic of Globalization: Reading the New North America," *Symploke* 9, nos. 1–2 (2001): 154, 148.

21. Yamashita, *Tropic of Orange*, 133.

22. Youngsuk Chae, *Politicizing Asian American Literature: Towards a Critical Multiculturalism* (New York: Routledge, 2008), 95.

23. Yamashita, *Tropic of Orange*, 126.

24. Laura Hyun-Yi Kang, *Compositional Subjects: Enfiguring Asian/American Women* (Durham NC: Duke University Press, 2002).

25. Julie Sze, "Not by Politics Alone: Gender and Environmental Justice in Karen Tei Yamashita's *Tropic of Orange*," in *New Essays in Ecofeminist Literary Criticism*, ed. Glynis Carr (London: Bucknell University Press, 2000), 30.

26. Rhacel Parrenas, *Children of Global Migration: Transnational Families and Gendered Woes* (Stanford: Stanford University Press, 2005).

27. Yamashita, *Tropic of Orange*, 15, 102, 12, 80.

28. Wallace, "Tropic of Globalization," 155.

29. Yamashita, *Tropic of Orange*, 203–4.

30. Yamashita, *Tropic of Orange*, 78.

31. Yamashita, *Tropic of Orange*, 199.

32. Yamashita, *Tropic of Orange*, 200, 198, 200, 201.

33. Yamashita, *Tropic of Orange*, 153, 11, 151.

34. According to the Pew Hispanic Center, in 2007 Hispanics constituted 47 percent of the population of Los Angeles County. http://pewhispanic.org/reports.

35. Yamashita, *Tropic of Orange*, 239.

36. Yamashita, *Tropic of Orange*, 151, 224, 211, 264.

37. Anzaldúa, *Borderlands/La Frontera*, 48.

38. Anzaldúa, *Borderlands/La Frontera*, 14.

39. Yamashita, *Tropic of Orange*, 265, 37, 265.

40. Karen Tei Yamashita, *Through the Arc of the Rainforest* (Minneapolis: Coffee House Press, 1990).

41. Yamashita, *Tropic of Orange*, 71.

42. Anzaldúa, *Borderlands/La Frontera*, 3.

43. Yamashita, *Tropic of Orange*, 268.

| Chapter 13

Chinese Migration to the Western Hemisphere
Multiraciality, Transgenerational Trauma, and
Comparative Studies of the Americas

Claudia Sadowski-Smith

Recent demographic changes in the Asian population in the United States have posed a serious challenge to academic formations concerned with studying these communities. Especially the concept of a pan-ethnic Asian American social formation consisting of Chinese, Japanese, Korean, and Filipino Americans, which has undergirded Asian American studies since its inception in the 1960s, appears in need of revision. As Wanni W. Anderson writes, the majority of Asians in the United States today do not articulate their experiences as Asian Americans, but instead tend to express their identity in terms of national origin with ties to a specific (if sometimes only imagined) national homeland.[1]

Several transnational approaches to theorizing connections between various U.S. Asian populations and their countries or areas of origin have recently emerged. Some of the most notable frameworks have focused on diasporic networks of family and identity among Chinese, Filipina/Filipino, and Japanese migrants in the late nineteenth and early twentieth century.[2] But, as Erika Lee has argued, this new emphasis on transpacific connections between the United States and Asia is still shaped by the originary U.S.-centrism of Asian American studies and its focus on the role of U.S. imperialism in creating diasporas. Lee has instead called for comparative work on the transpacific that can also encompass hemispheric perspectives.[3] Even though two such frameworks have emerged in the United States in the field of American studies, they have, like transpacific perspectives, also largely maintained a focus on specific racialized populations in the United States. New World studies emphasize the transnational African American experience of slavery as a point of intersection with plantation colonialism in the Caribbean and northern Brazil. And inter-American or hemispheric studies foreground the U.S. Southwest and its ties with Latin America through a focus on Latina/o and Chicana/o populations. Whereas New World studies have emerged from a fusion of black Atlantic, African American, and Caribbean studies, inter-American studies are largely conceptualized as a bridge across U.S.-based Chicana/o and Latina/o scholars and Latin American area studies.[4]

Contemporary representations of Chinese migration to several locations in the Americas may help us to imagine a more comparative perspective across existing transpacific and hemispheric models that can also decenter the United States from its prominent position and contribute to new frameworks for the study of the Americas. Cristina García's *Monkey Hunting* (2003), Sky Lee's *Disappearing Moon Café* (1991), and Karen Tei Yamashita's *Tropic of Orange* (1997) depict historical and partially ongoing Chinese migration to Cuba, Canada, and the United States via Mexico.[5] The three novels shed light on the emergence of overseas Chinese communities outside of Asia in the Americas as a result of migration that began in the nineteenth century and continues today. While contemporary Chinese migration to the Caribbean and Latin America has become numerically insignificant, people of Chinese descent constitute the largest so-called visible minority in Canada today, and Asian populations in the United States have doubled in each of past four decades.[6]

Together the three novels supplement the focus on U.S. imperialism and the role of U.S. immigration laws, policies, and practices in shaping Chinese movement to the Americas, especially to the U.S. neighbors Cuba, Canada, and Mexico, with attention to the role of transpacific and hemispheric factors in constituting Asian diasporic families and communities in the Americas. The novels employ the tropes of multiraciality and transgenerational trauma to shift the emphasis from Chinese American communities in the United States (largely perceived to be racially homogeneous) to an acknowledgment of multiracial Asian diasporic families and communities in Cuba, Canada, and the U.S.-Mexican borderlands. Set in the nineteenth century, when Chinese women remained largely absent from the Americas due to gendered exclusions, *Monkey Hunting* and *Disappearing Moon Café* depict relationships between Chinese immigrant men and women of other racialized communities that are situated at the bottom of the Cuban and Canadian socioracial hierarchies.[7] Focusing on the Mexican-U.S. border region, *Tropic of Orange* fictionalizes relationships among U.S. Asian Americans and Latina/os in a contemporary context. It is the collectively experienced trauma of Chinese immigration that enables the novels' protagonists to engage in relationships with Afro-Cuban, Native Canadian, and Latina women who have faced traumas of their own in the form of slavery, poverty, or migratory movement. As these three works show, the resulting interracial unions continue to be haunted by trauma, which is either consciously or unconsciously passed down to third- and fourth-generation descendants—either through stories told by parents and grandparents or through the efforts of descendants to piece together family histories despite gaps, holes, and distortions in family memory.[8]

Besides moving toward a comparative perspective that displaces the United States from its central role in transpacific studies and establishes connections to hemispheric work, the novels' emphasis on the importance of transgenerational trauma for the formation of Asian interracial families may signal the emergence of more comparative representations of racialized communities in the Americas, with far-reaching consequences for theories of migration, race, and nation formation. As the novels highlight the multiracial roots of various nation-states in the Americas, they challenge dominant narratives of nationhood in Cuba, Canada, and the United States.

These narratives affirm the existence of separate and distinct, biologically based white "majority" and racialized "minority" cultures, in which the majority culture represents the descendants of European settlers and immigrants. Notions of multiculturalism in the United States and Canada tend to treat racialized communities as distinct and internally homogeneous by marginalizing the more complex multi- and interracial histories of their populations. And official narratives of Cuban nationhood consider Cuban Chinese to be "exotic" and foreign and not inherently Cuban, in contrast to white Cubans and Afro-Cubans.

In their efforts to establish more complex national narratives, the three novels highlight forms of multiraciality that do not simply reaffirm notions of family or community as based on genetic commonalities. In these works multiraciality emerges as a response to various forms of collective trauma that cut across Asian, black, indigenous, and Latina/o communities in the hemisphere. An emphasis on the centrality of this response for the formation of what we now understand as separate racialized communities in various nation-states in the Americas can contribute to comparative studies of the Americas that acknowledge the role of U.S. imperialism in creating migratory labor movements, yet also calls attention to the policies of other nation-states in the Pacific and the hemisphere. Comparative perspectives across transpacific and hemispheric approaches question the continued focus on identity-based notions of affinity and thus point to the possibility of more inclusive forms of political alliance building.

Asian Afro-Cuban Families, Nineteenth-Century "Coolie" Labor

In *Monkey Hunting*, Cristina García creatively represents one of the earliest and most numerous forms of out-migration from China to Cuba and its effects on the formation of an interracial family, symbolized in a family tree at the beginning of the novel.[9] The collective trauma of Chinese overseas passage, indentured servitude, and racial discrimination upon arrival in Cuba is exemplified in the fictionalized history of the protagonist, Chen Pan. His experiences enable him to identify with the plight of African slaves in Cuba, and more specifically with the sexual slavery endured by his common-law wife, Lucrecia. Their traumas are passed down as far as their fourth-generation descendants, who live in China, Cuba, and the United States.

Chen Pan's story begins in 1857, when he is swindled into an eight-year contract by a Chinese recruitment agent and transported to Cuba. His narrative exemplifies the beginning of large-scale movement of Chinese labor to Cuba in the mid-nineteenth century, which responded directly to the abolition of the African slave trade. Instead of ending the transatlantic commerce of African slaves to Spanish America, however, abolition increased their purchase price to such a degree that Cuban sugar planters needed to search for alternative sources of labor. After China was forced to cede five of its major ports to British occupation in the aftermath of the first Opium War (1840–42) and to deregulate out-migration, impoverished males from the Guangdong and Fujian provinces presented themselves as the next source of cheap, durable, and exploitable labor to economies based on export-oriented agriculture.

Within this historical and economic context, the Cuban contract labor system was simply grafted onto the nearly defunct African slave trade. Chen and the other men are transported to Cuba on a prison-like ship, run by British shipping companies that had previously been involved in the African slave trade. During the four- to eight-month-long journey fictionalized in *Monkey Hunting*, the Chinese migrants are exposed to disease, hunger, and thirst; they are flogged and beaten to death for minor acts of disobedience; and several men commit suicide by jumping overboard. According to scholarly estimates, the mortality rates in the overseas passage of Chinese migrants hovered around 12 to 30 percent, sometimes reaching as high as 50 percent.[10]

The trauma of Chen's overseas passage is compounded by the conditions of his indenture upon arrival in Cuba. While Chinese migrants went to other nations in the hemisphere after slavery there had been outlawed, in Cuba the practice stayed in place until

1886, several decades after Chinese indentured laborers first arrived.[11] Though indentured servants were free men under contract rather than chattel for life, Chen and other Chinese laborers are sold on an auction block to work alongside African slaves cutting sugar cane. The Chinese indentured laborers live in slave quarters and are exposed to malnourishment and abuse. Their situation also approximates that of slavery because masters could invoke a clause in the contract or write a new contract when the laborers could not pay back their shipping cost, so that many were in fact kept unfree until death.[12]

García writes, "From his first hour in the fields, it is clear to Chen that he was in Cuba not as a hired worker but as a slave, no different from the Africans" (24). But unlike most other Chinese laborers, who "wanted nothing to do with the Africans" (26), he understands these parallels as opportunities for mutual exchange. He learns from African slaves how to work in the fields, and he teaches them Chinese physical exercises. The novel also highlights similarities in Chinese and African resistance to involuntary labor in Cuba, showing that Chinese laborers often rebelled, escaped, or committed suicide. In fact over 50 percent of Chinese indentured workers died before their eight-year contract ended.[13]

After two years on the sugar plantation, Chen escapes and eventually makes his way to Havana. There he works as a street peddler and then opens his own antiques shop in Havana's Chinatown, one of the earliest Chinatowns in Latin America. Despite widespread prejudice among Cuban *criollos* (Cubans of European descent), who "would have preferred that he still worked for them in the fields, or sold garlic at their kitchen doors" (66), he becomes a successful businessman and abandons his dream of returning to China. Six years after he escaped from indentured servitude he can afford to buy an African slave woman, Lucrecia, and her infant son from their criollo owner. The daughter of runaway slaves, Lucrecia was sold into slavery by her brother. Her trauma of sexual slavery, impregnation by her master, and eventual sale to Chen makes her want to "nail the worst of her memories to a cross" (123).

Chen does not buy Lucrecia to perpetuate her slavery, however, but to create a family. Unlike some of his wealthier Chinese fellow immigrants who import wives from China, Chen adopts Lucrecia's son and creates a multiracial family that cuts across Chinese Cuban and Afro-Cuban racial lines. Because of his experiences as a former indentured servant, he provides Lucrecia with the opportunity to symbolically buy her freedom from him before taking her as a common-law wife. The novel suggests that the traumatic experiences of indenture and slavery serve as a basis for the couple's relationship, to which both assimilate. While Chen decides it is easier for him "to be Cuban than to try to become Chinese again" (245), Lucrecia largely adjusts to the thriving Chinese community and becomes "Chinese in her liver, Chinese in her heart" (118).

A second narrative strand traces the contemporary effects of mid-nineteenth-century Chinese labor migration and Chen's creation of an interracial family in Havana's Chinatown. Chen's descendants settle outside of the ethnic enclave after the decline of Chinese immigration following the British prohibition of the "coolie trade" in 1874. Under pressure from the United States, Cuba further restricted Chinese migration after 1899 and passed legislation in 1902 prohibiting the entry of Chinese workers.[14] Chen's son creates two families with Chinese wives, one of whom stays in China. His children's lives continue to be marred by violence, and they are haunted by memories of family trauma, which they often experience as dreams or hallucinations. One of Chen's grandchildren, a teacher in a private school, ends up in a Communist Chinese prison, at least in part because her father "was a foreigner." Near her death, she dreams of searching for the descendants of her grandfather, about whose indenture she had heard many stories. After the 1959 Revolution under Fidel Castro, one of Chen Pan's grandsons is imprisoned in a mental hospital in Santiago de Chile on charges of "anti-revolutionary activities" for trafficking in contraband. His "treatment" with psychotropic drugs and electroshock therapy triggers memories of his grandfather's indenture and the belief that his grandfather is paying him visits.

After his release, this grandson becomes part of a significant Cuban Chinese exodus to the United States during the Castro regime. While Chinese workers had emigrated from Cuba to the United States as early as the 1860s, Castro's nationalization efforts threatened a large number of Cuban Chinese who owned small businesses and often disagreed ideologically with the new socialist regime. For the first decades of the Revolution, the Cuban government also restricted racial politics and cultural practices, and Cuba's primary ally, the Soviet Union, had problematic relations with the People's Republic of China, which further contributed to the repression of expressions of Cuban Chinese culture. In the late 1960s and early 1970s thousands of Cuban Chinese immigrated to the United States, particularly to New York City and Miami, and the number of Chinese living in Cuba dropped dramatically.[15]

As a fictionalized representative of this exodus, Chen Pan's grandson immigrates to New York City, where he ends up working in a restaurant. When he commits suicide, his own son, Domingo, the fourth-generation descendant of Chen Pan, reacts by enlisting in the Vietnam War. Intergenerational trauma also shapes Domingo's war experiences. A pair of his great-grandfather's spectacles repeatedly saves his life, and he enters into a relationship with a Vietnamese woman who had once been sold into sexual slavery and who "seemed familiar to Domingo, like he'd known her as a child" (155). When he fathers a child with her, Domingo places this event within the framework of his family history, asking, "Were people meant to travel such distances? Mix with others so different from themselves? His great-grandfather had left China more than a hundred years ago, penniless and alone. Then he'd fallen in love with a slave girl and created a whole new race—brown children with Chinese eyes who spoke Spanish and a smattering of Abakua" (209). Partially because of the army's explicit prohibition against relationships with Vietnamese women, Domingo eventually abandons his interracial family.

Monkey Hunting ends by moving backward in time to juxtapose Domingo's decision with Chen's joyful affirmation of his own mixed-raced family at the closing of his life in 1917, when, for a brief period, Chinese exclusion laws were repealed in response to labor demands at the onset of World War I and the expansion of U.S. commerce in Cuba. Chen's affirmation of multiraciality challenges official narratives of Cuban nationhood that rest on notions of distinct racial groups, such as white, Afro-Cuban, and, in part, Chinese Cuban. The mythology of a new Cuba developed under Castro has elevated black Cubans to integral participants in the creation of the Cuban nation alongside whites. The official recognition of African culture as an irreducible element in Cubanidad highlights experiences of black slavery during Cuba's colonial period and emphasizes slave rebellions as incipient explosions in the nationalist struggle against Spain, thus promoting black Cubans to a vanguard role in the new Cuba. While this narrative sometimes acknowledges the contributions of Cuban Chinese to the country's independence struggles,[16] it treats as more peripheral Chinese histories of (forced) migration and involuntary labor to the country. García's novel challenges this myth of a new Cuba by forging a comparative history of Chinese and black diasporic multiraciality and shared racialized trauma that calls for more inclusive accounts of Cuban nationhood and connects the country to transpacific and hemispheric frameworks of study.

Chinese Native Families and Nineteenth-Century Chinese Immigration

Like *Monkey Hunting*, Sky Lee's *Disappearing Moon Café* is organized around multiple, historically divergent narratives that focus on various branches of a mixed-race family. The novel begins about forty years later than García's and fictionalizes Chinese migration to Canada in the protagonist Wong Gwei Chang. Also like *Monkey Hunting*, *Disappearing Moon Café* highlights the traumatic effects of nineteenth-century Chinese labor migration and arrival in the hemisphere on third- and fourth-generation descendants. The novel focuses on a family whose complex multiraciality is mapped out in a genealogical tree at the beginning of the novel.

Disappearing Moon Café begins with an account of its protagonist's migration and ends with his memories of his interracial relationship with a Native Canadian. Gwei Chang arrives in Canada in 1892 at the behest of Victoria's Chinese Benevolent Association to collect the remains of Chinese workers who died building the western portion of the Canadian Pacific Railway between 1881 and 1885.[17] His traumatic experiences of poverty, starvation, and discrimination in China and Canada become the basis for his identification with his common-law indigenous wife, Kelora, with whom he has a son. But unlike García's protagonist, Gwei Chang soon abandons his interracial family and, because he feels he needs to follow tradition, enters into an arranged marriage in China. His silence about his mixed-raced family creates intergenerational trauma and leads to the decline of *both* his families and challenges notions of community formation based on shared genealogy and bloodlines.

Gwei Chang's charge to repatriate the bones of Chinese laborers responds to shifts in migration patterns as a result of changing British, U.S., and Canadian economic, political, legal, and social practices. Chinese migrants first went to Canada around 1858 from the U.S. West Coast or directly from China to work as miners, merchants, domestic servants, and service workers; their numbers grew following British legislation in 1874 to outlaw the global Chinese coolie trade and the U.S. passage of its first Chinese Exclusion Act in 1882.[18] While the 1874 law led to a decrease in Chinese migration to the Caribbean and Latin America, U.S. exclusion laws virtually banned all Chinese immigration to the United States. In the crucible of these two laws, elaborate smuggling networks emerged to transport labor migrants to the United States from Cuba (and other places) via the U.S.-Mexican and U.S.-Canadian borders.[19] In fact by the turn of the century Cuba had become a central transit point for the trafficking of Chinese immigrants who either were already living in Cuba or passing through the country on their way to other parts of the hemisphere.[20] Within this illicit labor network spanning the transpacific and the hemisphere, U.S. neighboring countries became passageways for Chinese entry as well as alternative locations for their settlement.

Because it did not have similar restrictive immigration legislation, Canada became a desirable location for immigration, especially after Canadian railroads and other companies began to recruit laborers directly from China. Unlike contract labor practices employed in Cuba, these recruitment schemes were not managed and controlled by European colonial powers, but by labor brokers and shipping companies in the United States and Canada. These entities advanced Chinese laborers the cost of their transportation and retained a line on the workers' services until they had repaid their debts. Because of agreements between shippers and labor brokers, Chinese laborers could not return to China until they had paid off these debts.[21] Once they arrived in Canada, they did not work alongside or replace African slave labor, as in the Caribbean plantation economy, but encountered mainly white workers in the context of unprecedented industrial development of the U.S. and Canadian West.

During his search for the remains of Chinese railroad workers, Gwei Chang falls ill and is nursed back to health by Kelora Chen, the offspring of an indigenous-white relationship. After the death of her parents, she was adopted by a Chinese laborer, Chen Gwok Fai. She speaks Chinese and, like Lucrecia in *Monkey Hunting*, has somewhat assimilated to Chinese culture. Gwei Chang's relationship with Kelora is partially based on their common poverty and her identity as an orphan, which resembles his status as an immigrant without a family. Gwei Chang observes similar levels of impoverishment and starvation in the remaining Chinese work camp gangs and among indigenous peoples, who, like black Cubans, have historically occupied a position at the very bottom of the country's racio-economic system. At first he understands that his survival as a new arrival in the Americas depends on interactions with Native people to keep from "starv[ing] like a chinaman" (234). But he soon begins to believe that, by abandoning Kelora, he can overcome his poverty and his orphan status. Lee poignantly writes, "He could see how famine was the one link that Kelora and he had in common, but for that instant, it made him recoil from her as surely as if he had touched a beggar's squalid sore. . . . In the next instant, he looked at Kelora and saw an animal" (234–35).

Under pressure from his family, Gwei Chang returns to China, enters into an arranged marriage, and sires a son. When he returns to Canada and learns that Kelora and her adoptive father are dead, he takes his mixed-race son, Ting An, as an apprentice, but fails to disclose his paternity to him. Unlike his fellow immigrant Chen Gwok Fai, who had adopted Kelora and her son in the absence of other family, Gwei Chang cannot bring himself to acknowledge his own mixed-raced son as his descendant and thus deepens Ting An's orphan status. As Gwei Chang moves up the social ladder in Chinatown from vegetable peddler to successful import-export businessman, he sponsors his Chinese wife's immigration to Canada as "a merchant's wife" as well as the arrival of their nearly grown son, Wong Choy Fuk. In conjunction with his rise in economic status, this second family appears to help Gwei Chang gain even more prominence in Chinatown, where he works to unify the Chinese community against restrictive immigration policies and other discriminatory laws that keep their numbers small and confined to an ethnic enclave.

Gwei Chang keeps from his new and "legitimate" family the existence of his "illegitimate," mixed-race son, whom he treats just like another worker. This family secret has destructive long-term consequences for the health of both families and for the Chinese community more generally. A second narrative strand in the novel focuses on the second generation's desperate attempts to produce an heir. Just as Gwei Chang had married a Chinese wife to create a "proper" family, a Chinese mail-order bride, Chong Fong Mei, is "bought" for the next male descendant, his son Choy Fuk. When the marriage does not produce an heir, the Wong family considers several options. Importing a second wife has become impossible because Canada had passed its own version of a Chinese exclusion law in 1924, under pressure from the United States and in the context of a postwar recession, when demobilized soldiers were looking for work and wartime industries closed.[22] A second option is to pay another woman to have Choy Fuk's child and give it to his wife to raise. Faced with this possibility, the former mail-order bride instead conspires to have children with Ting An, whom she does not know is her husband's half-brother. This obsession with having children at any cost (which resembles the efforts of *Monkey Hunting*'s protagonist to build a family by literally buying an infant and his mother) needs to be read as a reaction to the difficulties of forging Chinese families and communities in the Americas in the face of enormous gender imbalance, declining immigration, and, in the case of the United States, legal restrictions against interracial marriages.

In its third and dominant narrative, *Disappearing Moon Café* highlights the contemporary consequences of the silences and gaps in the family history that account for the trauma of immigration. Just as Ting An's lineage was suppressed in the Wong family history, the three children who are the product of the union between him and Fong Mei are passed off as legitimate Wong heirs. As the patriarch Gwei Chang did before her, Fong Mei chooses her loveless, arranged marriage over a relationship with Ting An, the beloved father of her children. Rather than aligning herself with a nameless and penniless orphan, she wants to partake in the wealth and the respectability offered by the Wong name.

Because they do not know that they share the same biological father, Ting An's daughter with Fong Mei and his son from another relationship commit incest. After their child, the last male Wong, dies at birth, his mother, Gwei Chang's granddaughter, commits suicide. This ultimate turning of the family upon itself also destroys the illusion of its pure lineage, revealing the family's mixed Chinese, white, and indigenous heritage. Even in the 1980s context of more open immigration legislation, the fourth-generation narrator of *Disappearing Moon Café* continues to be haunted by family trauma. As she says, "[It] has shaped so much of my own life, with evil tentacles that could have even wormed into the innocent, tender parts of my baby" (23).

Like *Monkey Hunting*, *Disappearing Moon Café* ends by moving back in time to the narrative of the interracial family's patriarch. In the novel's last chapter, set in 1939, the ailing Gwei Chang declares his undying love for his common-law wife, Kelora, and acknowledges his responsibility for the death of their son, Ting An. Coupled with the general orphan culture of immigrant men in which Ting An was brought up, his identity as an orphan contributed to his untimely death. Even on his deathbed, however, Gwei Chang does not realize or cannot admit that his rejection of his mixed-raced family ultimately also caused the end of his "legitimate" Chinese lineage when the last male Wong, himself of mixed race, dies at birth.

The destruction of this family, whose lineage was so carefully constructed to live up to the expectations of parents in China and of the Chinatown community, also questions Gwei Chang's belief in basing community formation on shared bloodlines and genealogies. After all, the desire to re-create Chinese family structures on foreign soil in order to battle immigration restrictions and pervasive discrimination based on essentialist notions of race also entailed or perhaps even necessitated denying connections to other racialized communities as another way of opposition and survival. While the ending of Lee's novel appears pessimistic, especially in comparison with the protagonist's reaffirmation of his interracial family in *Monkey Hunting*, *Disappearing Moon Café* highlights the existence of multiracial forms of family and community formations in Canada. A stress on multiraciality as an integral part of the Canadian national narrative could move the country beyond its somewhat limited official policy of multiculturalism. This policy reinscribes binary notions of biologically constructed majority and "visible minority" cultures. The emphasis on the Canadian multicultural nation has been widely critiqued as a means to undercut Québécois demands for special recognition by bestowing recognition on other cultural groups perceived as distinct from one another.[23]

Asian-Latina/o Families and Twenty-First-Century Chinese Immigration to the United States

Set in the borderlands of Mexico and the United States, Karen Tei Yamashita's novel *Tropic of Orange* fictionalizes Chinese immigration at the turn of the twenty-first century—often through Mexico—and its connection to the formation of interracial families. These families symbolize growing intersections among Asian and Latin American populations in the borderlands that are based on similar traumas of immigration and arrival in the United States. Rather than focusing on a generational model of family, such as the ones developed in *Monkey Hunting* and *Disappearing Moon Café*, *Tropic of Orange* depicts seven protagonists of different ethnic and national backgrounds, most of whom are not related to each other through biology or marriage. Instead of opening with a family tree, then, the novel begins with a "hypercontents" that traces the roles of African American, Mexican American, Mexican, Japanese American, Chinese American, and Chinese characters throughout the novel.

The marriage between the ethnic Chinese immigrant Bobby Ngu and his Mexican wife, Rafaela Cortes, symbolizes the notion of shared collective traumas of immigration and arrival that is at the heart of *Tropic of Orange*. Bobby is a "Chinese from Singapore with a Vietnam name speaking like a Mexican living in Koreatown" (15). He left Singapore because his father's bicycle-producing company could no longer compete with a U.S.-owned business and the family became impoverished. Immigrating under the guise of a Vietnamese refugee, Bobby ends up in Los Angeles, where he is socialized among growing populations of Latina/os. Throughout the various chapters in the novel that are devoted to Bobby, he asserts both the Asian and the Latino aspects of his identity. He speaks a Latino street slang and also visits Chinatown to get herbal remedies for several ailments.[24]

Like the immigrant protagonists in *Monkey Hunting* and *Disappearing Moon Café*, Bobby creates an interracial family by marrying Rafaela Cortes and siring a son, Sol. Rafaela immigrated to the United States for reasons similar to Bobby's: because the transnationalization of U.S. capital in Mexico created conditions for outmigration. Once in the United States as first-generation labor migrants and refugees, Bobby and Rafaela encounter similar difficulties when attempting to achieve upward mobility. Bobby's longer residency in the United States allows him to start his own janitorial business and sponsor his wife's immigration on a green card. But despite his hard work in two different jobs and Rafaela's pursuit of a college education, they remain at the bottom of the U.S. socioeconomic hierarchy.

The novel highlights the widespread nature of interracial relationships, independent of immigration and class status, by also portraying an upper-class Chicano reporter, Gabriel, and his Japanese American girlfriend, Emi, who are U.S.-born third-generation Americans. Both define themselves more in relationship to their high-paying jobs in the mass media than in terms of their ethnic identity. Emi and Gabriel largely mythologize or disassociate from their family history of immigration and its transgenerational traumatic effects. Gabriel's attachment to highly idealized notions of Chicana/o culture and its largely symbolic relationship to Mexico is represented in his acquisition of a house in his grandparents' hometown that he never even visits. Similarly Emi cannot fully acknowledge her connections to her homeless and estranged grandfather, who was born in a Japanese American World War II detention camp. She disavows the trauma of his detention, which has overshadowed his life, and its potential transgenerational effect on her. Emi is described as being so "distant from the Asian female stereotype . . . [that] it was questionable if she even had an identity" (19).

In addition to creating an interracial family, Bobby also adopts a twelve-year-old Chinese girl, who may or may not be his biological cousin. Xiaye's immigration from mainland China through Mexico exemplifies ongoing, contemporary Chinese movement to the United States and its intersection with immigration from Latin America. Although the majority of Asian immigrants (often ethnically Chinese members of professional and elite backgrounds from Taiwan, Singapore, and Hong Kong) enter the United States legally, hundreds of thousands of undocumented Chinese, most of whom are from Fujian Province and from economically poorer backgrounds, arrive as undocumented labor migrants every year.[25]

After the capture of several Chinese ships by U.S. authorities in the early 1990s, Chinese cartels began to employ more indirect routes from China to the United States that involve passage through Mexico and require travel across the Mexican-U.S. border. As the border has become one of the major transit points for Chinese immigration, this shift continues nineteenth-century Chinese histories of migration and settlement to Mexico as well as earlier manifestations of interracial family formation.[26] The passage of U.S. Chinese exclusion laws in the 1880s, the passage of the Chinese-Mexican Treaty of Amity and Commerce in 1893, and U.S. investment in Mexican mines and railroads stimulated more immigration from China to Mexico.[27] Brought to Mexico primarily by labor contractors and smuggling networks, the majority of Chinese immigrants continued on to the United States.[28] But others stayed in Mexico and moved into commerce and small business, and work in shoe and clothing factories, grocery stores, restaurants, laundries, and hotels.[29] Several immigrants also created interracial families with Mexicans. In response to anti-Chinese violence and the passage of anti-Chinese state laws in the 1930s, some of these families returned to China, creating Mexican barrios outside certain south China villages.[30] Chinese immigrants also formed relationships with Mexican (American) women in U.S. border states in the context of U.S. state laws prohibiting interracial unions with white women.[31]

The human smugglers extort Bobby for the transportation cost of his purported cousin, Xiaye, who arrived in Tijuana on a ship. To lower the price, Bobby decides to drive from Los Angeles down to Tijuana to smuggle his cousin across the border himself. In its focus on undocumented immigration from China, the novel highlights significant yet understudied parallels among Chinese and Latin American immigration. In the face of an increasingly militarized Mexican-U.S. border, undocumented immigrants from Asia and Latin American employ similar border-crossing methods, such as passing themselves off as U.S. citizens of Latino or Asian descent. To trick the border patrol, Bobby makes sure that his cousin gets rid of her "Chinagirl look" (204). He takes her to a beauty

salon where she gets a hair cut like that of his wife and buys her
new clothes and toys. After that they cross the Tijuana–San Diego
border without problems: the "official eyeballs Bobby's passport
and waves them through. . . . [They] drag themselves through the
slit jus' like any Americanos" (205).

Another of *Tropic*'s protagonists, the performer and laborer Arcangel, represents a composite undocumented border crosser who
bridges various ethnic and national communities. His character
draws on indigenous Aztec mythologies, Mexican performance art,
and the tradition of the trickster figure that is common in Asian
American, American Indian, and African American cultures. In
one of his performances, Arcangel pulls the Tropic of Cancer, the
line dividing northern from southern Mexico, across the Mexican-
U.S. border. As a result of this movement days become longer, geographic expanses stretch, and various cultural influences in cuisine
and language begin to merge. Toward the conclusion of the novel, Arcangel turns into another incarnation, "El Gran Mojado"
(the Big Wetback), in order to fight SUPERNAFTA in a wrestling
match. As a symbol of ongoing struggles over the representation
of the post-NAFTA Americas, the wrestling match ends undecid-
ed: SUPERNAFTA implodes after sending a missile launcher into
Arcangel's heart. Bobby is left straining to hold on to the two suddenly meaningless ends of the Tropic of Cancer. As he is the most
explicitly multiethnic figure in the novel and the patriarch of an
interracial family, his relationship to the Tropic of Cancer signals
a move beyond the dichotomous thinking represented in borders.
His family symbolizes the possibility that histories of interracial
individuals and communities will be more widely acknowledged
in accounts of U.S. nation formation. Bobby asks himself, "What
are these goddamn lines anyway? What do they connect? What do
they divide? What's he holding on to?" (270).

The Asian Americas in Comparative Studies of the Americas

Despite some emerging interest in *Tropic of Orange*, the novel's
explicit focus on multiraciality in the Americas has so far not lent

itself to exploration within Asian American studies frameworks that are moving toward internationalization.[32] Like the novels by García and Lee, *Tropic of Orange* models the potential emergence of comparative perspectives that center on the transpacific aspects of Asian immigration yet also account for multiracial interaction with other communities in various nations in the Americas. The fictionalized nineteenth-century histories of Chinese immigration in *Monkey Hunting* and *Disappearing Moon Café* correct amnesia about multiraciality and its connection to intergenerational trauma on the level of family, community, and nation. Lee's novel also suggests that interracial relationships may at times function as (perceived?) impediments to the survival of a racialized community under threat of extinction by exclusion and institutionalized racism, as in the Canadian case. However, García's fiction highlights that British regulation of the so-called coolie trade in 1874, which resulted in a decline of Chinese immigration to Cuba, may not have inspired the same efforts to rally around a shrinking community by reaffirming its racial purity. *Monkey Hunting*'s protagonist affirms his interracial family even in the face of a declining Chinese Cuban community. The novel may thus suggest that interracial relationships are more accepted when an ethnicized community diminishes in size and importance. In comparison, as fictionalized in Yamashita's novel, in today's U.S.-Mexican borderlands interracial relationships seem to have become so commonplace that they exist at every economic and social level of society and thus question the long-held notion of multiculturalism that emphasizes the existence of distinct ethnic communities.

A focus on interracial family formation and its effects on narratives of national identity in the hemisphere, designed to create "imagined communities," also opens the door for new approaches to the studies of the Americas.[33] Several comparative ethnic studies models have recently emerged that focus on connections among various U.S. racialized communities and sometimes also consider their interactions with other national contexts.[34] A reading of the three novels by García, Lee, and Yamashita contributes to such efforts by highlighting the role Asian immigration and multiracial Asian families have played in the histories of various hemispheric nations. While contemporary narratives of Cuban nationhood acknowledge the contributions of European and black populations to the country's history, they tend to treat Cuban Asians as marginal and do not acknowledge interracial Chinese-black formations. Mixed-race families of indigenous and Asian origin, such as the ones fictionalized in *Disappearing Moon Café*, are similarly not considered to be a central component of Canadian national narratives. In the contemporary Canadian census, no category of identification is available to indicate the status of such families and individuals. Similarly Yamashita's novel shows how widespread interracial family formations have become in the United States, despite the histories of legal prohibitions against interracial unions in several U.S. states. As the acknowledgment of multiraciality is missing from official accounts of U.S. nation formation, the U.S. census contains only the category "other" to describe mixed-race status.

Read together, these three novels show that diasporic multiracial families emerged in the crucible of global developments and U.S. imperialist policies — with often unintended effects on its neighbors — and the economics, politics, immigration laws, and racial relations of individual countries in the hemisphere. Chinese multiraciality in the Americas was shaped in the interplay of transpacific forces (affecting U.S. and Chinese relations), global currents (such as Britain's relationship with several nations in the Americas), and each individual nation-state's relationship with China, as well as, at times, with Britain and the United States. A multipronged emphasis on Asian forms of multiraciality acknowledges how the particularities of various American nation-states have shaped Chinese immigration and the subsequent emergence of multiracial families and communities in the hemisphere, while also paying attention to the role of U.S. (and British) dominance. This approach adds comparative perspectives on the national context in which racialized formations have emerged in the American hemisphere to the current emphasis on transpacific diasporas. Besides responding to questions of academic reorganization, fiction about Chinese movement to the hemisphere may thus also presage ongoing developments toward more inclusive forms of political alliance building that have become manifest in immigrant rights organizing across ethnic and transnational lines within the United States.[35]

Notes

1. Wanni W. Anderson and Robert G. Lee, eds., *Displacements and Diasporas: Asians in the Americas* (New Brunswick NJ: Rutgers University Press, 2005), 8–9.

2. See Erika Lee, *At America's Gates: Chinese Immigration during the Exclusion Era, 1882–1943* (Chapel Hill: University of North Carolina Press, 2003); Mae M. Ngai, *Impossible Subjects: Illegal Aliens and the Making of Modern America* (Princeton NJ: Princeton University Press, 2004); Dorothy B. Fujita-Rony, *American Workers, Colonial Power: Philippine Seattle and the Transpacific West, 1919–1941* (Berkeley: University of California Press, 2003); Eiichiro Azuma, *Between Two Empires: Race, History and Transnationalism in Japanese America* (New York: Oxford University Press, 2005); Henry Yu, "Los Angeles and American Studies in a Pacific World of Migrations," *American Quarterly* 56, no. 3 (September 2004): 531–43.

3. Erika Lee, "Orientalisms in the Americas: A Hemispheric Approach to Asian American History," *Journal of Asian American Studies* 8, no. 3 (2005): 235–56.

4. For examples of New World studies work, see Joseph Roach, *Cities of the Dead: Circum-Atlantic Performance* (New York: Columbia University Press, 1996); Deborah H. Cohn, *History and Memory in the Two Souths: Recent Southern and Spanish American Fiction* (Nashville TN: Vanderbilt University Press, 1999); Michael J. Dash, *The Other America: Caribbean Literature in a New World Context* (Charlottesville: University Press of Virginia, 1998); Vera M. Kutzinski, *Sugar's Secrets: Race and the Erotics of Cuban Nationalism* (Charlottesville: University Press of Virginia, 1993); George B. Handley, *Postslavery Literatures in the Americas: Family Portraits in Black and White* (Charlottesville: University of Virginia Press, 2000); Jon Smith and Deborah Cohn, eds., *Look Away! The U.S. South in New World Studies* (Durham NC: Duke University Press, 2004). For examples of inter-American

work, see Anna Brickhouse, *Transamerican Literary Relations and the Nineteenth-Century Public Sphere* (New York: Cambridge University Press, 2004); Kirsten Silva Gruez, *Ambassadors of Culture: The Transamerican Origins of Latino Writing* (Princeton NJ: Princeton University Press, 2002); José David Saldívar, *Border Matters: Remapping American Cultural Studies* (Berkeley: University of California Press, 1997) and *The Dialectics of Our America: Genealogy, Cultural Critique, and Literary History* (Durham NC: Duke University Press, 1991). For emerging work on connections among New World and inter-American studies, see José Eduardo Limón, *American Encounters: Greater Mexico, the United States, and the Erotics of Culture* (Boston: Beacon Press, 1998); Kirsten Silva Gruesz, "The Gulf of Mexico System and the 'Latinness' of New Orleans," *American Literary History* 18, no. 3 (2006): 468–95.

5. Cristina García, *Monkey Hunting* (New York: Knopf, 2003); Sky Lee, *Disappearing Moon Café* (Vancouver: Douglas & McIntyre, 1990); Karen Tei Yamashita, *Tropic of Orange* (Minneapolis MN: Coffee House Press, 1997). Subsequent references will be cited parenthetically in the text.

6. Wanni W. Anderson, introduction to *Displacements and Diasporas: Asians in the Americas*, ed. Wanni W. Anderson and Robert G. Lee (New Brunswick NJ: Rutgers University Press, 2005), 5.

7. While Chinese women's scarcity in the Americas has long been attributed to the patriarchal nature of Chinese society, which encouraged women to stay home, and to the sojourner status of Chinese immigrants, recent scholarship has highlighted the gendered nature of Chinese labor recruitment and exclusivist immigration laws, especially in the United States and Canada. The United States passed legislation prohibiting the immigration of prostitutes, which was liberally applied to all Chinese women. After the passage of nineteenth-century exclusion laws in the United States and the introduction of the head tax in Canada, Chinese women could come only as dependents of their "merchant" husbands. Canada's 1924 Exclusion Act prevented Chinese men from bringing in their wives and families. Indentured servants in Cuba planned to return to China, but usually ended up staying because they could not afford their passage home. Neither could they have afforded to bring their wives to join them.

8. My use of the term "intergenerational trauma" draws on Ann E. Kaplan, *Trauma Culture: The Politics of Terror and Loss in Media and Literature* (New Brunswick NJ: Rutgers University Press, 2005); Marianne

Hirsch, *Family Frames: Photography, Narrative, and Postmemory* (Cambridge MA: Harvard University Press, 1997); Gabriele Schwab, *Haunting Legacies* (Durham NC: Duke University Press, 2010).

9. An estimated one million Chinese emigrated between 1847 and 1874, when international pressure eventually halted the indentured Chinese labor trade. Chinese laborers went mainly to Peru, Cuba, and the United States, but were also recruited into plantations and other work sites in Brazil, Panama, Chile, and Ecuador. See Tamar Diana Wilson, "Chinese in Latin America," *Latin American Perspectives 136* 31, no. 3 (2004): 3–6.

10. In fact the overall mortality rate of Chinese passage to Cuba was markedly higher than that of African passage to Cuba. See Lisa Yun and Ricardo René Laremont, "Chinese Coolies and African Slaves in Cuba, 1847–74," *Journal of Asian American Studies* 4, no. 2 (2001): 110, 112.

11. Yun and Laremont, "Chinese Coolies and African Slaves in Cuba," 101.

12. Evelyn Hu-DeHart, "On Coolies and Shopkeepers: The Chinese as Huagong (Laborers) and Huashang (Merchants) in Latin America/Caribbean," in *Displacement and Diasporas: Asians in the Americas*, ed. Wanni W. Anderson and Robert G. Lee (New Brunswick NJ: Rutgers University Press, 2005), 88.

13. Yun and Laremont, "Chinese Coolies and African Slaves in Cuba," 114.

14. Lok Chun Debra Siu, "In Search of Chino Latinos in Diaspora: Cuban Chinese in New York City," in *Cuba: Idea of a Nation Displaced*, ed. Andrea O'Reilly Herrera (Albany: State University of New York Press, 2007), 126–28.

15. Siu, "In Search of Chino Latinos in Diaspora," 126.

16. Grant Hermans Cornwell and Eve Walsh Stoddard, *Global Multiculturalism: Comparative Perspectives on Ethnicity, Race, and Nation* (New York: Rowman & Littlefield, 2000), 194, 202.

17. About seven hundred Chinese workers died building the railway. See http://www.cbc.ca/news/background/china/chinese_immigration.html.

18. Peter S. Li, *The Chinese in Canada* (Toronto: Oxford University Press, 1998), 16.

19. Emily Ryo, "Through the Back Door: Applying Theories of Legal Compliance to Illegal Immigration during the Chinese Exclusion Era," *Law and Social Inquiry* 31, no. 2 (2006): 120.

20. Siu, "In Search of Chino Latinos in Diaspora," 126.

21. Patricia Cloud and David W. Galenson, "Chinese Immigration and Contract Labor in the Late Nineteenth Century," *Explorations in Economic History* 24, no. 1 (1987): 25. The system of Chinese recruitment to Canada (and for that matter to the United States) resembled conditions of indenture under which Europeans came to the United States and Canada in the seventeenth and eighteenth century, when they would pay shipping companies or labor agents the cost of the overseas passage plus profit after a term ranging from four to seven years.

22. After Chinese immigrants had fulfilled their function in the industrialization of the country and anti-Chinese sentiment and violence surged along the West Coast, Canada imposed a head tax on Chinese immigrants in 1885 rather than exclude them outright from entering the country, as did the United States. As Peter S. Li argues, the tax ensured a continuing supply of Chinese labor while officially endorsing second-class entrance status to sustain marginal participation in the Canadian economy. See Li, *The Chinese in Canada*, 41.

23. On this point, see, for example, Eva Mackey, *The House of Difference: Cultural Politics and National Identity in Canada* (London: Routledge, 1999); Donald C. Goellnicht, "A Long Labour: The Protracted Birth of Asian Canadian Literature," *Essays on Canadian Writing* 72 (2000): 1–41.

24. Bobby literalizes the pan-ethnic politics of Asian American civil rights struggles and its potential intersections with the 1960s Chicanismo movement. As David Palumbo-Liu argues, whereas Asian Americans were frequently evoked alongside other U.S. racialized groups in the framework of comparative internal colonialism theories in the 1960s, today Asian Americans are often omitted from cross-ethnic considerations. The economic ascension of some parts of the Asian American community has created assumptions of their full social, cultural, and political integration. Yet Asian American racial difference is, whenever politically exigent, still available for racist activation and mobilization. See David Palumbo-Liu, *Asian/American: Historical Crossings of a Racial Frontier* (Stanford: Stanford University Press, 1999), 4–5.

25. Paul J. Smith, introduction to *Human Smuggling: Chinese Migrant Trafficking and the Challenge to America's Immigration Tradition* (Washington DC: Center for Strategic and International Studies, 1997), x.

26. Sebastian Rotella, *Twilight on the Line: Underworlds and Politics at the U.S.-Mexico Border* (New York: Norton, 1998), 72–73.

27. Evelyn Hu-DeHart, "Immigrants to a Developing Society: The Chinese in Northern Mexico, 1875–1932," in *The Chinese Experience in Arizona and Northern Mexico*, ed. Wanni W. Anderson and Robert G. Lee (Tucson: Arizona Historical Society, 1980), 58.

28. Kennett Cott, "Mexican Diplomacy and the Chinese Issue, 1876–1910," *Hispanic American Historical Review* 67, no. 1 (1987): 70.

29. Wilson, "Chinese in Latin America," 6. As they prospered, an increasing number of immigrants, most of whom middle-class merchants, became Mexican citizens, whereas in the United States, Chinese immigrants were declared racially ineligible for citizenship. See Cott, "Mexican Diplomacy and the Chinese Issue," 79–80.

30. Hu-DeHart, "Immigrants to a Developing Society," 79.

31. Lawrence Michael Fong, "Sojourners and Settlers: The Chinese Experience in Arizona," in *The Chinese Experience in Arizona and Northern Mexico*, ed. Lawrence Michael Fong (Tucson: Arizona Historical Society, 1980), 25.

32. *Tropic of Orange* has finally begun to receive some attention from Asian American scholars. See Caroline Rody, "The Transnational Imagination: Karen Tei Yamashita's *Tropic of Orange*," in *Asian North American Identities: Beyond the Hyphen*, ed. Eleanor Ty and Donald C. Goellnicht (Bloomington: Indiana University Press, 2004), 130–48; Florence Hsiao-ching Li, "Imagining the Mother/Motherland: Karen Tei Yamashita's *Tropic of Orange* and Theresa Hak Kyung Cha's *Dictee*," *Concentric* 30, no. 1 (2004): 149–67.

33. Benedict Anderson, *Imagined Communities: Reflections on the Origin and Spread of Nationalism* (London: Verso, 1983).

34. For comparative work on intersections among Asian American and African American studies, see, for example, Heike Raphael-Hernandez and Shannon Steen, eds., *AfroAsian Encounters: Culture, History, Politics* (New York: New York University Press, 2006); Bill V. Mullen *Afro-orientalism* (Minneapolis: University of Minnesota Press, 2004); Jennifer Lee, *Civility in the City: Blacks, Jews, and Koreans in Urban America* (Cambridge MA: Harvard University Press, 2002). For work on intersections among Latina/o and African American studies, see Neil Foley, *Quest for Equality: The Failed Promise of Black-Brown Solidarity*

(Cambridge MA: Harvard University Press, 2010); Anani Dzidzienyo and Suzanne Oboler, eds., *Neither Enemies nor Friends: Latinos, Blacks, Afro-Latinos* (New York: Palgrave Macmillan, 2005).

35. Recent mass rallies for immigration reform in many U.S. cities have highlighted fledgling cross-ethnic coalitions among immigrants and immigrant organizations from Ireland, Eastern Europe, Latin America, Asia, and Africa, and some umbrella organizations have emerged to more formally unite diverse immigrant advocacy groups.

Chapter 14

Unequal Transpacific Capital Transfers
Japanese Brazilians and Japanese Americans in Japan

Jane H. Yamashiro and Hugo Córdova Quero

In Japan, *nikkeijin* refers to the descendants of Japanese emigrants, sometimes including Japanese emigrants themselves. Regardless of the country to which they emigrated, all nikkeijin have a common history that begins in the ancestral homeland and includes settlement outside of Japan. Although the term is commonly used in Japan, it is not always used in other countries.[1] Thus this socially constructed category is a by-product of Japanese racial formation and social stratification, and ethnic Japanese in the Americas may or may not be aware of the term and its implications.[2]

Lumped together as part of a single category, it would be easy to assume that nikkeijin in Japan have similar experiences, regardless of the country from which they migrate. On the contrary, the incorporation of migrants into Japanese society differs according to not only ethnic background, but also national background. In this sense, nikkeijin's distinctive national backgrounds are apparent.

The stereotypes of two nikkeijin groups reflect striking differences: Japanese Brazilians are often seen as unskilled manual laborers, while Japanese Americans are viewed as English-speaking middle-class Americans, if any image of them exists at all. Most research on nikkeijin in Japan focuses on the Japanese Brazilian experience due to their large population.[3] Since the late 1980s Japanese

Brazilians have been employed as unskilled workers in Japan in increasing numbers, despite their largely middle-class background in Brazil.[4] However, not all Japanese descendants fit this pattern.[5] The Japanese American case is quite different, and comparing the situations of the two groups can complicate research on nikkeijin migration to Japan. If Japanese Brazilians and Japanese Americans are predominantly middle-class in Brazil and the United States, respectively, how do the former become primarily blue-collar workers while the latter are largely able to retain their middle-class status and white-collar occupations in Japan?

To answer this question, this chapter explores Japanese Brazilian and Japanese American experiences in Japan, situating them in a stratified and globalizing world of unequal opportunities based not only on race, class, gender, and sexuality, but also on nationality.[6] Multiple empires have shaped the ways in which the uneven relations between nations have been conceptualized. Wallerstein theorizes the stratified world as a single "world-system" established in the fifteenth century by European expansionism.[7] Since the mid-nineteenth century, however, the United States has also gained imperial power, increasing its hegemonic global status. Therefore Wallerstein's world-system also suggests that both hemispheres have been separated into subregions, some more central to the global system than others. Several images have been used to describe this situation: core and periphery, first world and third world, and developed and underdeveloped.[8]

Based on this history of Euro-American imperial expansionism, our assertion is that compared to Japanese Brazilians, Japanese Americans' privileged position in Japan can be explained largely by the (un)translatability of wealth and skills from the home country. To demonstrate this, we briefly review the populations of Japanese Brazilians and Japanese Americans in Japan, then use Bourdieu's notion of different forms of capital to discuss how these two nikkeijin groups have different forms and amounts of capital in Japan due to the location of Brazilians and Americans within the global economy of the capitalist world-system. Our findings are based on two ethnographic fieldwork projects. Yamashiro conducted field-work in the Tokyo metropolitan region from 2004 to 20077, in-cluding interviews with fifty Japanese Americans.[9] Córdova Que-ro conducted fieldwork in the Kanto and Tokai areas from 2006 to 2008, including interviews with fifty Japanese Brazilians.[10]

Differential Incorporation into Japanese Society

"Migrations do not just happen; they are produced. And migra-tions do not involve just any possible combination of countries: they are patterned. Further, immigrant employment is patterned as well; immigrants rarely have the same occupational and indus-trial distribution as citizens in receiving countries."[11] Sassen points out the structured nature of not only international migrations, but of immigrant employment as well. These uneven experiences are marked by global and historical processes constructed on the ba-sis of colonial and/or racist ideologies (re)constructed in both the sending society and the host society.[12] This global capitalist struc-ture is what Wallerstein referred to as a world-system.[13] The mi-gration of Japanese Brazilians and Japanese Americans to Japan reflects the global inequalities of cultural and social capital, thus shaping the ways migrants from different countries can acquire economic capital in Japan.

Japanese Brazilians as Blue-Collar Workers

Most of the roughly three hundred thousand Brazilian nikkeijin in Japan work as unskilled laborers in Japanese factories, despite their middle-class and educated background in Brazil. In other words, these Brazilians are not simply unskilled laborers moving from one country to another; rather they are people with training and skills from Brazil whose educational and work backgrounds are not acknowledged in Japan when they take on manual labor.[14] The lack of recognition of social and cultural capital—with the consequence of downward social mobility—is not unique to Jap-anese Brazilians; other migrant groups experience this in the Unit-ed States and other industrialized countries.[15]

Japanese Brazilian labor migration to Japan began to surge in the late 1980s, with the coincidence of the Brazilian economic crisis, which pushed people out, and the rise of the Japanese bubble economy, which pulled people in, fitting Todaro's neoclassical economic explanation of migration as due to "income differentials."[16] The instability of their economy led many Brazilians to emigrate; those who had Japanese citizenship or whose parents were Japanese citizens could easily go to Japan. Japan was an attractive choice, for at the peak of the bubble economy a worker could earn five to ten times more doing unskilled factory work in Japan than working a white-collar job or owning a business in Brazil.

By the early 1990s many ethnic Japanese in Brazil were sansei, or third generation, and they could not readily obtain visas to Japan under the contemporaneous immigration law.[17] Luckily for them, at about the same time the Japanese economy was growing so fast that Japanese companies could not fulfill their cheap labor needs with domestic workers. Restrictive immigration laws made it difficult to legally import unskilled labor because the official stance of the government was that Japanese society was homogeneous and the acceptance of too many foreigners would disrupt the social harmony and integrity of the nation. Consequently the Japanese government added the *teijusha* (long-term resident) visa category as part of the 1990 revisions of the Immigration Control and Refugee Recognition Act, officially enabling people of Japanese ancestry up to the third generation to legally migrate to Japan. The lack of restrictions on their activities in Japan may suggest that government officials had Brazilians primarily in mind for Japan's unskilled labor needs.[18] The policy resulted in both increasing numbers of multigenerational Japanese Brazilians and their families migrating to Japan, and the policing of unskilled migrant workers from Southeast Asia in order to prevent the overflow of undocumented migrants.[19] Though the flow has decreased since the onslaught of the Japanese recession, Japanese Brazilians are now the third largest resident foreign national population in Japan, after Koreans and Chinese.[20]

During the 1990s Japanese Brazilians were mostly concentrated in industrial areas, often living in residential complexes near the factories where they worked. More recently an increasing number are residing in the Tokyo metropolitan area as well as many other regions of Japan.[21] Their significant presence in concentrated areas of Japan, combined with their cultural difference marking them as un-Japanese, has drawn attention, resulting in the emergence of stereotypes of Japanese Brazilians and Peruvians as criminals.[22]

However, the question remains: If Japanese Brazilians were formerly teachers or professionals back home, why aren't more of them utilizing those skills to find white-collar jobs in Japan? If working in a factory pays more than their jobs in Brazil, working in an office or at a school in Japan would ostensibly be even more fruitful. When Yamashiro asked this question to a Japanese Brazilian scholar who is renowned for his work on Japanese Brazilian labor migration to Japan, he replied that most Japanese Brazilians do not speak English. To get a good job in Japan, he explained, you have to speak either Japanese or English. In other words, being fluent in Portuguese (and sometimes additional languages as well) is generally not valued as cultural capital in Japan.

The economic situation for Japanese Brazilians in Japan is rapidly changing. By the end of 2008, due to the global financial crisis, thousands of Japanese Brazilian workers were becoming unemployed. The high rate of job loss has caused many families to return to Brazil, and it has mobilized hundreds of migrants to protest on the streets.[23] Meanwhile the Brazilian economy has become more stable. especially after the cancellation of its external debt by the International Monetary Fund and the World Bank.[24] This suggests that the "push/pull factors" encouraging the migration of Japanese Brazilians to Japan are reversing. The recession in Japan is leaving thousands of migrants unemployed.[25] Some cities are trying to keep their foreign migrants by temporarily hiring them at the prefectural level, by reducing their rent in public housing, or by giving them subsidies to help with their family's finances.[26] In contrast, the national government has developed a plan for reducing the migrant population by offering ¥300,000 per person (about $3,100) to Japanese Brazilian migrants to leave the country. This includes an explicit agreement never to come back under the same type of visa.[27] How this will impact the presence of Japanese Brazilians in Japan is still uncertain; however, it is clear that a new phase in the migration of Japanese Brazilians has started, perhaps redirecting the migration pattern again, from Japan to Brazil.

Japanese Americans as White-Collar Workers

The population of Japanese Americans in Japan is quite different from that of Japanese Brazilians. First, no one knows how many Japanese Americans there are in Japan, as there is no way to obtain those data. There are roughly forty-nine thousand registered American citizens in Japan, but there is no racial or ethnic data on them and there is no way to estimate the percentage of the total American population that is of Japanese ancestry.[28] In addition there are forty thousand U.S. military personnel in Japan, plus their families and civilian employees who hold various citizenships.[29] While the Japanese Brazilian population in Japan can be estimated based on the high percentage of Brazilian citizens of Japanese ancestry in the country, the same assumptions cannot be logically made about the percentage of Japanese Americans among all American citizens in Japan. In any case, we know that the number is thousands smaller than for Japanese Brazilians, leading to a smaller community and media presence and different kinds of treatment.

Another difference is that Japanese Americans are dispersed; there are no particular areas of the country or neighborhoods where Japanese Americans can be found. Their lack of visibility in Japan leads to the lack of an image of Japanese Americans and results in their being treated more as individuals than as part of a larger group. Sekiguchi has found that in a neighborhood where Japanese Brazilians compose 30 percent of the total residents, Japanese Americans are treated worse if thought to be Japanese Brazilian: "One Nikkei American resident of the area, who speaks limited Japanese but looks Japanese, claims being poorly served several times because he was mistaken as a Nikkei Brazilian. His claims gain credence because he once revealed that he was an American and a store clerk apologized saying, 'I am sorry, I thought you were a Brazilian.'"[30] In other words, in an area where Japanese Brazilians are concentrated, Japanese Americans are assumed to be Japanese Brazilian; in other areas their ethnicity is more ambiguously and they can be more flexible and strategic about their identity.[31]

In contrast to the predominantly blue-collar work that Japanese Brazilians do in Japan, Japanese Americans perform mostly white-collar work that takes advantage of their educational background. It is not uncommon to find Americans with bachelor's degrees working in offices or teaching English, while Brazilians with professional degrees and even PhDs may end up working in factories. Japanese American residents include more men than women and largely fall into the categories of businessperson, lawyer, white-collar office worker, student, Japan Exchange and Teaching Program participant (assistant language teachers and coordinators of international relations), English teacher, translator, homemaker, and U.S. military employee, though they also include a professional wrestler and other unusual occupations.[32]

One way to explain the lack of Japanese Americans working in factories might be that there is neither an economic push out of the United States nor a pull toward Japan. Another explanation comes from Bourdieu's notion of capital.

Bourdieu's "Forms of Capital"

The social world is accumulated history, and if it is not to be reduced to a discontinuous series of instantaneous mechanical equilibria between agents who are treated as interchangeable particles, one must reintroduce into it the notion of capital and with it, accumulation and all its effects. —PIERRE BOURDIEU, "The Forms of Capital"

In "The Forms of Capital" Bourdieu explains the distinctions between cultural, social, and economic capital, which is useful in comparing and explaining the relative situations of migrant Japanese

Brazilians and Japanese Americans in Japan. Bourdieu's notion of capital enables us to acknowledge the unequal histories and individual trajectories that differentiate the options of individuals as they participate in social exchanges. If "the social world is accumulated history" rather than simply rational actors involved in numerous calculated exchanges devoid of a larger cultural context, then inasmuch as individual histories diverge from one another, so the various forms of capital diverge from each other. Incorporating this sense of particularities and limited options and possibilities, Bourdieu helps us to see a stratified world where not everything is possible for everyone, despite what some would like to believe. In this way, the concept of capital makes social structures visible: "The structure of the distribution of the different types and subtypes of capital at a given moment in time represents the immanent structure of the social world." Moreover forms of capital can be seen as synonymous with forms of power.[33]

Cultural capital can exist in multiple forms. In the "embodied state," capital is internalized and incorporated. In other words, cultural capital can be acquired unconsciously through socialization.[34] So the mere fact of where one is raised—in what language and geopolitical space—affects one's accumulation and embodiment of cultural capital.

The way skills and traits are interpreted as cultural capital is context-dependent. For international migrants, this means that in different societies, their backgrounds and experiences may not be valued equally. According to Bourdieu, "Any given cultural competence (e.g., being able to read in a world of illiterates) derives a scarcity value from its position in the distribution of cultural capital and yields profits of distinction for its owner."[35] Rather than skills in and of themselves having inherent value, this suggests that what is considered cultural capital in each society varies, depending on how many others share the skill.

Language is one example of cultural capital. It is acquired, often unconsciously, through socialization. If "the link between economic and cultural capital is established through the mediation of the time needed for acquisition," then being a native or even a fluent speaker of a language should be greatly valued for the lengthy time needed to develop this skill.[36] However, scarcity value alone cannot explain how abilities are attributed social value. For international migrants who are one of only a few native speakers of their language in the host country, the scarcity of their linguistic abilities should increase their value. Yet being a native English speaker in Japan yields a higher profit than being a native Portuguese speaker, despite the ostensibly higher scarcity value of the latter. This reflects the unequal value attributed to language alone and the need to see valuation within a global framework.

Another example of cultural capital is academic qualifications. Bourdieu states that academic qualifications, as institutional recognition of cultural capital, can be compared and exchanged for economic capital, thus enabling the establishment of "conversion rates between cultural capital and economic capital by guaranteeing the monetary value of a given academic capital." But here again we see that for international migrants, the conversion rate may be arbitrarily biased against people from different parts of the world—in Japan a PhD from Latin America is not weighted the same as a PhD from the United States—despite the idea that academic certificates and degrees might hold some "constant" value due to their institutionalization.[37]

Social capital refers to one's group membership and is never completely independent of cultural capital because it matters not just to whom you are connected but also their cultural capital.[38] In this way, linguistic communities become sources of both cultural and social capital—which, not to be forgotten, are "disguised forms of economic capital" that have the potential to be converted as such. Language as a form of cultural and social capital in Japan differently shapes the opportunities and experiences of Japanese Brazilians and Japanese Americans migrating from one part of the world-system to another and their abilities to acquire economic capital.

Comparing Forms of Capital among Japanese American and Japanese Brazilian Migrants in Japan

Being able to speak English is a significant factor distinguishing Japanese Americans from Japanese Brazilians and greatly affects life chances and opportunities in Japan. Japanese Americans and Japanese Brazilians have different amounts of capital at their disposal, and English-language ability plays a part in this. The case of Japan makes clear that English has become "the hegemonic language of the contemporary world."[39] English has become the major language of communication in most industries, but has more than simply practical value. The cultural construction of English (i.e., the meaning and image attached to knowing and speaking it) and its role in an unevenly globalizing world are not inevitable; they reflect the power of English-speaking countries in the contemporary world. Japan is certainly no exception, and the social, cultural, and economic capital of knowing English is a major factor distinguishing most Japanese Brazilians from most Japanese Americans.

Cultural Capital

English has become the language of global intellectual discourse and the dominant language of intellectual communities involved in the production, reproduction and circulation of knowledge.
—JOHN RENNIE SHORT, *Global Dimensions: Space, Place and the Contemporary World*

Many Japanese people want to learn and practice their English because simply being an English speaker—and even more so if one is a native speaker—gives one cultural capital in Japan. One Japanese American man whom Yamashiro interviewed said that Japanese people sometimes befriended him simply to practice their English. He was not bothered by this; he actually saw it as a status symbol and enjoyed the attention. In this way a basic skill in the United States is transformed into a form of cultural capital in Japan. One Asian American man said that he was treated with more respect when he spoke English. Once, when he was on a train, a Japanese man near him seemed confrontational, or at least annoyed, perhaps because they bumped into each other in the crowd. When the Asian American spoke English to ask what was wrong and apologize, he said the other man's demeanor instantly changed and he became more polite and deferential. (An alternative explanation could be that the Asian American was recategorized as not-Japanese and was perhaps then forgiven for whatever had occurred.)

The valuing of English as a form of cultural capital depends on the host society and how it perceives the skills that migrants possess. As in Japan, in Brazil English is valued as cultural capital. Those who speak the language have some privileges that others do not have, such as being hired for better jobs, including management positions at transnational companies.[40] In Japan (and elsewhere) the value assigned to migrants' abilities and background experience depends on the context and assumptions about migrants. Referring to the specific case of Brazilian nikkeijin in Japan acquiring Japanese-language skills, Cornelius et al. state, "Japanese-language competence as human capital . . . does not influence wages positively even though language ability is the top criterion Japanese employers use when hiring foreign workers. Bilingual workers have an easier time finding employment, but not necessarily in higher-paying jobs; instead, they are employed as low-level, unskilled manual laborers. For instance, employers who hire [Brazilian] nikkeijin workers generally do not pay Japanese speakers better salaries because they do the same type of unskilled work as non-Japanese-speaking [Brazilian] nikkeijin."[41] In other words, once migrants are parceled into manual labor jobs, their additional language skills, whether preexisting or recently acquired, go unrecognized and unrewarded. This is also conditioned by the fact that, although in theory the long-term residence visa allows them to take on any kind of work, in reality the main jobs that Japanese Brazilians can secure are blue-collar jobs in small and medium-size factories. One explanation for this is the differential treatment of people depending on their citizenship and the assumption that migrants from third world countries do not have the background or knowledge to perform skilled labor.

Social Capital

> English is the language of international interaction.
> —JOHN RENNIE SHORT, *Global Dimensions: Space, Place and the Contemporary World*

English is an upper-class language in Japan. Japanese spend hundreds of thousands of yen to study it, and knowing English enables one to access higher class social networks, thus allowing social mobility. The upper class in Japan is increasingly educated abroad, usually in English-speaking countries such as the United States the United Kingdom. This experience and education abroad in a Western country is a status symbol and becomes a form of both social and cultural capital.[42]

English speakers possess not only cultural capital but also social capital, in that they are able to speak with and thus gain access to people in these higher echelons of Japanese society. In other words, there is a class dimension to speaking English in Japan. Most highly educated, upper-class people in positions of power can understand or speak English at least conversationally. Being able to access these social networks linguistically (though socially is another issue) thus encourages social mobility. In this way it represents a source of potential job opportunities, such as being recommended for a position by a prominent member of a social network. One Tokyo English-language magazine recently included an article on "U.S. university clubs in Tokyo," in which the author described several prestigious alumni clubs and their membership and activities. The Harvard Club "has about 400 members, with many Japanese and foreign members, including royalty, former Prime Ministers and other politicians, [and] leaders in finance and industry."[43]

In addition, people in Japan, for various reasons (school exams, jobs, leisure, etc.), pay a significant amount of money to improve their English. This commodity value adds to the image of English as a desirable skill and status symbol. In his research Córdova Quero came across a Japanese college student who introduced himself as "proudly speaking English two weeks in a row" both at home and at college. When asked why he did not speak Japanese despite being in Japan, the student boldly replied, "It is because I want to be American. I don't want to be Japanese, and in order to be a good American, I need to speak English fluently." For this student, speaking English represents Americanness, and both are highly valued traits. His comment about rejecting his Japaneseness and instead embracing Americanness reflects the dominant dichotomization of Japaneseness and foreignness in Japanese society.[44]

A Brazilian woman who taught Spanish at a woman's university and had hoped to expand to teaching about Brazilian and other Latin American cultures and histories summarizes her disappointment about the situation: "Portuguese? This language I never had the opportunity to speak, much less to teach . . . There is no interest in Japan for countries which are not the United States — which the Japanese simply call 'America' — or for any language which is not English." Though she admits that this is a generalization, she adds that those who speak English, and especially those from the United States, are in a privileged position in Japan.[45]

Economic Capital

> English is required to be competitive in global markets. Many countries have adopted it as a second language and emphasize it as an important subject in their schools. . . . For individuals in many countries, English skills are an invaluable asset in the job market. . . . English has become a form of cultural capital for both national governments seeking to produce a globally competitive workforce and for individuals eager to achieve a better position in a globalizing world.
> —JOHN RENNIE SHORT, *Global Dimensions: Space, Place and the Contemporary World*

Whereas international migrants who do not speak English (or Japanese) are usually forced into blue-collar or manual labor industries, native English speakers have many more employment options in Japan, based on language ability alone. This gives them more flexibility economically. Many Americans go to Japan with the backup plan of teaching English if things do not work out in other employment areas. Some Japanese Americans are in Japan to learn cultural arts or to study other subjects and earn money teaching English to support these other activities. A recent article in a Tokyo English-language magazine reported, "Being a foreigner in Japan does have many advantages, particularly as a musician. If you look and sound good here, there are many potential jobs that you will be hired for ahead of a Japanese musician. The fact that you are a native speaker is in itself a valuable commodity. For example, narration. A friend of mine from London read three articles from the Yomiuri Shimbun [a major daily] and was paid ¥120,000 [about $1,250] for 25 minutes work!"[46] Being a native English speaker is like an occupational safety net in Japan: you know you can always find a job teaching English or doing other work, and this will not only keep food on the table and a roof over your head, but will also keep you from having to work in a factory.

Native English speakers can easily find jobs teaching English, especially in, but not limited to, urban areas like Tokyo. There is an abundance of English teaching jobs at various levels—private English schools, elementary through college-level English classes, one-on-one tutorials, and more—with corresponding job stability. Linguistic ability is not the only factor that matters, however; in Japan many English-language schools do not hire non-native English-speaking foreigners who are fluent in English (i.e., they hire native English-speaking foreigners or non-native English-speaking Japanese). Córdova Quero spoke to the director of an English-language school who was recruiting prospective English teachers. Knowing many Japanese Brazilians who are fluent in English, he asked the director if he would like to contact them. The director's answer was clear: "No, not [Japanese] Brazilians, please, as people will not feel comfortable being taught English by someone who is not American. If you know Americans, please recommend them, but not [Japanese] Brazilians."

It is possible to find well-paying jobs in Tokyo that require English skills but do not require Japanese skills; besides jobs teaching English there are also upper-level management jobs in American and other foreign and multinational companies. Of course, these jobs require additional types of cultural capital as well and are not necessarily open to English-speaking Asians, Africans, or Latina/os as they are to English-speaking Americans, Europeans, and other Westerners. Some international lawyers and businesspeople interviewed by Yamashiro said they do not need to know much, if any, Japanese for work. Especially at American and multinational corporations, meetings with clients and upper-level managers might be conducted entirely in English—especially if participants come from multiple countries. One man Yamashiro spoke with told an anecdote about an Italian executive who ran meetings with Japanese employees in English. One day the Japanese employees complained about having to conduct meetings in English. The Italian's response was something like, "Don't complain to me—if I had it my way, we'd be speaking in Italian!"

More and more Japanese are motivated to improve their English-language skills because high scores on the Test of English for International Communication might mean a promotion, depending on the industry. In this way, English has become a form of cultural capital, easily convertible into economic capital.

Conclusion

This chapter contributes to the study of transnational and transpacific migration patterns by crossing the boundaries of multiple area studies. Most research in Latina/o American studies focuses on migration to and experiences in the United States. Moreover the point of origin tends to be Mexico, the Caribbean, or Central America rather than South America. Similarly in Asian American studies most work has focused on migration to and experiences in the United States. Research that explores transnational ties to Asia tends to look at first-generation migrants and their ties to the country from which they emigrated. In Asian studies, more specifically Japanese studies, there is a growing interest in the so-called return migration of nikkeijin. However, their histories and identities are filtered through the point of view of Japanese society and constructions of who the "Japanese" are. We have comparatively examined ethnic Japanese North and South American return migrants to Japan, locating them within a hierarchical world-system where their national background translates into unequal social, cultural, and economic capital in their ancestral homeland.

The discourse on nikkeijin in Japan often refers to their migration as a "return to the homeland." While this is certainly part of the picture and one useful paradigm for understanding Japanese American and Japanese Brazilian experiences, focusing on national (and linguistic) differences reveals the diversity of nikkeijin in Japan. We point out that differences exist between nikkeijin from North and South America, but future research needs to further examine the diversity among South Americans, showing that Brazilian experiences differ from those of Spanish-speaking Peruvians, Bolivians, and Argentineans. Regional differences within each national group might also be worth pursuing (e.g., comparing Japanese Americans from the East Coast and the West Coast, Japanese Brazilians from urban and rural areas). Each national and linguistic community includes not only nikkeijin, but also their spouses (many of whom are not of Japanese ancestry) and children (many of whom are of mixed ancestry).

This chapter has shown how Japanese American and Japanese Brazilian opportunities and positionalities in Japan, though part of a larger nikkeijin history and community, are very uneven due to global inequalities in cultural, social, and economic capital within the world-system. These cases reveal the importance of seeing these groups not simply as ethnic return migrants, but as stratified ethnic groups in a larger global economy of which Japan is a part. The employment hierarchy in Japan reflects larger economic and labor inequalities in the world today that are shaped by and contribute to "unequal transpacific capital transfers." Rather than viewing globalization as a social process that merely promotes increasing flows of people, cultures, and capital, these findings suggest the need to acknowledge that even the so-called return of the diaspora is structured by and reflects a stratified global economy and world-system.

Notes

1. Jane H. Yamashiro, "Nikkeijin," in *Encyclopedia of Race, Ethnicity, and Society*, ed. R. T. Schaefer (Thousand Oaks CA: Sage, 2008).

2. Hugo Córdova Quero, "'To Be Nikkeijin or . . . Not to Be': Identity Formation Dilemmas among Brazilians of Japanese Ancestry Migrating to Japan," in *From Nikkeijin to Nikkei: Searching for New Approaches to Studying Nikkeijin*, ed. M. Iijima and T. Watarai (Kyoto: Center for Integrated Area Studies, Kyoto University; Japan Consortium for Area Studies, 2008).

3. Joshua H. Roth, *Brokered Homeland: Japanese Brazilian Migrants in Japan* (Ithaca NY: Cornell University Press, 2002); Takeyuki Tsuda, *Strangers in the Ethnic Homeland: Japanese Brazilian Return Migration in Transnational Perspective* (New York: Columbia University Press, 2003).

4. Jeffrey Lesser, ed., *Searching for Home Abroad: Japanese Brazilians and Transnationalism* (Durham NC: Duke University Press, 2003); Daniel Touro Linger, *No One Home: Brazilian Selves Remade in Japan* (Stanford: Stanford University Press, 2001); Keiko Yamanaka, "'I Will Go Home, but When?' Labor Migration and Circular Diaspora Formation by Japanese Brazilians in Japan," in *Japan and Global Migration: Foreign Workers and the Advent of a Multicultural Society*, ed. Mike Douglass and Glenda S. Roberts (London: Routledge, 2000).

5. Edson Mori, "The Japanese-Brazilian Dekasegi Phenomenon," in *New Worlds, New Lives: Globalization and People of Japanese Descent in the Americas and from Latin America in Japan*, ed. L. R. Hirabayashi, A. Kikumura-Yano, and J. A. Hirabayashi (Stanford: Stanford University Press, 2002); Masato Ninomiya, "The *Dekasegi* Phenomenon and the Education of Japanese Brazilian Children in Japanese Schools," in *New Worlds, New Lives: Globalization and People of Japanese Descent in the Americas and from Latin America in Japan*, ed. L. R. Hirabayashi, A. Kikumura-Yano, and J. A. Hirabayashi (Stanford: Stanford University Press, 2002); Yoko Sellek, "Nikkeijin: The Phenomenon of Return Migration," in *Japan's Minorities: The Illusion of Homogeneity*, ed. M. Weiner (London: Routledge, 1997).

6. Vilna Bashi and Antonio McDaniel, "A Theory of Immigration and Racial Stratification," *Journal of Black Studies* 25, no. 5 (1997): 668–82; Wayne A. Cornelius, Takeyuki Tsuda, and Zulema Valdez, "Human Capital versus Social Capital: A Comparative Analysis of Immigrant Wages and Labor Market Incorporation in Japan and the United States," IZA Working Paper No. 476, Forschungsinstitut zur Zukunft der Arbeit, Bonn, 2002; Hirohisa Takenoshita, "The Differential Incorporation into Japanese Labor Market: A Comparative Study of Japanese Brazilians and Professional Chinese Migrants," *Japanese Journal of Population* 4, no. 1 (2006): 56–77.

7. Immanuel Wallerstein, *The Modern World System: Capitalist Agriculture and the Origins of the European World Economy in the Sixteenth Century* (New York: Academic Press, 1976); Immanuel Wallerstein, *The Capitalist World-Economy* (Cambridge, England: Cambridge University Press, 1979); Immanuel Wallerstein, "Class Conflict in the Capitalist World-Economy," in *Race, Nation, Class: Ambiguous Identities*, ed. E. Balibar and I. Wallerstein (London: Verso, 1988). According to Wallerstein, the unit of social scientific analysis is neither the "state" nor the "nation" but the entire world, since the world constitutes a single capitalist economy where even the socialist and communist countries play a role (*The Modern World System*, xi). See also Alvin Y. So, *Social Change and Development: Modernization, Dependency and World-system Theories* (Newbury Park CA: Sage, 1990), 172. Wallerstein's work is indebted to theories developed in the 1960–70s by, among others, Paul Marlor and Paul Baran, *Monopoly Capital: An Essay on the American Economic and Social Order* (New York: Monthly Review Press, 1966); André Gunder Frank, *Capitalism and Underdevelopment in Latin America* (New York: Monthly Review Press, 1967); Samir Amin, *Imperialism and Unequal Development* (New York: Monthly Review Press, 1977).

8. The center/periphery metaphor comes from Vladimir Il'ich Lenin, *Imperialism: The Highest Stage of Capitalism* (1917; repr., Chippendale, Australia: Resistance Books, 1999); Nikolai Bukharin, *Imperialism and World Economy* (1917; repr., London: Merlin Press, 1972); Immanuel Wallerstein, "World System," in *A Dictionary of Marxist Thought*, ed. Tom Bottomore (Malden MA: Blackwell, 1991), 590–91. In his book *Imperialism*, Lenin analyzes the repercussions of World War I, explaining that capitalist countries (center) need colonies (periphery) in order

to sustain and expand their economic power. In this light, World War I was an excuse to redistribute the world among capitalist countries. Other metaphors come from dependence theory, developed by Gunder Frank in *Capitalism and Underdevelopment in Latin America* to explain why underdeveloped countries continuously lack development due to their dependence on more developed capitalist countries. Underdeveloped or third world countries are a consequence of developed capitalist (first world) countries' policies of decapitalization produced by their exploitation of third world countries. See Tony Lawson and Joan Garrod, *Dictionary of Sociology* (London: Fitzroy Dearborn, 2001), 63–64.

9. The Tokyo metropolitan region includes Tokyo, Saitama, Chiba, and Kanagawa prefectures.

10. The Kanto and Tokai areas include Tokyo as well as the prefectures of Chiba, Ibaraki, Saitama, Gunma, Tochigi, and Shizuoka.

11. Saskia Sassen, *Globalization and Its Discontents: Essays on the New Mobility of People and Money* (New York: New Press, 1998), 56.

12. This follows the work of Grosfoguel, whose analysis focuses on the cases of Puerto Ricans in New York and Algerians in France. See Ramón Grosfoguel, "Race and Ethnicity or Racialized Ethnicities? Identities within Global Coloniality," *Ethnicities* 4, no. 3 (2004): 315–16; Ramón Grosfoguel and Ana Margarita Cervantes-Rodríguez, eds., *The Modern/Colonial/Capitalist World-system in the Twentieth Century: Global Processes, Antisystemic Movements, and the Geopolitics of Knowledge* (Westport CT: Praeger, 2002).

13. Globalization from a world-system point of view articulates the context within which migrations occur as part of a long historical, political, economic, and increasingly global process whose roots date back to the fifteenth century. See Wallerstein, *The Capitalist World-Economy*; Walter D. Mignolo, *Local Histories/Global Designs: Coloniality, Subaltern Knowledges, and Border Thinking* (Princeton NJ: Princeton University Press, 2000). According to Harumi Befu, globalization in East Asia may have occurred at the same time as its counterpart in the West. In fact he sees the attempts of Toyotomi Hideyoshi to expand Japanese territory into Korea in 1592–93 as the beginning of globalization in Japan, which in turn was "interrupted" during the Edo period, 1603 to 1868. Harumi Befu, "Globalization as Human Dispersal: From the Perspective of Japan," in *Globalization and Social Change in Contemporary*

Japan, ed. J. S. Eades, Harumi Befu, and Tom Gill (Melbourne: Trans Pacific Press, 2000), 17–40.

14. Yamashiro, "Nikkeijin." It is important to point out that not all Japanese Brazilians work in factories in Japan. The film *Mundo Nikkei: Os Brasileiros do outro lado do mundo*, produced by Vera Sanada and directed by Yuri Sanada (70 minutes, AVENTURAcomBR Productions, 2008, DVD), for example, shows Japanese Brazilians whose occupations include scuba diving instructor, rap singer, and speed racer. Moreover some Japanese Brazilians may work at factories during the week but spend weekends and free time practicing their vocations (e.g., as painters, artists, photographers, Protestant ministers).

15. Seymour Martin Lipset and Reinhard Bendix, *Social Mobility in Industrial Society* (New Brunswick NJ: Transaction, 1992); George J. Borjas, "Making It in America: Social Mobility in the Immigrant Population," NBER Working Paper No. 12088, National Bureau of Economic Research, Cambridge MA, 2006; Rebeca Raijman and Moshe Semyonov, "Modes of Labor Market Incorporation and Occupational Cost among New Immigrants to Israel," in *Immigration to Israel: Sociological Perspectives*, ed. Elazar Leshem and Judith T. Shuval (New Brunswick NJ: Transaction, 1998), 111–34; Thomas Bauer and Klaus F. Zimmermann, "Occupational Mobility of Ethnic Migrants," IZA Working Paper No. 58, Forschungsinstitut zur Zukunft der Arbeit, Bonn, 1999; Li Zong, "International Transference of Human Capital and Occupational Attainment of Recent Chinese Professional Immigrants in Canada," PCERII Working Paper No. WP03-04, University of Alberta, Edmonton, 2004.

16. Michael P. Todaro, "A Model of Labor Migration and Urban Unemployment in Less Developed Countries," *American Economic Review* 59, no. 1 (1969): 138–48. It is important to note, however, that Todaro looks at rural to urban migration, which is not the same as international migration from "peripheral" nations to "core" nations. As pointed out earlier, though there may be wage differentials between Brazil and Japan, many migrants have educational backgrounds and training that simply go unrewarded in Japan or even fail to be commodified beyond the need for a labor force. For further analysis on this issue, see Wallerstein, *The Modern World System*, 349–50 and "Class Conflict in the Capitalist World-Economy," 115–24. One clear consequence is that the perceptions of social, cultural, and economic capital are not the same for the migrants in the host society as in the homeland.

17. It should be noted that although there are Japanese descendants in Brazil up to the sixth generation, only those from the second and third generation were granted the opportunity to obtain the long-term resident visa. See Paula Harumi, "100 anos depois: O primeiro rokussei," *Made in Japan*, April 10, 2008, 34–41.

18. Ayumi Takenaka, "Ethnic Community in Motion: Japanese-Peruvians in Peru, Japan, and the U.S." (PhD diss., Columbia University, 2000), 128.

19. Yamanaka, "'I Will Go Home, but When?'" 123–52.

20. There were 599,000 registered Korean nationals (from both the Republic of Korea and the Democratic People's Republic of Korea) and 520,000 Chinese nationals registered in Japan as of December 31, 2006 (Statistics Bureau, 2007).

21. Ewerthon Tobace, "Eles moran na capital," *Higashi Alternativa*, March 20, 2008, 18–29.

22. Solidarity Network with Migrants Japan, *Living Together with Migrants and Ethnic Minorities in Japan: An NGO Policy Proposal* (Tokyo: SMJ, 2007).

23. Cristiane Tobace, "Brasileiros protestam em Tokyo contra demissões em massa," *International Press*, January 19, 2009, http://www.ipcdigital.com/br/Noticias/Crise-no-Japao/Brasileiros-protestam-em-Tokyo-contra-demissoes-em-massa (accessed April 29, 2009).

24. For decades that external debt forced Brazil to follow economic decisions made at the IMF and World Bank, which caused the country great economic instability. The cancellation of the external debt not only has lessened the demands of the IMF and the World Bank but has produced socioeconomic changes under President Lula that have allowed many migrants to return to Brazil.

25. Osny Arashiro, "Brasileiros ocupam vagas temporárias em serviço de limpeza," *International Press*, February 25, 2009, http://www.ipcdigital.com/br/Noticias/Crise-no-Japao/Brasileiros-ocupam-vagas-temporarias-em-servico-de-limpeza (accessed April 27, 2009).

26. "Komaki dá subsídio para famílias com dois ou mais filhos," *International Press*, April 21, 2009, http://www.ipcdigital.com/br/Noticias/Comunidade/Aichi/Komaki-da-subsidio-para-familias-com-dois-ou-mais-filhos (accessed April 27, 2009).

27. Arudou Debito, "'Golden Parachutes' Mark Failure of Race-Based

Policy," *Japan Times*, April 7, 2009, http://japantimes.co.jp/cgi-bin/
fl20090407ad.html (accessed April 8, 2009); Hiroko Tabuchi, "Japan
Pays Foreign Workers to Go Home, Forever," *New York Times*, April 22,
2009, http://www.nytimes.com/2009/04/23/business/global/23immigrant
.html (accessed April 23, 2009). This type of voluntary repatriation with
economic incentives is similar to what Filipinos experienced in the United States during the Great Depression with the Filipino Repatriation Act
of 1935. See Casiano Pagdilao Coloma, *A Study of the Filipino Repatriation Movement* (San Francisco: R&E Research Associates, 1974). It is
different from the forced repatriation of Mexicans in the United States in
the 1930s and Romani (Gypsies) in France especially during 2010, which
was due to anti-immigrant sentiments. See Francisco E. Balderrama and
Raymond Rodríguez, *Decade of Betrayal: Mexican Repatriation in the
1930s* (Albuquerque: University of New Mexico Press, 2006); Margaret
Brearley, "The Persecution of Gypsies in Europe," *American Behavioral Scientist* 45, no. 4 (2001): 588–99; Marie Bidet, "Will French Gypsies Always Stay Nomadic and out of the Law-making Process?" in *Proceedings of the International Conference "Romani Mobilities in Europe:
Multidisciplinary Perspectives," January 14–15, 2010* (Oxford: Oxford
University Press, 2010), 20–27.

28. Statistics Bureau and Statistical Research and Training Institute,
Japan in Figures 2007 (Tokyo: Ministry of Internal Affairs and Communications, 2007). Whereas racial and ethnic data are regularly collected on people in the United States, for Americans abroad it seems that
background data are collected by the country in which they are residing.
Japan collects data on citizenship but not ethnic or racial background.

29. Fur further details, see the U.S. Forces Japan website, http://www.
usfj.mil/.

30. Tomoko Sekiguchi, "Nikkei Brazilians in Japan: The Ideology and
Symbolic Context Faced by Children of This New Ethnic Minority," in
*Exploring Japaneseness: On Japanese Enactments of Culture and Con-
sciousness*, ed. Ray T. Donahue (Westport CT: Ablex, 2002), 199.

31. See Jane H. Yamashiro, "Racialized National Identity Construction in the Ancestral Homeland: Japanese American Migrants in Japan,"
Ethnic and Racial Studies 34, no. 9 (2011): 1502–21.

32. Ayako Takamori, "Japanese American Women in Japan: Gender and Ethnicity in a Transnational Context," paper presented at Asian

Studies Conference Japan, Tokyo, 2007; Donna Fujimoto, Susie Sakayori, Ken Fujioka, Ken Ikeda, and Laura Kusaka, "Nikkei Perspectives: Emerging Narratives," in *JALT Conference Proceedings*, ed. K. Bradford-Watts, C. Ikeguchi, and M. Swanson (Tokyo: JALT, 2006), 928–39; *Finding Home*, 52 minutes, produced and directed by Art Nomura, Arrupe Productions, 2006, DVD; Jane H. Yamashiro, "Rethinking the Japanese/Foreigner Distinction," *Japan Times*, March 22, 2007, B10; Jane H. Yamashiro, "When the Diaspora Returns: Transnational Racial and Ethnic Identity Formation among Japanese Americans in Global Tokyo" (PhD diss., University of Hawai'i at Mānoa, 2008).

33. Pierre Bourdieu, "The Forms of Capital," in *Distinction: A Social Critique of the Judgement of Taste*, trans. Richard Nice (London: Routledge, 1984), 241, 242, 243.

34. Bourdieu, "The Forms of Capital," 245, 245–46.

35. Bourdieu, "The Forms of Capital," 245.

36. Bourdieu, "The Forms of Capital," 247, 246.

37. Bourdieu, "The Forms of Capital," 248.

38. Bourdieu, "The Forms of Capital," 248, 249.

39. John Rennie Short, *Global Dimensions: Space, Place and the Contemporary World* (London: Reaktion Books, University of Chicago Press, 2001), 129.

40. Interestingly some Japanese Brazilians counted their proficiency in English as a tool for success in Brazil, though it did not benefit them in Japan. Hirohisa Takenoshita has stated that the possibilities for the insertion of migrants into a new culture and society as well as their employment opportunities are already conditioned prior to their arrival, and do not depend on the traits that were recognized as cultural or social capital in the country of origin. Takenoshita, "The Differential Incorporation into Japanese Labor Market," 62.

41. Cornelius, Tsuda, and Valdez, "Human Capital versus Social Capital," 10–11.

42. There is also an economic relationship between where different Japanese go and why. Japanese who go to the United States tend to be relatively wealthier than Japanese who go to Australia or other countries that provide them with working holiday visas. Because of the restriction on their work activities in the United States, only middle- and upper-class Japanese can afford to live and often study without working. Those who

do not have the financial means to live abroad without an income tend to be attracted to countries that have these special visa agreements with Japan. See Kumiko Kawashima, "Ōsutoraria no wākinguhoridē rōdōsha: Rosujene sedai no ekkyō to kikan" (Australia's working holiday laborers), in *Rōdō sanshin 2: Ekkyō suru rōdō to "imin,"* ed. Yasumasa Igarashi (Tokyo: Otsuki shoten, 2001).

43. George P. Taylor, "U.S. University Clubs in Tokyo," *Weekender* 4, no. 6 (2005): 12.

44. While this student associates Americanness with speaking English, other ways Japanese express and identify with Americanness include consuming American goods, listening to American music, having American friends, and owning American property.

45. Eva Paulino Bueno, "Japanese Brazilian, Stay Off Japan!" *Brazzil,* September 2003, http://www.brazzil.com/2003/html/articles/sep03/p130sep03.htm.

46. Ben Meehan, "Start Your Music Career in Japan," *Tokyo Weekender* 4, no. 6 (2005): 7.

| Chapter 15

Ganbateando
The Peruvian Nisei Association and
Okinawan Peruvians in Los Angeles

Ryan Masaaki Yokota

On April 19, 1990, more than five hundred Okinawan and Japanese Peruvians came together in a crowded ballroom in Los Angeles at a *fiesta de reencuentro* (reunion party) to celebrate the revival of the Peruvian Nisei Association (PNA), an organization dedicated to providing a social space supportive of the particular needs and interests of the Okinawan and Japanese Peruvian community in Los Angeles.[1] Accompanied by copious amounts of food, vigorous dance music, and the sounds of talking and laughter, old friends rekindled their ties and were able to catch up on the latest news, while children and young adults met and formed new relationships based on a shared familial experience of migration and cultural change. The mood was festive, and appropriately so, considering the large size of the community that had developed and the solid planning and organization that had gone into the event. One can safely say that the attendees represented about two hundred families who were members of the PNA. Of note is that a large proportion of these members (roughly half) were of Okinawan descent.

How these Okinawan Peruvians and their friends ended up at this fiesta de reencuentro on a warm spring night in Los Angeles brings up a range of questions related to the larger issues of imperialism, migration, war, and ethnic identity. In addressing these issues, this study deals with the history of the Okinawan Peruvians in Los Angeles, gathered in oral history interviews of multiple generations of Okinawan Peruvians and archival materials of the Peruvian Nisei Association, an organization that existed in Los Angeles in the 1980s and 1990s. I look at the way diverse processes of Japanese imperial formation and modernization initially drove Okinawan Peruvian migration to Peru, only to be forcibly removed from Peru in the U.S.-directed incarceration and relocation of approximately 1,800 Okinawan and Japanese Peruvians during World War II. During the postwar resettlement process, approximately 300 internees fought their "repatriation" to Japan, and some eventually settled in Los Angeles. Later this presence allowed for further migration under the provisions of the 1965 Immigration Act; thus the incarceration process initiated a chain migration to the United States that continues to this day.

I also look at questions of identity and ethnic formation and discuss the Okinawan Peruvians and their process of cultural adjustment in the United States. Beginning immediately after the war, the former internees found it quite difficult to adjust to their new surroundings. Successive migratory waves, from students in the 1960s to families seeking to escape economic upheaval in Peru in the 1970s and 1980s, eventually shaped the need for an organization to help provide the social and economic support critical to survival and success in the United States. Additionally issues of cultural acculturation and racialization came to the forefront when the children of these migrants had difficulty adjusting in the United States. I also address relations between the migrants and the larger Peruvian American community and the homeland politics relating to communities in Peru. In considering these issues, I hope to raise important questions about the linkages between ethnic and area studies in order to suggest some areas of additional research in need of investigation. I conclude by arguing that a unique diasporic Okinawan Peruvian identity has emerged in these Okinawans (Uchinānchu), as a minority within a minority, experiencing multiple migrations.[2]

Okinawan Migration to Peru

The Okinawan community has been defined by migration since the beginning of the Meiji period and the forced integration of the Ryūkyū Kingdom first as a domain (*han*) of Japan in 1872, and later as Okinawa Prefecture in 1879. Despite the fact that as the Ryūkyū Kingdom, Okinawa had existed as a unified independent state prior to colonization, Japanese incorporation of Okinawa involved initiatives to imprint the Japanese character on the religious, educational, linguistic, and governmental fabric of the Okinawan people, as symbolized in assimilation policies (*dōka seisaku*, 同化政策) that stressed the cultural transformation of the colonized into Japanese.[3] Despite moves to assimilate as Japanese citizens, however, Okinawans found themselves consistently regarded as "inferior" Japanese, unable to fit in as legitimate members of the Japanese Empire, much less allowed to govern their own affairs. It was in this context of Japanese colonization that many Okinawan migrants left for Peru. Although a minority emigrated for political reasons, most emigrated for economic reasons stemming from the overpopulation and underdevelopment of the islands. Given the consistent lack of local opportunities caused by population issues and tax burdens, emigration presented one of the few options for economic advancement.[4] In fact pooled resources invested in an emigrant family member often represented one of the main hopes that a family had for both survival and success, so that "in 1929, 66.4 percent of the prefecture's entire revenue consisted of funds sent from overseas."[5] Because of this unusually high rate of remittances, the generation of Okinawans who left their homeland for resettlement throughout the Americas and the Pacific profoundly aided in the development of their local communities.

Immigration to Peru occurred largely as an acceptable alternative following the closing of the United States, Canada, and Australia through racially discriminatory immigration legislation passed because of rising fears of Japanese immigrants and the growth of Japanese military might.[6] From this transnational perspective, Okinawan migration to Peru can be seen as an outgrowth of the racially motivated bar against Asian migrants to "white" countries. In Peru, by 1941 "the total number of Japanese immigrants was approximately 29,000, with one-third originating from the island of Okinawa."[7] These migrants to Peru represented close to a fifth of the total of all Okinawans abroad, and by 1940 made Peru the third largest foreign destination for Okinawans, after Hawai'i and Brazil.[8] Originally consisting primarily of male migrants, the immigration of more women to Peru soon signaled a shift from a sojourner mentality to a perspective favoring settlement and greater local community engagement.

Okinawan-Naichijin Relations in Peru

Upon arrival in Peru, many Okinawans found themselves the targets of discrimination from some of their Naichijin (non-Okinawan Japanese) peers, due to assumptions of racial superiority imported from colonial Japan. Many Naichijin looked on Okinawan migrants as inferior; they led many of the main Japanese organizations and discouraged intermarriage with Okinawans.[9] This historical differentiation between the Okinawans and Naichijin was also expressed in the development of separate Okinawan institutions for much of the early migratory history of the Japanese and Okinawan communities in Peru. Over time, however, differences between the two groups gradually lessened, perhaps owing to the growth of the Okinawan population in proportion to the Naichijin population and the integration of the younger generation. Additional Okinawan influence came through their economic success. The most widespread form of mutual assistance used by the Okinawan Peruvians, the *tanomoshi* (頼母子), or revolving credit association, served to provide startup funds that, combined with the diligence and strong work ethic of the Okinawan immigrants, succeeded in stimulating a successful entrepreneurial class in the community.[10] Okinawan community influence and representation in the mainstream Japanese associations and newspapers eventually increased as well.[11] Additionally, with the growth of anti-Japanese sentiment in Peru and because local Peruvian racism failed to distinguish between the two groups and targeted Okinawans as Japanese, Naichijin sentiments against Okinawans eventually lessened in importance.

Anti-Japanese Hostility in Peru

Peruvian racism and discrimination against Asian immigrants had existed prior to the Japanese arrival into the country, as evidenced by earlier patterns of anti-Chinese sentiment. With the rise of Japanese imperialism during the 1930s and the impact of the Great Depression, local Peruvian distrust of the seemingly closed Japanese and Okinawan Peruvian community eventually developed into outright anger and persecution. For many Peruvians, the dual citizenship possessed by many of these immigrants suggested the potential for treachery and suggested the existence of a "fifth column" that could potentially arise and take over the country.[12] Local politicians used this anti-Japanese xenophobia to exact political gains over the immigrant population most disenfranchised at the time. Despite perceptions to the contrary, Okinawan and Japanese Peruvian community members were far from dominating any particular industry, though they were concentrated in certain occupational areas, such as merchants, bazaar owners, barbers, coffee shop owners, and charcoal dealers. Rather they essentially served as convenient scapegoats for Peruvian economic woes.[13]

These fears eventually caused the Okinawan and Japanese Peruvian communities to be targeted for attack. In 1940 a local incident involving a dispute between two Naichijin barbers turned into a feud for control of the Japanese Central Association, with the Japanese consulate taking sides and trying to forcibly deport one of the barbers. In the ensuing scuffle a Peruvian servant named Marta Acosta was killed. When news of her death reached the public, pent-up animosities against the Japanese quickly reached a crescendo, culminating in days of rioting throughout the cities of Lima and Callao. Hundreds of businesses were destroyed, at the cost of $7 million.[14] For Okinawan Peruvians like Chieko Kamisato, who was about six at the time, these riots proved to be a rude awakening:

> In 1940, they had a huge riot against the Japanese community and
> we had to close our store because they started throwing rocks and ev-
> erything at our store. And they started coming inside the house, and
> started looting everything. So we had to sort of run away and thank
> god we had a second floor and third floor, so we all sort of hid our-
> selves up in the third floor and went into hiding. And the police never
> came till much, much later, when everything was completely looted.
> And at that time that's when the Nakada side of the family all joined
> us because their house was completely looted and they didn't have any
> place to stay. So they stayed with us for a while until they were able
> to find a place again.[15]

The riots were profoundly traumatic for local community members,
especially Okinawans. Indeed of the 620 households that reported losses in the riots, 500 of these households were Okinawan.[16]
Such impacts were lessened in force only because families and the
community as a whole shared resources afterward.

From Peru to the United States: Forced Incarceration during World War II

With the heightening of U.S.-Japanese hostilities following Japan's
invasion of China and alignment with the Axis powers, the United States increasingly drew Latin American countries into the war
effort by urging the freezing of Japanese financial assets, many of
which had been sheltered in Latin American financial institutions.[17]
After the bombing of Pearl Harbor on December 7, 1941, the United States exerted pressure throughout the Americas in an effort to
shore up support for the war effort. In complying with U.S. interests, Peruvian officials quickly froze Japanese and Okinawan domestic bank accounts, closed Japanese-language schools, and shut
down businesses.[18] In large part the political weakness of the Japanese and Okinawan community, combined with their immigrant
status and lack of integration, meant that they had little recourse
against the abrogation of their rights.

The Peruvian government, acting under the prodding of U.S. officials, eventually rounded up and deported Okinawan and Japanese

Peruvians to the United States. Taking a page from the Japanese
American internment program already initiated in the United States
and in countries like Panamá, U.S. Ambassador R. Henry Nor-
web urged the Peruvian government to develop such a program as
their contribution to the war effort. Other officials, such as Sec-
retary of State Cordell Hull, even suggested the internment of all
Japanese Latin Americans in the United States.[19] Along with those
from Peru, the United States succeeded in interning Japanese and
Okinawans from throughout Central and South America and the
Caribbean. Despite the Americas-wide nature of the internment
and incarceration process, "of the 2,264 interned, approximately
1,800 were from Peru, and an estimated half were Okinawans."[20]
Thus Peruvians in general and Okinawan Peruvians in particular bore a disproportionate burden in the internment experience.

Among those Okinawan Peruvians deported to the United States,
some were single male heads of households whose families were
later allowed to join them; in other cases entire families were deported. In Kamisato's case, the government deported her father
immediately and her mother had to negotiate numerous processes
in order to reunite with him: "When my father was taken to prison, we wanted to go on the next boat right away but unfortunately it was all filled up and they told us we had to wait for the next
boat and we didn't know when it was going to be. And my mother just insisted that she wanted to go. We had an English-speaking person living next door to us, so she took her to the American
Embassy and talked to the person there and he was able to get us
on the ship, to go right away . . . so we didn't have to be separated for so long."

Others were not as lucky and had scant information on the whereabouts of their loved ones and how to reunite with them. In fact of
the earlier groups that were rounded up, "some were sent to concentration camps in Panamá, where they were treated like convicts.
They were forced to perform hard labor under armed guard. Some
died under the horrible treatment."[21] U.S. authorities eventually
shipped the Okinawan and Japanese Peruvians to the Crystal City,

Kennedy, Seagoville, and Missoula internment camps, in Texas and Montana.[22] The main differences between the Peruvian and American internment experiences, however, were in terms of the scale of the operation and the fact that the Peruvian internees were incarcerated not in the War Relocation Authority camps, but in secret Department of Justice camps, the existence of which was censored for the duration of the war. Despite the desire of U.S. officials for a larger program, logistical issues alone, not humanitarian considerations, complicated the Peruvian program.[23] With the war effort in full force, the United States could hardly afford to divert precious maritime resources to a larger scale operation in Peru.

Upon landing in the United States, internees soon found themselves stripped of their personal dignity and devoid of significant rights under international or American law. As Kamisato said of this process, "On the ship, we didn't have freedom because there were soldiers and there were sailors, and so when we arrived in New Orleans that's when they took all the women on one side, and all the men on the other side and they put all of us in this huge room and we had to take a shower. . . . In those days I don't know if they knew about Auschwitz, but it was almost like that. We were all put into one room, but actually what they were doing was cleansing us and spraying us with DDT. It was a little bit humiliating for the women folks."

At the Department of Justice Immigration and Naturalization Service camps internees found themselves in cramped quarters, under terrible conditions, and with scant comfort. Beyond the personal violations associated with the internment process, they also had their passports confiscated upon arrival, in essence making them illegal aliens.[24] The full importance of this aspect of the internment process, however, did not become clear until after the war ended, when they sought to rebuild their lives in the United States.

Postwar Legal Battles and Resettlement

For many of the internees, the internment process lasted two to three years, during which they faced deportation to Japan as part of the hostage exchanges arranged by the United States. By September 1943, for example, more than 1,300 Latin American internees were sent to Japan, almost half of them from Peru.[25] The fate of those deportees to Okinawa proved especially tragic, as many suffered in the devastating Battle of Okinawa, in which a third of the local population died.[26] Those still remaining in the United States soon faced a range of difficulties related to their legal status, with the passage of Proclamation 2655 by President Truman in 1945, which authorized the deportation of enemy aliens. For the Okinawan and Japanese internees, this proclamation turned jubilation at the war's ending to frustration at internees' inability to return home to Peru, compounded by their lack of legal status in the United States. Additionally the Peruvian government refused to let any former internees return "unless they had been born in Peru, were naturalized, or had a Peruvian spouse," so that only about a hundred ended up returning to Peru despite the fact that many internees of German descent were allowed to return.[27] Even those lucky few able to return received no compensation for their loss of freedom and property.

Because of restrictions set by the Peruvian government, those remaining in the United States had little legal recourse, until receiving support from the American Civil Liberties Union attorney Wayne Collins. While Collins was working with other clients in the Crystal City internment center, the Japanese and Okinawan Peruvians approached him about their plight, and he agreed to help them. Initially this aid came in the dispensation of work furloughs to a produce-processing plant called Seabrook Farms, in New Jersey.[28] While a welcome relief from the camps, the workers soon found life on Seabrook Farms particularly arduous. As Kamisato relates, "We were sent to Seabrook Farms, and that's actually when the hardships started because . . . I mean we had nothing. I mean we had no money, we had nothing. And we had to start from scratch and it was very, very difficult for our parents." Because Kamisato's businessman father had never been a laborer, he found it especially difficult to adjust to factory work. The cold winters and communal toilets and baths also contributed to making the experience very difficult. From that point forward, Chieko Kamisato had to attend English schools, and her parents had an extremely difficult time in the winter, when the work stopped and finances ran low.

Despite these difficulties, the Okinawan Peruvians at Seabrook Farms still felt a strong attachment not only to Peru, but also to their ancestral homeland, as evidenced by relief efforts initiated to help rebuild Okinawa. As part of a larger national and international fund-raising effort, this relief campaign had a profound impact on rebuilding Okinawa, and despite their own difficulties, Okinawa Peruvians gave generously. When members of the Okinawa Washington DC committee of the Okinawan relief effort went to Seabrook Farms to talk to the Okinawan Peruvians there, they quickly responded. Eventually they even organized their own group to raise funds in 1947. Their donation letter stated, "Recalling the sufferings of the Okinawans who survived the horrors of war, we find in ourselves only tears of deep emotion; there are no words, other than to acknowledge you as the ones who have truly suffered. . . . As far as we are overseas, our feelings of affection for Okinawa remain unchanged. When we are repatriated to Peru we will call upon all Okinawans to work for relief."[29]

This letter, signed by the Okinawan Peruvians at Seabrook (including Chieko Kamisato's father), included a donation of $200. Later in 1949 Peruvian Okinawans at Seabrook made an additional $10 donation to the relief effort.[30] Although these Okinawan Peruvians were living a very difficult life and often lacked financial resources, they recognized the tragedy that had occurred in their ancestral homeland as even more profound than their suffering in the incarceration process.

In the spring of 1949 the U.S. State Department finally allowed the Japanese Latin Americans to remain in the country, giving them the status of "permanent legally admitted immigrants." This allowed them to move and resettle while working out the final issues related to their deportation proceedings. A record of that time explains, "Most of the Peruvian group who had been working in

Seabrook Farms in New Jersey eventually resettled in Los Angeles or Chicago. In Los Angeles they formed the *Perú Kai*, or Club, to maintain contact with their lawyer, Wayne Collins, but also for the sake of mutual friendship and contact within the group." For the former internees located in Los Angeles, their meetings "were tremendously enjoyable and significant and included the children, who were born in America, and the families of those who married Nisei."[31] In 1953 Congress suspended the deportation proceedings, and the Japanese and Okinawan Peruvians were finally free to continue with their lives, and even apply for naturalization.

Despite these advances, however, the early years in Los Angeles proved difficult for many of the Okinawan Peruvians. Kamisato describes the experience: "When we came [to Los Angeles] we lived on 5th and Wall Street, right on [laughs] skid row. . . . And I think we lived there for almost three years I guess. And it was very, very hard because my parents had to look for a job and not being able to speak the language, my father, he was always working as a dishwasher or as a janitor. I mean that's the only type of job that he was able to get, which was very pitiful to see. . . . My mother was working as a maid in the hotel, cleaning the rooms and things. And it became very, very hard for them." Aside from the downward mobility precipitated by the postinternment process, family life proved especially difficult. For one dishwashing job her father often had to stay in Malibu for the week due to limited access to public transportation. Despite these early difficulties, however, some of the Okinawan friends and relations of the Kamisato family were able to help them to find better jobs and living arrangements. Kamisato said, "In fact, once we came to the United States, most of our associations were with Okinawans." As in the broader Okinawan and Japanese American community, these extended family networks proved crucial in providing support through the resettlement process, especially considering the hostile attitudes that many internees faced. Eventually the Kamisato family operated a boarding house serving a large Japanese and Okinawan clientele, which helped them to acclimate to their new lives in Los Angeles.

Kamisato attended Polytechnic High School near downtown Los Angeles. She found that her background made it difficult to integrate with other students at her school: "Most of my friends were Hispanic-speaking friends, because in high school people were kind of cliquish, and since I had this Spanish accent it was difficult for me to be friendly with the people here. It was much easier to be friendly with the Hispanic people. So I think most of my friends were Hispanic, or some were the people that were from Peru that went to Poly High. And we always sort of stuck together, people from Peru. We never really lost touch with each other even though we all went to different schools." For Kamisato, however, who had to help her parents in their business, there was often little time to socialize outside of school and home. The main exceptions to this were the few friends that she and her family were able to meet on the weekends, with whom they mostly spoke Spanish.

Postwar Peruvian Community Dynamics

Those Okinawan Peruvians left in Peru underwent many changes due to the trauma of the war and the Peruvian perception of the Japanese and Okinawan Peruvians as perpetual foreigners. Postwar migration to Peru had slowed significantly, and the community's attitude shifted toward support of greater integration into the cultural life of Peru. In the prewar period, many Okinawan Peruvians had enrolled their children in Japanese schools, thinking that they would eventually return to Okinawa, but as a consequence of wartime experiences, there was a growing recognition of the need to be seen as Peruvians, not as Japanese, and after the war many children were enrolled in Peruvian schools and universities.[32] Alex Nakada, a Nisei (second-generation) Okinawan Peruvian, and the biological brother of Chieko Kamisato, describes his experience: "Prior to the war, most of the names were in Japanese—Toshiro, Kunio, Yamamoto—but after the war it changed. Everybody has a Spanish name now, and the reason is that there was no reason for going back. So they said 'Hey, we are here. I think this is going to be better than going back to Japan.' So we were assimilated as

Peruvians."[33] Intermarriage with non-Okinawans, which had been
rare before the war, also increased, along with a shift toward Catholicism and a more mixed cultural outlook.[34] Thus Okinawan
and Japanese Peruvian communities drastically changed their social and cultural norms as they sought to rebuild their lives.

Student Migrants to the United States

During the 1960s the Okinawan Peruvian community became interested in sending their young people to study in the United States.
Due to the visa restrictions at the time, however, students needed
sponsorship. Interestingly many of the formerly interned Okinawan
Peruvians ended up sponsoring their relatives. These family connections allowed Alex Nakada, who was related to the Kamisato
family, to immigrate temporarily. As he relates, "Most of us came
over here just to study. [Some] people could afford to send kids
over here. [But] I was the least likely to come over here because if
not for my aunty, I wouldn't have had the money or the desire to
come here to pursue higher education." In the case of Pedro Agena, these same connections facilitated his journey to Belmont High
School in Los Angeles; he was able to obtain a student visa through
a friend of his mother's who had been interned during the war.
Some of these Okinawan Peruvian students, such as Alex Nakada, stayed in Los Angeles on a permanent basis, and eventually a
large enough group existed for social networks to develop. As Nakada says, "When I came over here, that's when I met all the Peruvian Nikkei.[35] There were like ten or fifteen or more Peruvians.
Because we were Nikkei from Peru, we stuck together. . . . Most of
them were Okinawan. People from Naichi, they were only a few.
. . . Mostly they had relatives. I can't think of anyone who didn't,
and that's why I guess they came over here. . . . Mostly they were
like my uncle, who relocated during the war and didn't go back to
Peru." In many ways the relationships that these students developed from their earlier sojourns in the United States would help to
create transnational networks that lowered the costs of migration
in terms of information and community resources. As economic

conditions in Peru worsened, such networks decreased the cost of
frequent returns to the United States and eventually helped lead to
further visits and more permanent settlement later.

Post-1970s Migrants to the United States

The 1970s and 1980s represented a period of instability for Peru,
both economically and politically. Following the seizure of military power by Gen. Juan Velasco Alvarado in 1968, military government reforms radically destabilized the economy. Even after
the eventual return of the administration to civilian control in
1980, the leadership of Fernando Belaúnde Terry and his succes-
sor, Alan García, failed to revive a faltering economy. Inflation
climbed over 7,000 percent.[36] Economically and socially the dras-
tic shifts in the Peruvian economy created a continual dilemma,
encouraging emigration in search of better opportunities. With the
passage of the Immigration Act of 1965, U.S. immigration policy
had changed its focus to emphasize family reunification, and many
used this reason to migrate to the United States during this time.
The decision of Agena's family to migrate in 1978 came at a time
when a large number of his friends were leaving the country. His
marriage to one of Alex Nakada's sisters facilitated his journey to
the United States, and other family members used their connections to migrate to the United States. Gisela Shimabukuro, a Sansei (third-generation) Okinawan Peruvian, was born in Peru and
emigrated to the United States with her family: "We came here in
1982 when I was three years old, mainly for economic reasons.
My mother's family, or her brothers and sister, the majority were
already in Los Angeles, and my uncle Alex Nakada, was the one
who motivated my mother to join him in L.A. My mother believed
that my older brother and sister and I wouldn't have much of a
future in Peru as far as higher education, so she believed that we
would get a better education in the states. And she was right."[37]
Like Agena, Gisela's family emigrated to the United States through
familial connections to Alex Nakada, who in turn had emigrated through his relationship to his sister Chieko Kamisato. These

experiences are evidence of the opportunities provided by processes of chain migration.

For many of these immigrants, their relatives' job connections enabled them to find temporary employment until they got settled. By this time Chieko Kamisato had started her own fashion design company and was among the very first Nikkei to enter that industry. Alex Nakada worked as a manager at Fish King, a shrimp and fish processing company owned by a second-generation Japanese American named Masashi Kawaguchi, who himself had been interned at the Minidoka, Idaho, concentration camp. Nakada's job at Fish King proved to be a boon for his relatives, for it allowed him to hire many family members and other Okinawan Peruvian immigrants. Agena says, "In my case I think I was very lucky because I came in June '78 and I worked for a couple of months with Alex. Alex used to be a manager at a shrimp company. . . . [My wife] didn't speak any English so she had to go to adult school for probably a year and a half before she could communicate. . . . She stayed at home for maybe the first two or three years, and then she started working for Chieko for a couple of years. After that she found a job in different T-shirt companies."[38]

Other relatives also found temporary work at Fish King. Shimabukuro says of her parents' situation, "We came to L.A. and stayed with my uncle Alex. I think we lived with him for about a year until my father got a job at a seafood factory which my uncle Nakada managed, called Fish King." In fact Fish King became a hub of sorts for recent Okinawan and Japanese Peruvian immigrants to find temporary or even permanent employment as they adjusted to being in the United States. Nakada says, "The funny part was, since I went to work at the company my status was changing a little bit at that time. And I was able to hire Peruvian Nikkei over there, so a lot of people went to work over there. So my sphere of influence was expanding so much that people from Peru, you know, they would hear, 'Hey, if you want to work, go to Alex, and you can work at his place.'" Thus basic family and community connections played a critical role in allowing migrants to find employment at a time when they spoke little English and had few opportunities.

Following these temporary arrangements, many of the Okinawan Peruvians still ended up having a hard time adjusting, either in the workplace or in society at large, though interactions with the large Latina/o population lessened their difficulties. Shimabukuro says, "My mom worked at home for a little bit until I got into kindergarten. That's when she got a job doing other labor work, working alongside other Latinos, so it wasn't necessary for her to learn how to speak English. Same with my dad, he worked alongside a lot of Latinos." Many of these immigrants found employment in a range of markets, though in general they worked in industries dominated by Latina/os or in Japanese or Japanese American companies.

Beyond their employment issues many families experienced great difficulties adjusting to their life in the United States. These difficulties became especially pronounced among the children, who had often grown up entirely in Peru, speaking only Spanish. The presence of a large Spanish-speaking population did help to make adjusting a little easier. Agena describes his children's experiences: "In the beginning it was really tough for [them]. They didn't know any English. The first two or three days at school, they came back home crying [laughs] because they were scared and they didn't know the language. But I think that one of the benefits of being in California is you find a lot of Spanish-speaking people, so once they found some friends that spoke Spanish they were more at ease I guess. . . . But in the beginning it was hard for them."

Gisela Shimabukuro's siblings also had a difficult time adjusting, as she relates: "When they came to school here, they put them in those ESL [English as a second language] classes, and it was funny because my sister was telling me that when my uncle Alex first enrolled them in the schools, he told them that they were second-language learners so they needed to be put in ESL classes. So the teachers put them in with the Chinese kids. [laughs] But then my uncle told them that 'No, they need to put them with the Mexican kids cause they speak Spanish, not Chinese.'"

In some families the lack of language skills caused changes in family relationships. When parents did not speak English, their English-speaking children were forced to assume greater responsibilities, as Shimabukuro relates:

> [My parents] lived in the U.S. for about twenty-three years, and out of those twenty-three years they didn't really develop any kind of English skills, so growing up, my brother, sister, and I would always have to translate for my parents. My brother and sister did a lot. They had to always call the banks, call the telephone companies, help my parents pay for bills, help my parents write checks. I remember doing that too in junior high, helping them take care of a lot of bills and stuff because they couldn't read any English. Or when we'd go shopping I'd always have to translate for my mom or my dad. In school at parent-teacher conferences I always had to be there as well, which was always frustrating for me as a kid.

Much like other immigrant youth, Shimabukuro's experiences demonstrate that the cultural acclimation process proved to be extremely difficult for family relations, with a large part of the burden borne by the children. Their parents soon began to recognize the need for a network that could help their children find other youth who shared their experiences and could help them cope with their difficulties.

The Peruvian Nisei Association in the Early 1980s

The desire to create a space for Okinawan Peruvian youth in Los Angeles to get together crystallized in July 1981, with the idea of having an *undōkai* (sports meet). Following the success of the undōkai, the idea of creating a permanent group grew until the network of family members and relations decided to form the Peruvian Nisei Association.[39] Nakada explains, "In 1981, I decided to make a little association, so we had the first session at my house and we decided to found the association. I was their first president for the first eight years, I guess because everybody was busy and didn't have the time and didn't have the facilities. We used to have the sessions at the Fish King cafeteria." Though composed largely of Okinawan Peruvians, the group included other Japanese Peruvians as well, though this was less common since many Japanese Peruvians lacked the family ties that would have allowed them to immigrate.

As described in a letter by Nakada, the PNA had four guiding philosophies: to provide more interaction between the families, develop more cultural and social events, give moral and also material support toward the recently arrived, and "most importantly, [support] the development of all our children, who are the future generation, so that they will go on knowing, one to all the rest, the teachings and delegation of the oriental traditions that our parents gave us and that we are passing to them, and this will be through social functions and the teaching of the language, dances, and customs."[40]

From the very beginning, the group focused on creating a range of social and cultural activities, including additional undōkai, an annual New Year's Eve dance, *fiestas de carnavalito*, Mother's Day lunches, *bailes de fiestas patrias*, and a trip to Las Vegas.[41] The PNA set up committees for sports, social events, women, youth, cultural programs, membership, and finance to facilitate the operation of the organization. Membership dues were set, and a tanomoshi was organized by the Women's Committee in March 1982. The Youth Committee even organized a ski trip. The PNA provided financial support by raising funds for a member with cancer and organizing a blood drive for a member whose child had leukemia. Newsletters from the PNA publicized weddings, communions, and other information of interest to members. In many ways, this organizing represented the first attempt to bring together the widely dispersed Okinawan and Japanese Peruvian community in Los Angeles.

Rebirth of the PNA in the Early 1990s

Sadly, however, this first incarnation of the PNA was unable to sustain itself for long, and in the late 1980s lapsed in operation for a range of reasons, including a failure on the part of members to take up leadership and the difficulties of overcoming the community's geographic dispersion. In January 1990 the group reorganized itself and held the fiesta de reencuentro (reunion party) mentioned at the beginning of this chapter. In preparing for the event, organizers had broken the large southern California region into five geographic areas, consisting of Los Angeles, Gardena, Orange County, the San Fernando Valley, and the San Gabriel Valley.[42] A quick count from a planning meeting for the event determined that 152 families were members, though organizers at the time were unable to include firm numbers for the large Los Angeles area. This event proved to be a complete success, with more than 335 adult and 150 junior pre-sale tickets sold and international coverage in the local *Rafu Shimpo* newspaper in Los Angeles and the *Perú Shimpo* and *Prensa Lima* in Lima, Peru. In many ways this event signaled the rebirth of the newly reformed PNA. Nakada stated at the time, "Now, a little bit older, but perhaps wiser, we find ourselves once again with this desire, or longing, to continue this dream that we've never been able to make completely real, this dream of having something of our own, that we'll belong to an association that will bring together all the Nisei, so that we'll have a more unified social life. If we can, it'll be not only for ourselves, but for our children as well."[43]

Eventually the group reorganized and held elections to bring in a board of directors; it existed relatively continuously from 1990 until about 1999. This reorganized group maintained a range of social and cultural events, much as its earlier incarnation had in the 1980s, such as regular board member elections, undōkai, New Year's Eve parties, Mother's Day picnics, *peña criollas*, and other events.[44] Regular newsletters reported births, deaths, weddings, and other family-related news in the community. Later the newsletter contained articles on relief efforts in Peru, commentary on political developments in Peru, and tips to help recent immigrants adjust, thus providing a communal space where PNA members could find a sense of identity with others of similar backgrounds and experiences.

Of interest is the way the PNA Youth Committee began to organize itself. Sponsoring Halloween parties, Christmas parties, and other social events, the PNA youth group provided a place where these youth could share their unusual background. Shimabukuro describes her siblings' experiences: "My brother and sister, they were in the same circle of friends. There were a lot of them their age. There was a big group. They were teenagers at the time, so I was always jealous because they got to go to movies, or eat out at restaurants, and they had house parties, and they went clubbing. And every time we had these social events, that circle of friends would always hang out together. . . . I would say it was a group of maybe twelve to fifteen."

According to the August 1990 PNA newsletter, the youth group counted more than fifty members. Quite a bit of dating occurred within this circle of friends, yet not all of the youth group's activities were purely social in nature. In 1990, for example, the youth group went Christmas caroling at the Gardena Keirō Nursing Home, and according to a newsletter from January 1992, the group planned a fashion show fundraiser to benefit City of Hope Hospital in Los Angeles. Through all of these activities, the youth group provided a space for PNA youth to socialize and contribute to the larger community.

Relationships with Other Peruvian Americans

Another impact of the PNA was to raise the profile of Okinawan and Japanese Peruvians within the larger Peruvian and Peruvian American community. Following the rebirth of the PNA in the 1990s, the high-profile Peruvian presidency of Alberto Fujimori, and the 1984 election of Alex Nakada as the only Okinawan Peruvian member of the Peruvian Chamber of Commerce in LA, relationships between the PNA and the broader Peruvian community continued to grow. Much of this relationship building occurred through PNA fundraising for the relief of those Peruvians hardest hit by the economic instability of the time. The November 1990 edition of the *L.A. Peruvian Times*, for example, contained a picture of Nakada with the president of the Un Día Por El Perú

Committee, a group dedicated to relief work in Peru, thus highlighting PNA participation in these efforts. Additionally, according to an August 1990 newsletter, the PNA donated $2,000 to the
Pan American Nikkei Association fund drive to support Peruvian
aid organizations. Through the course of its existence, the group
worked on a number of fundraising efforts that contributed to the
redevelopment of Peruvian society.

News of PNA events often received coverage in the local Peruvian American press. An October 1990 edition of *Maxi's Magazine* carried pictures of members with the singers Luz Palomino
and Arturo "Zambo" Cavero. A March 1991 edition of *L.A. Peruvian Times* noted the recent formation of a youth group in the
PNA. In August 1991 the *L.A. Peruvian Times* had a number of
pictures of one of the peña criolla events. In January 1992 the *L.A.
Peruvian Times* recognized Alex Nakada and Luis Yamakawa for
their work in reporting on the activities of the PNA, and in July
1991 the *L.A. Peruvian Times* reported that Iván Yonemine, an
Okinawan Peruvian Desert Storm veteran, had recently returned
to his parents in Garden Grove, and that the son of Cesar Kochi, a
(PNA member), had recently graduated from Carnegie-Mellon University. Thus the presence of the PNA served to draw attention to
the Okinawan and Japanese Peruvian community within the larger Peruvian community in Los Angeles.

Much of this coverage proves particularly interesting in terms of
how Okinawan Peruvians had to constantly position themselves as
legitimate members of the Peruvian community. In an article published in a local Peruvian American magazine, the author, Carlos
Pongo, asked Nakada if he had been able to visit the land of his ancestors. Nakada replied, "Before anything, I want to say that I am
a Peruvian, because it is there that my parents wanted to emigrate
and put down roots, though I have had the opportunity to visit
Okinawa, the land of my ancestors."[45] An article in the Los Angeles Peruvian American magazine *Revista del Perú* had this description of the PNA: "The majority of them don't have a single drop
of 'Peruvian' blood flowing through their veins; they're children,

grandchildren, and great-grandchildren of the first Japanese immigrants that arrived at the beginning of the century in search of
better horizons. But they love the land that they were born into,
passed through their difficulties, assimilated *our culture* [empha-
sis mine], and share the responsibility of reconstructing the country and contributing towards its development."[46]

Most interesting about this article's description of the PNA is
the way it framed the Okinawan and Japanese population as an
"other" vis-à-vis the "Peruvians." Much like U.S. perceptions of
Okinawan and Japanese immigrants as "perpetual foreigners," the
local Peruvian community seemed to mirror this sentiment in discussing the way Okinawan and Japanese Peruvians had successfully assimilated "our culture," meaning the culture of non-Asian
Peruvians. In fact in one of the articles in the *L.A. Peruvian Times*
covering the PNA's peña criolla event, the newspaper printed a picture of Alex Nakada dancing with the caption "Andean music has
a great affinity to Japanese music. Because of this the Nisei like
the Huaynito so much. The expression of Alex Nakada reaffirms
this."[47] This caption suggests that the PNA and other Okinawan
and Japanese Peruvians may connect with and adopt an authentic
Peruvian culture, but they will never be considered a part of it. As
was true in Peru, the Okinawan and Japanese Peruvian community
in the United States continually faced the dilemma of gaining legitimacy in the larger Peruvian community as Peruvians themselves.

The PNA's Decline and the Future Generation

Eventually the organization stopped operating, probably due to a
combination of factors, such as the fact that its original purpose of
providing mutual assistance to recent immigrants and support to
the youth lessened in importance with declining immigration, and
because most of the younger generation had reached college age.
Additionally the difficulties of bringing geographically dispersed
people together undoubtedly contributed to its decline. With the
eventual dissolution of the PNA in the late 1990s, a vacuum existed regarding the status of its former members. In the end a large

number of the Okinawan Peruvians who had formerly been involved in the PNA joined the Okinawa Association of America (OAA). Agena recalls, "About three years ago [around 2002] we had a friend that knew Mr. [Haruo] Yamashiro [then president of the OAA], and he was asking 'Why don't we join the OAA?' ... So we actually had a dinner at Happa (an Okinawan-owned restaurant in Gardena), and about thirty to forty people attended. And most of the people who attended agreed to join the OAA. And even more than the people who attended, many heard by word of mouth, so we encouraged them to join the OAA. . . . I would say about sixty people [are now in the OAA]." Reflecting a new openness in the organization, the OAA has become the main organization reflecting the Okinawan Peruvian community in Los Angeles, and with Pedro Agena having served on the membership committee for the organization, Okinawan Peruvians have been represented within the leadership as well.

As for the PNA, some of the remaining funds of the organization were recently donated to the development of a hospital in Peru, showing that the PNA continues to have an impact on the community there. And there has even been talk of reviving the PNA, or at least an incarnation of it. Nakada continues, "So right now when we have get-togethers, reunions for weddings or whatever, and half the people I don't know. So I'm trying to revive the club, making it a little more like they have in Peru, like a senior citizens club, and from then we can inquire about all the family. Because when we go to parties or weddings we see a lot of children, I mean the young kids are married and have kids. And I guess there's a big population right now. It would be interesting to investigate and see how many."

Although there has been some movement to bring back some level of organization to the Okinawan and Japanese Peruvian community outside of the OAA, for the next generation of youth there remain a number of problems related to maintaining a sense of identity as Okinawan Peruvians. Agena says, "I think it's harder here to get the younger third and fourth generation of Okinawans to get into the OAA organization or to have this feeling of belonging in being Okinawan. . . . I think we need to work more on the parents to give the kids the sense of being Okinawan."

Mirroring these sentiments, Shimabukuro remarked that she didn't have much of an Okinawan or Japanese identity growing up, or many Nikkei friends at school: "So I didn't really have much of a Japanese identity. I mean growing up we spoke Spanish at home and we ate Peruvian food, and we had Peruvian decorations all over the house. I didn't really grow up with the Japanese culture. I never took off my shoes in the house, I never ate with chopsticks, and my mom never prepared Japanese meals. The only thing Japanese we ate was rice. But we always had Peruvian food." In fact many of Gisela's friends growing up were other Latinos who spoke Spanish. It wasn't until her enrollment at UCLA that she began to learn more about Japanese culture through her involvement with the Nikkei Student Union, a Japanese American student group. In the end Shimabukuro seemed to identify with the idea of being Okinawan, though without projecting a clear sense of what that means. She says, "I don't really know much about Okinawan history or Japanese history. But I have family in Okinawa more than in Japan. So I guess I would identify more as Okinawan than Japanese." All told, the younger generation of Okinawan Peruvians probably know more about Peru than they do about their Okinawan ancestral homeland, contributing to further questions about their identity.

Conclusion

This study reveals the convoluted migratory history of the Okinawan Peruvian community in Los Angeles. Far from occurring as a result of simple push and pull economic factors, the migration history of this group reveals how state processes in the form of Japan's occupation and colonization of Okinawa initiated a range of modernization programs borne by an island region overpopulated and burdened with economic instability. Subsequent to their move to Peru, Okinawan immigrants and their descendants found themselves caught up in the political machinations of the United States in its war against Japan, which forcibly uprooted the Okinawan and Japanese Peruvians from their adopted homeland to be incarcerated in the United States. Soon after the war and the resettlement process, the presence of these migrants set in motion a chain of migration that began with student sojourners in the early 1960s and culminated with a larger wave of permanent migrants in the 1970s and 1980s. Yet as Donna Gabaccia notes, "While transnational history allows us to mount a critique of the immigrant paradigm that shares so much with existing ones, it also offers something new. Through an incredible sleight-of-historiography, the immigrant paradigm forces into the American nation migrants that the nation not only sought to exclude but whose histories are scarcely paeans to the promise and triumph of American democracy."[48] Looking at the transnational history of the Okinawan Peruvian community can reveal the way U.S. hegemony forced a range of migratory movements, with these migrants eventually settling in the United States. Through their continued presence, these Okinawan Peruvian immigrants, especially those incarcerated during World War II, serve as a stark reminder of and contrast to the declarations of democracy and respect for human rights embodied in U.S. principles and law.

Beyond that, however, this study points out the complexity of the Okinawan Peruvian community's existence as a diasporic community. As Lane Ryo Hirabayashi notes, "The immigrants in Latin America from the prefecture of Okinawa are perhaps the only population from Japan who could be properly conceptualized in terms of a diaspora, at least if one adopts the criteria specified by William Safran."[49] Safran's definition, the subject of much scholarly debate, argues that diasporic peoples are defined by an association with an ancestral land, a collective myth of homeland, a sense of alienation from their current location, and a wish to return to their "home."[50] The Okinawan Peruvian community fulfills all of these categories; the least applicable is the category related to the myth of return. At the same time, support for the homeland was amply seen through the development of Americas-wide relief efforts for Okinawa initiated after the end of World War II, suggesting the strength of continuing diasporic sentiments.

The conflicted diasporic Okinawan position has been further complicated by the particular conditions of inclusion and exclusion in both Peru and the United States, and has informed the development of a transnational identity. Due in large part to the memory of belonging to a formerly sovereign nation (the Ryūkyū Kingdom), combined with the historical existence of racism against the Okinawan and Japanese immigrants in Peruvian society, these immigrants were at first unwilling and unable to fully adopt a Peruvian identity. Some have argued that when alienated from both the sending and the receiving countries, migrants are more likely to develop a transnational identity.[51] For Okinawans, already marginal within Japanese society, viewed as the "other" in Peruvian society, and later phenotypically racialized as Asian but feeling culturally Latina/o in the United States, it was not easy to simply adopt an "American" identity. Neither did it help for the Okinawan Peruvians to adopt a simple definition of themselves as Nikkei, or Japanese Americans, which homogenizes identity in its own way, flattening Okinawan identity as coterminous with being Japanese.[52] In daily negotiations the Okinawan Peruvians in Los Angeles have been forced to continually carve out an identity for themselves that bridged the categories of being Okinawan, Japanese, Peruvian, and American.

Considering the role of "print-capitalism" as defined by Benedict Anderson, the creation and formation of the PNA and its newsletter proved especially crucial in developing sentiments of connectedness to their fellow "nationals."[53] For with the formation of the PNA and the development of regular newsletters to foster a sense of collective identity out of a conjoined awareness of being Okinawan, Japanese, Peruvian, and American, PNA members began the process of "imagining" their sense of connectedness despite any differences of class, regional origin (in Peru), or linguistic proficiency (in terms of proficiency in Uchināguchi, Japanese,

Spanish, or English).[54] With the formation of the PNA, an attempt to map out issues and a sense of identity began to develop, beyond the organization's immediate goals of providing assistance to the recently arrived. The most interesting aspects of this identity occur on those boundaries, or *fronteras*, as noted by Gloria Anzaldúa, where these Okinawan Peruvians either related to or distanced themselves from other Uchinānchu, Nikkei, Peruvians, and Americans. All told, these issues point out the basic inability of nation-state boundaries to provide an overarching definition for the Okinawan Peruvians in Los Angeles. As Arjun Appadurai notes, "No idiom has yet emerged to capture the collective interests of many groups in translocal solidarities, cross-border mobilizations, and postnational identities. Such interests are many and vocal, but they are still entrapped in the linguistic imaginary of the territorial state."[55] Even further, these limitations are most interesting in the U.S. context in describing how they interrogate the mythology of the American assimilation process. Indeed with so many migratory paths having been traveled and so many different perspectives, the history of the Okinawan Peruvian community clearly demonstrates that the United States has become just one more nodal point in the global story of migration.

At the same time, however, this story also serves to interrogate the very idea of what it means to be American, especially considering the ways the American melting pot strips away nationalities and racializes people. Steven Ropp explains, "Persons of Asian descent, by laying claim to their *Latinidad*, occupy an important part of this contested space, especially as they negotiate their positioning by Latin American societies that may see them only as Asian and an American society that often privileges Asians as a so-called 'model minority' over Latinos."[56]

By maintaining their connection to their Peruvian identity, these Okinawan Peruvian community members continually challenge and expand the definition of what it means to be an American by rejecting easy racializations of their identity into being considered Asian or Asian American. Even further, their presence also contests the notion of what it means to be a Latina/o. Shimabukuro says, "When I tell people about my background, it's funny to get their responses, because a lot of them don't know there are a lot of Japanese people in Latin America, and when I open my mouth and speak Spanish they're stunned. Or even when I'm out in public talking to my mom in Spanish I get second glances. But I think I'm very lucky to have these three cultures. It's very diverse, three very different cultures." Far from falling into easily racialized definitions of identity, Shimabukuro's quote demonstrates that she has carved out a more heterogeneous definition of cultural identity than the simple categories of Asian, Latina/o, or American.

In many ways the study of the Okinawan Peruvian community of Los Angeles is of particular significance to Asian American studies in helping to expand historical notions of both Japanese American studies and the general pan-Asian leanings of Asian American studies. Too often categories of what it means to be "Japanese American" have been limited by a homogenizing process that has mirrored the assimilation practices imposed by the central Japanese government in Okinawa. Additionally when talking most discussions about a "Japanese American" experience of migration and the World War II incarceration process fail to mention how Americas-wide and interconnected both the migratory and relocation processes actually were. By looking at the Okinawan Peruvian experience, scholars can begin to address these shortcomings. Even further, by looking at the history of the growing numbers of Asian Latina/os in the United States, scholars can reconceptualize Asian American history as being more than just a history of Asians in the United States, and instead begin to visualize Asian migration to the Americas as less bounded by the theoretical limitations produced by the myopia of living in the U.S. nation-state or by the political dimensions of area studies.[57]

Ultimately this study has served as a preliminary overview of the Okinawan Peruvian community in Los Angeles and has sought to outline the various aspects of their migratory, political, and social history, though more work needs to be done. Yet beyond the limitations of this study, this analysis has been an attempt to supply an additional element in the project of recovering the Uchinā nchu voice from history, entangled as it has been in the Japanese colonial project and subsumed under the particularities of adjusting as a diasporic people to multiple new environments. For members of the Uchinānchu diaspora, this does not have to mean that all Uchinānchu will necessarily share the same sense of cultural identity, however. Indeed many of my interviewees cited a range of cultural characteristics that they used to define an Uchinānchu identity, including traditional customs and cultural practices, such as the *sanshin* or Okinawan dance, or social practices or sentiments, such as the feeling that Okinawan people are more friendly and outgoing than Naichijin. Among the younger generation, raised in the United States, such sentiments seem less pronounced. Despite these differences, homogeneous cultural integrity may not be absolutely necessary,[58] and can point out the strengths of cultural flexibility, as can perhaps best be seen in the Okinawan concept of a *chanpur* (mixed) culture. The Okinawan Peruvian community in Los Angeles points out that despite the differences among them and other Uchinānchu in the homeland or the diaspora, and allowing for the difference engendered by the course of various migrations, scholars can begin to define a larger sense of Uchinānchu identity, delimited by the confines of nation-state boundaries. For the Uchinānchu, simply fighting an erasure from history can be a part of this project, and it is in that spirit that I have sought to write this community history as a testament to a voice in history long overlooked and a contribution to a growing appreciation of who the Uchinānchu are.

Notes

This chapter has been developed from research conducted while in the MA program in Asian American studies at the University of California, Los Angeles. I would like to acknowledge and thank my advisor, Professor Valerie Matsumoto, along with Professors Clara Chu, Mariko Tamanoi, and Henry Yu, who served on my thesis committee. Much appreciation also goes to Professor Ben Kobashigawa for suggesting this topic in the first place. Additional thanks to Steven Masami Ropp for his suggestions related to sources of interest. Profound thanks to the Okinawa Association of America, Pedro Agena, Chieko Kamisato, Gisela Shimabukuro, and Alex Nakada for opening up their homes to me in conducting this research. Final thanks to my partner and wife, Tina Bhaga Yokota, for her support and companionship throughout this project.

1. *Ganbateando* is a portmanteau bridging both Japanese and Spanish that was used as the title of a song by the Okinawan Peruvian group the Diamantes. It combines the Japanese admonition *ganbatte*, roughly meaning "Keep struggling!" with the *-ando* suffix of the Spanish present participle conjugation, to suggest "continuing to persevere." Though the song refers to *dekasegi* who leave Peru to work in Japan, the meaning of struggling through migrations mirrors the experiences of the Okinawan Peruvians of this chapter.

2. Throughout this chapter I use the terms "Uchinānchu" and "Okinawan" interchangeably, though Uchinānchu is more inclusive. "Okinawan" often refers only to people from the main island of Okinawa or only to the people of modern-day Okinawa Prefecture (to the exclusion of outlying island groups or the Amami Ōshima island group in present-day Kagoshima Prefecture, all of which had been part of the former Ryūkyū Kingdom). I ask the reader to please bear these considerations in mind so as not to unconsciously reify Japanese colonial nation-state demarcations.

3. For a discussion of the particularities of the dōka seisaku and its effects on Okinawa, see Alan Christy, "The Making of Imperial Subjects in Okinawa," *Positions* 1, no. 3 (1993): 141–69.

4. For information on political aspects of migration, see Robert K. Arakaki, "Theorizing on the Okinawan Diaspora," in *Okinawan Diaspora*, ed. Ronald Y. Nakasone (Honolulu: University of Hawai'i Press, 2002), 36. For information on the tripling of the Okinawan population between 1881 and 1914, see Wesley Ueunten, "Japanese Latin American Internment from an Okinawan Perspective," in *Okinawan Diaspora*, ed. Ronald Y. Nakasone (Honolulu: University of Hawai'i Press, 2002), 94. For information on the tripling of Okinawan tax burdens during that same period, see Masato Masukawa, "The Modern State and Nationals beyond Its Boundaries: Reflections on Japanese Nationals in Peru Who Left Japan before World War II" (PhD diss., University of California, Los Angeles, 2000), 233.

5. Makoto Arakaki, "The Uchinānchu Diaspora and the Boundary of 'Nikkei,'" in *New Worlds, New Lives,* ed. Lane Ryo Hirabayashi, Akemi Kikumura-Yano, and James A. Hirabayashi (Stanford: Stanford University Press, 2002), 307.

6. Ueunten, "Japanese Latin American Internment from an Okinawan Perspective," 96.

7. James L. Tigner, "Japanese Immigration into Latin America: A Survey," *Journal of Interamerican Studies and World Affairs* 23, no. 4 (1981): 465.

8. Tomonori Ishikawa, "Rūtsu toshite no Okinawa: Nanbei imin o chūshin ni," in *Okinawa shakai to Nikkeijin/Gaikokujin/Amerajian,* ed. Yumi Andō, Noriyuki Suzuki, and Naomi Noiri (Tokyo: Kubapuro, 2007), 89–98.

9. Steven Masami Ropp, "The Nikkei Negotiation of Minority/Majority Dynamics in Perú and the United States," in *New Worlds, New Lives,* ed. Lane Ryo Hirabayashi, Akemi Kikumura-Yano, and James A. Hirabayashi (Stanford: Stanford University Press, 2002), 284.

10. James L. Tigner, *The Okinawans in Latin America* (Washington DC: Pacific Science Board National Research Council, 1954), 16. The tanomoshi usually involved a set number of participants joining by mutual assent, who would contribute a monthly fee to a financial pool. Monthly recipients would be determined depending on need or by lot, until each member had their turn. In the absence of access to credit in a foreign country, such an arrangement, operating largely on trust, would provide members with the necessary funding for startup entrepreneurial ventures and necessities. Japanese, Korean, and other Asian immigrants also utilized similar organizational structures to help them succeed in foreign lands.

11. Tigner, *The Okinawans in Latin America,* 609.

12. C. Harvey Gardiner, *Pawns in a Triangle of Hate: The Peruvian Japanese and the United States* (Seattle: University of Washington Press, 1981), 8.

13. Daniel M. Masterson and Sayaka Funada-Classen, *The Japanese in Latin America* (Urbana: University of Illinois Press, 2004), 66.

14. Masterson and Funada-Classen, *The Japanese in Latin America,* 156–57.

15. Chieko Kamisato, interview by author, May 26, 2005, Los Angeles,

tape recording. All subsequent quotations of Kamisato are from this interview. Japanese names are given in the American fashion of given name followed by surname, in accordance with the sources. Chieko, a Nisei (second-generation) Okinawan Peruvian, had been adopted from the Nakada side of the family into the Kamisato side when she was very young. Her biological father had a sister in the Kamisato family who adopted her and raised her as a Kamisato. Alex Nakada, who is referenced later, is her biological brother, but she was raised to consider him a cousin.

16. Seiichi Higashide, *Adios to Tears: The Memoirs of a Japanese-Peruvian Internee in U.S. Concentration Camps* (Seattle: University of Washington Press, 2000), 110.

17. Masterson and Funada-Classen, *The Japanese in Latin America*, 115.

18. Mary Fukumoto, *Hacia un Nuevo Sol: Japoneses y Sus Descendientes en el Perú* (Toward a new sun: The Japanese and their descendants in Peru) (Lima: Asociación Peruano Japonesa del Peru, 1997), 250.

19. For information on Peruvian contributions to the war effort, see Gardiner, *Pawns in a Triangle of Hate*, 13–14. For information on the proposal to intern all Japanese Latin Americans, see Masterson and Funada-Classen, *The Japanese in Latin America*, 161.

20. Ueunten, "Japanese Latin American Internment from an Okinawan Perspective," 92.

21. The Okinawa Club of America, *History of the Okinawans in North America*, trans. Ben Kobashigawa (Los Angeles: Asian American Studies Center, UCLA, 1988), 100.

22. Akemi Kikumura-Yano, ed., *Encyclopedia of Japanese Descendents in the Americas* (Walnut Creek CA: AltaMira Press, 2002), 253.

23. Masterson and Funada-Classen, *The Japanese in Latin America*, 161.

24. Ayako Hagihara and Grace Shimizu, "The Japanese Latin American Wartime and Relocation Experience," *Amerasia Journal* 28, no. 2 (2002): 208.

25. *Personal Justice Denied: Report of the Commission on Wartime Relocation and Internment of Civilians* (Seattle: University of Washington Press, 1997), 310.

26. Ueunten, "Japanese Latin American Internment from an Okinawan Perspective," 109.

27. Fukumoto, *Hacia un Nuevo Sol*, 253; Kikumura-Yano, *Encyclopedia of Japanese Descendents in the Americas*, 253.

28. *Personal Justice Denied*, 313.

29. The Okinawa Club of America, *History of the Okinawans in North America*, 127, 142.

30. The Okinawa Club of America, *History of the Okinawans in North America*, 549.

31. The Okinawa Club of America, *History of the Okinawans in North America*, 101.

32. Raúl Araki, "An Approach to the Formation of Nikkei Identity in Perú," in *New Worlds, New Lives*, ed. Lane Ryo Hirabayashi, Akemi Kikumura-Yano, and James A. Hirabayashi (Stanford: Stanford University Press, 2002), 83.

33. Alex Nakada, interview by author, May 17, 2005, Los Angeles, tape recording. All subsequent quotations of Nakada are from this interview unless otherwise noted.

34. Ropp, "The Nikkei Negotiation of Minority/Majority Dynamics in Perú and the United States," 292.

35. "Nikkei" refers to Japanese-descended people outside of Japan. In general I have tried to avoid this term as it tends to homogenize people of Okinawan ancestry as Japanese.

36. Masterson and Funada-Classen, *The Japanese in Latin America*, 229.

37. Gisela Shimabukuro, interview by author, May 27, 2005, Los Angeles, tape recording. All subsequent quotations of Shimabukuro are from this interview.

38. Pedro Agena, interview by author, April 14, 2005, Los Angeles, tape recording. All subsequent quotations of Agena are from this interview. Pedro Agena is a Nisei/Sansei (second/third-generation) Okinawan Peruvian. His father was born in Okinawa, but his mother was born in Peru. He is married to one of Alex Nakada's sisters.

39. Of note is that most of the organizational newsletters until about 1996 called the organization the Peruvian Nisei Association, though later newsletters referred to it as the Peruvian Nikkei Association, perhaps representing a move to be more inclusive of the younger generation.

40. Alex Nakada, letter to the Peruvian Nisei Association, January 16, 1982, in author's possession.

41. The fiestas de carnavalito are the equivalent of Mardi Gras in the United States. It is celebrated prior to Easter Sunday. The bailes de fiestas patrias is a social gathering to celebrate Peruvian Independence Day.

42. Peruvian Nisei Association Meeting Minutes, February 3, 1990, in author's possession.

43. "Nikkei Peruanos se Activan" (Peruvian Nikkei get active), *Prensa Nikkei*, May 15, 1990, my translation. Unless otherwise noted, all translations are my own.

44. The peña criollas were parties with traditional Peruvian songs and dances.

45. Carlos Pongo, "Entrevista a Alex Nakada" (interview with Alex Nakada), *Perú en USA*, December 15, 1985, 5.

46. "Niseis Peruanos: Criollos Con Sabor Oriental" (Peruvian Nisei: Creoles with an Oriental flavor), *Revista del Perú*, December 1994.

47. *L.A. Peruvian Times*, August, 1991.

48. Donna R. Gabaccia, "Is Everywhere Nowhere? Nomads, Nations, and the Immigrant Paradigm of United States History," *Journal of American History* 83, no. 3 (1999): 15.

49. Lane Ryo Hirabayashi, "Reconsidering Transculturation and Power," *Amerasia Journal* 28, no. 2 (2002): xviii.

50. William Safran, "Diasporas in Modern Societies: Myths of Homeland and Return," *Diaspora* 1, no. 1 (1991): 84.

51. Takeyuki Tsuda, *Strangers in the Ethnic Homeland: Japanese Brazilian Return Migration in Transnational Perspective* (New York: Columbia University Press, 2003), 255.

52. M. Arakaki, "The Uchinānchu Diaspora and the Boundary of 'Nikkei,'" 306.

53. Benedict Anderson, *Imagined Communities* (London: Verso, 1991), 6.

54. Uchināguchi is the main Ryūkyūan/Okinawan language.

55. Arjun Appadurai, *Modernity at Large: Cultural Dimensions of Globalization* (Minneapolis: University of Minnesota Press, 1996), 166.

56. Steven Masami Ropp, "Secondary Migration and the Politics of Identity for Asian Latinos in Los Angeles," *Journal of Asian American Studies* 3, no. 2 (2000): 220.

57. In fact many scholars have criticized traditional area studies disciplines such as East Asian studies and Latin American studies as supporting American colonialism, conjoined as they have been by historical linkages with U.S. government military and economic policy objectives.

58. Jeremy Waldron, "Minority Cultures and the Cosmopolitan Alternative," in *Rights of Minority Cultures*, ed. Will Kymlicka (New York: Oxford University Press, 1995), 108.

Contributors

MAILE ARVIN grew up in Richmond, Kentucky, and Kāneohe, Hawai'i. A graduate of Swarthmore College, she now resides in San Diego and is a PhD student in UC San Diego's Ethnic Studies Department. Her research focuses on race in Hawai'i, the history and present of the Kānaka Maoli (Native Hawaiian) sovereignty movement, and global indigenous rights. A poet and essayist, she has also published work in Kearny Street Workshop's *Same Time, Same Place* (2006) and *12 Ways: An Anthology of the Intergenerational Writer's Workshop* (2007).

FAYE CHRISTINE CARONAN is an assistant professor of ethnic studies at the University of Colorado, Denver. She specializes in comparative ethnic studies and the study of U.S. imperialism. Currently she is working on two research projects. The first examines how Filipino American and U.S. Puerto Rican performance poets participate in a politics of representing U.S. imperialism. The second looks at the role that race played in the imagining of the U.S. nation and its empire in the Pacific in the first half of the twentieth century.

LAURA E. ENRIQUEZ received her BA from Pomona College and her MA from the University of California, Los Angeles. Currently she is a doctoral student in sociology at the University of California, Los Angeles, specializing in immigration, race/ethnicity, and gender. Her work focuses on the educational experiences and political incorporation of undocumented young adults, where she engages in issues of racialization, social capital formation, citizenship, and political and civic participation.

CAMILLA FOJAS is Vincent de Paul Professor and the director of Latin American and Latino studies at DePaul University. Her main areas of research are cultural, film, and media studies of the Americas and the American Pacific, especially with regard to the construction of race and national borders. Her books include *Cosmopolitanism in the Americas* (Purdue University Press, 2005), *Mixed Race Hollywood* (coedited with Mary Beltrán, New York University Press, 2008), and *Border Bandits: Hollywood on the Southern Frontier* (University of Texas Press, 2008).

VERNADETTE VICUÑA GONZALEZ is an assistant professor of American studies at the University of Hawai'i at Mānoa. She is currently working on a book titled "Securing Paradise: Tourism and Militarism in Hawaii and the Philippines." Her latest essays, a collaborative effort with Robyn Magalit Rodriguez, appear in Duke University Press's *Alien Encounters: Asian Americans in Popular Culture* (edited by Mimi Nguyen and Thuy Linh Tu) and in *Frontiers: A Journal of Women Studies.*

RUDY P. GUEVARRA JR. is an assistant professor of Asian Pacific American studies at Arizona State University. His main areas of research are comparative and relational examinations between Asian Americans, Pacific Islanders, and Chicana/os and Latina/os, multiracial and multiethnic identity, labor history, immigration and transnational migration, and community formations. He is the author of *Becoming Mexipino: Multiethnic Identities and Communities in San Diego* (Rutgers University Press, 2012) and the coeditor (with Marc Coronado, Jeffrey Moniz, and Laura Furlan Szanto) and a contributing author of *Crossing Lines: Race and*

Mixed Race across the Geohistorical Divide (Alta Mira Press, 2005). He has also published essays in the *Journal of San Diego History* and the *Journal of Asian American Studies.*

SANDRA HAMADA received her BA in sociology at Pomona College, where as a research assistant with Dr. Gilda Ochoa she studied the educational experiences of Asian American and Latina/o high school students. As an undergraduate she became passionate about and involved in feminist, race, and class politics. As a Claremont Graduate University Ronald E. McNair scholar, she presented and published a study on Asian American student activism. Motivated by her research and her own educational experience, she currently fights for quality education in South Los Angeles as a community organizer.

KUʻUALOHA HOʻOMANAWANUI is a Kanaka Maoli (Native Hawaiian) woman born in Kailua, Oʻahu, and raised in Wailua, Kauaʻi. A scholar, poet, musician, and artist, she is also the chief editor of *ʻOiwi: A Native Hawaiian Journal,* the first contemporary journal featuring Native Hawaiian writers and artists. With a PhD in English, an MA in Hawaiian religion, and a BA in Hawaiian studies from the University of Hawaiʻi at Mānoa, she has taught a variety of courses at different levels over the past decade focusing on Native Hawaiian mythology, literature, and indigenous perspectives on literacy. A Ford Foundation predoctoral and doctoral fellow, she is currently an assistant professor of Hawaiian literature with the Department of English at the University of Hawaiʻi at Mānoa in Honolulu. She also works with different Native Hawaiian community groups to develop the next generation of Hawaiian artists and writers.

BIANCA ISAKI received a PhD in political science from the University of Hawaiʻi at Mānoa in 2008. She continues to edit her manuscript, "A Decolonial Archive: The Historical Space of Asian Settler Politics in a Time of Hawaiian Nationhood," while attending the William S. Richardson School of Law in Honolulu and working at KAHEA, a community-based group that advocates at the intersections of environmental justice and Hawaiian rights.

JINAH KIM was born in Seoul, South Korea, and moved to the United States when she was eight. After graduating from Columbia University, she worked as a union organizer for UAW-clerical workers. She received her PhD in cultural studies from the Department of Literature at UCSD in 2006. As assistant director of the Asian American studies program at Northwestern University, she is currently working with the Latino/a studies and African American studies programs to develop a new major in comparative race and diaspora that will open new theoretical and practical ground for understanding race, identity, and global movements in historical, cultural, and analytical contexts. In her current book project she examines how Asian and Latina women's migration from home and nation since the 1970s has enabled new transnational structures and ties. She is also conducting research for her second project, which looks at the relationship between the Mexican bracero project and the internment of Japanese Americans during World War II. Her teaching focuses on representations of the Korean War, the impact of Asian and Latina labor on U.S. domestic practices, how Asian American and Latina/o literature and film represent the neoliberal city of Los Angeles, and comparative Pacific and Atlantic studies.

ERIKA LEE is a professor of history and the director of Asian American studies at the University of Minnesota, where she teaches Asian American studies, immigration history, and transnational American history. She is the author of two award-winning books, *At America's Gates: Chinese Immigration during the Exclusion Era, 1882–1943* (University of North Carolina Press, 2003) and (with Judy Yung) *Angel Island: Immigrant Gateway to America* (Oxford University Press, 2010), sponsored by the Angel Island Immigration Station Foundation, as well as many articles on immigration history and policy. She is currently completing a book titled "Asian Americas: A History of Asians in the Americas."

GILDA L. OCHOA is a professor of sociology and Chicana/o and Latina/o studies at Pomona College, where she teaches courses on race/ethnicity, education, Los Angeles communities, Chicana/os and Latina/os, qualitative research methods, and sociological theory. She is the author of *Learning from Latino Teachers* (Jossey-Bass, 2007) and *Becoming Neighbors in a Mexican American Community* (University of Texas Press, 2004) and the coeditor of *Latino Los Angeles* (University of Arizona Press, 2005). She has also written essays on critical pedagogy and Mexican American women's activism. Her most recent research involves working with a southern California high school to enhance the educational and social experiences of the predominantly Asian American and Latina/o students at the school.

STELLA OH is an associate professor and the chair of women's studies at Loyola Marymount University. Her areas of specialization include Asian American literature, critical theory, and feminist theory. Her research has appeared in several journals and anthologies, including LIT: *Literary Interpretation Theory*, AJWS: *Asian Journal of Women's Studies*, *Concentric: Literary and Cultural Studies*, and *Mine Okubo: Following Her Own Road* (University of Washington Press, 2007). Her current book project, "The Spectacle of Race," explores issues of race, gender, visibility, and consumption. She teaches Women of Color in the United States, Feminist Theories, Feminist Research Methods, Asian Pacific American Women, and Literature by Women of Color.

JOANNA POBLETE is an assistant professor of history at the University of Wyoming. She received her MA and PhD in U.S. history from UCLA. From 2006 to 2008 she was a postdoctoral fellow for the Department of History at the University of North Carolina at Chapel Hill. Her research focuses on issues of U.S. empire and the impact of government structures and labor migration policies on the everyday lives of people who have come under U.S. authority, such as Filipinos, Puerto Ricans, and American Sāmoans. Her book manuscript, "Neither Citizens nor Foreigners: Filipino and

Puerto Rican Labor Recruits to Hawai'i, 1900–1940," is currently under review for the American Encounters/Global Interactions
series at Duke University Press. She is also working on a book on
immigration, tuna canneries, and U.S. authority in the unincor-
porated U.S. territory of American Sāmoa.

HUGO CÓRDOVA QUERO holds a PhD in interdisciplinary studies in religion and ethnic studies from the Graduate Theological
Union in Berkeley. His areas of specialization are religion and theology, ethnic and migration studies, cultural studies, and critical
theories (feminist, queer, and postcolonial). From 2006 to 2008 he
conducted fieldwork in eight Roman Catholic parishes, interviewing Japanese Brazilian migrants who reside in the Tokyo Metropolitan Area, while he was visiting researcher at the Center for Lusophone Studies at Sophia University in Tokyo. After graduation
he was a postdoctoral visiting researcher at the Iberoamerican Institute, Sophia University. He is currently adjunct faculty at Starr
King School for the Ministry, Graduate Theological Union. He is
the coeditor of *Sociedade Japonesa e Migrantes Brasileiros: No-
vos Caminhos na Formação de uma Rede de Pesquisadores* (Japanese society and Brazilian migrants: New paths in the formation
of a researcher's network; Center for Lusophone Studies, Sophia
University, 2008) and *Transnational Faiths: Latin American Migrants and Their Religions in Japan* (Ashgate, 2012).

JENNIFFER ROJAS graduated from Pomona College in 2009 with
a dual degree in Spanish literature and public policy analysis, with
a concentration in sociology. While at Pomona College her course-
work was primarily focused on the educational experiences of students in inner-city schools. For the past two years she has been an
executive assistant at Inner City Law Center, a nonprofit that focuses on housing and homelessness issues and provides legal services to low-income individuals and families.

CLAUDIA SADOWSKI-SMITH is an associate professor of English
at Arizona State University. She is the author of *Border Fictions:*

Globalization, Empire, and Writing at the Boundaries of the United States (University of Virginia Press, 2008) and the editor of *Globalization on the Line: Culture, Capital, and Citizenship at U.S. Borders* (Palgrave, 2002). She has published several essays on immigration, border theory, literatures of the U.S.-Mexican border, and the internationalization of American studies in such journals as *American Quarterly, South Atlantic Quarterly, Comparative American Studies, Arizona Quarterly,* and *Diaspora.*

JANE H. YAMASHIRO has a PhD in sociology from the University of Hawai'i at Mānoa. Her dissertation, "When the Diaspora Returns: Transnational Racial and Ethnic Identity Formation among Japanese Americans in Global Tokyo," draws from her background in Asian American and Asian studies to examine how Japanese Americans reconstruct their racial and ethnic identities by living in Japan. Her areas of specialization include race and ethnic studies, international migration, globalization, transnationalism, diaspora, ethnic identity, and cultural studies. She is currently a visiting researcher and lecturer at the Faculty of Liberal Arts at Sophia University in Tokyo.

RYAN MASAAKI YOKOTA is currently a PhD candidate in Japanese history in the Department of History at the University of Chicago. His dissertation research focuses on post–World War II Okinawan nationalisms, including independence movements, movements for regional autonomy, diasporic nationalism, and indigenous nationalism. He received his MA in Asian American studies at the University of California, Los Angeles. His articles include "'Transculturation and Adaptation: A Brief History of Japanese and Okinawan Cubans," published in *Afro-Hispanic Review,* and "Interview with Pat Sumi," published in *Asian Americans: The Movement and the Moment* (UCLA Asian American Studies Center Press, 2001).

Index

To order or obtain more information on these or other University of
Nebraska Press titles, visit nebraskapress.unl.edu.